Be Not Afraid to Follow the Footprints from Heaven

JOHN S. CARPENTER

Copyright © 2016 John S. Carpenter
All rights reserved
First Edition

PAGE PUBLISHING, INC.
New York, NY

First originally published by Page Publishing, Inc. 2016

ISBN 978-1-68348-201-7 (pbk)
ISBN 978-1-68348-202-4 (digital)

Printed in the United States of America

DEDICATION

My
Thanks
To my Ruthie,
Beloved Soulmate.
You inspire me every day
With your gentle, thoughtful love,
Unwavering support and encouragement
While suffering with grace and dignity
With your own pain and illness.
You quietly saved my life,
showed me *true* LOVE,
and led me back
to our God.
I LOVE
You.

CONTENTS

Contents 5

Preface..7

Acknowledgements...9

Chapter 1:   The Awakening..11

Chapter 2:   Disbelief and Disorder...18

Chapter 3:   Marian Apparitions...26

Chapter 4:   The Search for Truth...35

Chapter 5:   The Realm of the Visionary 55

Chapter 6:   Witnessing the Supernatural 74

Chapter 7:   More Than One Miracle of the Sun 96

Chapter 8:   The Great Evangelist...116

Chapter 9:   Accurate Heavenly Predictions..........................140

Chapter 10: Altering History..159

Chapter 11: Undeniable Miracles 177

Chapter 12: Evidence Left Behind..203

Chapter 13: Science Validates the Supernatural 230

Chapter 14:	Heaven is for Real…but so is Hell	269
Chapter 15:	The Role of Angels	295
Chapter 16:	Angelic Protection	323
Chapter 17:	Messages for Mankind	334
Chapter 18:	"Just Wait Till Your Father Comes Home"	355
Chapter 19:	Darkness…Then Light	375
Chapter 20:	The Meaning of Life	413
Appendix 1:	Eighty-Nine Marian Apparitions Chart	431
Appendix 2:	"Dessert for Catholics"	437
Bibliography		451
About The Author		469

PREFACE

"BE NOT AFRAID…"

This book is written for the reader to experience supernatural events in a credible fashion. For those of you who are uncertain of the existence of God, this book may shed some positive light on that idea for you. Do not be afraid to stretch the boundaries of your beliefs.

"TO FOLLOW THE FOOTPRINTS…"

For those of you who demand evidence and scientific proof, this book may give you plenty to think about. There is stunning physical and correlational evidence of these "footprints." For those who are detective minded, you should find a feast of data to feed upon. We are tracking the evidence that suggests something supernatural has passed our way and still exists in our present day.

"…FROM HEAVEN"

For those of you of varying religious backgrounds, this information may validate, enrich, or challenge your beliefs. For "fallen-away" Catholics, it is time to awaken to your own rich history and return to Jesus in the Eucharist. For Protestants, these are some of the reasons that I converted to Catholicism. And for all the practicing Catholics who can only name or describe a few Marian apparitions—or are unaware of the scientific studies on Eucharistic Miracles—this book is your next course in learning some important discoveries to grow your faith.

As for atheists and other nonbelievers, welcome to a new reality, but "be not afraid" to read this book. I hope it rocks your world and puts you on a path toward heaven. Just "follow the footprints" and open your heart and soul to these new possibilities.

ACKNOWLEDGEMENTS

First of all, I wish to thank Guy Duncan Carpenter and Jane Elizabeth Mohler Carpenter for falling in love and giving me life. They provided a stable, loving home environment that gave me the strong foundation to venture out into the world with an open mind to help troubled souls and explore unexplained mysteries. They gave me the secure beginning of a wonderful religious life. Thank you, Mom and Dad, as you smile down from heaven.

I wish to thank those who read my words, gave me constructive feedback, and offered loving support as I wrote and pieced together this project over thirteen months after five years of research. They are Susan McMan, Loretta McCullough, Diana Edgington, Georgia Latourette, Sharon Lorry Davis, and Christy Carender.

I especially am grateful for the biblical and spiritual support from Father Rick Jones of Our Lady of the Lake in Branson, Missouri, Dr. Gregory Thompson of the Marian Association, and Donald Hartley, a.k.a. *The Catholic Defender* from the *Deeper Truth* website. Father Rick supported my weekly e-mail research newsletter, promoted my church lectures, and encouraged my spiritual growth.

Gregory asked me to be his codirector for the planning and development of statewide conferences, parish missions, and inspiring pilgrimages. He is a devoted warrior toward the saving of as many souls as he can with his humble yet deeply felt words. Donald gave me the opportunity to spread my research to the world through an Internet-broadcast, weekly radio show called Journey with Mary through Deeper Truth Blog Talk Radio. Listeners tune in from the

Philippines, Australia, India, Hong Kong, Africa, Peru, Europe, Brazil, Saudi Arabia, Canada, all over America, and many other countries every week.

I thank God for opening these doors for me to spread His message to humanity. I thank Blessed Mary for persistently nudging me along. I am grateful for the Holy Spirit that others say has entered within me and "caught me on fire." (I wondered where that driving obsession came from!) And last, but certainly not least, I wish to thank my loving Ruthie, my spiritual partner who guided me gently back to God, and to whom this book is dedicated, forever and ever.

CHAPTER 1

THE AWAKENING

Growing up in the Methodist Church as the son of a Methodist minister was a wonderful collection of beloved memories. The church was warm and friendly with many social events, church dinners, youth groups, and the annual "Hanging of the Greens" to decorate and celebrate the Christmas season. There were beautiful stained glass windows, a booming pipe organ, and fun times in the Sunday school classes. My father was well liked and greatly appreciated for his relevant sermons to today's issues. Sometimes, my own behavior as a child was used as an example to illustrate some point in his preaching. But sometimes, I was not listening well as I was busy drawing little pictures on the small pad of paper my mother would supply to keep me quiet and occupied. At other times, I would gaze at the beautiful thirty-foot stained glass panels and lose myself in the biblical stories represented.

I went through confirmation classes in the sixth grade but was already getting distracted by pretty girls. We knew that Mary was the mother of Jesus, miraculously conceiving him through the power of the Holy Spirit. In later years, when I heard the term Immaculate Conception, I thought it was referring to that process of how Mary conceived Jesus through God. We never heard of Mary's Assumption into heaven. We never learned about her being crowned the Queen of Heaven. We never considered the idea that Mary had been given to us by Jesus as the Heavenly Mother for all of us on Earth. The Miracle at Fatima was never mentioned, nor the idea that any Marian apparitions had ever occurred. I did see some mention of Fatima in a book about unexplained mysteries, but it just seemed like a bunch of religious people in Portugal got worked up into a religious frenzy or hysteria over some unexplained light in the sky—probably a UFO sighting. We did not understand the saints at all—and just passed it off as "some Catholic thing."

We knew the basic Bible stories, how to say a few prayers, and how to sing "Jesus Loves Me!" Our family would have a special acting out of the Nativity at home on Christmas Eve with hand-carved wooden figures. As my father would read the key Bible verses, each of us would take turns placing another figure, animal, or angel into the Nativity scene. Then we would eagerly get ready for the reading of "The Night Before Christmas" with magical visions of Santa Claus coming that night. Sometimes, I would awaken early, listening for the jingle bells of reindeer on our roof. I could swear that I heard them one time!

Carpenter family with nativity figures in 1961.
(left to right: Paul, Mom, Ann, John, Dad)

Years later, my father retired, and I had gone off to college. The church and its memories were fading. But it was difficult to attend another church—and without my father as the pastor, who could possibly take his place? I admired and looked up to my dad. Could **anyone** ever take his place? I probably stopped going to church for about six years. I was beginning to accept that I would just have to find a church that "felt right" to me...somehow.

I explored many other versions of Christianity for the first time—Congregational, Baptist, Presbyterian, Church of Christ, Lutheran, Assembly of God, Catholic, Unitarian, and even Morman. Where I went often related to who I knew at that point in time. With a tour group to Mexico City, I even visited the Catholic Basilica in 1995 where the image of Our Lady of Guadalupe is enshrined. However, I was only a Methodist tourist and did not fully comprehend the miraculous significance of the story or how Mary could actually be appearing to people. Another "Catholic thing," I assumed.

Then, two major events changed my world. First, I met Ruthie, a new love in my life. She had been Catholic all of her life and gently led me back to church. She patiently explained why Catholics do what they do—especially all of the rituals, kneeling and standing during a service. I learned that every bit of the Mass comes from Biblical scripture and is considered "the greatest prayer." I was taught that the Communion bread or wafer actually becomes Jesus' body when consecrated by the priest – and is then called a Host (Although this process still seems symbolic, *science will tell us differently* later in this book). As I got accustomed to the practices, I became intrigued at how much depth, symbolism, and rich history exists in the Catholic faith. It was not really that different from the Methodists—just more complete and in-depth! The Eucharist was the biggest difference—and I felt sadly left out as I could not partake in it as a non-Catholic. My participation would not be allowed until I became Catholic. I began to feel that as a Methodist, I had only received the introductory course to religion. Becoming Catholic would be like taking the advanced or masters level course in religion!

The second life-changing event was travelling on a lecture trip to Italy. This took me to Milan, Tuscany, and Florence. There was a Catholic church of some type on almost every city block in the old historic section of Florence. I was surrounded by Catholicism! There were grand cathedrals, beautiful statues, historical relics, and even "a dead guy under the altar" in one church! Okay, let me explain. Some bodies of Catholic saints do not decay with death; this is a supernatural mystery that science has not been able to explain. To honor these holy figures, a body may be displayed under an altar or significant area of the church (more about this phenomenon later).

Cathedral (Duomo) in Florence, Italy
photo by author

It was all of this amazing Catholic history that impressed me. "Catholic" actually means "universal"—and I was amazed that the Italian Mass had the same scripture readings for that day as did the parishes back home in Missouri. I began to see that the Catholic Church is truly the original church, started by Christ with Peter as its first pope. I began to see that all of its rituals are *preserving* original practices while Protestants and others were removing, editing, or modernizing aspects of these practices. I knew now that this was my church—and that nothing else could ever replace it.

I gladly began the RCIA process to finally become Catholic. There was so much to learn in such a short time that it was basically a grand yet brief overview of everything important about Catholicism. I learned that we don't worship the Virgin Mary or the saints—but that we ask them to pray for us to Jesus in the same way that we might ask a good friend to do. I had begun to hear more about Mary than ever before. I was intrigued that appearances of the Virgin Mary had been logged into history a few times. It still felt like some kind of old legend, mythical story, or fairy tale—not a real event. But this enticed me toward learning more, so I borrowed a DVD on Fatima from the church library.

Wow! I had no idea that she had actually appeared to three children on numerous occasions, talked with them, and predicted events. I had no idea that the Miracle of the Sun was a real event attended by over seventy thousand people because it had been foretold by Our Blessed Mother. Kids could not make this stuff up and then have supernatural events actually take place on the stated date and precise hour as predicted! It was also exciting that Fatima had occurred in 1917—less than one hundred years ago! Could Mary *really* be around us—that recently?

Now I wanted to know so much more! Religion was *coming alive* for me in a fascinating way. It was here and now—*in the present.* I had a new awareness that was changing my whole life. Religious concepts and ideas had been only that—words and ideas. Now they suddenly had a new meaning and purpose for me in my present life. It is hard to explain—but it reminds me of the 1962 movie, *The Miracle Worker*, which starred Patty Duke and Anne Bancroft. Helen Keller, the famous blind, deaf, and mute girl had been learning how to spell words but had not yet made the connection to what those words actually meant. Suddenly, as the water is pumped from the family well and she feels it flowing through her hands, *she makes the connection*—and all of those words suddenly come alive and have meaning for her. It is an emotional moment of great awareness and deep meaning for her life, and she would never be the same again.

And that is *exactly* what I felt and experienced *so profoundly* with my own religious awakening! Words, concepts, ideas, and religious teachings had jumped off of the pages and become three-dimensional figures of meaningful reality for my life. The Holy Spirit entered my soul, flowed into my heart, and ignited the passionate fire for my religion. My eyes were opened, and I was "on fire" with the Holy Spirit for the praise of God! Even my Ruthie commented on my new enthusiasm and identified it as the Holy Spirit within me now.

But then, I looked around me and saw the many hundreds of sleeping souls, living a mechanical existence, lost in meaningless materialism, and absorbed in themselves and their devices for superficial amusement. Families have disintegrated. Relationships are suffering. Souls are losing worthwhile focus. We have become lost children, aimless on a path going nowhere, and not even realizing that we are lost without any *real* purpose in life.

We could really benefit from Our Heavenly Mother's guidance and Her Son's infinite love! Blessed Mary even predicted these current troubling times in her statements to two children in the French Alps in 1846:

> **"The true faith of the Lord having been forgotten, men will abolish civil rights as well as ecclesiastical. All order and all justice will be trampled underfoot, and only homicides, hate, jealousy, lies, and dissension would be seen without love for country and family. All the civil governments will have one and the same plan—which will be to abolish and do away with every religious principle, to make way for materialism, atheism, spiritualism, and vice of all kinds… There will be a time of false peace in the world. People will think of nothing but amusement. The wicked will give themselves to all kinds of sins" (10:89–90).**

A passionate desire began to burn within me to awaken other sleeping souls to what I have so joyously experienced. I decided to make it my perpetual mission to bring others to the infinite love of God through Jesus and his Blessed Mother Mary. But *how* do I approach a doubting, defiant, and violent world that may be blind, deaf, or aggressively opposed to such ideas?

If these present generations need convincing proof and "evidence," then ***that is what I shall give them***! If they can at least be willing to look—and "not be afraid" of challenging their own beliefs, then maybe this book can help them "follow the footprints" that I have discovered "coming from heaven." Then, they, too, can awaken with a new passion for life and love for their fellow man. By following that newly discovered path toward heaven, they could save themselves—and also the souls of others—before it is too late.

> **"Sometimes the devil allows people to live a life free of trouble, because he doesn't want them turning to God. Your sin is like a jail cell—except it's all nice and comfortable, and there doesn't seem to be any need to leave. The door's**

wide open…until one day, time runs out. The cell door slams shut—and, suddenly, it's too late!" (82)

Are we *too* comfortable in a self-absorbed life without any belief in God? Are we lured into that deceptive jail cell of sin—enjoying ourselves and not feeling any pain yet? Are we apathetic about religion—and unaware of the trap that we are setting for ourselves?

It is NOT too late to wake up…

And follow the footprints…

CHAPTER 2

DISBELIEF AND DISORDER

People are claiming that the Virgin Mary, the Mother of Jesus Christ, is visiting them. That just **cannot** be possible! These people **must** be delusional or psychotic. The Virgin Mary has been dead for two thousand years. How could they *even begin to believe* such a thing? How could they ever expect us to accept such a wild claim? *This has to be complete nonsense!*

And yet, these claims persist—not only in recent years, but in almost every year since the Virgin Mary went to Heaven. The International Marian Research Institute in Dayton, Ohio contains the largest collection of written materials on the Blessed Mother in the world (6). They list over 2,554 reported appearances in just under two thousand years. And 386 of them have reportedly occurred in just the last one hundred years. **Impossible! This can't be!** What is *really* going on?

Perhaps, these are just religiously obsessed people who want to see her so badly that they *actually believe* that they have. History, however, does not support this theory. Most witnesses had absolutely no expectation that she was going to appear. Some were not even religious. Some did not recognize her or establish her identity until much later. Others who saw her had hated Catholics and placed no special importance on the Virgin Mary at all. And still others, who were atheists, did not believe in *any* divine beings at all—that is, until they actually witnessed her for themselves. It is very hard to accept that you just saw something *that you never thought could even exist!*

Other witnesses, who did *not* recognize her, thought that she might be a ghost, a restless soul, or a demon. They even threw holy water at her to see what would happen. Others **did** recognize her and then humbly asked for her to please appear to somebody else—as they did not feel worthy or "religious enough" to be receiving a visit from her. Many of these witnesses were fearful about telling anyone, ***knowing*** that nobody would ever believe them!

None of these reactions are typical of delusional people. A disturbed mind creates whatever it desires and needs. The delusional person will fearlessly boast of having such a visit and would not be lacking in any details or understanding. The delusional mind always has all of the answers that it needs to satisfy itself—not necessarily to convince anybody else. In contrast, the typical healthy witness to an appearance of Mary is often reluctant to tell anyone because they don't understand it themselves and are afraid of ridicule and disbelief from others.

Could they just be crazy? Or suffering a temporary split from reality due to stress? Psychotic hallucinations are a private, individualized experience due to that person's own personal disturbance, chemistry, genetics, and psychiatric issues. Hallucinations are creative, unique, and personalized; therefore, they would rarely be exactly alike between two people, let alone among the many members of a group. By definition, a group of people could not have the same experience or ever share a hallucination. Therefore, a group of teenagers experiencing a visit from Mary cannot be hallucinating and then claim all the same exact details, same words spoken, and same actions observed. Even if they were able to hallucinate simultaneously in an individual manner, the onset would never be at the same moment, nor end at the same second. Yet, these groups have been witnessed to do exactly that—even within a fifth of a second when scientists were observing.

At one time, years ago, I had three patients claiming to be Jesus Christ on a closed hospital psychiatric unit. One was a healer; another was a preacher; and the third was a great carpenter—according to them! They were vastly different in their perspectives, words, and actions—despite choosing the same mental deviation to be

Jesus Christ. *People just do not share hallucinations.* Therefore, if a crowd of people witness an appearance by Mary, that disorder can immediately be ruled out. Quite often, there are multiple witnesses or "visionaries" numbering anywhere from three to eight, all seeing her at the same time. In a suburb of Cairo, Egypt in 1968, as many as 250,000 people of all faiths witnessed her all at the same time for hours—cheering as she waved to them and blessed them! (59)

Furthermore, witnesses to her appearances have been psychologically evaluated and tested since the 1800s. There is not a single credible event of seeing the Virgin Mary that has been proven to originate from the existence of a psychological disturbance or mental disorder. In fact, all witnesses have been assessed as quite "normal" in their thoughts and behavior. They are not religiously obsessed, hysterical, or prone to fantasy. They are judged to be typical, healthy adults or children who have been functioning well in everyday life and continue to do so. They have not fallen into the dark abyss of mental deterioration with unpredictable or disturbing activity. In fact, any changes in behavior have only been positive ones—becoming kinder, more humble, generous, unselfish, thoughtful, loving, as well as more spiritual and dedicated to their faith. For many, it became a life-changing event that enhanced their lives for the rest of their years. These are *not* signs of a mental disturbance!

Consider the report by Agostino Gemelli, a world-famous psychiatrist, on his evaluation of the visionary, Adelaide Roncalli, from Ghiaie di Bonate, Italy (1944):

> "Lying can be absolutely ruled out...her personality is dominated by spontaneity, simplicity, directness...We are witnessing a precociously positive type, realistic and concise—that is furthermost from the hysterical type...We can declare that the claimed visions of Bonate are true and are not the fruit of a sick mind, neither an effect of imagination, nor an effect of suggestion" (110).

And from Medjugorje, Bosnia (1981) comes this report from a Muslim psychiatrist, Dr. Mulija Dzudza. After harsh interrogations, attempts at frightening the six visionaries by exposing them to severely demented hospital patients, a trip to the mortuary, and thorough psychiatric examinations, they passed every test and answered all questions without guile or hesitation. He declared that these six visionaries were sound and healthy—and added,

> "I have not seen more normal children than these. It is those who brought them here who should be declared insane!" (48:43)

Dr. Giorgio Sanguinetti, a professor of psychiatry at the University of Milan, Italy, specialized in the study of delirium—especially religious delirium. He traveled to Medjugorje, Bosnia in 1985 to study the six visionaries and their patterns of behavior. He knew that certain patterns are observed over and over in "delirious people with a mystical bent." He concluded:

> "I consider it of fundamental importance to emphasize that in all my conversations with the young visionaries of Medjugorje, I have never discovered any thought, look, conversation, attitude, or behavior similar to these pathological states which I have researched. It must be made clear that the visionaries live a normal life…they relate to others as if they were no different…their behavior is discreet and polite…they are not effusive, nor are they withdrawn or exhibitionist. On the contrary, they look calm, peaceful, and gentle. They do not try to convince anyone…their smile is not smug or malicious or artificial. They certainly are not looking for attention or for an audience. They do not offer interpretations or personal opinions about their mystical experiences. All they want to do is report the facts and admit that they are happy" (8:206–207).

Yet, the generations of today believe that everything can probably be explained in some manner by scientific reasoning. Perhaps this can all be explained by an undiscovered neuropsychological disorder of the brain. They would insist that any supernatural event can probably be accounted for by natural causes. They would proclaim that any mystery on our planet could be eventually explained through science. Something in the environment *must* be creating such ridiculous illusions. Some chemical interaction in the brain *must* be causing such visions. With careful and persistent analysis, they choose to believe that science will eventually explain *everything* that we do not fully understand yet. And if science cannot do so, then the events must be clever fakes or orchestrated hoaxes that have fooled all of us.

What are we to believe? Science has yet to find any explanation for any of these events. What benefit would anybody gain from a clever hoax? There is no money or profit to be gained. The typical reaction is usually ridicule, disbelief, or patronizing laughter. There would be no positive recognition, praise, or fame to be acquired. And most hoaxes are usually revealed or eventually discovered at some point in time. Yet, not one alleged visit by the Virgin has ever been proven to have been faked.

If these appearances are not real, then how could such a mistaken perception inspire so many people in a similar positive fashion for centuries—changing lives in wonderful and productive ways, converting millions to Christianity—especially Catholicism? After Our Lady of Guadalupe appeared in Mexico, over nine million Indians converted to the Catholic faith. After the Virgin appeared in Lourdes, France and created a new spring of water, over seven thousand miraculous healings have been carefully examined and documented as legitimate by medical investigation teams. What delusion or hoax could ever produce such incredible benefits?

In Fatima, Portugal, the Virgin told three shepherd children that she would perform a miracle at noon on October 13, 1917, **so that everyone could believe** that she had really been visiting them. Many skeptics, doubters, journalists, doctors, officials, investigators, and atheists gathered in that amazing crowd of over seventy thousand on a cold, miserable, rainy day. Many expected that a hoax would be revealed as there was no way that three little kids could produce anything amazing or supernatural at a designated time. Instead, at the predicted time of 12:00 noon, the clouds suddenly parted, and the entire crowd witnessed an amazing display in the sky as the sun pulsated, "danced," emanated a rainbow of enveloping colors, and zigzagged toward the ground, frightening everyone within 650 square miles of Fatima (29:199–202).

BE NOT AFRAID TO FOLLOW THE FOOTPRINTS FROM HEAVEN

Huge, diverse crowd at Fatima, October 13, 1917

Was this just a clever optical illusion? One might assume so until one understands that this solar display completely dried up all of the muddy ground, countless puddles, and the entire rain-drenched crowd who truly felt the intense heat when the sun dipped from the sky toward them. *Hardly just an illusion.* (Scientists have estimated that it would take the energy equivalent to a two megaton nuclear explosion to completely vaporize the water accumulated at Fatima.) Skeptics were now on their knees praying as recounted by one young man witnessing the solar spectacle from a town ten miles away:

> "Nearby, there was a godless man who had spent the morning making fun of the simpletons who had gone to Fatima just to see a girl. I looked at him, and he was numbed, his eyes riveted on the sun. I saw him tremble from head to foot. Then he raised his hands toward heaven, as he was kneeling there in the mud, and cried out, 'Our Lady, Our Lady'" (32:57).

Not a single witness that day proposed any explanation other than it being "a miracle from God." The Virgin Mary kept her word in giving everyone a sign that would strongly encourage them to finally believe in her presence and her messages for mankind. Mass hysteria requires a group to be comprised of like-minded people who closely share the same beliefs and experiences. The huge crowd at Fatima was far from that in its varied composition and diverse characters. But when they all left that day, there was no lingering debate, no confusion, nor any disagreement over what had happened. For such diverse and different-minded people, it is astounding that there was no continuing controversy or doubts expressed over what had happened that day. Even secular newspapers had no choice but to describe "the miraculous dancing of the Sun" at Fatima.

Despite the fact that we can rule out psychological disorders, natural phenomena, hoaxes, illusions, and religious hysteria, there will be many who will ***still*** choose to **not** believe in these supernatural appearances. Despite good evidence, reliable witnesses, and impressive, repeating patterns of data, those who choose to not believe are amazingly unaffected by such evidence. But why? Personally, they just cannot accept, comprehend, or cope with such a notion—so, they will push it away, deny it, avoid it, and ridicule anyone who *does* choose to believe. It overwhelms them emotionally and heightens their anxiety and insecurities. They become defensive and deny such supernatural events could ever exist.

If a person already has their mind steadfastly determined to disbelieve, then no amount of evidence will *ever* make one bit of difference. Their mind has essentially become firmly closed to any considerations that might "rock their world" and open them up to internal fears and unwanted anxieties. Instead, they may become loud opponents of this research because they know that an unexplained mystery still exists that could create unwanted tension within them. They would prefer to eliminate or keep at a distance anything that might challenge their predictable and secure little world. "Don't confuse me with the facts!"

I also have to comment on those who readily believe *anything* without any discernment, investigation, or interest in acquiring evidence. We could call that a form of faith, but I am actually referring to a group of people who go to the *other* extreme in believing *everything* without any question. They see the image of the Virgin Mary in a deformed pancake, a pool of oil, an odd-shaped vegetable, a unique rock formation, a twisted tree trunk, or within particular clouds in the sky. These people draw laughter and disbelief, causing the actual appearances of the Virgin Mary to be taken less seriously. They are eager to believe and look for examples of her presence everywhere. Their claimed experiences are vastly different from the patterns of data that have arisen from historical accounts of seeing the Virgin.

The visits of the Virgin Mary are not delusions or psychotic mental disturbances. They are not fantasies or religious obsessions. They are not illusions or the product of a mass hysteria. Science has not been able to explain *any* of these events thus far. If this phenomenon is *not* due to any psychological disorder, then it must be *some kind* of reality. But **what** is it? How do we find the truth—especially when many people have already decided that it is not possible and are in adamant disbelief at the outset? And if it "cannot be possible," then no one will be willing to seriously discuss it or ever look further at any historical evidence.

"Be not afraid." Let us take a closer look…

CHAPTER 3

MARIAN APPARITIONS

"We are the children of Mary. Mary is the Mother of Jesus and the Mother of us all. If Christ is ours, then his mother, therefore, is also ours. She, the Lady above heaven and earth—here passes the woman who is raised far above all women, indeed, above the whole human race. No woman is like unto thee. Thou art more than an empress or a queen, blessed above all nobility, wisdom, or saintliness (88:11)" **(Martin Luther, ten years *after* he left the Catholic Church and began the Protestant Reformation).**

In my first year of being Catholic, I decided to learn more about these supposed appearances of the Virgin Mary. As a psychiatric therapist, I find that people often have many unusual experiences that are quite interesting to study. If these "visionaries" or witnesses who encountered the Virgin were not crazy, then I wanted to know what was going on! If they *were* delusional, then I would want to understand how that could be happening as well. The term "apparition" can be misleading as it suggests a ghostlike appearance. Mary has appeared vividly in dreams, as an image in the sky, or most frequently as a very real, touchable, huggable, three-dimensional presence.

Could there really be more than the few, well-known, apparition cases? Many Catholics do not believe that there are any other apparitions worthy of consideration other than the handful that they have already been told about. Most Catholics cannot name more than three or four appearances—usually Fatima (Portugal), Lourdes (France), and Guadalupe (Mexico). After first watching that revealing DVD documentary on Fatima from the church library, my research began with the book, ***Those Who Saw Her***, by Catherine Odell (11). Here were detailed accounts of fifteen, church-approved appearances of Blessed Mary! This took me way beyond the traditionally described accounts of Fatima, Guadalupe, and Lourdes. I began to see patterns of data developing in how and why she appeared. It began to feel very real and believable for the first time. Mary was no longer just a biblical character from two thousand years ago. She was now a real presence in today's world through mystical and supernatural means. If we declare her to be real, then Jesus would be just as real also. And God would not be dead after all. In fact, **we** have been the ones dead in spirit, ignorant of this knowledge, and lost on our paths. **We** are the ones not listening, not paying attention, and asleep at the wheel.

In a very general sense, this is what a "Marian apparition" could be like. You would be in the middle of a normal daily activity when something would distract you and gain your attention. It might be a flash—like lightning—or perhaps a very intense light "like the sun" from which a figure of a beautiful lady emerges. Her appearance is both regal, probably with a crown on her head, but also very loving, tender, and motherly. She may float on a small wispy cloud several feet above the ground or over a small tree or bush. You drop to your knees, entranced and humbled by her presence. Her light may surround you as well as you become oblivious to anything or anybody else around you. She may or may not speak, but if she does, you will hear messages regarding prayer, sacrifice, confession, penance, or conversion. She may request that a church be built in this place. She may give you some warning for mankind or a prediction of future events. Then she will fade away as quickly as she arrived. You are stunned but very moved by the experience. You also know that **nobody** is *ever going to believe you*!

Artist's perception of a "typical" Marian apparition
(Photo-Art created by author)

"And a great sign appeared in heaven: a woman adorned with the sun, and the moon was under her feet, and on her head was a crown of twelve stars" (**Revelation 12:1**).

A quick search on the Internet took me to several great sources of historical information. The International Marian Research Institute at the University of Dayton in Ohio has the largest collection of printed materials in the whole world on the Virgin Mary. From various historical sources, they list around 2,160 reports before 1900 and then another 386 sightings in just over the past one hundred years. This totals over 2,546 reports! A number of those reports have an unfavorable ruling based on various factors. However, of those 386 incidents from the past century, only seventy-seven have had a negative ruling, leaving over three hundred cases still open for potential approval (6).

The approval process by the Catholic Church is a careful, meticulous, and conservative process. It begins with the local bishop in every case. He is to launch an investigation utilizing experts from the fields of medicine, science, and theology. Unfortunately, this does not always happen. Sometimes, the verdict stems only from the personal opinion of the bishop, which then might depend **less** upon facts and **more** on his own beliefs, opinions, and personality. It is not always an objective decision; several cases have contained unethical scandals that forced unfair and unfavorable conclusions.

Such was the case with the 1944 encounters in Ghiaie di Bonate, Italy. A seven-year-old visionary had the classic trancelike experience and messages from Mary while crowds as great as 350,000 people witnessed supernatural solar displays and other incredible events as well as miraculous healings. Despite all of this, a bold and arrogant scholar gained the trust of the bishop and sequestered the young girl away for months, drilling her, pressuring her, and demanding that she sign a statement that he had written, claiming she had lied about it all. At such a young age, she was traumatized and in fear of going against his wishes. She signed his statement against her will. For conservative reviewers, this cast enough confusion and doubt upon the events that the apparition received a "negative ruling." But this was finally reversed in 2003 with the first phase of approval granted for faith expression (110; 9).

Another case in Lipa, Philippines in 1948 was placed under great doubt when six bishops declared that the events were phony. The official church investigation in April 1951 was rather suspicious in that key witnesses were not interviewed, diaries and evidence were destroyed, and the six bishops who signed the negative report admitted later that they had been coerced to do so under *threat of excommunication*. This would be another case that should be removed from the "negative" pile and closely reviewed. That did happen, eventually, on September 12, 2015 with official approval finally granted by the archbishop (9; 126).

There are four listed norms for discernment (6):

1. Something of a supernatural or miraculous nature has taken place—not easily explained by way of science, psychology, a hoax, or other means. It *must* be beyond human explanation.
2. The witness or visionary must be mentally sound, honest, sincere, cooperative, obedient to ecclesiastical authorities, and able to return to normal practices of the faith. There must be no financial gain, selfish motive, or suggestion of profit with those involved.
3. The content of any revelation or message must be theologically acceptable, morally sound, free of doctrinal error, and not in contradiction with religious practices.

4. The apparition must result in positive spiritual assets which endure (prayer, conversion, increase in charity, etc.), perhaps bearing spiritual fruits for many.

A committee is supposed to report its findings to the bishop who then decides whether or not to allow public worship at the apparition site. If the committee is undecided or waiting for further developments, the bishop can still allow public worship if he so chooses. Apparitions are classified as either (1) "not worthy of belief," (2) "not contrary to the faith," or (3) "worthy of belief." The messages of an approved apparition cannot have any content that is contrary to the teachings of the Church.

There are several types of church approval.

TRADITIONAL - This usually pertains to more ancient visitations. In these cases, there was never any organized investigation, but the credibility of the reporting sources and documentation was good enough to warrant belief in the apparition and its visionaries.

IMPLIED - Although no formal declaration of approval has yet been made regarding these incidents, religious figures such as the pope may visit, pray, hold Mass, or simply honor the apparition site with their presence. The pope is unlikely to visit a location that is questionable, scandalous, or controversial because just his very presence would give credibility to and more acceptance for that apparition.

BISHOP LEVEL - As established in the Council of Trent (1545–1563), the local bishop is the first and main authority in the judgment of the authenticity of apparition claims. Vatican approval is **not required** for an apparition to be considered authentic. After an episcopal approval, the Vatican may do nothing. Pope Paul VI made it clear in 1969 that the main acceptance for any apparition lies with the local bishop. The Vatican only gets involved when it needs to or chooses to—much like the Supreme Court in the United States hears only the legal cases that it chooses to consider. Because there are so many reports worldwide to pursue and investigate, if the Vatican were to actually become involved in investigating every single case itself, this would essentially become all that the Vatican would be doing.

Pope Paul VI also deleted certain canons in the Code of Canon Law in 1969 that had previously forbidden publications to describe new miracles, messages, or apparitions. Thus, the increases today in the reporting of apparitions might appear suspicious until one realizes that the freedom to publicly report them was changed, which would create, at least in part, a natural increase in the numbers.

VATICAN LEVEL - This is when the Vatican does get involved, perhaps doing their own private study and eventually rendering an opinion in order to either approve public devotion or discourage it. Many Catholics erroneously think that ***only a Vatican-approved apparition can be believed***. If so, then there are only about fifteen or so that have Vatican approval. Of course, that is a very conservative number out of over 2,500 reports but consider those fifteen approvals in this fashion:

> "The Virgin Mary is real. The Virgin Mary is real. The Virgin Mary is real. The Virgin Mary is real. The Virgin Mary is real. The Virgin Mary is real. The Virgin Mary is real. The Virgin Mary is real. The Virgin Mary is real. The Virgin Mary is real. The Virgin Mary is real. The Virgin Mary is real. The Virgin Mary is real. The Virgin Mary is real. The Virgin Mary is real."

How many times does a visit by the Virgin Mary need to be declared "real" in order to be fully accepted as a real phenomenon?

In their 1973 pastoral letter, *Behold Your Mother: Women of Faith*, the American bishops called authenticated appearances of Mary "providential happenings which serve as reminders of basic Christian themes such as prayer, penance, and the necessity of the sacraments" (9).

The approval process has rarely been a quick process. Much caution and care is given so as to not hastily reach a decision that could mislead people to an unworthy place of devotion. If quickly or carelessly approved—and problems did develop later on—then people would not trust such decision-making by the church and would be unlikely to believe any future decisions. Many Catholics are fiercely adamant that one should not even mention, refer to, or acknowledge an apparition that has not been approved—so as to not prematurely excite or influence others in an unacceptable manner. In fact, when I mention the name of an apparition event that someone is unfamiliar with, the first question I most frequently hear is, "Is that one approved by the Vatican?"

The fastest approval on record was within one month by the Coptic Pope in Egypt. This was because many bishops, investigators, and thousands of people of different faiths all witnessed Our Lady in Zeitoun, a suburb of Cairo. One of the longest periods of time waiting for approval involved apparitions in Laus, France. They happened in 1664 but did not receive official approval until May 4, 2008—some 344 years later! The first approved apparition in the United States occurred in 1859 in Champion, Wisconsin but did not receive local bishop approval until 2010—some 151 years later. Doing some basic math with forty of the better-known apparitions revealed that it takes the church an **average** of fifty-seven years to grant approval. We would most likely be dead then before we could even discuss it...right?

Other factors can clearly affect the objective, fair, and efficient process of approving apparition events. The differences in the cultures and governments of so many countries around the world have a major impact on how objective, professional, and expedient any investigation might be. Much depends upon the political climate and structure of how each country operates. Much also depends upon whether a war is going on or a difficult religious upheaval is taking place at the time. And in what century or period of time did these events happen? Could there even have been a fair or judicial appraisal conducted at those times of instability or transition?

Events in Medjugorje in Bosnia-Herzegovina provide a classic example for demonstrating a number of different interfering factors. When the appearances of the Virgin Mary to six children began in Medjugorje in 1981, the local bishop, Bishop Zanic, was very impressed, enthusiastic, and excited, claiming that these incidents were just as credible as Fatima or Lourdes. But then, the Communist government was opposed to this religious excitement, fearing a rebellion of some sort. The bishop was threatened with severe imprisonment if he supported the apparitions. The bishop greatly feared going to prison, so he reversed his opinions and would not support these heavenly visits. Years later in 1993, his replacement, Bishop Peric, openly did not believe in **any** Marian apparitions anywhere—*not even Fatima, Lourdes, or Guadalupe!* This new bishop would not even interview the children or consider any evidence. This was certainly not an objective or judicial effort. Yet, over fifty million pilgrims have flocked to Medjugorje and experienced many spiritual wonders. In a completely unprecedented manner in 2009, the Vatican decided to block a negative judgment of the apparitions from that bishop and take the matter out of the bishop's hands by performing their own three-year independent investigation from 2010–2013. A decision could be rendered sometime soon. It is unlikely that the Vatican would have done all of this if they had not thought that there was something quite worthy of careful investigation (45:64–65, 72, 75, 76).

Even Pope John Paul II had stated in June 1987, "Aren't you aware of the marvelous fruits it is producing?" Later in April 1989, he told Paul Hnilica, a close confidant and auxiliary bishop of Rome, "If I wasn't a pope, I'd have been in Medjugorje long ago" (8:211). The Swiss Archbishop Hans Balthasar blasted Bishop Zanic's first published position by saying,

> "My Lord, what a sorry document you have sent throughout the world! Medjugorje's theology rings true. I am convinced of its truth. Everything about Medjugorje is authentic in a Catholic sense. What is happening there is so evident, so convincing...a theater of holiness" (8:211–212).

Pope Benedict XVI (then Cardinal Joseph Ratzinger) spoke about visions and apparitions: "To all curious people, I would say I am certain that the Virgin does not engage in sensationalism; she does not act in order to instigate fear. She does not present apocalyptic visions, but guides people to her Son. And this is what is essential. The Madonna did not appear to children, to the small, to the simple, to those unknown in the world in order to create a sensation. 'Mary's purpose' is, through these simple ones, to call the world back to simplicity, that is, to the essentials: conversion, prayer, and the sacraments. A private revelation can have a prophetic character and can be a valuable aid for better understanding and living the Gospel at a certain time. Consequently, it should not be treated lightly. It is a help which is offered but its use is not obligatory" (9).

Another website, The Miracle Hunter, has done extensive gathering of information and lists details of even the earliest reports. Synopses of reports are presented from various historical sources and grouped for every hundred years or so (9). It is an impressive effort and a careful collection of data for these historical incidents. The Mary Pages website also does a nice job of collecting historical accounts (7).

With these large collections of historical accounts, how do we discern the truth? How do we decide what is real and worthy of belief? What account might be simply a legend, myth, tall tale, or an example of popular folklore? Or are people truly documenting reality as it happened? Are there patterns of data—descriptions, behavior, and actions—that repeat and run through these historical accounts to give credibility and reality to this phenomenon?

Let's "follow the footprints"…and see where they take us…

CHAPTER 4

THE SEARCH FOR TRUTH

Faith does not seem to be enough to believe in anything of a religious nature today. Present generations desire proof or evidence before being willing to believe. They expect that science can explain anything which presents itself as inexplicable or supernatural. They do not seem to believe that there is any proof for the existence of God—*or are they even looking*?

Belief is a direct result from finding truth. We will choose not to believe, most likely, if anything is proven to be false.

However, as children, we were often fed the fantasy that Santa Claus existed—and that we *should believe* in that fantasy. It felt wonderful to believe this story, trusting in our parents and *wanting* to believe this annual showering of gifts from an obese elf hauled around the planet by his glorious flying reindeer. (Seems silly now, right?) In fact, radio and television stations would add to this fabricated myth by broadcasting the latest tracking on radar of Santa's journey from the North Pole. We were taught to believe whatever they reported on TV as truth. We felt happy, were motivated to behave better, had great expectations, and were delightfully rewarded on Christmas morning with the truth of receiving gifts. Because gifts did seem to magically appear, the myth appeared to be a genuine reality, reinforced by the loving deception of the adults.

To see the glowing faces of children entranced by this fairy tale is a memorable joy for adults as well. We love perpetuating this myth because of the magical dreams, joyful anticipation, and happiness that it brings each year. In fact, despite the sobering disappointment of learning the truth, these joyful and happy memories cause us to want to deceive our own children next—so that they, too, can enjoy the magical fantasy that was never based in any reality whatsoever.

The point is that when we discover the truth that Santa Claus is not real, we stop believing in Santa Claus. Once a person realizes that Santa Claus is a fantasy, just try to get them to buy into that fantasy a second time. It will never happen because now they know the truth. We only take the risk of believing in anything as adults whenever we think that we have discovered the truth.

People are not sure what to believe about the existence of God. Is it another myth or legend? Another story promoted to give us false feelings of hope and joy? Where is the truth—the evidence or the reasons to truly believe? These are not readily obvious to today's generations of young adults, so they choose to believe whatever they want. They will probably consider only that which can be observed and proven with scientific evidence. The adults promoted Santa Claus, so why should we believe the incredible Jesus story? Is there truth—*enough truth*—for them to believe?

Blessed Mary, Jesus, and Joseph statues in Our Lady of the Lake Catholic church in Ashland, Wisconsin (photo by author)

BE NOT AFRAID TO FOLLOW THE FOOTPRINTS FROM HEAVEN

The first problem is that the story is two thousand years old. This creates a great sense of disconnection because it happened so very long ago. How can we relate to something that far into our past? How can we personally comprehend the customs, culture, thinking, and behavior of those times? How can we possibly know what is true and genuine? At this point, most people would not even go a step further to find any truth. They might choose to believe, blindly, without evidence, because they simply want to—perhaps out of faith. But the younger generations do not seem interested, probably assuming that any story from two thousand years ago is irrelevant to their current lives and their self-directed interests in the present. They doubt that rules, customs, or commandments from ancient times would have any relevant bearing on their modern lives rooted in technology, independent free will, and personal career goals.

So what would it take to convince modern generations that Jesus, Mary, Satan, and God are all very real and active in our present lives?

That would seem to be a monumental and impossible task!

It even sounds crazy and delusional—but what if we *could* provide evidence of their supernatural presence? If we could produce some truths, then belief is possible. If we provide an impressive collection of historical facts and undeniable truths, then belief becomes much easier and more likely to happen. There will always be those who have already made up their minds—no matter how much truth is presented to them. And there will always be those who will look at the truth but deny that it is there—probably because they are uneasy, frightened, or not ready to accept it because it challenges their present beliefs. Fear and insecurity can produce strong opposition to obvious truths. People don't like their world being changed by unexpected information. Keep that in mind.

How do we find **truth** in these historical accounts so that we can **believe** them?

Repeating patterns of details establish reality. If Santa Claus was actually observed in the sky by 230 people on the ground in Poland as his reindeer hauled his sled and gifts overhead, that would be a very unique and extremely unusual event. It would still be a "one-of-a-kind" incident that many sources would try to explain in terms of science, weather anomalies, an advertising gimmick, optical illusion, projected hologram, or grand hoax. But then, Santa's magical ride through the sky is again witnessed over Saudi Arabia, Ireland, and Nigeria. Many witnesses describe the same exact details of his appearance, performance, and actions. No longer is this event a "one-of-a-kind" quirk or fluke. It is now less likely to be labeled as a hoax due to the vast physical distance between sightings and different cultures involved. Other explanations also begin to fail as believable answers. With over a one thousand credible witnesses now from four different countries, fantasy and illusion are becoming less likely of an explanation. We may not be able to prove yet whether or not it is really Santa, but we can be more certain that it is not an unusual weather condition, an airplane, a meteor shower, a hot air balloon, an advertisement, or a unique illusion to one location. We have a better idea—through repetition of details—of **what it's not**, even though we still cannot be certain of **what it is**.

In contrast, fantasy is a creative story unique to an individual. If one asked a hundred people to create a story of how God would visit our planet, one would receive a vast variety of fascinating tales—all unique to the individual perspective and experience of those one hundred people who fantasized such an event. It would be very unlikely that we would obtain repetitious details or matching descriptions of any specific nature. The imaginations of a hundred people are never going to be exactly alike. By chance, there might be some similarities, but no two stories would ever be exactly alike.

If FBI agents were trying to track a serial killer across America, they would search for unsolved murders which have similar details. Exact details might include the hair color or style of each victim, the age of the victim, the sex of the victim, the type of unmarked van seen in the area, the precise method of killing, the types of materials used, a killer's "signature" or specific mark or item left behind, etc. When unsolved murders in Utah, Texas, Arizona, Nevada, Oklahoma, and New Mexico reveal matching details, it suggests a reality that these murders are possibly linked and perpetrated by the same criminal. Many specific details are not publicized so that detectives can be more certain of their results. If they would not compare details and link these unsolved cases, the killer would not likely be discovered. Repeating specific details compose a precise picture of reality that leads to truth!

Social sciences often rely on statistical probability, based on how often a detail or aspect appears and repeats. For example, if 3 percent represents the statistic for a "chance occurrence," and the detail repeats in its appearance 72 percent of the time, we can conclude that the detail did not appear *by chance*—but rather is a **significant** occurrence (and part of a pattern of reality). Therefore, when we examine encounters with the Virgin Mary by various cultures and people of the world over twenty centuries, specific details are likely to repeat—**only if it is a *real event***. Details are *not* going to repeat with any significance if the source is an imagined fantasy, myth, legend, delusion, hoax, or psychological disturbance. Those are all created and personalized experiences unique to the individual and highly unlikely to repeat with any significance. If you asked a hundred children to draw God, you would get one hundred different and very creative drawings as each child imagines what God would look like. Each drawing would reflect that child's experience, learning, perspective, and imagination. Therefore, each drawing should be as unique as each child and their creative approach.

Throughout the thousands of alleged visits by the Virgin Mary, there are definite and specific patterns of repeating details. This becomes compelling evidence for a reality—real events, credible truth, and the opportunity for belief to thrive because there is a reasonable certainty that these appearances have **really** happened. Eyewitness testimony will be presented. Physical evidence is occasionally available. Scientific examinations have taken place. Psychological evaluations have been done. Theologians have been consulted. Heavenly predictions have come true and correlating biblical references add credibility to these being real appearances by the true Mother of Jesus.

Take a look at some of the specific details that are repeating throughout the reported accounts. For example, when the Blessed

Mother speaks, her voice has a unique quality that many witnesses have tried to describe with some difficulty:

TLAXCALA, MEXICO (1541): Juan Bernardino describes, "A soft, almost musical voice" (3:38).

RAPALLO, ITALY (1557): Giovanni Chichivola states, "The sound of a sweet voice called my name" (4:112–114).

VINAY, FRANCE (1649): Pierre Port-Combet hesitated, "Hearing the sweet sound of her voice" (3:69).

QUERRIEN, FRANCE (1652): As Jeanne Courtel is miraculously healed from her lifelong condition of being both deaf and mute, she recalls hearing the "sweet voice" of the Virgin Mary (3:73).

LOURDES, FRANCE (1858): "It is not necessary," said Mary in a soft, musical, mysterious voice to Bernadette. It had a wonderful quality that she could find no words for (11:102).

CHAMPION, WISCONSIN (1859): "She spoke in a soft, sweet voice—the sound was heavenly" (20:11).

HERAULT, FRANCE (1873): "The Blessed Virgin, dressed now in gold and holding a rosary in her right hand, spoke in a sweet voice" (3:135).

FATIMA, PORTUGAL (1917): "They were terrified, but her soft voice calmed them and melted their fears away" (29:68).

GHIAIE DI BONATE, ITALY (1944): "At first, I was scared and was on the point of running away, but the Lady called to me in a sweet voice...Her voice sounded so harmonious and sweet that, so far as I tried to reproduce it, I was never able to" (110).

GARABANDAL, SPAIN (1961): "Her voice was sweet and pure—and not like any other voice that they had ever heard" (34:13).

CUAPA, NICARAGUA (1980): "She answered me with the sweetest voice I have ever heard from any woman—sweeter than the softest voice" (2:158).

MEDJUGORJE, BOSNIA-HERZEGOVINA (1981): Blessed Mary spoke simple messages of reconciliation in a voice that "was like a bell that rings softly" (11:220). "The young woman smiled at each of them and then spoke in a voice more like singing than speech" (8:77). "She spoke in a singing voice" (8:84).

KIBEHO, RWANDA (1981): (1) She heard a strong but lovely voice—"soft as air and sweeter than music"—say, "My child…" (2) The soft sweet voice filled with motherly love called her name again (39:35, 59).

Obviously, these witnesses were intrigued by the unique quality of her voice—"a soft, sweet, musical tone." These quotes span nearly five hundred years from countries all over the world! This is the kind of detail that suggests that they are all experiencing the same supernatural visitor in the same manner.

I have tracked hundreds of details from eighty-nine of the best documented apparition accounts in order to see if a pattern of reality continues to emerge. Here is another example, in this case, a supernatural detail: the inability to move an object or person due to some kind of an invisible force.

ORBEY, FRANCE (1491)

"Suddenly, he was dazzled by a bright light. In the brilliant light he could distinguish the figure of the Blessed Mother dressed in a long white veil. She was holding three ears of corn in her right hand while the other hand held a clump of ice. Without identifying herself, she began to speak,

"Arise, brave man. See these ears? These are the symbols of fine harvests that will reward virtuous and generous people and bring peace and contentment in the homes of faithful Christians. As to the ice, it means hail, frost, flood, famine and all its attendant misery and desolation that will punish disbelievers with the gravity of their sins which tire the Divine Mercy. Go down to the village and announce to all the people the meaning of these prophecies."

When the vision disappeared, the blacksmith became terribly frightened, and upon reaching the village, he said nothing—in disobedience of Our Lady's wishes. He went inside the market, purchased a sack of wheat, and started to prepare it for placement on his horse.

But the sack of wheat became uncommonly heavy and could not be lifted. Even with the help of others, the sack could not be

moved. **The villagers wondered if witchcraft was involved!** It was then that he remembered the words of the Virgin, and realizing the weight of the sack was a signal to him, he loudly shared the message that had been entrusted to him by Our Lady. Many people heard the message spoken with sincerity and took it to heart, resolving to do better in the future. When he had finished telling of his experience and the message given to him, he easily lifted the sack of wheat and secured it onto his horse, and left for home" (3:19–20).

RAPALLO, ITALY (1557)

The Blessed Virgin Mary appeared to Giovanni and reassured him by saying,

> "Do not fear, Giovanni. I am the Mother of God. I have chosen you to be a messenger of my motherly will. Visit the ecclesiastics of Rapallo and let them know that the Mother of God has chosen this place as her perpetual dwelling place and would like a church to be erected here. I leave here a pledge of my love."

The vision then directed his attention to a small picture propped against one of the rocks where he had been resting.

> "Tell the people that this picture was brought here from Greece by the angels. I leave it here as a token of my love for them. Fast on Saturday."

The vision then disappeared as if carried away in a cloud. The farmer Giovanni studied the icon on the rock. The picture depicted Our Blessed Mary lying on a bier at the time of her passing from this world on to the Heavenly Kingdom. The Holy Trinity was represented by figures in the central part of the icon. Surrounding the Virgin in a mournful attitude were several saints and two angels. **Giovanni attempted to pick the icon up off the rock, but he could not budge it at all.** Much to his surprise, a spring had begun flowing from the dry ground by the rock—the exact spot where the Blessed Virgin had appeared.

He went to the village and told the people what had happened. The priests to whom he told his story were skeptical, but because of Giovanni's excitement, they reluctantly followed him to the place of the apparition. **There they saw the picture which none of the peasants could lift**, and the spring which had mysteriously appeared. **One of the priests raised the portrait without difficulty** and carried it in procession to the parish church, where it was carefully locked up pending further investigation. But the next morning, the icon had disappeared from the church—only to be found back on the rock up on the wooded hill (3:43–44).

PELLEVOISIN, FRANCE (1876)

"The next night, on the 15th of February, the Virgin appeared.

> "Be not afraid, for I am here. This time My Son is showing His Mercy. He will let you have life; on Saturday you will be healed."

Mary responded with a smile. Estelle saw a marble tile wrapped in white silk paper **but found it impossible to pick up.** Then Mary said it was time to look into the past. Estelle's past mistakes were reviewed. Stunned at what she had done over the years, she felt great sadness. Mary just remained silent and then left with an expression of goodness on her face" (137).

KIBEHO, RWANDA (1981)

"On one occasion, Alphonsine was walking along with a group of girls when she suddenly dropped to her knees as though she had been shot. She landed heavily on her knees and stared at the ceiling exactly as she had the day before. Her face lit up in ecstasy, smiling peacefully with tears of joy running down her cheeks. The transformation was so sudden and dramatic that some girls began to believe. Others howled with laughter, waving their hands in front of her eyes and shouting in her ears. But she did not blink, flinch, or react. She didn't see the girls any longer—only the beautiful lady hovering above her again in the same soft, glorious light. Mary was the "most beautiful woman" she had ever seen—and said her skin was neither black nor white but "shined like polished ivory."

On another occasion, her classmates tossed rosaries at her while she was in an ecstasy, trying to hook them on her head like a ring-toss game. Some girls were respectful and laid their rosaries in front of her, hoping that Mary might bless them. When Mary told Alphonsine to pick them up so that she could bless them, the girl reached blindly into the pile of all the rosaries, unaware of the girls around her, and managed to only select those that were from the respectful girls. **Those from the hecklers "stuck to the ground like anchors" and could not be lifted** (39:40, 43).

This interesting phenomenon, directly related to these heavenly visits, suggests a kind of deliberate divine intervention. It especially gets interesting *when the visionaries cannot be moved*, either, while they are in the realm of visiting with the Blessed Virgin.

LOURDES, FRANCE (1858)

"Just three days later, she felt compelled to return (with father's permission) and took a bottle of holy water and a group of her curious classmates with her down the path to the Grotto of Massabielle. She fell into a mesmerized trance in front of the grotto as she saw the Lady again. Others could not see or hear anything but were impressed by her gaze that could not be broken with distractions. When Bernadette was done praying and the Lady had vanished, **friends could not move her physically from her spot. They ran to the sawmill, and the operator of the nearby mill struggled to move the girl as she suddenly seemed incredibly heavy and hard to move.** He was able to finally drag her back up the footpath" (11:100).

TRE FONTANE, ROME, ITALY (1947)

On the Saturday after Easter Sunday, April 12, 1947, Bruno took his three children (Isola-ten, Carlo-seven, and Gianfranco-four) for a picnic to Tre Fontane. One of his children lost his ball and asked for his help. He followed this child but saw his youngest child kneeling at the entrance to a cave. The child's face was radiantly joyful as he stared into the cave, repeating, "Beautiful lady, beautiful lady." His hands were folded as if engrossed in deep prayer. Bruno looked into the cave and could see nothing that would account for the boy's action. He then turned toward his other two children, but by then, they too, had dropped to their knees, hands folded in prayer with their eyes transfixed on someone in the cave. The three children were mesmerized by something supernatural that he could not see. **Seized with fright, Bruno tried to grab his children and carry them away, but he could not move them! It was as if they were glued to the ground.** Then, in the midst of an intense perfume of flowers, Mary appeared to Bruno as well. An intense light filled his eyes for a moment, and then everything in front of him disappeared—his children and the cave (153).

GARABANDAL, SPAIN (1961)

By Sunday, June 25, people, including five priests and many doctors, were coming from all the nearby villages as word of the visions spread. **One doctor tried to lift Conchita during her kneeling ecstasy, getting her only barely off the ground**, and dropped her hard on her knees. Others could hear the sound of bones breaking. Yet, Conchita remained unaware of that action, and the villagers found her unharmed without a scratch or bruise after her ecstasy was over (34:9–10). When the girls were not in ecstasy and they would try to lift each other up, they would struggle and fall, laughing like all children. But during an ecstasy, they lifted each other up with ease. **If, however, during an ecstasy, someone else tried to move them or lift them, it was very hard (34:25).** Perhaps most peculiar of all was the way **the force of gravity seemed to increase around the girls whenever they saw the Virgin.** They became so heavy that even the largest man in the village could not lift them an inch off the ground. Basque laborers who prided themselves on their strength were brought in to give it a try. Witnesses watched man after man fail in attempts to raise the girls during their ecstasies, then walk away trembling with fright (8:181).

ZEITOUN, EGYPT (1968)

In the early hours of April 13, Wagih Rizk Matta, a photographer, succeeded in photographing the vision for the first time—**overcoming an inexplicable sensation of immobility which prevented the vast majority of people from operating their cameras**. Having taken the pictures, he then became aware of being completely healed from an old injury to his arm! (Doctors confirmed his miraculous healing.) (59:21, 80)

AKITA, JAPAN (1973)

"On June 12, 1973, Sister Agnes Sasagawa (age forty-two) entered the convent chapel, focused on preparing for the Eucharist. She was still adjusting to her recent loss of all hearing. Suddenly, as she approached the altar to open the tabernacle door, a brilliant light broke forth—brighter and whiter than the sun. Overwhelmed, she dropped to her knees and prayed for the next hour—**feeling as if she was being held there by some heavy force**. She was able to leave after that. The next day, as she opened the tabernacle door again, the brilliant light poured forth once more" (11:190–191).

KIBEHO, RWANDA (1981)

"Three of the visionaries took mystical journeys with Mary. Before Alphonsine went on her journey, Mary instructed her to inform the school director 'not to bury her—even if she appears dead.' The stunned director knew by now to take Alphonsine seriously. She told them that she would be away for the whole weekend. Failing to show for the Friday evening meal, a nun went to check on her on Saturday morning. She was stunned to find her lying unresponsive on her bed—**unable to be awakened or even budged an inch**. The director grabbed the school nurse and summoned Abbot Augustin

Misago, a leading member of the Commission of Enquiry. Soon, there were many concerned officials, priests, and others in attendance as Alphonsine truly appeared dead. Medical experts concluded that she was still alive, but that her pulse rate was impossibly slow, and her blood pressure too low with breathing almost nonexistent—a shallow breath once a minute. **As many as six men tried with all their might to roll her over, separate her clasped hands, or lift her from the bed, but without any success!** Eighteen hours later, Alphonsine awoke, livelier than ever—with sparkling eyes, relaxed muscles, and a glowing face. Later, she described her journey with the Blessed Virgin" (39:133–134).

ZAKARPATTYA, UKRAINE (2002)

On another occasion, Olenka kissed the feet of Christ when he appeared before her—but then felt a sharp pain stab her in the hands, feet, heart, and head. She collapsed to the ground, and the other **children had difficulty raising her.** She stretched on the ground, spreading her arms out, assuming the position of someone being crucified. **Again, she could not be lifted from the ground.** A young boy ran back to the village for help, returning with Reverend Atanasy Chiypesh and a watchman. They eventually got her to her home after sprinkling water from the spring on her face (159).

A final example of a repeating phenomenon—correlated with the appearances of Blessed Mary—involves the sudden and intense fragrance of roses. Note how this reoccurs over hundreds of years throughout countries around the world:

VICENZA, ITALY (1426)

She had "the likeness of a most beautiful queen with garments more resplendent than the sun, wreathed in a **fragrance of a thousand scents**" (3:10).

SAVONA, ITALY (1536)

Then Mary asked the farmer to return to this same place on the fourth Saturday to receive another message meant for the Curia and the people of Savona. When she vanished from his sight, a **sweet fragrance of flowers** lingered for some time (162).

MADRID, SPAIN (1610)

Looking for shelter, they saw a mysterious light coming from a cave. They hurried to it and found a beautiful statue of the Virgin Mary holding the Child Jesus. Surrounding it was a shimmering light and a **heavenly fragrance of flowers** (3:55).

LAUS, FRANCE (1664)

The chapel appeared to look like all the other small houses in the village, so Benoite had a terrible time the next day trying to locate it in a town she had never travelled to. She stopped at the entrance to every poor dwelling, trying to detect that **"sweet fragrance"** that she associated with the Blessed Virgin. Finally, she detected the fragrance at a doorway where the door had been left ajar. Inside, she found the beautiful Lady standing on the dust-covered altar.

Within four years, the church was completed. The hands of the poor had gathered its materials; donations had dug its foundations. The earliest historians of Laus are unanimous in reporting the **sweet, heavenly fragrance** of the place. A great number of people attested to the **strong fragrances** coming from the church. It was so intense that it spread from the church all over the valley. Judge Francois Grimaud claimed,

> "During the Easter season of 1666, I smelled a **very sweet fragrance** for around seven minutes. I had never smelled anything like it in my life, and it gave me such deep satisfaction that I was enraptured."

From March 24 until the end of May 1690, the Laus church was so pervaded with this **fragrance** that *all the pilgrims* attested to it. This phenomenon is still experienced today. To avoid any possibility or claim of deception, *flowers are not usually allowed* at the shrine. The manuscripts of Laus report:

> "Every time the Blessed Virgin honored her with Her visit, people smelled a **heavenly fragrance** that pervaded the entire church. Sometimes the shepherd girl's clothing was deeply permeated with the **heavenly scent** for up to eight days. These **supernatural fragrances were so sweet** and delightful that they uplifted many souls" (123:4, 6).

FATIMA, PORTUGAL (1917)

August 19: Jacinta broke off a small branch that Our Lady had rested her feet upon, which had been touched by her magnificent robe, and took it home. On the way, Lucia's mother demanded, skeptically, to hold the branch. She was shocked to behold a **"magnificent fragrance"** that she could not identify—and was a changed woman from this point forward (29:178) (32:42).

September 13: Lucia shouted to the people as Blessed Mary rose to leave, "If you want to see Our Lady, look that way (to the East)." When the crowd looked, hundreds or more saw the luminous globe ascending toward heaven. But thousands who were present also witnessed other supernatural details: a sudden cooling of the air, a dimming of the sun—so much so that thousands could see the stars at midday, a white mist surrounding the holm oak and the children, and a **shower of white, iridescent flower petals** that vanished upon reaching the ground (32:47).

February 20, 1920: Jacinta died at 10:30 p.m., alone, in her hospital bed. Doctors were amazed that after three days, her body smelled **"as sweet as a bouquet of roses."** This was a surprising and drastic change in fragrance from the horrible, repulsive stench of her illness. She still looked alive in her coffin with cheeks and lips of a beautiful pink color. A number of witnesses testified to the **extraor-**

dinary sweet odor emanating from her body. It was clearly the fragrance of flowers! (29:267–268)

TRE FONTANE, ROME, ITALY (1947)

Then, in the midst of an **intense perfume of flowers**, Mary appeared to Bruno as well. An intense light filled his eyes for a moment, and then everything in front of him disappeared—his children and the cave (153:2).

LIPA, PHILIPPINES (1948, 1990)

In August, when Our Lady first appeared to her, there was an **overpowering but pleasant fragrance of flowers**.

August 20, 1948: Teresita saw **showers of rose petals** for the first of many times. They occurred both outside in the garden and inside the convent. Many clergy, pilgrims, and religious witnessed these **rose petal showers**. The rose petals contained miraculous images of Jesus, Mary, and other holy scenes. They were collected, saved, and cherished by many—even to this present day.

Saint Therese of Liseux accompanied Our Lady during some of the apparitions. She had been known for saying, "From the heavens, I will let fall a **shower of roses**."

Bishop Alfredo Verzosa ordered the Carmelite nuns to withdraw the statue of Mary from public veneration because of all the commotion it had caused. He personally went to the convent on November 19, 1948, determined to do this, himself. When he opened the door and entered the convent, a ***shower of rose petals*** fell on him. He fell to his knees and could not utter a word. From that moment on, Bishop Verzosa supported the apparitions with official approval.

Many cures have been reported using the rose petals.

And "showers" of rose petals have often fallen inside Teresita's home as well. Several witnesses, including a priest, were present when ***full roses materialized out of thin air*** and landed on the stairs, altar, and bedroom of Teresita's home.

May 1990: The next day—after forty years—Archbishop Gaviola finally ordered the statue to be displayed again. **Showers of rose petals began again.** As Teresita and two others were praying in front of Mary's statue in the chapel, a **shower of pure white rose petals** fell *inside* the chapel.

Other reports include the "spinning of the sun" and **strong smell of roses** again. Water gained healing powers if the rose petals had been dipped into it (126).

GARABANDAL, SPAIN (1961)

With so many people and so many items piled up for blessing, it would be impossible for the girls to know what item belonged to whom. But during their ecstasies, they not only returned every item correctly to each individual, but their eyes never left Mary—as if she was guiding them to the rightful owners! And despite some people and priests trying to trick or test the girls, they *never* made a mistake. Many times people would notice the **sweet smell of roses** coming from an object kissed by Our Lady. Sometimes Mary would ask the girls to "have (name) kiss the crucifix," and they would always go right to that stranger in the crowd (34:17–18).

SAN DAMIANO, ITALY (1961–1970)

Many have smelled the **strong and exquisite fragrances of roses** in Mama Rosa's chapel and in the waiting room next to it. Sometimes the **sweet perfume (from invisible flowers)** could be smelled all the way from Mama Rosa's house to the local church on the way to Mass. (58:7).

AKITA, JAPAN (1973)

On September 29, with another nun at her side, Sister Agnes saw the statue of Mary ablaze with light again. For the first time, the companion with her was able to see the unearthly light and gasped with excitement. The statue's hands glowed brightly, and the wound was healed finally. But later that night, when the statue glowed again, tears began flowing from the statue's eyes. The tears had a wonderful *fragrance of flowers* that persisted for seventeen days! (11:200)

MEDJUGORJE, BOSNIA (1990)

Only minutes after an apparition with Mirjana Dragicevic, Janet Knez was impressed by the depth and luminosity of Mirjana's eyes, the chalky transparency of her skin, and the serenity of her expression, and most of all—the **overpowering scent of roses** now present around Mirjana. **The aroma was so intense that it almost made Janet feel drunk**. She shook Mirjana's hand and afterwards could smell **roses** on her own fingertips—which lingered for days! (8:21)

CUENCA, ECUADOR (1988)

On August 28, 1988 at 4:50 a.m., a great light invaded her bedroom at home, and Blessed Mary first appeared to this sixteen year old out of the light. Patricia was very startled—but not afraid. When asked to pray, she began to quickly say Our Father, but Mother Mary told her to pray it more slowly and with feeling. Then Our Lady vanished, leaving a **soft scent of flowers**, which remained for three days in the whole house.

On December 15, 1988, family and close friends noted something different when Patricia went into an ecstasy in her bedroom. The ladies immediately placed their rosaries on the altar for Mary to bless. As they finished praying the Rosary, the **beautiful smell of flowers** was present in the room! On December 25, 1988, the **scent of fresh flowers** and candles (neither was present or lit) preceded Blessed Mary's visit as a group gathered to pray. The day after Christmas, when this group was praying again, the **strong odor of incense and flowers** permeated Patricia's house again (23:1–2, 19–22).

AGOO, PHILIPPINES (1989)

Just before the Virgin Mary would appear, her presence could be detected through the **extraordinary fragrance of roses**. People would kiss the ground when they perceived this. A flash of light usually preceded her appearance.

Large crowds were present during each apparition. Tens of thousands of people converged on this small community, causing traffic jams for scores of miles. Those present were often treated to spectacular signs and visions in the sky as well the "miracle of the spinning sun," the **aroma of roses**, and a mysterious blue light whenever Mary would appear to Judiel.

February 6, 1993: The statue of Our Lady cried tears of blood after the regular First Saturday apparition at Apparition Hill. Later that night, the statue was brought to the bishop's palace in San Fernando. Bishop Lazo reported that he witnessed with his own eyes the statue shedding tears of blood. He said that the room filled with the **strong fragrance of roses**, "and we knelt and prayed" (98:1, 2, 7).

STEUBENVILLE, OHIO, USA (1992)

"I could hear the voice of some young lady that sounded like she was singing or crying. Then I **smelled these roses. I mean the place just reeked of roses. It was so strong...I couldn't believe it...** Then I peeked through the open door of the church, and I saw this lady dressed all in red, standing with her hands open in front of the altar. She was saying over and over, 'My Son's heart is broken'" (2:302).

PERRYVILLE, MISSOURI, USA (2003)

Neal and a few others decided to make one last trek, stopping at the various Stations of the Cross along the way. At the fourth station (where Jesus sees his Mother), Neal suddenly was overwhelmed by a **strong scent of roses—"so intense that you could almost taste them!"** He fell down on the large rocks as if unconscious but suffered no cuts, bruises, or injuries. He had an intense desire at that moment to be with Mary and Jesus in heaven. He felt like "a million bits of information were being dispersed all at once." Then he heard Blessed Mary say to him,

> "I have much for you to do…Never waste a moment to serve God" (84).

There are many more examples of these kinds of repeating details throughout the historic literature. Certain patterns are definitely developing. Repeating patterns suggest a reality. Reality is truth. Truth promotes belief. But are **you** ready to believe, yet?

The footprints are right in front of us and becoming clearer and easier to track.

Follow them with me—as we proceed deeper into these mysteries!

CHAPTER 5

THE REALM OF THE VISIONARY

What does it take to be a visionary?
Do we have to act like a saint?
Do we have to be religious and very devoted?
Do we have to be a certain age?
Do we have to be interested or have a desire to become involved?
Do we need to have an upstanding character?
Do we have to be Catholic?
What if we don't wish to be involved?

We would probably assume that any visionary would be a devout, religious, prayerful person who would delight in such a holy visitation. We could assume that the person would be a mature, responsible, dedicated individual with an upstanding character. We would expect that any such visionary would therefore love the opportunity to serve Jesus and Mary.

And we would be wrong.

Many visionaries were between the ages of ten and sixteen; others as old as seventy. Some had no religious training at all. Most were ordinary people with ordinary problems. Some were anti-Catholic or nonbelievers. Some asked Mary to select somebody else for her requests as they did not feel adequate for the tasks. Some did not even recognize her or know who she was for months. Many were frightened, uncertain, confused, and uneasy about such visions. In short, they were basically normal, everyday people who were suddenly thrust into the amazing position of dealing with the Virgin Mary from two thousand years ago!

Their human reactions were quite normal and believable. But the transformation in their lives was truly remarkable and often miraculous. Some would eventually become great religious leaders or even saints. Others would completely change their careers, life directions, or religious practices. All of these "average" people would change dramatically, suggesting that they had indeed been transformed by some amazing life encounter. Even very young children would suddenly become devout or dedicated to their religion and saintly in their transformed personalities. And not just for a few weeks—but for the rest of their lives. *They clearly encountered **something** life altering!*

When experiencing an appearance by the Virgin Mary, the visionaries found themselves truly in another realm. Many times, the light surrounding Mary encompassed them as well—and they would see nothing else but themselves alone with her. When Mary arrived, they would suddenly drop to their knees, often in precise union if in a group. The following are, again, excerpts taken from accounts of Marian apparitions.

BEAURAING, BELGIUM (1932)

Adults began to suspect tricksters perpetrating a hoax, so at least six adults trailed the children in a protective and investigative manner on the third night. The five children shrieked with delight when they saw the Virgin Mary—even closer this time where they could see her beautiful features in greater detail. Her feet were hidden by a little cloud as she floated only a couple feet above the ground in front of them. She was dressed in a glowing white gown, hands joined in prayer, blue eyes raised toward heaven with rays of light surrounding her head. Then she reached outward with her arms and disappeared. The children ran to find the adults who had spread out to watch for pranksters. Suddenly, the children were overwhelmed as Mary appeared again near the shrubs of the convent's entry gate. But the adults could not see what all the children had reacted to. One mother decided to return later that night with three of the older kids to investigate further. When the Virgin appeared, **the three dropped hard to their knees, simultaneously, on the cobble-stoned street, reciting the Hail Mary "as one voice" of a high pitch.** The mother was impressed that they seemed to be looking at the same exact yet invisible object. As she approached where they were gazing, her own daughter cautioned her not to walk into Mary as it might offend or disrespect Mary. The mother began to believe. The apparitions did not occur every night, but the children assembled and prayed the Rosary anyway. **When she did appear, they would all drop to their knees in unison. They all went down as if pushed by a strong force.** Witnesses commented that the noise made by their knees hitting the ground made enough pressure to break the kneecaps of other people. Yet the children never felt any pain (5:175) (11:164–170) (101).

HEEDE, GERMANY (1937)

More than seven thousand returned to the site the next day on November 8. But the civil authorities forbade Father Staelberg from accompanying the girls. Another priest was present that day from Herkenhoff and reported these details:

> **"Suddenly, the (four) girls fell to their knees, all together, without one or another making a signal to her companions...** They posed several questions to the apparition. After a quarter of an hour—during which they continued to be constantly stiff, eyes fixed on a precise point—their questions seemed unanswered" (115).

GARABANDAL, SPAIN (1961)

The girls described "three warnings" that they would receive to indicate that Mary would be coming soon. The first was a slight feeling of joy and anticipation. The second call was more like an overflowing of happiness with a great desire. The third calling was a feeling of urgency, and the girls would rush to the place where the apparition was to occur. Father Valentin decided to test the girls one day without their knowing it. He had the girls separated in different homes to see if they were influencing each other in any way. By the "third call," the girls all left their homes simultaneously, arriving at the rocky lane at the same moment and **falling to their knees into an ecstasy all at the same time!** On another occasion, both priests closely observed all four girls in an ecstasy in the church. The girls were begging Mary for proof or some miracle because so many people still did not believe them. They made an ecstatic march, backward, to the altar, **dropped to their knees in unison**, and recited a rosary beautifully (34:22, 39).

MEDJUGORJE, BOSNIA (1981)

Medjugorje visionaries Ivanka, Mirjana, Marija, and Ivan with eyes focused on the Virgin Mary in 1981.

"When we were about two meters (six feet) away from the Madonna, **we felt as if we were thrown to our knees. Jakov was thrown kneeling into a thorny bush**, and I thought he would be injured. But he came out of it without a scratch" (52:15).

When the children arrived at the hill that evening, a large crowd was already on the hill, awaiting them. The three flashes of light were often visible to many in the crowd. When Mary arrived, **the children would suddenly stop the group prayer on the exact same word and drop to their knees in uncanny synchronization**. It was very crowded, so when Mary appeared to them, the mass of praying, singing witnesses was a bit too close. When they saw the crowd accidentally step on the Virgin's long veil, she would disappear. When some order was established, she would reappear. But then a boy stepped on her veil, and she disappeared again. With tears in their eyes, the children cried out, "Be careful! You are standing on parts of her gown, and she keeps disappearing each time you do that!" (45:38) (52:24)

A team of specialists from the University of Montpellier, France ran many tests on five of the visionaries *during their apparitions*. Note this particular finding:

"Within one-fifth of a second, they simultaneously knelt and looked precisely at the same spot in the air without any visible reference point when the Virgin Mary appeared to them" (132).

LITMANOVA, SLOVAKIA (1990)

Finally, Ivetka's father urged her to share what had transformed her behavior and attitude. Upon learning of the visitation from the Beautiful Lady, he gathered his wife and the two girls and headed for the woodcutter's shack on August 5, 1990. No sooner did they enter the door of the shack than a brilliant light **sent the group to their knees**. Immediately, both Ivetka and Katka saw the Beautiful Lady in the dazzling light (2:329).

LUZON, PHILIPPINES (1982)

One teacher, who *had seen* the vision along with the children, said that **she had felt an awesome force making her kneel down on the ground** (129).

Even if the terrain is rugged or harsh, slamming to their knees never injures or bruises them. They stare at a certain point in space, and their faces reflect a joyous countenance. Bystanders are emotionally moved by their transformed appearance.

BANNEAUX, BELGIUM (1933)

Nobody believed Mariette's story except her father. It was he who accompanied her to the garden three nights later on January 18 at seven in the evening to observe her next encounter. She **suddenly knelt on the frozen ground**, started praying the Rosary, and saw the "Lady in white" descending from the sky in the distance. The image was small at first but glowing brightly and getting closer as she floated down between two pine trees. Her father watched in amazement as she raised her arms as if greeting someone. Mariette was delighted at how close Mary was this time—hovering just a few feet above the ground on a small gray cloud of smoke.

The father was impressed by his daughter's words and behavior, so he rode on his bike to get others as witnesses. As they returned, they found her leaving the garden area and entering the road, drawn down the road as if in a trance. Mariette said, "She is calling me." **They watched in amazement as she was thrown to her knees twice on the pavement in the cold, twelve-degree air and started praying earnestly. It sounded like her knees cracked on the frozen ground.** But she never experienced any injuries (11:180).

GARABANDAL, SPAIN (1961)

By Sunday, June 25, people were coming from all the nearby villages as word of the visions spread—including five priests and many doctors. One doctor tried to lift Conchita during her kneeling ecstasy, getting her only barely off the ground, and **dropped her hard on her knees. Others could hear the sound of bones breaking. Yet, Conchita remained unaware of that action, and the villagers found her unharmed without a scratch or bruise** after her ecstasy was over.

The physical actions of these girls impressed many doctors and specialists. **As they would fall to their knees with each ecstasy, they would often land on sharp stones and rocks and remain kneeling for extremely long periods of time without moving—with no bruising, cuts, scrapes, or marks.** The girls would look in the same direction, at the same spot, and would change direction simultaneously as if watching something that had just moved (34:9–10, 20) (33).

KIBEHO, RWANDA (1981)

When Alphonsine told of her experience, nobody believed her. As more experiences continued, so did the harsh ridicule, teasing, and hurtful comments. On one occasion, she was walking along with a group of girls **when she suddenly dropped to her knees as though she had been shot. She landed heavily on her knees** and stared at the ceiling exactly as she had the day before. Her face lit up in ecstasy, smiling peacefully with tears of joy running down her cheeks. The transformation was so sudden and dramatic that some girls began to believe (39:40).

CUENCA, ECUADOR (1988)

The next day, Saturday, October 8, the group was visiting the Shrine of Our Lady of Guadalupe when Patricia **suddenly fell to her knees**; her body became rigid, tilting her head far back, and she held out her arms, palms upward, toward the sky. Other tourists became startled—but she was completely unaware of them (23:8).

Witnesses hear a change in their voices—a husky whisper or soundless moving of lips. If in a group, all will speak, pray, or sing in perfect unison at times. Witnesses note that they can move effortlessly over difficult terrain, never falling or getting cuts, bruises, or other injuries. Walking through muddy areas, their feet have remained impossibly clean. Their gaze stays on Mary even if they are moving across terrain where they should watch where they step—and they never fall or stumble. Sometimes, they move at a supernatural speed, well witnessed by others.

GARABANDAL, SPAIN (1961)

Villagers noted many other odd behaviors—being thrown backward to the ground simultaneously without injury or pain, levitating off the floor several inches, **moving at incredible speed either forward or backward over the rugged terrain with heads looking up the whole time, never running into anything, never falling or stum-**

bling. Despite adults running at full speed to try to keep up, the girls were never tired or winded—it was as if they were gliding along effortlessly without even looking at the ground **as long as they kept Mary in their vision.** On one occasion, observers saw two of the girls walk over a small footbridge while the other two **just glided over the small stream as if walking on air**! (33) Even when barefoot, their feet were never harmed by sharp rocks, glass, and dangerous terrain. In fact, their bare feet stayed very clean despite the dirty village streets—something that nobody there could fake (34:23–24).

MEDJUGORJE, BOSNIA (1981)

Excitedly, Vicka ran back to get Marija and Jakov, and now all six of these kids became filled with joy—not fear—at seeing the Virgin Mary. Mary summoned the children to come up to her. They were **utterly amazed at the ease and speed with which they advanced up the steep and treacherous slope**—full of sharp-edged stones and prickly, thorny briers. Vicka describes that moment:

> "We ran quickly up the hill. It was not like walking on the ground. Nor did we look for the path. We simply ran toward her. In less than five minutes we were up the hill—**as if something had pulled us through the air.** I was afraid. I was also barefoot, but no thorns had scratched me (52:15). We went straight up through the brambles. We ran as if borne along. We felt neither stones nor brambles. Nothing. As if the ground were covered with sponge or rubber. Impossible to explain" (8:76).

The other kids described it *as if they were flying* up the rugged hillside. Those who were watching from below were **astonished at the speed of the children's ascent** and did not even try to follow them (usually took fifteen to twenty minutes to climb—not two minutes!) (45:32). Jozo Ostojic, age twelve, had recently set a regional record for the hundred-yard dash. He recalls:

> "Little Jakov Colo was two years younger than me—and not really athletic. Normally, I can outrun him by a huge distance. But on this day, I can't come close to keeping up with him.

He and the others seemed to be flying up that hill. There is no path, just rocks and thornbushes, but all six of them are moving at an incredible speed, bounding from rock to rock, taking enormous strides. I am running as fast as I can, but falling further and further behind, and so are the grown men running with me. We are gasping for breath, almost in tears, unable to believe what is happening" (8:79).

HERAULT, FRANCE (1873)

Believers, skeptics, and the curious all gathered on July 8, 1873 in his vineyard for the predicted second appearance of Mary. Auguste's wife worried about what might happen if the Virgin failed to appear, and this crowd of five hundred would become disappointed and perhaps angry. But Auguste had plenty of faith and no fear at all. After a few minutes, Auguste removed his hat and raised both arms high in the air. He seemed transfixed by what he was able to see, while everybody else saw nothing. With his arms still raised, **he was suddenly carried *with uncommon speed* by some invisible force to the cross about forty yards away.** He prayed silently while gazing at the Blessed Virgin before him, dressed now in gold and holding a rosary in her right hand (3:135).

LA CODOSERA, SPAIN (1945)

It was 3:00 p.m., May 27, 1945, when ten-year-old Marcelina Exposito, accompanied by her cousin, Augustina, was walking to the village on an errand for her mother. The girls were walking through the area known as Chandavila when they noticed something strange in the distance. **They were about to ignore it, but then a strange force somehow propelled them to a chestnut tree in the distance.** There, a little above the ground, was a vision of Our Lady of Sorrows. She was easily identified by the black robe and mantle she wore, the stars that sparkled around her, and the stars that embellished her gown. Her hands were joined, and her beautiful face bore every mark of deep pain and overwhelming sadness (3:195).

BANNEUX, BELGIUM (1933)

The three spectators arrived at the house in time to see Mariette walk out of the yard and head down the wintry road. She walked past the three **as if she were being pulled**. Her father became frightened. "Where are you going? Come back." Mariette responded, "She is calling me..." (11:179–180)

Visionaries seem oblivious to pain and unable to be harmed. Scientists and doctors have tried to distract their heavenly gaze with bright lights, loud sounds, pin pricks, electrical shocks, candle flames, harsh pinching, touching of their eyes, and other distracting actions. Here are some documented examples.

LOURDES, FRANCE (1858)

On April 7, the Tuesday after Easter, Bernadette prayed at the grotto in the early morning. Several hundred watched—including Dr. Dozous who was there to examine her during her visionary experience. Bernadette took a large candle and encircled the flames with her hands and fingers. It was hot enough to scorch human flesh. With her fingers laced around the wick, the flames were licking up into and around the girl's unprotected hands. This should have severely burned anyone, but she had no physical reaction or evidence of any burns as the stunned doctor examined her closely (11:109).

BEAURAING, BELGIUM (1932)

By December 8 on the Feast of the Immaculate Conception, up to fifteen thousand were in attendance near the convent. During this beautiful visitation only visible to the five children, Dr. Maistriaux studied the children carefully—lighting a match under Gilberte's hand, but getting no response or evidence of any burns. Pinching, pin pricks, and high-powered flashlights never affected the five children's eyes nor broke their concentration (11:168).

BE NOT AFRAID TO FOLLOW THE FOOTPRINTS FROM HEAVEN

GARABANDAL, SPAIN (1961)

Visionaries Mary Loli and Conchita are entranced by the Virgin Mary's appearance in Garabandal, Spain in 1961.

Their eyes did not blink or react to efforts to make them blink. Their heads were often tilted backward in very awkward positions, looking upward for long periods without any discomfort. They were pinched, poked, stuck with needles, and had bright lights shined in their eyes—but none of the four girls ever reacted during their ecstasies. A group of strong men would lift them and drop them—but never would they become hurt, bruised, or injured as anybody else would have. Their reflexes, heartbeats, eyes, ears, noses, and sensitivity to pain were all monitored by specialists who concluded that these girls did not react to any outside stimuli. Not even the heat of summer or the bitter cold of winter affected them.

The girls found lumps, marks, and pin pricks where they had been tested during their ecstasies by the doctors. The doctors were amazed that none of the girls reacted in any fashion yet displayed the marks and bruises from their tests. During an ecstasy, they reported that they could only see Mary, each other, and anything that her brilliant light illuminated. They were unaware of other people, doctors running tests, large crowds, the time of day, or type of weather. It was as if they had entered into a divinely protective and supernatural realm as long as Mary was present. When they spoke with Mary, others present could hear a low, guttural, husky voice or whisper instead of their normal voices (34:20–21) (33).

MEDJUGORJE, BOSNIA (1981)

During the first apparition on top of the mountain, Ivanka and Mirjana each fainted briefly. Jakov was so overwhelmed that he reeled and fell backward into a dense bramble of thornbushes, disappearing from sight. The others doubted that he could get out without being slashed to ribbons, but a moment later, Jakov scrambled out of the brambles without a scratch. Later, witnesses were amazed that Marija and Vicka—who had lost their shoes in that amazingly fast ascent—did not have a single scratch or cut from the jagged rocks and treacherous terrain (8:77).

On Monday, June 29, the children were again summoned by the authorities and sent to the neuropsychiatric department at the hospital in Mostar. They were subjected to harsh interrogations. Attempts were made to frighten them by exposing them to severely demented patients at the hospital. They were shown dead bodies in the mortuary. But they passed every test, confidently answering every question without hesitation.

They were subjected periodically to every type of medical and scientific examination available. On January 14, 1986 in Paina, Italy, near Milan, the following comments were the conclusions of seventeen renowned scientists, doctors, psychiatrists, and theologians following their long and detailed research.

> "The results proved that the apparitions, to which the visionaries testify, are a phenomenon that surpasses modern science—and that all points toward some *other level of happening*" (132).

Another team of specialists from the University of Montpellier, France, ran many tests on five of the six visionaries *during their apparitions*. Here are their findings:

1. Within one-fifth of a second, they simultaneously knelt and looked precisely at the same spot in the air without any visible reference point when the Virgin Mary appeared to them.
2. All eye movements ceased in a time period lasting from three minutes up to forty-five minutes.
3. Nobody blinked in response to any eye being touched.
4. They did not react to any pain they were subjected to—including an algometer which causes lesions or skin burns.
5. There was a complete absence of sensitivity.
6. They showed no reaction to a hearing test—an input of ninety decibels in their ears (equal to a loud explosion).
7. They did not blink when a one thousand-watt light bulb was placed in front of their eyes.
8. Their regular voices stopped during the vision—yet all muscles of the mouth, jaw, and throat that are involved in speech continued, but the larynx (voice box) was shut off. This is physically impossible.

The French team of scientists concluded,

> "Nothing in the physical realm interferes with their experience. This phenomenon seems to be a state of active, intense prayer, partially disconnected from the external world, in a state of contemplation with a separate person whom they alone can see, hear, and touch" (132).

KIBEHO, RWANDA (1981)

Alphonsine's face lit up in ecstasy, smiling peacefully with tears of joy running down her cheeks. The transformation was so sudden and dramatic that some girls began to believe. Others howled with laughter, waving their hands in front of her eyes and shouting in her ears. But she did not blink, flinch, or react. She didn't see the girls any longer—only the beautiful lady hovering above her again in the same soft, glorious light.

Word spread like fire to many other villages, and school officials were afraid that an attention-seeking teenager was going to turn their school and parish into a national embarrassment. One of the priests gave permission for the harshest heckler, Marie-Claire, to go ahead and torment her even further! So she organized a group of tormenters to pull her hair, twist her fingers, pinch her very hard, scream in her ears, and shine a powerful flashlight into her eyes. But Alphonsine had no reaction whatsoever to any of this because she was in an ecstasy with the Virgin Mary. One day, Marie-Claire held a burning candle under her right arm, but still there was no reaction. The priest, who was encouraging the harassment in order to expose her as a fake, now told Marie-Claire to stick a long needle several inches deep into her arm during the next ecstasy. Alphonsine still showed no response as she continued to happily chat with Mary. But she started begging Mary to let other students see her, too, because Alphonsine was tired of the disbelief and ridicule. (The Virgin complied by involving seven more children.)

Investigators and doctors continued to monitor and test the eight visionaries, pinching the girls with pliers, sticking them with needles, twisting their arms behind their backs, and shoving them hard to the ground. One very large man, a doctor, kneeled on top of one of the teenagers and bounced up and down on her chest! None of the visionaries ever reacted or were ever injured. In fact, they didn't even seem to notice as their faces beamed with love and joy, chatting and singing to the Virgin (39:40, 44–45,128–129).

It is truly as if visionaries are temporarily in a protective bubble—as if in the divine hand of God. This supernatural realm begins with the appearance of Mary and ends with her departure. Further evidence suggested that something akin to an invisible protective shield came about during these encounters, as some instances occurred during rainfall and yet no one or anything became wet within that specific area of divine contact.

KNOCK, IRELAND (1879)

The crowd witnesses a supernatural scene in Knock, Ireland in 1879.

The figures of the Virgin Mary, St. Joseph, St. John, several angels, and a lamb on an altar were witnessed in a glowing tableau by fourteen residents during a pouring rain.

> "The figures were full and round, three-dimensional, as if they had a body and life. They were about two to three feet out from the church wall. They said nothing, but as we approached, they seemed to go back a little toward the gable. I could see the pupils and iris of Our Lady's eyes. I could see the smooth texture of her milky skin. I was so close that I could see the lines and letters inside the book that St. John held. I also saw the wings of the angels fluttering!"

All of the witnesses agree that they saw the figures move in the hour and a half that they knelt before them. All noted that, **despite the pouring rain, the three figures all remained dry. The ground beneath them and the church wall behind them also remained completely dry**. All who passed by were blessed with the ability to see this event (40:153) (11:131).

FATIMA, PORTUGAL (1917)

Promptly at noon, the Virgin Mary arrived with the usual flash of light. Her snow-white feet rested upon the flowers and ribbons which adorned the tree's upper branches where she hovered. The faces of the children assumed an unworldly expression. Their features appeared more delicate, their color mellow, their eyes intent upon the Lady. **And they were strangely dry in the pouring rain** (32:53).

KIBEHO, RWANDA (1989)

Thirty thousand were in attendance for that final contact with Alphonsine on November 28, 1989. After several hours, as the Queen of Heaven began to leave, Alphonsine's face became grief-stricken. She probably didn't notice that she had **mysteriously remained dry in the pouring rain** (11:239).

CUENCA, ECUADOR (1990)

Over 115,000 people gathered for the final apparition on March 3, 1990. There was a grand procession with flower-decked litters carrying statues of Jesus and Mary. Once inside the "Garden" area, Patricia's body arched backward as she looked up to the sky and went into the usual ecstasy. She stared at a single spot in the sky, became unaware of anyone around her, and was **unaffected by the sudden drenching downpour of rain**. She spoke Mary's message without any conscious recollection afterwards (23:61–62,105).

The visionaries are clearly moved and inspired by their experiences. Their lives seem changed forever. Here are a few examples.

CASTELPETROSO, ITALY (1888)

The priest in the diocese treated the whole affair as delusional and preached against it. A second priest, Don Luigi Ferrara, was also a disbeliever—*until he saw her too*!

"I had many times derided those who visited the mountain on which these wonderful apparitions took place. On May 16, 1888, however, I felt a desire to visit the place. When I arrived, I began to look into one of the fissures, and I saw with great clearness Our Lady, like a statuette, with a little Child in her arms. After a short interval I looked again at the same spot, and, in place of the Most Holy Virgin I saw, quite clearly, the dead Savior bearing the crown of thorns and all covered in blood. Whenever I think of these visions on this mountain, I am moved to tears and cannot speak" (9, 19).

FATIMA, PORTUGAL (1917)

Visionaries Lucia, Francisco, and Jacinta in Fatima, Portugal in 1917.

Lucia later reported that the children were ushered off to Ourém where they were locked in a room and told that they would not be let out until they revealed the secret that Our Lady had entrusted in them. They were shown a cauldron of oil placed over a fire and told that if they had not revealed the secret by the time the oil boiled, then they would be either hung or beheaded.

They were taken to a foul-smelling detention cell and thrown in with adult male prisoners. The other prisoners became impressed—even inspired—by the strong religious conviction of the young visionaries (ages seven, nine, and ten) and their lack of fear in the face of death threats. The children decided to recite prayers, recognize their suffering as necessary, and got the other prisoners on their knees to pray with them. Afterwards, the prisoners decided to cheer up the children with songs, harmonica music, and dancing.

The children realized that if they were put to death, it would be the ultimate sacrifice, and they could go to heaven sooner! When they faced the authorities at the crucial moment of decision—as the oil finally boiled—they were filled with sweet peace, fearless conviction, and steadfast devotion to Mary's wishes. Santos had lost his advantage over the children since they had decided to become joyous martyrs, so he drove them back home on August 15 (29:150–166).

BANNEAUX, BELGIUM (1933)

Mariette's behavior and attitude had dramatically changed. She decided now to not skip school as she had been doing, take her studies seriously and prepare thoroughly, and attend the local parish to pray every morning before school. No longer was she a mischievous, unruly, careless truant (11:178–179).

HEEDE, GERMANY (1937)

But news of these events was received in the village with the predictable skepticism and laughter. It was not until the villagers started noticing the dramatic change in the four girls' behavior did they begin to consider the appearances more seriously. The usual playful and giddy girls had changed their manner of living to a more serious demeanor with fervent and long prayers while impatiently anticipating Our Lady's next appearance (3:191).

CUENCA, ECUADOR (1988)

Pachi (Patricia) began to experience dramatic changes within herself. Normally, she would have spent her free time shopping for new clothes. Now, she spent her time in church, in prayer. Patricia felt a great love pouring into her along with the Virgin's promise to be with her forever. She took the responsibility of retaining the great secret very seriously. Pachi felt her life changing, and she no longer wanted to be a glamorous fashion model. It was hard to give up her fun-loving activities and stubborn independence. She found a way to still have fun but with a new emphasis in life. Patricia married her boyfriend, Andres Cordova, in 1991, and they dedicated their lives toward helping the poor and sick as well as teaching youth groups and young couples how to grow deeper in their Catholic faith (23:10, 17).

LITMANOVA, SLOVAKIA (1990)

Although they could not explain their feelings, they had been transformed forever by this experience. They now saw the world in a whole new perspective and decided not to share this with anyone. But their parents noticed the changes in their behavior and appearance. The girls were often seen sitting on the front steps of their small church (usually locked) with their hands folded in prayer and their eyes staring far into the distance. They were more withdrawn at home from friends and family—usually in quiet meditation (2:328–329).

What if you still believe that they all must be crazy and delusional?

If you were just a skeptical bystander in the crowd, would you have experienced anything that would lead you to develop any acceptance and belief?

Would you have seen anything that you could not have explained?

Keep following these "footprints"…more clues ahead…

CHAPTER 6

WITNESSING THE SUPERNATURAL

> "Then the LORD said: 'I am making a covenant with you. Before all your people I will do wonders never before done in any nation in all the world. The people you live among will see how awesome is the work that I, the LORD, will do for you.'"
> **(Exodus 34:10)**

What if you are *not* the visionary? As a bystander, priest, family member, or good friend, do you get to experience anything? Is there anything that you get to see, hear, or feel that helps you believe that something supernatural or heavenly is actually taking place? You may *want* to believe that these things are truly happening, but you would probably desire **your own** validation or confirmation of these alleged visits by the Virgin Mary.

The good news is that witnesses *have been able* to experience supernatural signs and events.

FATIMA, PORTUGAL (1917)

When June 13 arrived, the three children and a number of bystanders returned to the site for Blessed Mary's second visit—and they were not disappointed. Although only the children saw the light approach, bystanders noted that the sun seemed to dim in the cloudless sky. And although the adults could not see Mary, they did witness a wispy pillar of smoke next to the holm oak. They could not clearly hear Mary's voice, but they did report a small sound—"like the buzzing of a bee." At the end of her visit, a crowd of about fifty witnesses observed the little cloud (that Mary had stood upon) rise slowly and retreat toward the east. The top branches and leaves of the holm oak were also bent as if a weight had just been on top (where Mary had appeared) (32:22–23).

On August 13, news of the children's abduction by the authorities reached the eighteen thousand waiting for the children, nearly inciting a riot among those who had gathered with great anticipation at the apparition site. But these many thousands were not to be disappointed as Blessed Mary did give them a number of signs to show that she had kept her promise to be present. There were two loud explosions—"like cannon fire"—that came from the holm oak where she had always appeared. People began to flee in fear. But then, strangely, the people were pulled toward the tree as if by an electric current. Some fainted—others were afraid. The clouds took on a fantastic sequence of colors: blood red to pink to blue to indigo. There were flashes like lightning. A wispy pillar of smoke rose next to the tree. Some spoke of a falling of roses! Every person had some level of experience that day and came away feeling great awe and inspiration (29:152) (32:37).

On September 13, it is estimated that as many as thirty thousand people awaited the children. Lucia was almost finished reciting the Rosary when the flash of light came. Then a globe of light appeared before the crowd—but this time, thousands could witness it, including three priests: Vicar General of Leiria, Monsignor John Quaresma, and Father Manuel do Carmo Gois. Here is the Monsignor's detailed eyewitness account:

"At noontime, silence fell on the crowd, and a low whispering of prayers could be heard. Suddenly, cries of joy filled the air, many voices praising the Blessed Virgin. Arms were raised to point to something above, 'Look! Don't you see?' I, too, raised my eyes to probe the amplitude of the skies, hoping to see what the other fortunate eyes were seeing before me. There was not a single cloud in the whole blue sky, yet to my great astonishment, I saw clearly and distinctly a luminous globe, coming from the east to the west, gliding slowly and majestically through space. My friend also looked up and had the happiness of enjoying the same unexpected but enchanting apparition. Suddenly, the globe with its extraordinary light disappeared before our eyes. There was a little girl near us, about the same age as Lucia. She was excited with joy and kept saying, 'I still see Her...now She is coming down to the foot of the hill'" (32:47).

Lucia shouted to the people as Blessed Mary rose to leave, "If you want to see Our Lady, look that way (to the east)." When the crowd looked, hundreds saw the luminous globe ascending toward heaven. But thousands who were present also witnessed other supernatural details: a sudden cooling of the air, a dimming of the sun—so much so that thousands could see the stars at midday—a white mist surrounding both the holm oak and the children, and a shower of white, iridescent flower petals that vanished upon reaching the ground (32:46–47).

JANONIS, LITHUANIA (1962)

On July 15, many uniformed military men chased people and beat them to keep them away from the apparition site on the farm of the eighteen-year-old visionary, Ramute Macvyte. The state authorities had forbidden people to go there to pray. But on July 25, Marijona Tamasoniene and her two daughters, Aldona and Elizabeth, with their children, Genute and Stasyte, traveled from Zaltiskiu to seek the apparition site on the farm in order to pray there. Cautioned by the visionary's parents not to do so, they begged to hide in a haystack near the barn and pray there instead. Ramute's mother and sister, Anna, coaxed them to come out of the haystack; and, as they did, *the haystack and clover disappeared*, and a bright light appeared. Ramute's mother fell to her knees—feeling "as if she were thrown to the ground by its brilliant projections." All of them saw the strange light. The visionary's sister, Anna, ran back into the house to tell visionary Ramute and her father what all of them had seen. The father ran out of the house just in time to see the light fading away (59:181).

ZEITOUN, EGYPT (1968)

On Tuesday, April 2, 1968, at 8:30 p.m., two Moslem workmen, standing at the gate to their work garage across from St. Mary's Church, were startled by the appearance of a "lady in white," kneeling beside the cross at the top of the church's dome. One of the workmen, Farouk Mohammed Atwa, pointed his bandaged finger toward the lady, fearing that it might be a nun about to commit suicide, and said, "Lady, don't jump! Don't jump." Feeling a sense of desperation, he dashed off to call the fire brigade and the rescue squad while others ran across the street to summon the priest, Father Constantine. At that moment, the lady rose to her feet, revealing herself as a luminous being, dressed in shimmering robes of light. One woman cried out, "Our Lady Mary!" At that moment, a flight of glowing white doves appeared from nowhere and hovered around the apparition. Then everything faded away into the dark sky, leaving spectators below speechless. Farouk Atwa's bandaged finger was full of gangrene and due to be amputated the next day. But when he arrived at the hospital the next morning, the surgeon was astonished to find his finger completely healed—the first recorded miraculous healing in Zeitoun (59:17–18).

The image of the Virgin Mary materializes in the air over St. Mary's Church in Zeitoun, Egypt, 1968, in front of 250,000 witnesses.

JOHN S. CARPENTER

Large crowds enthusiastically greeted the
Virgin Mary's appearances in Zeitoun from 1968-1971.

Exactly a week later, there was another apparition, then another and another in rapid succession. They always took place at night and were generally preceded by mysterious lights, flashing silently over the church like a canopy of shooting stars or "a shower of diamonds made of light." Minutes later, formations of luminous doves would appear and fly around the floodlit church. Eyewitnesses described them as "strange birdlike creatures made of light" which flew with "astonishing swiftness without moving their wings." They always maintained a definite formation and then disappeared "like melting snowflakes." Shortly after, a blinding explosion of light would engulf the church roof. As it diminished, it would shape itself into the brilliant form of Our Lady. She would be seen in a long white robe and veil of bluish-white light. The stunned spectators below could see her garments blowing in the warm night breeze. A dazzling halo shone around her head. Her radiance was so intense—"like the sun in human form"—that it was almost impossible to discern her features. The vision would glide with effortless ease across the domes, bowing and greeting the amazed crowds below. Occasionally, she would appear above or between the palm trees in the church courtyard or emerge in a globe of light from either one of the four corner domes or other structures (59).

A dazzling crown of light sometimes shone above her head, giving an impression of unearthly and sublime majesty. News of the apparitions spread like fire across Egypt, attracting multitudes of Christians, Jews, Moslems, other religions, and even disbelievers and atheists. Within a few weeks, the crowds reached an estimated 250,000 people every night! These differing religions had all come together, praying together, singing together—in praise to Blessed Mary. She would acknowledge the massive crowds below, waving at them, holding out an olive branch—which would generate an ecstatic cheer from the masses (59:86–88).

The Coptic Pope personally sent Bishop Athanasius to make a detailed investigation—and then the bishop had his own experience:

Two children gaze at the Virgin Mary praying on the roof of St. Mary's in 1968 in Zeitoun, Egypt.

"Suddenly, there she was—standing in full figure. The crowd was tremendous. It was too difficult to move among the people. But I worked my way to in front of the figure. There she was, five or six meters above the dome, high in the sky, full figure—like a phosphorescent statue, but not stiff like a statue. There was movement of the body and clothing...Our Lady looked to the north—she waved her hand. She blessed the people, sometimes in the direction where we stood. Her garments swayed in the wind. She was quiet, full of glory.

It was something really supernatural…very, very heavenly…Some people were reciting verses from the Koran. Some were praying in Greek. Others were singing Coptic hymns…I tried to distinguish the face and features…there was something about the eyes and mouth I could see…the apparition slowly faded away…"

Often in a burst of light, she would appear out of what seemed to be nothing. A cloud that would form and become brighter and brighter—and eventually, she would appear in this great illumination. Then, within this illumination, the outline of her figure would appear brighter and brighter. She bowed her head, moved her hands as to bless the multitudes, turned from side to side, and moved as if gliding on the church roof and domes. When she turned to move to the other side of the church, the back of her head could be seen. On some occasions, she appeared to be ascending above the large dome into the sky. There were times when it appeared as if a door—a crack of light in the sky—would open, and she would "step out of heaven" or a "sanctuary door" and then leave by the same means. Other times she would fade into a silhouette, then a cloud, and then disappear. Those who saw her features the clearest report a youthful, healthy looking, beautiful lady with beautiful eyes, hair, and hands. At the time of her visits, most people became transfixed in wonder, amazement, or a state of ecstasy to the degree that all actions became impossible. Arms and fingers could not move to adjust cameras or take pictures (59:80–82).

Authorities wanted to rule out any pranks, hoaxes, or clever light shows. Police extensively searched a fifteen-mile radius of the church, seeking any kind of device that might create such an effect. At one point, they initiated a power blackout in the area so that nothing electrical could be possibly utilized to create these images. And the radiant Virgin Mary, her flying luminous doves, and the eerie heavenly lights continued to materialize just as brilliantly as ever during the power outage—much to the delight of thousands in the dark (59:25).

By early 1970, the frequency of the apparitions had diminished to an average of one per month. The last glorious and final public sighting was on May 29, 1971. Crowds thinned out over those years, but it is estimated that three out of every four Egyptians had seen the Virgin Mary by then—many had numerous sightings. Approximately forty million people encountered her heavenly presence—including even President Nasser of Egypt! (158)

MEDJUGORJE, BOSNIA-HERZEGOVINA (1981)

A local pediatric specialist from Citluk, Dr. Darinka Glamuzina, an atheist, was sent by the authorities to observe the children visionaries. She came forward, skeptically, and asked the children if she could touch "this heavenly person" that they claimed to be seeing. One of the visionaries, Vicka, decided to first obtain Blessed Mary's permission:

Vicka: "May this lady touch you?"
Blessed Mary: "There have always been unbelieving Judases, but let her touch me. She may come closer."

Vicka showed the lady where to stretch out her hand; the doctor moved her hand to touch the Blessed Virgin. Suddenly, Dr. Glamuzina became instantly fearful, stunned, and jerked her hand away. The Virgin then disappeared. The doctor left abruptly, refused to speak, but told authorities that she would not return again. Later, the doctor described her experience:

"I felt something metallic and shocking…It sent shivers throughout my body. It was at that moment that I knew *something was really happening* here!" (45:45)

Later, it was learned that Dr. Glamuzina returned to her faith in the Catholic Church.

One evening in Medjugorje, Our Lady told the visionaries to come to the apparition site on Mount Podbrdo at about 11:00 p.m. and to invite a select group of "believers" to attend. About forty people gathered on the mountainside and began praying. One man, Marinko, looked up and saw the sky apparently opening up some nine to twelve feet and a great intense light coming toward him and the others. Everyone exclaimed together, "Look at the light!" It seemed to them that a globe of light came out of the wooden cross and burst in their midst into thousands of bright stars. Some of the children became panicky and started to scream. Immediately, Marija cried out, "Calm down. Our Lady is with us." Then they prayed for forty minutes.

Then the visionaries declared, "Our Lady is looking at all of you and telling you that those who would like to touch her may do so." The children led the others to her, but if they stepped on her veil, she would disappear momentarily. Those that touched her described a "numbing of the hands." If a sinner touched her, her dress would turn darker; and if too many sinners touched her dress, it would turn black, and she would disappear. The nearby neighborhood of Cilici saw this area encircled with light, drawing them to also come observe (45:59) (52:53–54).

Father Jozo preached passionate and inspired messages during those days. But the government authorities ordered him to stop these church services. His refusal to cease and his loyalty to the children led to his arrest on August 17, 1981. The Virgin reassured the children that she would watch over Father Jozo in prison. And there were indeed signs of her supernatural presence: prisoners and guards claimed they could see a glowing aura around the priest. The guards would turn off all the lights in his prison cell—yet his cell was always strangely illuminated by a supernatural light! The guards would lock his cell door, but it would always swing open as they started to walk away. No matter how hard they tried, they could never keep his cell door locked. Frightened and shaken, the guards quit trying. When Vicka asked Blessed Mary about this, she told the children on August 30 that she had been responsible for those tricks! He was finally released eighteen months later (48:61) (45:100–101).

A number of times in the early years, the word "MIR" ("peace") was written in large bright letters in the evening sky above the cross on Mount Krizevac (52:77). The pastor and many others witnessed this phenomenon on many occasions. The most frequently observed phenomena have involved the cross on Mount Krizevac. People have seen this huge, thirty-foot tall, concrete cross transform into a column of light. At other times, the whole thirty-foot tall cross had changed into the bright, luminous form of a young lady that matched the description of Mary given by the children—but with less clear detail. This occurred with most intensity for thirty minutes during the trial of Father Jozo on October 21–22, 1981 (52:77). Father Luka Vlasic gives the following report:

> "I noticed that the cross **was gone** from the mountain! In its place was now a large, white bright column. Soon this changed into a statue with the contour of a woman. She had her hands extended. She was looking toward the parish church. At times, it appeared as if she was bowing to the left, then to the right. A strong thought came to my mind, 'This is a reward from Our Lady for the long and exhausting four months of hearing confessions in Medjugorje.' (He and three other priests had traveled to help with that.) Many pilgrims around the church and coming out of the church witnessed the supernatural sights. Their faces were aglow with exultation. I am willing to confirm the truthfulness of this testimony by oath at any time" (52:78–79).

Father Janko Bubalo described his own moving experience as well.

> "I looked out the rectory window a little after 5:00 p.m. and saw two of the nuns kneeling on the wet ground with their arms wide open. Near them were some seventy men and women, kneeling and quite oblivious of the falling rain. Some were crying, some praying, and others singing religious hymns. They were all looking toward the cross (on the mountain), **but it had disappeared!** In its place was a strange, pale, rose-colored light without equivalent in real life. Through binoculars, I saw the silhouette of a woman. Her arms were open, and her feet were hidden in a luminous cloud at the base of the pedestal of the cross. I was filled with joy! All the villagers who looked were able to see her. The people prevailed upon the seers to ask Our Lady about the significance of this happening, and she told the children that *it had been Her* appearing on the mountain" (52:79).

Father Stanko Vasilj added a few more details from his perspective through binoculars:

> "I saw the silhouette of a woman with a very light and luminous grey cape. At a certain moment, a ray of sparkling light issued from her right cheek. Everyone was on their knees outside. Three Carmelite priests arrived by car at that moment, having witnessed her from their car for the last mile and a half. At the end, a cloud rose up from the site of the cross. It was clear and transparent and divided in two, in the form of a fan. It was followed by another cloud, dark and somber, that came down like a curtain on each side of the cross. The cross finally reappeared, resuming its usual appearance. I affirm all of this, fully aware of my great responsibility before God and the church" (52:79–80).

The visionaries added that Blessed Mary told them that "*all of these signs are meant to reawaken the people's faith. Every day I pray to My Son in front of that cross, asking Him to forgive the world*" (52:81).

In 1988, Dr. Marco Margnelli concluded that "we were certainly in the presence of an extraordinary phenomenon." Having witnessed everything from the uncanny "synchronous movements" of the visionaries to the miraculous healing of a woman with leukemia, what affected him most deeply was *the birds*. During the late afternoon, flocks of birds would gather in the trees outside the rectory where the visionaries shared their apparitions. They would chirp and coo and call *by the hundreds*—at times deafening to the ears. But as soon as the apparition began, **"they would suddenly and simultaneously all go silent."** This "absolute silence of the birds" haunted the doctor for a long time. After returning to Milan, he became a practicing Catholic again (8:208).

L'LLE-BOUCHARD, FRANCE (1947)

The church of St. Giles was packed and overflowing with two thousand people for this greatly anticipated last apparition on December 14. The Virgin appeared to the four girls again and asked for more prayers for sinners—and in response to a request for a miracle, Mary smiled and replied, **"Before I go, I will send a bright ray of sunlight."**

As Our Lady vanished, a mysterious bright ray of sunshine streamed through a window and settled on the very place of the apparition. It grew in such bright intensity and size that all had to shield their eyes. The four girls were surrounded by sparkles of various colors. The ray of light was later determined to be inexplicable in natural terms since its path would normally have been interrupted by some of the pillars of the church. Further tests proved that it was physically impossible for a normal ray of sunshine to have entered that part of the church at that time of year because of the position of the sun. It was declared to have been miraculous (3:207).

CUAPA, NICARAGUA (1980)

On October 13, 1980, on the Feast of Our Lady of Fatima, a large glowing circle appeared above the ground in front of fifty people that had gathered to say the Holy Rosary. Everyone saw the light that came from the sky—a single ray—like a powerful spotlight that illuminated the circle in front of them (2:162–163).

GHIAIE DI BONATE (1944)

Visionary Adelaide Roncalli in ecstasy in
Ghiaie di Bonate, Italy, 1944.

Doctor Eliana Maggi testified under oath on January 16, 1946, before the Episcopal Committee.

> "That Saturday was a rainy day. At the outset of the apparition a sun ray shone on the child's head. I raised my eyes to the sky and saw a cross-shaped rift in the sky and a shower of golden and silvery spots for a minute or two, and everybody hailed it as a miracle."

Don Luigi Cortesi wrote,

> "Somebody noticed a strange beam of light shining upon the child (visionary) and reverberating over the surrounding faces. Others noticed the sun had a cross shape. Others saw the solar disc whirl dizzily, forming a ring not larger than half a meter. In the lower layers of the atmosphere some people saw a rain of golden stars, small yellow clouds in the shape of hoops—so thick and near that somebody tried to catch them in full flight. On the onlooker's hands and faces the most various colors shaded off with the yellow color prevailing over the others. Phosphorescent hands were seen; light globes in the shape of Hosts…" (110)

GARABANDAL, SPAIN (1961)

On June 22, 1962, St. Michael told Conchita that he would give her a visible Host during Communion—which was when she first learned that the Hosts had NOT been visible when given by the angel. The Virgin Mary told Conchita that the date for this miracle would be July 18, 1962. Word of this spread like fire, and there was a joyous celebration and much anticipation on that day. However, as the day wore on, many people became disappointed and went home. Finally, at 1:40 a.m., Conchita left her home in ecstasy, and the lingering crowd eagerly accompanied her in the dark. Several eyewitnesses reported seeing this miracle:

> Benjamin Gomez: "I was so close…inches from her face…I looked in her mouth…nothing…I turned my head just for an instant. When I looked back, the Host was on her tongue. It

was white—out of this world…like snow, a snowflake upon which the sun's rays were striking…"

Pepe Diez: "I was scarcely eighteen inches away from her face…She kept her tongue out like that for about a minute. As I stood there—my eyes riveted to her, something incredible happened! Without moving my eyes for a fraction of a second, suddenly a neat, precise, and well-formed Host appeared miraculously on Conchita's tongue…Her tongue was out and bare, and then all of a sudden the Host was there! I did not see how it came. It was instantaneous!…It was just there!"

Alejandro Damians: "There was a great deal of confusion—crowding, pushing, people trying to see…I crouched over, and Conchita was on her knees. I took the (movie) camera out of the bag and looked through the lens without making any adjustments…I was sure I could see her head and shot. I caught the last seconds of the miracle (on movie film). I would not exchange the bliss which I felt in those moments for anything in this world. It was a joy, deep and intense, which I cannot explain."

This was the evidence that so many people had been looking for! (34:45–51) (33)

AGOO, PHILIPPINES (1992)

December 13, 1992: A Eucharistic Miracle was witnessed by Father Cortez and nuns at the convent. A statue of Mary, carved according to Judiel's description of her, was brought to the convent and shed tears to the amazement of the nuns and Father Cortez. When Father Cortez placed a Host on Judiel's tongue, witnesses reported that they saw it "turn into flesh and blood." When Judiel went back to his pew after Communion, he felt liquid dripping from his mouth. Then the Host swelled in his mouth, and the person next to him alerted Father Cortez, who urged him to spit it out. The Communion Host had transformed into pulsating flesh and blood. Father Cortez wanted to preserve this Eucharistic Miracle, but Our Lady intervened and said that Judiel must swallow it. As a concession, however, the nuns were allowed to press and imprint the bloody Host onto their white handkerchiefs. Each nun did receive an imprint on each handkerchief. Then Judiel put the Host back on his tongue—at which time it slowly turned back into a white Host—just before he swallowed it, according to witnesses. When Father Cortez asked him to open his mouth afterwards, there was no trace now of any blood, flesh, or pieces of the Host (98:6) (97).

BETANIA, VENEZUELA (1984)

It was a gorgeous spring day for a large church picnic on March 25, 1984 for the 108 people in attendance. A grotto nearby with a spring-fed waterfall attracted the active children. Around 3:00 p.m., one of the children ran excitedly back to the resting adults to proclaim that the Blessed Mother was appearing to them above the waterfall near the grotto. Word spread quickly, and soon, everybody was rushing to see what the child was talking about—and they ALL saw the incredible sight! The glowing white figure of Our Lady stood out against the dark green trees. Many saw a blue sash around her waist, and she was holding the baby Jesus. Many were able to see the clear, beautiful features of her face. She was silent like a statue, causing some to search for tricks or natural explanations. Fifteen minutes later, she evaporated or "was absorbed into the trees." But she appeared six more times that day to the delight of the onlookers. The seventh appearance, right before sunset, was very clear and detailed so that nobody could doubt that it was a strikingly beautiful woman—not a statue or foggy illusion. All of the 108 people at this church picnic saw her clearly—not just children and poor people, but doctors, lawyers, a judge, priests, an army general, and even a few atheists! (11:263–265)

CUENCA, ECUADOR (1988)

Another six thousand people climbed the mountain for the first Saturday in December 1989. At 7:00 p.m., Blessed Mary appeared to Patricia and told her,

"Forgive one another and remove resentment from your heart. Days of darkness are near, but greater than the darkness of the earth is the darkness of the soul. Why? Because you do not keep lit the lamp of the heart with the light of My Son Jesus. You must learn how to make amends for your faults. When you fall, you must not remain sitting, but you must get up. The greatest fault is when you realize that you have fallen and you don't get up."

A phenomenon was witnessed on that day by thousands of persons. The clouds parted, and a great light formed the image of Our Lady of the Miraculous Medal in the sky. Hands and faces sparkled with a golden glow—as if from glitter. This amazing celestial image converted many people who had been "just curious" until that moment (23:53–54).

L'ILE BOUCHARD, FRANCE (1947)

Halfway through praying a decade of the Rosary in front of the altar, the four girls looked up and were astonished to see a "beautiful lady" with her hands joined in prayer. To the left of the lady was an angel, holding a lily while his eyes were fixed in contemplation of the lady. The lady was wearing a brilliant white dress with gold trim at the neck and wrists. There was a blue sash around her waist and a veil covering her head. She radiated a strong golden light. Jacqueline asked the lady if she might be the Heavenly Mother. The Virgin quickly affirmed that she was indeed. The angel announced that he was Gabriel. Blessed Mary then turned and asked to kiss the hand of each girl, bending low to reach the hands of Jacqueline and Nicole. But the other two girls were much smaller and could not reach high enough. Jacqueline took them up, one after the other, and lifted them up at arm's length *as though they were practically weightless*. All four testified to the solidity and warmth of Mary's hand and the touch of her lips.

On the next day, December 9, the four girls assembled at the appointed time and began praying the Rosary. Blessed Mary appeared and showed the girls the golden cross of her rosary. When she asked them to kiss it, Jacqueline and Nicole were able to stand up to do so.

Madame Trinson was amazed to see Jacqueline repeat her feat of the previous day, lifting up the two younger girls as though they were featherweight dolls so that they could also kiss the golden cross. The metal was cold to their lips, and they were penetrated with a sense of Mary's grief. Approximately 150 people gathered on the next day and were amazed to see Jacqueline repeat her feat of effortlessly lifting the two youngest girls again in order to kiss Mary's hand. (3:204-206)

GARABANDAL, SPAIN (1961)

Sometimes, during their ecstasies, the four girls would lift each other up without any difficulty to receive a kiss from Mary. After their ecstasies, they could not even begin to lift each other up without struggling and falling. They maintained an aura of peacefulness and normality during the rest of their day—which amazed and inspired villagers. Mercedes Salisach, a writer from Barcelona, was present when Mary Loli rose from a position of lying on the floor into the air—levitating about ten inches above the floor. She reports:

> "I took a stick and passed it under her. There was nothing but air underneath her! The expression on her face as she gazed upward was beautiful—*just beautiful…*" (33)

BETANIA, VENEZUELA (1978)

Many more apparitions occurred in the following years. On one occasion on this farm, March 25, 1978, many saw a radiant mist coming from the woods. As the mist settled on top of a large tree, Maria—with fifteen others—saw Our Lady materialize with hands on her chest. Maria heard, "**Little daughter, this is not a dream. My presence among you is real**" (68:202).

> "Then her hands opened up, and I saw what appeared to be rays coming from her hands. They came directly toward us, bathing us with light—and one man cried out, 'Everything is burning up!' The whole area appeared to be on fire. It was beautiful. The sun began to gyrate, and everyone was shouting with emotion."

Maria was overwhelmed and fell to the ground. But in front of everybody's eyes, her body was raised up into the air—causing her daughter Maria and goddaughter Jacqueline to cry inconsolably from fear. During the levitation, the soft, tender voice of the Virgin Mary had asked her to accept the difficult task of bringing the message of peace and reconciliation to all nations. Word spread of these amazing sights (11:276–277).

CUENCA, ECUADOR (1989)

From the beginning, Patricia had made a small altar or shrine in her bedroom where she had arranged pictures and statues along with blessed candles. On January 15, 1989, these pictures and statues began exuding oil and tears. Droplets of blood formed on the crucifix. Regarding this phenomena, Blessed Mary revealed to Patricia on February 1, 1989 that the oil was an oil of salvation for those with strong faith—and that the sick should be blessed with this oil.

> "The Father has allowed the grace of the holy oil, and my tears have been shed for the ingratitude of my little children due to the lack of unity, lack of love, and because each nation opens its doors to evil and to its own destruction. Love one another, children, and do not hurt the Father. I am the Guardian of the Faith."

Patricia's boyfriend, Andres, had been out of the country for much of this time and was not sure what he believed. Taking a dry picture of the Holy Shroud of Christ, he held it in his own hands while the group prayed. He was amazed to see oil coming from the eyes in the picture and droplets of liquid forming from around the crown of thorns. All of his doubts about the apparitions vanished with this stunning event (23:31–33).

DAMASCUS, SYRIA (1982)

A small, three-inch-tall icon of Mary with the Christ child in Myrna's bedroom began oozing enough oil to fill a saucer! Confused, family members were summoned—and they all began praying. Within one hour, four more dishes of oil came from the small picture. The icon poured forth oil for the next four days. The clergy and civil authorities all investigated for any evidence of a fraud or trick. They could only conclude that oil was indeed coming from the icon. When they asked Myrna to pray in front of them, having washed her hands well, the oil would flow from her palms again. They were impressed that she was not more religious than most others. She prayed very little, only went to church once a week, and loved to dance, swim, and laugh like other young people.

One day a priest was kneeling near Myrna while she was praying, and he heard her say, "Father, I feel like the Virgin has entered into me!" Then he saw a "brilliant liquid" flowing abundantly from her palms. A bishop who was also present in the room noted that the oil had the scent of myron—or holy oil. Medical doctors and scientists gathered to decipher the origin of the healing oil that continued to exude from Myrna's hands when she prayed. Thousands of people began to visit the icon in her home. The sick gathered in her courtyard, asking to be anointed with the healing oil. Phenomenal cures resulted for many of them (2:249–250).

AGOO, PHILIPPINES (1993)

March 6, 1993: It is estimated that one million people gathered that day for the anticipated apparition. The crowd included top Philippine government officials, journalists, and the local bishop—acting as a representative for the pope. Father Cortez conducted a noontime Mass at Apparition Hill with this massive assembly. At one point, Father appealed for silence from the crowd, calling for them to feel the presence of Christ in their hearts. Suddenly, the silhouette of the Virgin Mary appeared for five seconds above the guava tree. Two government officials, the Speaker of the House and the Senate President Pro Tempore, attested to seeing this manifestation in Agoo. A radio reporter, Mon Francisco, described the apparition to listeners of Manila's radio station DZXL.

"I saw a silhouette of a woman wearing a dark waistband. I had not expected to see any apparition—and I was *not* hallucinating!"

About ten minutes afterwards, visionary Judiel was reading a message he had just received from the Virgin when "lights of different colors came from various directions and moved toward the sun," according to the Manila Bulletin (129).

ASSIUT, EGYPT (2002)

Since mid-August 2000, the Egyptian city of Assiut has experienced unusual lights, glowing figures and luminous doves over St. Mark's Church—a large Coptic church in the center of Old Town. Hundreds and sometimes thousands prayed, sang, and danced around the church. It was initially suspected that somebody was perpetrating a clever hoax with lasers or a light effects show. But when the local government ordered the electricity for the entire area to be switched off for one night in order to uncover any deception, the unusual lights returned as bright as ever. Next, the officials evacuated the area from 10:00 p.m. until 6:00 a.m. each night, but the spiritual lights were stronger and brighter than ever.

It began at 11:30 p.m. on August 17, 2000, while hundreds of thousands of Copts from all over Egypt were celebrating St. Mary's Lent. Residents around St. Mark's Church of both Coptic and Muslim faith watched the apparition of the Virgin Mary above the dome and between the two towers until 3:00 a.m. Then again, from 4:00 a.m. until 6:00 a.m., she appeared along with blue-green flashes of heavenly lights and glowing doves. Thousands gathered as the news spread like wildfire. After the officials gave up trying to find any evidence of a hoax or clever light display, the figure of Mary along with incense, celestial lights, and flying luminous doves continued every night from 2:00 a.m. until 6:00 a.m. On one occasion, the shadow of a monk appeared next to Mary.

On September 6, 2000, one woman told the BBC that she had seen the Virgin Mary with outstretched hands, and a light emanating from them, accompanied by a smell of incense and large numbers of glowing pigeons. Sarwat Hani Marzouk said, "I saw Mary. She was so beautiful, wearing a blue veil. Light was emanating from her hands. Then doves started flying—they were as big as ducks."

On September 15—with thousands headed to rooftops for the best views—one eyewitness files this report from his position across from the south side of the church.

> "The two church towers—especially the south one—were a festive theater of heavenly lights and flying doves for more than four hours! Very amazing! Very touching! Very impressive! Explosions of light come from each of the eight sides of the second level of the tower. Other flashes stem from the left tower, across the roof, ending in the main dome and illuminating the cross above it. Something like a spot of light could be seen inside the center of the cross above the tower—from which a storm of light would burst forth. Lights vary in intensity…to a very bright shining light that is so intense that it illuminates the surrounding buildings and faces of the people! The most touching feature that occurred many times was a burst of light coming forth from inside the dome, passing through the eight columns…From inside, that light comes something like doves—seen at first still continuous with the light, then separated in a sparklike fashion to fly for a short distance—then disappear."
>
> "As for the doves, I could see them in many formations… flying above the church, between the towers—they don't flap their wings. What is astonishing is that the chest of each dove is luminous like a lamp. They fly and then disappear after a while. Doves continued to fly with the bursts of light for a couple of hours. When you look around, you see the thousands of people over hundreds of roofs or hanging out windows—praying, singing hymns, or applauding" (100).

WARRAQ AL-HADAR, EGYPT (2009)

The apparitions began at the Church of the Virgin Mary and Archangel Michael in Al-Warraq. Hassan, a Muslim neighbor, was sitting at his local coffee shop across the street when he saw a strong light coming from the church around 8:30 p.m. More people on the street began to notice the light and saw a glowing bird circling above the church. Around 2:00 a.m., a vision of the Virgin Mary appeared in her blue-and-white robes (158). Anba Dumadius, Archbishop of Giza, issued this statement:

> "On Friday, December 11, 2009, at 1:00 a.m., the Holy Virgin appeared in her full height in luminous robes above the middle dome of the church named after her. She was described as wearing a pure white dress with a royal blue belt. She had a crown on her head, above which appeared the cross on top of the dome. The crosses on top of the church's domes and towers glowed brightly with light. Blessed Mary moved between the domes and on to the top of the church gate between its two twin towers. All of the local residents saw her! The apparition lasted from 1:00 a.m. until 4:00 a.m. on Friday. Many cameras and cell phones took pictures. Some three thousand people from the neighborhood, surrounding areas, and passersby gathered in the street in front of the church to see the apparition. Since Friday, the huge crowds gathered in the vicinity of the church have been seeing luminous white pigeons soaring above the church during various times of the night. They also saw a star emerge suddenly in the night sky and travel some two hundred meters across the sky and disappear. The huge crowds never stopped singing hymns and praises for the Holy Virgin" (156).

Seeing is believing…and hundreds of these witnesses are no longer skeptical. Therefore, curious or doubting bystanders *are able to witness* a multitude of amazing signs—signs that suggest that heaven is very much present and active in our lives.

There was one grand event that happened in Fatima in 1917—"the Miracle of the Sun." The next chapter will detail its miraculous occurrence and reveal that such a grand event was not a one-time event but has actually happened many more times since that first amazing day in 1917…

CHAPTER 7

MORE THAN ONE MIRACLE OF THE SUN

"And I will show wonders in the heaven above and signs on the earth beneath, blood, and fire, and vapor of smoke; the sun shall be turned into darkness and the moon into blood, before the day of the Lord comes, the great and manifest day" **(Acts 2:19–20).**

Thus says the Lord: "I will rescue you and this city from the hand of the Assyrians, and I will protect it." And this will be a sign for you from the Lord that the Lord will do this word which he has spoken: "Behold, I will cause the shadow of lines, which has now descended on the sundial of Ahaz, **to move in reverse** for ten lines." And so, **the sun moved backward** by ten lines through the degrees by which it had descended **(Isaiah 38: 6–8).**

The Miracle of the Sun has been historically associated with Fatima, Portugal as a one-of-a-kind supernatural event. Allegedly, the Virgin Mary had been appearing to three small children on the thirteenth of every month from May to October 1917. Blessed Mary promised the children that a miracle would occur with the October visit "so that all may believe." Skeptics did not believe that three little kids could arrange for a stunning miracle to occur on a stated day and time, twelve noon, on October 13. They were certain that a hoax or grand charade would finally be exposed to everyone. Atheists did not believe that *anything* of a divine nature could possibly happen.

Investigators were there to objectively observe whatever was to take place and look for rational or scientific explanations. Journalists were ready to spin their own stories for the public based on *whatever* was to be experienced.

Shortly after the predicted time of noon on that miserably rainy, windy, bone-chilling cold day, the clouds parted, and the sun was now visible. Despite the large crowd of well over seventy thousand individuals—containing skeptics, atheists, journalists, investigators, anti-Catholics, and people of other religions, this "miracle" was so impressive that not one of those people doubted or debated it afterwards. No explanations were offered; nobody argued that it was anything other than simply amazing and miraculous.

FATIMA, PORTUGAL (October 13, 1917)

The huge crowd at Fatima, Portugal during the Miracle of the Sun on October 13, 1917.

Let us first take a closer look at the details from the actual eyewitnesses from that day:

> "Suddenly the people broke out with a cry of extreme anguish. The sun, still rotating, had unloosened itself from the skies and came hurtling toward the earth. This huge, fiery millstone threatened to crush us with its weight. It was a dreadful sensation. During this solar occurrence, the air took on successive different colors. While looking at the sun,

I noticed that everything around me darkened. Everything had the color of an amethyst—the sky, the air, everything and everybody. A little oak nearby was casting a heavy purple shadow on the ground. This did not give the impression of being an eclipse. While still looking at the sun, I noticed that the air had cleared. Everything far and near had changed now. Now everybody and everything looked yellow!" (32:56)

"The sun was sometimes surrounded by blood-red flames. At other times, it was aureoled with yellow and soft purple. Again, it seemed possessor of the swiftest rotation and then seemed to detach itself from the heavens, come near the earth, and give forth a tremendous heat" (32:57).

"The sun came out with a well-defined rim and seemed to come down to the height of the clouds. It started to rotate intermittently around itself like a wheel of fireworks for about eight minutes. Everything became almost dark, and the people's features became yellow. All were kneeling in mud" (32:57).

"The sun cast different colors, yellow, blue, and white. It trembled constantly. It looked like a revolving ball of fire falling upon the people. As the sun hurled itself toward the earth in a mighty zigzag motion, the multitude cried out in terror, 'We are all going to die here.' At last the sun swerved back to its orbit and rested in the sky. Everyone gave a sigh of relief. We were still alive" (32:54).

"We could look at the sun with ease. It seemed to be continually fading and glowing in one fashion, then another. It threw shafts of light one way and another, painting everything in different colors—the people, the trees, the earth, even the air. Everybody stood still and quiet, gazing at the sun. At a certain point, the sun stopped its play of light and then started dancing. It stopped once more and again started dancing until it seemed to loosen itself from the skies and fall upon the people. It was a moment of terrible suspense" (32:54).

"Suddenly, at noon, the clouds drew away, and the sun appeared as if it were trembling. It seemed to come down. It began spinning like a fire-wheel in the pagan feasts. It stopped for a few minutes and again started rolling…we could look at it as though it were the moon. Things around turned into different colors. I was afraid—I thought the sun would fall upon us. My clothes were wet—then suddenly dry! I resolved to lead a better life and amend for my sins" (27:45).

"We got close to the tree where the children were. Now it was raining harder. There was a good three inches of water where I stood—and mud on the ground. I was soaking wet. It was raining just like when you open a faucet at your house. And then, suddenly, the rain stopped. The sun started to roll from one place to another place, and changed to blue, yellow—all colors! Then we see the sun come toward the children. Everyone was hollering out. Some start to confess their sins 'cause there were no priests around there. Even my mother grabbed me to her and started to cry, saying, 'It is the end of the world!' I could look at the sun without pain in the eyes. Everyone around me was making a tremendous noise. I was looking at the crowd as the sun was actually falling. As soon as the sun went back in the right place the wind started to blow real hard, but the trees didn't move at all. In a few minutes the ground was as dry as this floor. Even our clothes had dried. I thought that either I was out of my mind or this was a miracle…a real miracle" (27:7–11).

The Baron of Alvaiazere was an atheist who carefully had taken many precautions to avoid being influenced by the large crowd. The baron had not expected anything to happen and wanted to be certain that he would not be the victim of suggestion. He gave his reaction to the canonical committee as follows:

"An indescribable impression overtook me. I only know that I cried out, 'I believe! I believe! I believe!' And tears ran from my eyes. I was amazed, in ecstasy before the demonstration of Divine Power…I was converted in that moment" (27:17).

Several other men of science were actual witnesses and testified to the objective reality of the phenomenon. They added that no natural explanation could be given. One scientist, Pio Sciatizzi, stated:

"Of the historic reality of this event there can be no doubt whatsoever. It was outside and against known laws (of science and nature) and cannot be proven by certain simple scientific considerations. Given the indubitable reference to God, and the general context of the event, it seems that we must attribute to Him alone *the most obvious and colossal miracle of history…*" (27:17)

Two other transformed disbelievers testified:

"I did not believe in the apparitions. So I sat inside my car. Then, all at once, I noticed that everybody looked at the sky. Natural curiosity attracted my attention, so I got out of my car and looked at the sky, too. I saw in a clear area of the sky—where one should not be able to stare at the sun—the very sun. It was like a disc of smoked glass, illuminated from behind, and turning over itself, giving us the impression that it was coming down over our heads. I could then see the sun more easily than I can see the moon on a full moon night. From those hundreds of mouths I heard words of belief and of love for the Blessed Virgin. And then I believed. I was sure that I had not been the victim of suggestion. I saw that sun as I never saw it again" (27:59).

"At first I did not believe. But I looked at the sun—it did not hurt my eyes. I saw it spinning like a disc, rolling on itself. I saw the people changing color. They were stained with the colors of the rainbow. Then the sun seemed to fall down from the sky. I was afraid that the sun would fall down—as the people said that the world was going to end. Everyone was afraid and screaming. I thought that it was a great miracle!" (27:61)

Two prominent newspapers of Portugal at that time were *Diario de Noticias* (*The Daily News*) and *O Seculo* (*The Century*). Both were predominantly antireligious. Yet, here is an excerpt from each of their firsthand accounts:

Diario de Noticias: "The sun seemed veiled in gauze. We could look at it without strain. The gray tint of mother-of-pearl began changing as if into a silver disc that was growing and growing…until it broke the clouds! Then the silvery sun, still shrouded in that grayish light, began to rotate and wander about within the circle of the receded clouds! The people cried out with one voice. Thousands, transformed by ecstasy, fell to their knees upon the muddy ground. Then, as if it were shining through the stained glass windows of a great cathedral, the light became a rare blue, spreading its rays upon the nave… Slowly, the blue faded away and now the light seemed to be filtered through yellow" (27:74).

O Seculo: "We saw the immense crowd turn toward the sun at its highest, free of all clouds. The sun seemed to us like a plate of dull silver. It could be seen without the least effort. It did not blind or burn. All of a sudden, a tremendous shout burst forth, 'Miracle, miracle!' Before the astonished eyes of the people, whose attitude carried us back to Biblical times, and who, white with terror, heads uncovered, gazed at the sun— which trembled and made brusque and *unheard of movement beyond all cosmic laws*. The sun seemed literally to dance in the sky. They swore that the sun turned around on itself as if it were a wheel of fireworks and had fallen almost to the point of burning the earth with its rays" (27:74–75).

And from another town, ten miles away, came the report from a young boy who later became a priest, Father Joaquim Lourenco, after his inspirational encounter:

"About noon, we were startled by the cries and exclamations of the people going by our school. The teacher was the first to run outside to the street with all the children following her. The people cried and wept on the street; they were all pointing toward the sun. It was the Miracle promised by Our Lady. I feel unable to describe it as I saw it and felt it at the time. I was gazing at the sun; it looked so pale to me—it did not blind. It was like a ball of snow, rotating upon itself. All of a sudden, it seemed to be falling, zigzag, threatening the earth. Seized with fear, I hid myself amidst the people. Everyone was crying, waiting for the end of the world. During the minutes that the miracle lasted, everything around us reflected all the colors of the rainbow. We looked at each other, and one seemed blue, another yellow, red, and so on. After ten minutes, the sun resumed its place as pale and without splendor" (32:57–58).

Obviously, something dramatic, terrifying, undeniable, and inexplicable took place. Not only was it impressive, but it happened *as predicted*—as a sign from heaven—just as the children had recounted from the words of the Virgin Mary. The Blessed Mother had told the children:

"In October, I will perform a miracle so that all may believe."

Others might argue that it was still just an amazing coincidence—an unusual solar phenomenon that just happened to occur at that specific time and not due to any divine promise.

But what if this incredible display has happened again—and in correlation with other religious events? Has that ever occurred? Would that not be significant and extremely important for our consideration? Would that not add support for the idea of Divine Intervention instead of a quirky, natural, yet unexplained phenomenon?

Here, then, are excerpts from other Miracle of the Sun occurrences, reported with similar descriptions from around the world.

GHIAIE DI BONATE, ITALY (1944)

Crowds up to 350,000 gathered in Ghiaie di Bonate to see a Miracle of the Sun when the Virgin was appearing to Adelaide Roncalli in 1944.

BE NOT AFRAID TO FOLLOW THE FOOTPRINTS FROM HEAVEN

The appearances of the Virgin Mary to Adelaide Rocalli, age seven, in Ghiaie di Bonate, Italy began on May 13, 1944 (the same exact date of May 13 as at Fatima). She appeared thirteen times in that month of May, giving important messages about family values. Crowds gathered in the thousands as word spread of these appearances. But nobody had anticipated the solar phenomenon that began on May 20, 1944 in front of thirty thousand people.

"Somebody noticed a strange beam of light shining upon the child and reverberating over the surrounding faces. Others noticed the sun had a cross shape. **Others saw the solar disc whirl dizzily**, forming a ring not larger than half a meter. In the lower layers of the atmosphere some people saw a rain of golden stars, small yellow clouds in the shape of hoops. On the onlooker's hands and faces the most various colors shaded off with the yellow color prevailing over the others…"

The next evening, on May 21, many testimonies from the site of the apparition *and from surrounding villages* as two hundred thousand witnesses described an impressive solar phenomenon. The sun came out of the clouds, whirled dizzily on itself, and projected beams of yellow, green, red, blue, and violet light in all directions. The beams of light colored the clouds, fields, trees, and the stream of people. After a few minutes, the sun stopped its whirling, and then those phenomena began soon again. Many noticed that the sun had turned white like a Host. The clouds seemed to be lowering down on the people. Some noticed a rosary in the sky. Others saw a majestic Our Lady with a trailing cloak. Some people, who were at a greater distance, saw Our Lady's face looming in the sun. From nearby Bergamo, many witnesses observed the sun become pale and radiate all of the rainbow's colors in all directions. They also noticed a large yellow light beam falling over Ghiaie, perpendicularly.

On May 28, the solar phenomena repeated itself in front of three hundred thousand people—seen not only in Ghiaie, but from very distant locations. The parish journal of Tavernola, dated June, 1944, described:

> "At 18 hours sharp (6:00 p.m.), people noticed a fading of the solar light together with a flash—similar to sudden lightning.

The sun looked green, then bright red, then gold yellow. Furthermore, **it whirled dizzily**. On seeing that spectacle, people poured into the streets."

The solar phenomenon was observed also on the 31st of May, both at Ghiaie and from other nearby towns. Because of these supernatural solar displays, crowds had grown to an amazing size of 350,000 in attendance. Similar to the appearances of Mary on the thirteenth of each month at Fatima, these solar displays repeated on both June 13 and July 13, 1944 (110).

Coincidence? Here, we have six evenings of supernatural displays involving the sun, all promptly occurring at the same predicted time, always in correlation with appearances of the Virgin Mary. No weather phenomenon or freakish solar activity could ever be so organized, structured, on time, and predictable—and just happen to coincide with reported appearances of Our Lady!

LA CODOSERA, SPAIN (1945)

Although there are not many details, it was reported that several occurrences of the **sun spinning in the sky "like at Fatima"** occurred during the series of apparitions that occurred in Spain (9).

ROME, ITALY (1980, 1982)

Bruno Cornacchiola, an outspoken anti-Catholic who had threatened to kill the pope, was amazingly changed forever when he and his three young children were stunned with a visit from the Virgin Mary in Rome on April 12, 1947. After being confronted and then "schooled" for hours by Blessed Mary, Bruno repented, converted, and became a devout Catholic. On April 12, 1980, on the thirty-third anniversary of the Virgin's visit, approximately three thousand people, including twenty-five priests, had gathered to hear Bruno recall the first apparition and attend a Mass. Suddenly, during the Holy Sacrifice, they were astounded by a supernatural display in the sky.

"Strange images appeared in the sky above the Grotto. **The sun seemed to turn backward in the heavens and then began to draw near the earth.** It could be seen without straining the eyes. It appeared bigger than normal, and showed within its corona brilliant and diverse colors. In rapid movements, as an incandescent magma forming diverse figurations, the sun appeared as a cross, an 'M', a heart surrounded with stars or dripping with blood, the monogram of Christ (IHS), hands joined in prayer, the Holy Family, etc. Some saw the sun separate into three circles, then come back together again. In spite of the numerous trees which should have impeded vision, the sun stood out clearly and brightened the chapel, faces, and the clothing of the people."

The phenomenon lasted about thirty minutes. Meanwhile, the Mass that had been in progress was halted so that the people could calm down and return their attention to the service. Two years later, on the same anniversary date, April 12, 1982, the phenomenon of the Miracle of the Sun was repeated. Again, the people could look directly at the sun without hurting their eyes (57).

SEREDNE, UKRAINE (1955)

In Seredne, Ukraine, Anna saw the Virgin Mary on sixteen occasions in 1954. Many of these apparitions were accompanied by phenomena such as **a spinning sun**, shooting stars, powerful winds, and unusual cloud formations. The signs in the sky made believers out of most of the people.

On May 15, 1955, as Anna gazed at the flaming heavens, the Blessed Mother appeared in the center of immense rays of brilliant light. As **the pulsating rays spun and danced**, Anna saw Mary attired in her traditional robes and tiara as Queen of the Ukraine. She stood on a black serpent—rendering it powerless with the point of her shoe if it tried to move (2:270).

SAN DAMIANO, ITALY (1961–1970)

During many of the apparitions, the sun would spin or whirl in its orbit and throw out multicolored shafts of light. At times, it would be dimmed to such a degree that gazing at it did not have any ill effect in the least on the eyes. Sometimes, this phenomenon would last throughout the entire apparition. On one occasion, it was shaded so much that only a thin ridge on the outer section (of the sun) could be visible—like a glowing ring (58:6–7). On December 8, 1967, on the feast of the Immaculate Conception, about two thousand were present for the apparition (half had come from at least nine foreign countries). For this occasion, the sun was spinning for over an hour and throwing out multicolored rays (58:10).

CUAPA, NICARAGUA (1980)

During 1980, Bernard Martinez had visits from Our Lady in Cuapa, Nicaragua. On October 13, 1980, the Feast of Our Lady of Fatima, a large glowing circle appeared above the ground in front of fifty people that had gathered to say the Holy Rosary. Everyone saw the light that came from the sky—a single ray—like a powerful spotlight that illuminated the circle in front of them. Then the people noticed that a circle had also formed in the sky. "It was like a ring around the sun—but it's not the sun!" **The circle began to radiate all the colors of the rainbow (at exactly 3:00 p.m.)—which danced about the sky.**

> "It was 3:00 p.m. in the afternoon. One could feel a small breeze that moved softly. Pleasant—like a fresh shower—but which did not wet us. While we observed this, we were silent and continued seeing that circle of light which gave off colored lights from the exact center, where the sun is at twelve noon. All of a sudden, a lightning flash—the same as the other times—then, a second flash. I lowered my eyes, and I saw the Lady."

She appeared on her little cloud which rested above a pile of flowers that the group had brought. She extended her hands, and rays of light reached out to everyone, causing some to cry with joy (2:163).

MEDJUGORJE, HERZEGOVINA (1981–present)

On August 2, 1981 (Feast of Our Lady, Queen of Angels), a series of celestial displays began and have continued to the present day. Just like at Fatima in 1917, **the sun was seen to spin on its own axis** just before sunset. Witnessed by 150 people that day, they could stare at the sun without hurting their eyes. **It seemed to come toward those who were watching it** and then recede back to its position in the sky. As it came closer, great darkness appeared behind it. The reaction of the 150 witnesses varied from praying to crying to panic and running away. After fifteen minutes, it ceased spinning and a white cloud was seen coming down over the mountain and toward the sun. A large number of people also saw numerous globes of different colors moving around the sun, while others claimed they saw Our Lady, the Sacred Heart, a great number of angels with trumpets coming out of the dimmer sun. Others also saw a large heart with six smaller hearts beneath it (for the Virgin and the six children?) (52:74).

Father Umberto Loncar, a Franciscan priest, describes the supernatural events of August 3 & 4:

> "Many pilgrims observed that the sun had become pale, and that it had bright rings around it. These rings were casting reddish rays on the parish church of Medjugorje. A little later, they saw bright globes of different colors rotating around the sun. All of this was seen while Our Lady was appearing to the seers from 6:20 to 6:40 p.m. I, myself, had not bothered to look at the sky and so I didn't really believe in them. The next day, I did gaze carefully toward the sun and did observe what the pilgrims had been reporting, but I assumed there must be natural explanations. But the next day was a different matter: At exactly 6:20 p.m. the sun paled, a breeze sprang up, and a most unusual, reddish-violet cloud traveled with considerable speed—much faster than clouds usually do—toward the huge cross on Mount Krizevac. It hovered over the huge cross for a minute or two, then started to move eastward and down

toward the earth. I was awe-struck with what I saw next: a magnificent, reddish-violet figure of Our Lady, rising from Mount Crnica (Podbrdo). As it rose majestically in the sky, it slowly lost its delightful reddish-violet color and began slowly disappearing. But, I saw her unusually white veil, fluttering elegantly in the air under Our Lady's feet for about a half-minute" (52:75–76).

On December 9, 1983 (Feast of the Immaculate Conception), a group of pilgrims reported their deeply-moving experience:

"We had a sun miracle at 1:00 p.m. We had just walked behind the church when a storm commenced...the church seemed to shake. Clouds as dark as night were driven across the sky by this brief storm. Suddenly, the sun broke through with spectacular rays. Then **we saw the sun spin**—seen most clearly by our most skeptical members! Everyone got on their knees because we all saw the darting and fiery rays breaking through the dark clouds in various directions. As the clouds disappeared, the sky became rose-red, and the sun paled. Seen in the sun was the Andrew cross. As it disappeared, a huge cross made of light began to be raised above the sun, peaked by a crown. Around it the darkness grew again—as though the judgment of God was at hand. ***All of this time, the huge cross on the mountain was invisible!*** The spectacular rose colors grew brighter and brighter, twirling around the cross of light above the sun" (52:76–77).

On December 11, the eve of the Feast of Our Lady of Guadalupe, a "dance of the sun" took place shortly after 3:00 p.m. as described by an American woman:

"**The sun started to quiver and shake as if it wanted to rip itself loose from the sky**. It looked like it had a disc covering it—which also shook. The natives call this "the Host." Then the sun **started to rotate clockwise** toward us. It was spectacular and awesome! **It came toward us and then spun back, counterclockwise**. It lasted until about 3:40 p.m." (52:117)

At 2:50 p.m. the next day, she and her friends were treated to another performance:

> "**The sun started to quiver and shake and then spin toward us**. The more we prayed, the more spectacular the sight became. The sun started to spin faster and faster, and all of a sudden, we could see a beautiful red glow around it. This changed to yellow, orange, and a most beautiful violet. It started back again, and it came toward us, again changing colors around it. The lady next to me from England was bathed in the colors that the sun was throwing off. I also saw the ground bathed in red, yellow, orange, and violet. **Suddenly, the sun jumped across the sky as if it were going down in the West behind the mountain. But just as fast as it jumped over, it jumped back. After that, it zigzagged up and down**. My husband and all the others saw it, too! This spectacle lasted one full hour." (52:117–118)

Professor Courtenay Bartholomew, MD was on top of Podbrdo Hill when it started raining heavily. Here is his account of experiencing unexpected supernatural events:

> "As my clothes were drenched with rain, I did not stay long on the hill and returned to the church after a slow and careful trek down the slippery slope of Podbrdo. At 2:10 p.m.—just as I was about to enter the church in my wet clothes, I saw about seven people standing at the right side of the church, looking up at the sky. I approached them just in time to hear one American pilgrim exclaim, 'Look at the sun.' It was then that I saw the **sun spinning rapidly** and changing colors as it disobeyed all the cosmic laws of nature. Occasionally, the various colors of the sun would be reflected on the faces and clothes of the spectators of this great miracle. Within three minutes, my clothes felt quite dry. On that day, the miracle of the Sun continued for longer than one hour, and we all looked steadily at it for that period of time without hurting our eyes in the slightest. This is not possible under ordinary circumstances as the retina can easily be damaged after a brief period of staring at the sun" (68:151–152).

RWANDA, AFRICA (1981–1989)

Beginning in 1981 and continuing through 1989, Our Blessed Mary made countless visits to as many as eight teenagers in Kibeho, Rwanda in Africa. Many thousands attended the public apparitions of visionary Agnes and were often amazed at celestial displays that accompanied her visits from the Virgin Mary.

> "**The sun danced across the sky** right before my eyes! It danced and changed into many colors, like a rainbow swirling in a glass circle, and then it became as gray and pale as the moon. There was suddenly another sun behind the first one, illuminating it. On the face of the moon was a giant Eucharist and chalice, and then the colors changed again—like a third sun had emerged that was red, green, and gold. And the face of the Virgin Mary appeared in the center of the sun—just as clear as day!"

> "Thousands started looking up—when I looked up, I'd thought I'd gone crazy. I blinked and rubbed my eyes again…**the sun really was dancing! It moved back and forth as though God Himself were tossing it from one hand to the other**. And then another sun emerged from the dancing light. There were two suns in the sky! They spun in circles of opposite direction. One spun clockwise and the other counterclockwise. But then they spun into each other, reuniting as a single sun" (39:126).

Agnes pointed to the sky as Jesus spoke to her and said to the crowds:

> "Behold what you see. Are there any among you who can deny now that they have a sign? Watch closely and remember what you witness. Believe your eyes or deny what you are seeing."

> "There, far above our heads, was an image of Jesus on the cross with the Blessed Mother standing below him with her head bowed in grief. When I checked to see if others were witnessing the same scene, I saw 15,000 people dropping to their knees, many making the sign of the cross as they looked to the sky through tears of love" (39:127–128).

BE NOT AFRAID TO FOLLOW THE FOOTPRINTS FROM HEAVEN

BETANIA, VENEZUELA (1978–1993)

A number of memorable appearances by Our Lady to Maria Esperanza occurred from 1976 through 1990 with hundreds of other witnesses in Betania, Venezuela in South America. On one occasion on this farm, March 25, 1978, many saw a radiant mist coming from the woods. As the mist settled on top of a large tree, Maria—with fifteen others—saw Our Lady materialize with hands on her chest. Maria heard, "**Little daughter, this is not a dream. My presence among you is real.**"

> "Then her hands opened up, and I saw what appeared to be rays coming from her hands. They came directly toward us, bathing us with light—and one man cried out, 'Everything is burning up!' The whole area appeared to be on fire. It was beautiful. **The sun began to gyrate**, and everyone was shouting with emotion" (11:277).

As many as thirty thousand people gather on the twenty-fifth of each month. On one occasion, Dr. Arrieta, stricken with prostate cancer which had metastasized to his spine, was in attendance. In the morning, thousands saw the sun lose its light and turn green in its center. Then, like at Fatima, **the sun seemed to come down toward the screaming, fearful crowds**. Dr. Arrieta felt an infusion of heat throughout his body and believed he was being healed at that very moment. Medical tests confirmed he was now completely free of cancer (11:283).

On March 25, 1993, author, scientific researcher, and physician, Professor Courtenay Bartholomew, MD, heard thirty pilgrims shouting with joy near the grotto, and he turned in time to catch a glimpse of Mary—"wearing a beautiful chiffonlike long veil of light blue which floated majestically in the gentle breeze." Immediately afterwards, the sun appeared to shed smaller golden suns which moved swiftly across the sky in various directions, and then suddenly disappeared. He was impressed that **"all known laws of science had just been altered by the Creator"** (68:206).

CUENCA, ECUADOR (1988–1990)

Appearances to Patricia Talbot in Cuenca, Ecuador in South America from 1988 to 1990 altered forever this young woman's career and dreams. The massive crowd witnessed supernatural events in the sky—**like the sun changing colors and hurtling toward them!** These celestial miracles were repeated on other occasions and witnessed by many (23:49).

About six thousand people climbed the mountain for the first Saturday in December 1989. At 7:00 p.m., Blessed Mary appeared to Patricia. A phenomenon was witnessed on that day by thousands of persons. The clouds parted and a great light formed the image of Our Lady of the Miraculous Medal in the sky. Hands and faces sparkled with a golden glow—as if from glitter. This amazing celestial image converted many people who had been "just curious" until that moment (23:53–54).

NAJU, KOREA (1995)

At about 3:00 p.m. on June 30, the shape of the sun was changing gradually. By 3:30 p.m., it became a clear image of the Host. **It was also spinning and pulsating like a heart.** It was radiating different colors—blue, green, purple, yellow, red, and gold. These colors were reflected on people's clothes. Many who witnessed this were screaming with joy, and some were crying. The light was shining upon the roof of the Chapel and upon the people on the ground. Visionary Julia Kim said, "I saw Jesus and the Blessed Mother near the image of the Eucharist in the sky. There were also angels. The Blessed Mother began speaking in a most merciful, loving, kind, and soft manner. She was extremely beautiful." Blessed Mary said,

> "My beloved children! I bless you in a special way today, bestowing all the light from Heaven on you so that you may now live in the light of the Lord and myself and may become the apostles of the light that radiates from My Immaculate Heart. If you follow me completely, you will soon see the day when the darkness that is covering the Church will disappear.

The light of love from the most merciful and loving Sacred Heart of Jesus and My Immaculate Heart is bestowed upon you so that peace instead of suffering and anxiety may be given to you. In this desolate world, the danger of a new war is turning into a reality. But the power of God's love cannot be blocked… Now, all My children! Do not approach me because of curiosity and as spectators, but follow me with complete trust. You may not understand My words well now, but will some day. It is not too late yet. If you believe, follow, and trust My words as true messages originating from God, you will enjoy eternal happiness."

LIPA, PHILIPPINES (1990)

With the apparitions at Lipa in the Philippines concluding in May 1990, it was mentioned that a number of observers had witnessed the **"spinning of the sun"** (126).

AGOO, PHILIPPINES (1989–1993)

From 1989 through 1993, large crowds were present during each apparition with a young man named Judiel in Agoo, Philippines. Tens of thousands of people converged on this small community, causing traffic jams for scores of miles. Those present were often treated to spectacular signs and visions in the sky as well the "**miracle of the spinning sun**," the aroma of roses, and a mysterious blue light whenever Mary would appear to Judiel. **The miracle of the "dancing sun" was witnessed by many thousands of people on several occasions**. First, the sun would change from its usual radiant glare to a softer glow covered by a disc. Then different colors would radiate from the sun, spinning these rays of predominantly blue, green, red, and yellow colors onto the crowds as colored discs. These colors would remain on the disc-shaped objects for a few seconds after the disc was touched. Images of angels, the Holy Family, Jesus, and Mary with Joseph would appear from the pulsating sun.

Interest had grown tremendously in the apparition occurrences to the point that countless thousands started gathering in the days preceding an event. On March 5, 1993, the day before the next apparition, a *Manila Bulletin* reporter covering the events said that he personally witnessed **"a spinning and dancing of the sun"** for about fifteen minutes. And at dawn of the apparition day, **"the sun again moved and danced"** for a brief time (129).

SANTA MARIA, CALIFORNIA (1990)

In 1990, in Santa Maria, California, twenty thousand people—mostly of Spanish descent—had assembled on a hill where a large cross had been erected according to the messages from Mary received by a local visionary. They were all dressed in their Sunday best clothing—the men in suits, the women in beautiful attire as if attending a wedding, and the children exquisitely dressed in white clothing, dresses, white shoes, and white veils. They were praying the Rosary and singing hymns. It was very hot with no room to sit as everyone was standing on the hill. There was an air of expectation and a spirit of joy in the air.

Suddenly, people began to exclaim, **"Look at the sun!" It was spinning and pulsating.** Great rays of light of every possible color streaked from the center of the sun across the sky like lightning. Some people wept; others tried to film the phenomenon; others just gazed in wonder. A little girl about seven years old suddenly fell to her knees and stretched her arms toward the sun, crying, "Madre de Dios!" (Mother of God). Two little boys, probably two and three years old, also fell to their knees. Great tears of joy fell to the ground from their little cheeks as they, too, cried out, "Madre de Dios!" Their little arms reached up to a figure only they could see (2:313–314).

DONG LU, CHINA (1995)

In China, over thirty thousand Catholics from the unofficial Catholic Church had gathered for Mass on May 23, 1995, at the Dong Lu shrine on the vigil of the Feast of Our Lady, Mary Help of Christians.

There were four bishops of the unofficial Catholic Church concelebrating the Mass, and nearly one hundred unofficial priests standing in the open field. Suddenly, during the opening prayer and again during the consecration, **the people observed the sun spinning from right to left.** Light rays of various shades of color emanated from the sky. Participants saw Our Lady of China and the child Jesus in the sky. The Virgin Mary appeared as a beautiful lady in white, surrounded by light. They also saw the Holy Family, the Heavenly Father, and the Holy Spirit. The phenomenon lasted about twenty minutes (106).

From a research perspective, it is significant that these undeniable supernatural events are occurring many years apart and at great distances from each other—from Asia to South America, Europe to Africa and to the South Pacific, etc. It is also significant that they are always linked to a religious event, visionary, or prayerful gathering. Unquestionably, these witnesses are attempting to describe the same kind of supernatural experience! "With God, nothing is impossible."

> "Then Joshua spoke to the Lord, on the day that he handed over the Amorite in the sight of the sons of Israel, and he said before them: "O sun, you shall not move toward Gibeon! O moon, you shall not move toward the valley of Aijalon!" And the sun and the moon stood still, until the people had avenged themselves of their enemies. Has this not been written in the book of the just? And so **the sun stood still** in the midst of heaven, and it did not hurry to its rest **for the space of one day**. Never before and never after was there so long a day, as when the Lord obeyed the voice of a man, and fought for Israel." (**Joshua 10:12–14**)

We are finding some big "footprints" now!
But why would the Virgin Mary be visiting us?
What is her purpose?
What does she want?
Heaven begins to reveal its goals in the next several chapters…

CHAPTER 8

THE GREAT EVANGELIST

"The Blessed Virgin Mary is like the Moon in the night sky, shining brightly down on us, illuminating our path through the darkness. But the moonlight is not her own, but merely the reflection of the Sun's brilliance. Her Son's divine light illuminates her and then through her to us. When we shine with the light from Christ, others will see Christ in us. Our Blessed Mother is that reflection of her Son's Light."

—John Carpenter

When I think of a "great evangelist," what comes to my mind is the image of an outspoken, Bible-thumping, assertive individual who draws curious crowds and commands attention while enthusiastically delivering inspiring rhetoric. The image of Mary is traditionally one of quiet humility, gentleness, silent obedience, and never seeking attention. So when I heard that Mary was considered "The Great Evangelist," I really had to stop and contemplate that idea.

In reading many historic accounts of her appearances with mankind, it became very clear how she could viewed as a "great evangelist." First of all, *just appearing* to people all over the planet in many different nations is a deeply spiritual and memorable event. Hundreds and thousands of people wanted to commemorate those wonderful heavenly appearances by building a shrine or a bigger church at those locations. People were deeply moved and would sacrifice their time and precious pennies to make it happen. Priests, bishops, and even popes would celebrate Mass at those locations, adding to the special holiness already felt at those sites. Countless conversions or renewals of faith would happen for pilgrims.

Appearing to a wealthy couple, the Virgin Mary designates where a church should be built through the location of a miraculous snowfall in Rome. (painting by Mino da Fiesole, 1470)

Yet, Blessed Mary *made certain* that these things would happen. In an overwhelming and impressive majority of her visits, **she requested that a church be built** in a certain location. Sometimes, she even designated the exact spot, outlined the boundaries, and listed details of its structure and design. Despite many difficult challenges, people who encountered Our Blessed Mother became determined to fulfill her wishes. Many structures were very simple and small shelters for prayer in the beginning. Dedication to Mary's wishes usually led to additions, enlargements, extensions, and often completely new structures. Although not realized by most people, many of the grand and breathtaking Catholic basilicas and cathedrals around the world originated with a visit from Our Blessed Mother many years ago.

Our Lady did not need to be an outspoken, attention-drawing orator. Just her beautiful appearance, often holding baby Jesus in her arms, was inspiring enough. Her humble yet persistent requests for churches to be built were respectfully received—despite any doubts as to whether it was a realistic or feasible possibility to pursue. Sometimes, she would appear again to confirm her intention and emphasize her sincere desire. She would reassure those listening that resources of materials and money would "not be a concern" with her help. Despite all of the difficult odds and negative doubts, the churches would *somehow* get built and survive through time.

Working under the direction of God and Her Son, Blessed Mary was dedicated and determined to see different regions of the Earth grow in devotion—sometimes become reborn where devotion to her Son had withered, become forgotten, or had been deliberately suppressed. Here are some examples from history where Our Lady's intervention helped to develop great churches.

ROME, ITALY (352 AD)

In August of that year, a wealthy man named John and his wife had a dream that the Virgin Mary wanted a church built in her honor in Rome. He was told that they would know where to build it because snow would fall on that spot. Amazingly, Pope Liberius had the same dream on the same night. Despite it being a very hot summer in Rome, snow fell the next day on Mount Esquiline, one of the famous Seven Hills. However, it fell into a precise rectangular pattern—as if outlining the boundaries of the church Mary desired to have built.

When Pope Liberius showed up on Mount Esquiline to witness the miraculous snowfall, he found John and his wife already there, kneeling in prayer to the Virgin. People crowded to see the rectangular patch of snow, which would not melt despite the hot summer heat of August. John was convinced that its shape and size indicated that a church should be built on that precise spot. **As soon as the plot for the building had been staked out, the snow melted.**

John met the costs of building this church, which was completed in 354 AD. It was dedicated as the Basilica Liberiana after Pope

Liberius. Seventy years later, it was rebuilt on a grander scale by Pope Sixtus III, who added decorations and ornaments of silver. It was renamed the Basilica Sixti at that time. Today, it is called the Church of Santa Maria Maggiore (**St. Mary Major**) and is one of the largest basilicas in the world. They celebrate the "Miracle of the Snow" every year on August 5 (4:115–118).

VICENZA, ITALY (1426)

On March 7, 1426, at 9:00 a.m., Vincenza Passini (age seventy) encountered a beautiful woman on her path up the hill. She had "the likeness of a most beautiful queen with garments more resplendent than the sun, wreathed in a fragrance of a thousand scents." Overcome by the beauty of the woman, Vincenza fell to the ground. The beautiful woman spoke:

"I am the Virgin Mary, the Mother of Christ who died on the Cross for the salvation of men. I beg you to go and say in my name to the people of Vicenza that they must build in this place a church in my honor if they want to recover their health. Otherwise, the plague will not cease. As proof of what I say, let them dig here, and from the rock, living water will spring. As soon as the building begins, money will not lack."

After saying this, Blessed Mary took a twig, and with a graceful movement, traced the sign of the cross on the ground. Then she also drew the shape of the church to be built. Finally, she planted the twig in the ground where the high altar of the shrine stands today. As soon as the church was completed, the plague disappeared, and the region no longer suffered from it. Two large chapels were added to this grand basilica in 1972 along with thirty additional confessionals. The Servants of Mary took possession of the shrine in 1435 and are still ministering to pilgrims today, almost six hundred years later (3:10–12).

JOHN S. CARPENTER

ROME CITY, INDIANA, USA (1956)

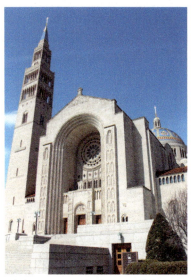

Basilica of the National Shrine of the Immaculate Conception in Washington D.C. (photo by author)

Interior of the National Shrine in Washington D.C. (photo by author)

October 13, 1956: Our Lady appears to Sister Mildred Neuzil and describes her desire for a National Basilica to be constructed in Washington DC while holding a replica in both of her hands (146):

> "This is my shrine, my daughter. I am very pleased with it. Tell my children I thank them. Let them finish it quickly and make it a place of pilgrimage. It will be a place of wonders. I promise this. I will bless all those who, either by prayers, labor, or material aid, help to erect this shrine."

Three years later on November 20, 1959, the Shrine of the Immaculate Conception in Washington DC was completed. It is the largest Catholic Church in the United States and in all of North and South America. It is the eighth largest Catholic Church in the world (144).

SAN NICOLAS, ARGENTINA (1983)

When Blessed Mary appeared to her on October 7, Gladys Quiroga de Motta asked her what she wanted her to do. Mary's image faded away and an image of a chapel appeared. Our Lady was requesting that a church be built. On the evening of November 24, Gladys and a small group had walked to the location where Mary had stated that she wanted a church. As they stood there, a powerful shaft of light pierced the darkness and struck the soil. The only other witness to this in the group besides Gladys was a nine-year-old girl (11:251).

CUENCA, ECUADOR (1989)

When the Holy Virgin asked for Patricia to find a remote location for prayer in the mountains, she and several friends began the search. Because Patricia had no idea where to look, she prayed for God to lead them. They headed for Turi, one of the beautiful mountains surrounding the city of Cuenca. As they neared the top of Turi, they heard bells—loud church bells coming from the northeast, the direction of a different mountain. There was *nothing* in the area that could be responsible for the ringing of bells. And no church bells would be ringing at that time of day.

So, they took it as a sign and drove up the other mountain in the direction of the bells. They observed a strange light in the shape of an arrow that pointed to a place high on that mountain. The light was so unusual that they drove to where it pointed downward toward a huge rock in the middle of a large open area. They decided to pray the Rosary at this boulder and wait for a confirming sign. Almost immediately, Patricia felt the wind on her face, and looking up, saw the Holy Virgin standing over the rock. Smiling, Blessed Mary told Patricia that she had found the place where Our Lady would give her blessings to her children and lead souls to conversion. Later, on March 3, 1990, the Holy Virgin gave her instructions for how to build that sanctuary high in the mountains at El Cajas—*complete with dimensions and descriptive details*! (23:35–37, 63)

ZARAGOZA, SPAIN (40 AD)

On January 2, 40 AD, while St. James was deep in prayer by the banks of the Ebro, the Mother of God appeared to him and gave him a small statue of her image holding Jesus and also a six-foot column of jasper. She instructed him to build a church in her honor.

> "This place is to be my house, and this image and column shall be the title and altar of the temple that you shall build. The faith of the people will become as strong as this pillar."

About a year after the apparition, James arranged to build a small chapel in Mary's honor—the first church ever dedicated to the honor of the Virgin Mary. Today, a Baroque-style church, completed in 1686, exists on this site and houses the precious items given to James by the Virgin Mary in 40 AD. During the Spanish Civil War of 1936–1939, three bombs were dropped on the church, but *none of them exploded* (160).

GENOA, ITALY (1490)

On August 29, 1490, Benedict Pareto was grazing his flock on the mountain when his attention was drawn to a brilliant movement of light. Within this heavenly glow was the image of a woman holding a child on her arm. Although he did not know who she was, he felt compelled to kneel as she approached him. Standing before him, the "beautiful lady" assured him with these words:

> "Do not be afraid. I am the Queen of Heaven and have come to you with My Divine Son for this reason: You are to arrange for a church to be built on this spot, to be dedicated in My name."

Poor Benedict protested that he had no money with which to build a church. But the Lady calmed his confusion with these words:

> "Trust me, Benedict. The money will not be lacking. Only your good will is needed. With My aid, all will be easy."

The basilica of della Guardia was built in 1923; the greatest day in its calendar is August 29 when there are colorful celebrations and torch-lit processions at night to commemorate Benedict Pareto's original encounter. The walls of the church are inlaid with marble with the perpetually-lit, crowned, marble statue of Mary in its niche near the high altar. Six popes from Clement XVI to Benedict XVI have honored the shrine in various ways (3:15–18).

MEXICO CITY, MEXICO (1531)

On December 9, 1531, Juan Diego was traveling his daily route past the hill of Tepeyac when he saw a cloud encircled with a rainbow of colors and heard strange music. A woman's voice was calling above the music. Ascending the crest of the hill, he encountered a strikingly beautiful woman standing there, beckoning to him. She radiated such light and joy that he dropped to his knees and smiled at her in wonderment.

"You must know and be very certain in your heart, my son, that I am truly the perpetual and perfect Virgin Mary. I wish and intensely desire that in this place my sanctuary be erected so that in it I may show and make known and give all my love, my compassion, my help, and my protection to the people. Here I will hear their weeping, their sorrow, and will remedy and alleviate their suffering, necessities, and misfortunes. And so that my intention may be made known, you must go to the house of the bishop of Mexico and tell him that I sent you, and that it is my desire to have a sanctuary built here" (11:40–41).

Because the bishop was not easily convinced that the Virgin Mary had been visiting this poor Indian, heaven chose to miraculously imprint the Virgin's image on Juan Diego's cloak so that there would be no doubt of his claims. The bishop was overcome with amazement over the stunning divine image, and the church was built where she had requested it to be placed. Today, it has evolved into the magnificent Basilica of Mexico City where that miraculous image of Our Lady of Guadalupe is preserved and displayed (more on that "physical proof" later...). Pope John Paul II beatified Juan Diego in 1990 and raised him to sainthood in 2002. Our Lady of Guadalupe inspired over nine million conversions in Mexico (11:52).

RAPALLO, ITALY (1557)

On July 2, 1557, a farmer named Giovanni Chichizola was walking on a donkey trail on a wooded hill overlooking the city of Rapallo. Coming upon a cool, shady spot, he paused for his noonday rest. The sound of a sweet voice calling his name startled him to alertness. There, standing close beside him, was a beautiful lady surrounded by an intense light. The Blessed Virgin Mary appeared to him and reassured him by saying,

"Do not fear, Giovanni. I am the Mother of God. I have chosen you to be a messenger of my motherly will. Visit the ecclesiastics of Rapallo and let them know that the Mother of

BE NOT AFRAID TO FOLLOW THE FOOTPRINTS FROM HEAVEN

God has chosen this place as her perpetual dwelling place and would like a church to be erected here."

The very next year in 1558, the Archbishop of Turin authorized the building of a church on the hill where Mary's visit had taken place. Construction began immediately, and during the following year, the church opened and was dedicated to Our Blessed Mother. The shrine found acceptance with the Vatican when Our Lady of Montallegro was crowned in solemn ceremonies on July 7, 1767 by the Bishop of Ajaccio, Corsica. Pilgrims can approach the site on foot by way of an old mule track or by cable car from Rapallo. Pilgrims are intrigued with the beauty of the sanctuary in the basilica which replaced the original chapel (3:43–46).

VAILANKANNI, INDIA (1580)

Basilica in Vailankanni, India inspired by the Virgin Mary in the 1600's.

A lame boy had been helping his mother in Vailankanni by selling her daily pot of buttermilk to travelers along the main road. One day, as he sat along the side of the road, a strange and brilliant light surrounded him. A beautiful lady appeared in the light, holding an infant in her arms. She asked if she could have some buttermilk for her child. Without hesitation, he poured her a cup, and she gave it to her child. Then she asked the lame boy if he would deliver a message for her to a certain Catholic gentleman in nearby Nagapattinam. The boy replied that he wanted to do her the favor but could not because of being so lame. She smiled and told him to stand up. Immediately, he was surprised that he could walk, jump, and run—for the first time in his life! She again commanded the boy to contact the Catholic gentleman in the nearby town of Nagapattinam to build a church in her honor. He was so excited that he ran down the road, thrilling the villagers who knew he had been unable to walk. The gentleman had no trouble believing the young boy because he had had a dream in which Blessed Mary had also told him to build a church in her honor. He asked the boy to take him to the spot of this apparition. The first thatched church was built on that very spot by this Catholic gentleman (1:77–78).

September 8 is now the feast day for Our Lady of Good Health. Every year, a procession begins on August 30, and people come from all over India—some walking as much as two hundred miles on foot—because of their devotion and sacrifice to Mary. As many as five hundred thousand pilgrims visit every day during this week-long celebration. Ironically, very few are Christians—most are Hindu, Muslim, Parsee, Egyptian, etc. The little church is now a magnificent basilica with at least eight million visitors every year (154).

QUERRIEN, LA PRENESSAYE, FRANCE (1652)

On August 15, 1652, Jeanne Courtel, age twelve, was a poor shepherdess tending her father's flock of sheep. She had been both deaf and mute ever since her birth. She was reciting her prayers when she was surprised by the sudden appearance of the Blessed Virgin. Our Lady was holding the Child Jesus on one arm and holding a stalk of lilies in the other. Blessed Mary had only spoken a few words when Jeanne suddenly realized that she could actually hear her! The twelve year old had been miraculously healed. Our Lady spoke in a sweet voice,

> "I choose this place to be honored. Build for me a chapel in the middle of this village and many people will come."

On September 20, after conducting his investigations, the bishop formally recognized the validity of the apparitions and blessed the first stone of the future chapel. The chapel was begun that year in 1652 and was completed four years later. It was enlarged in 1779 because of the large crowds that visited the shrine. On August 14, 1950, some twenty thousand pilgrims visited Querrien for the coronation of the statue by the local bishop. The shrine of Our Lady of Eternal Aid is proud to announce that it is the only one in Brittany that has been authenticated by the Catholic Church (3:73–75).

LAUS, FRANCE (1664)

The Virgin Mary appears to Benoite Rencurel in Laus, France, 1664.

As the unschooled shepherdess, Benoite Rencurel, arrived in front of a small grotto, a lady of incomparable beauty appeared, holding the hand of an equally beautiful child. The naïve shepherd girl just could not believe that she was actually in the presence of the Mother of God.

> "I want a large church built on this spot, along with a building for a few resident priests. The church will be built in honor of my dear Son and Myself. Here, many sinners will be converted. I will appear to you often here."
>
> Benoite: "Build a church? There's no money for that here!"
>
> "Do not worry. When the time comes to build, you will find all that you need, and it will not be long. The pennies of the poor will provide for everything. Nothing will be lacking."

Although there were no resources at all, construction of a much-needed, larger church was undertaken with great enthusiasm. It was the poor who took up the challenge. Many of the pilgrims as well as the local people would carry one or more stones from the streams to the construction site. Thanks to Father Gaillard's tenacity, **the construction was built according to the indications Our Lady had given to Benoite**. On October 7, 1666, Father Gaillard laid the first stone of the building at the Feast of the Holy Rosary. Within four years, the church was completed. The hands of the poor had gathered its materials; donations had dug its foundations (123:4, 6).

LICHEN, POLAND (1850)

Our Lady appeared in 1850 to Mikolaj Sikatka, who was pasturing his cattle. She called for people to come to conversion, penance, and prayer. She informed about the punishment which would come—predicting wars and an epidemic of cholera.

> "When hard days will come, those people who will come and will pray and do penance. Whenever this nation will come to Me and ask for help, I will never leave this nation. On this place will be built a magnificent church for My veneration. **If people will not build this church, the angels will build it.**"

The Holy Virgin predicted the formation of the sanctuary and the monastery in Lichen from which her glory would flow. Thanks to the generosity of visiting pilgrims, a new Sanctuary of Our Lady of Lichen was built, modeled after St. Peter's Basilica at the Vatican.

Pope John Paul II consecrated this church—Poland's largest—on June 7, 1999. It is the seventh largest church in Europe (125).

The list of churches Our Lady asked to be built goes on and on. It is impressive how many grand basilicas and beautiful cathedrals in the world were "breathed into life" as the result of an inspiring appearance by Our Blessed Mother Mary. And each church became a new home for Her Son Jesus with each new tabernacle that was constructed within each new church.

The Virgin Mary, under heaven's direction, was also a great evangelist with some very difficult antagonists and stubborn disbelievers. She had a way, whether it be subtle and indirect, or confrontational and persistent, to inspire people to come to know Her Son Jesus. Here are some examples taken from the history of our world.

LAUS, FRANCE (1664)

Benoite Rencurrel's employer, Mrs. Rolland, was a woman who had no interest whatsoever in religion, but she wanted to see for herself what was going on at the site of these apparitions. One day before dawn Mrs. Rolland entered the grotto and hid behind a rock. Shortly afterwards, Benoite arrived and the Virgin Mary appeared to her. Our Lady reported:

> "Your mistress is over there, hiding behind the rock. Tell her not to curse with the name of Jesus, because if she keeps it up, there will be no paradise for her. Her conscience is in a very bad state; she should do penance."

Mrs. Rolland heard every word clearly and tearfully promised to amend her ways—which she did, faithfully, after that day (123:3).

KIBEHO, RWANDA (1981)

A priest at the high school didn't believe any of the visionary schoolgirls, calling them "a pack of liars" and wanting these three "seers" thrown out of the school. Visionary Marie-Claire approached him with a message from Our Lady about his "unjustly tormenting her children" and needing to do penance. "She wants you to kneel down tonight, hold your arms open to God, and pray your rosary three times." But the priest called her a liar and ordered her to stay in her dormitory room until morning when he would then deliver a "proper punishment."

That night, the priest decided to play it safe—*just in case the visions were authentic*, locking himself in his room, drawing the curtains shut, and kneeling on the floor. He spread his arms wide and recited the rosary three times. When he finished, he placed his rosary into his nightstand, placing some books and magazines on top of it before closing the drawer. The next morning, he summoned Marie-Claire for her punishment. But she was smiling cheerfully when she arrived, and before he could speak, she exclaimed:

> "Father—the Blessed Mother is very pleased that you prayed your rosary exactly as she asked you to, but she told me this morning that you shouldn't have piled all those books and magazines on the rosary when you put it back in the drawer. She says to keep it with you at all times and pray with it every day."

The priest was stunned at this amazing validation, and his heart was immediately converted, becoming a huge supporter of the visionaries from then on! (39:26–27)

GARABANDAL, SPAIN (1961–1965)

Two Jesuit priests, Father Luis Andrei and his brother Father Ramon had gone to Garabandal out of curiosity. As Father Ramon watched an apparition event with the four girls in ecstasy, he began to have serious doubts. He thought to himself, "If this is authentic, let the apparition cease for one of them." Amazingly, at that very moment, Mary Loli came out of her trance and looked at Father Ramon, smiling. A few moments later, she went back into her ecstasy—and Jacinta asked her why she had left. Mary Loli asked Blessed Mary what had happened. Father Ramon was able to hear Mary Loli say, "Oh! That's why? **It was so he would believe!**" (34:37–38)

LIPA, PHILIPPINES (1948)

August 20, 1948 - Teresita saw ***showers of rose petals*** for the first of many times. They occurred both outside in the garden and inside the convent. Many clergy, pilgrims, and religious witnessed these rose petal showers. The rose petals contained miraculous images of Jesus, Mary, and other holy scenes. On January 23, 1949, the cornerstone was laid for the new church, Our Lady Mediatrix of All Grace—with up to fifty thousand present. But Bishop Alfredo Verzosa ordered the Carmelite nuns to withdraw the statue of Mary from public veneration because of all the commotion it had caused. He personally went to the convent on November 19, 1948, determined to do this, himself. When he opened the door and entered the convent, a *shower of rose petals* fell on him. He fell to his knees and could not utter a word. From that moment on, Bishop Verzosa supported the apparitions with official approval (126:2–3).

ZEITOUN, EGYPT (1968)

Several high-ranking officials obtained a private story while visiting the home of one of the district's leading Muslims. He admitted that he had been antagonistic toward visitors in the beginning because his house was near the church where the apparitions were happening. He would throw stones at the pilgrims as they had to pass close by his house. He even called the police to try to have them arrested. But then, much to his surprise, he said that *Our Lady appeared to him* and asked him why he behaved in this manner. She begged him not to continue in this fashion and commanded him to paint the sign of the cross on his house. Although remaining a practicing Muslim, he is now convinced of the authenticity of the visits and, in fact, he painted ***forty*** *huge white crosses* on his house! (68:182)

BETANIA, VENEZUELA (1984)

It was a gorgeous spring day for a large church picnic on March 25, 1984 for the 108 people in attendance. A grotto nearby with a spring-fed waterfall attracted the active children. Around 3:00 p.m., one of the children ran excitedly back to the resting adults to proclaim that the Blessed Mother was appearing to them above the waterfall near the grotto. Word spread quickly, and soon, everybody was rushing to see what the child was talking about—and they ALL saw the incredible sight! Bishop Ricardo wanted to investigate the events of March 25, 1984 himself and was most impressed by the reports that actually came from several atheists and agnostics (11:264, 280, 282).

> "One of them was minding his own business, drinking water from the waterfall when he saw the apparition without any preconception or expectation—and he was not psychologically prepared for this!"

They are believers now! One can only imagine that amazing transformation—to witness something that you never had believed to be possible, *and then to see it* with your own eyes.

STEUBENVILLE, OHIO, USA (1992)

Tony Fernwalt was not a spiritual or holy man. In fact, he had suffered many hardships, including raw poverty, violence, and imprisonment. He was not expecting what he experienced on March 10, 1992, as he was doing some cleanup work at St. Jude's Orthodox Church in Steubenville, Ohio. As he climbed the stairs from the church basement where he had been working, he described:

> "I could hear the voice of some young lady that sounded like she was singing—or crying. Then I smelled these roses. I mean the place just reeked of roses. It was so strong…I couldn't believe it…Then I peeked through the open door of the church, and I saw this lady dressed all in red, standing with her hands open in front of the altar. She was saying over and over, 'My Son's Heart is broken.'
>
> I thought, Oh boy! Her kid's been in an accident or something. Maybe he's in the service, or sick, or getting a divorce. Anyway, it was none of my business. I shut the door to the basement. I figured to go to the back of the church and not bother her. As I

walked past her, she said again, 'My Son's Heart is broken.' She looked like she was from India or some place like that. Long dress, draping veil, funny clothes. Everything was red. When I got to the back of the church, I sat down to rest on an old folding chair. She was suddenly right there! It scared me! First thing she says to me is, 'As you know, My Son is Jesus.'

That bothered me. I said, 'Yeah, and I suppose you're the Virgin Mary.' I figured she was nuts and belonged in the state hospital, Fallsview or Massilon or someplace like that. I looked at her pretty close. Then I started noticing the beauty of her. She looked too young to have a son in the service. I looked at her real close now. She looked too tall for her body. 'Something's wrong here,' I said to myself. I started going down from her head, down her whole body, till I got to her feet. They were standing on a mist that was resting on the floor. Her feet were maybe a foot off the floor on the mist! She looked me right in the eye and said, 'Yes.' (responding to his question about being the Virgin Mary)

Something in me told me that this was serious. It gripped me—choked me—I couldn't breathe. I'm sitting in the chair—I felt like I was dying. I grabbed my neck. She said, 'Do not be afraid.' I was scared—but some kind of peace came to me when she spoke. 'Do not be afraid. You have sinned against God. You have sinned against My Son, and you have sinned against God's children.'

I knew that I had whipped my kids and my wife. Then she started to tell me about other things I had done. She said that I wanted to be cruel. I figured anybody can look up the court records. It's all there. Then she said, 'You need to pray. Pray that people come back to church. Pray that people come back to My Son. Pray for forgiveness. Ask My Son for forgiveness.'

Then I started to see my sins unfold in front of me. Only now I wasn't thinking about how I felt. I could **feel** how the others felt when I was hurting them. I **felt** their pain. I even **felt** their fear. If I hit somebody, I **felt** the hurt. I could **feel** their mental and physical pain when I hurt them. She kept asking me to ask Jesus for forgiveness for each thing that I did that I was seeing. She told me things about things I did that nobody ever, ever knew! I thought that I must be dying. I can't stand this! I didn't see anything good that I had ever done in my life. Only the bad stuff. And there was plenty of bad stuff. I was kind of mad.

I said, 'If you are who you say you are, I want to know about the world—things that they say are going to happen.' We talked about wars, riots, violence in the cities. She said that God does not cause these. We do. She told me about lots of things that are going to happen on the earth. I said to her, 'I've been bad all my life. Why would you care about me? I would have sold your Son for thirty pieces of silver too, maybe less.'

She looked at me—I could see her love for me! She said, 'No, you are only a child. People will come and teach you love. They will help you to love and understand. I will take you from a Saul to a Paul. I will leave signs to prove that I was here, and believers will come and see and believe.'

She promised that the scent of roses would be a sign. Things would turn gold. The sick would be healed, and weak faith would become strong. She said, 'My Son wants all people to return to Him. Pray that sinners will be converted. Pray that their hearts turn back to My Son. My Son wants all souls. He does not want to lose even one soul.'"

This encounter changed Tony's life forever. He was a devoted Catholic afterwards (2:302–306).

CASTELPETROSO, ITALY (1888)

The priest in the diocese treated the whole affair as delusional and preached against it. A second priest, Don Luigi Ferrara, was also a disbeliever—*until he saw her, too*!

> "I had many times derided those who visited the mountain on which these wonderful apparitions took place. On May 16, 1888, however, I felt a desire to visit the place. When I arrived,

I saw with great clearness Our Lady, like a statuette, with a little Child in her arms. Whenever I think of these visions on this mountain, I am moved to tears and cannot speak" (3:154).

ROME, ITALY (1842)

An Austrian Jew named Alphonse Ratisbonne was the youngest son of an important banking family in Strasbourg. Alphonse was a Jew by race and religion and was very well off in material possessions. He harbored a great hatred for Catholics and anything to do with the Catholic Church—largely due to his brother George converting and becoming a priest. He blamed the Catholic Church for "bewitching" his brother. A series of mishaps brought him to Rome, a city he had vowed to never visit. He became acquainted there with Baron Theodore de Bussières, a very fervent Catholic.

One afternoon, during a raging argument with Bussières in which Ratisbonne was ridiculing the superstitions of the Catholic religion, the baron challenged him to submit to a simple test and wear the Miraculous Medal. Ratisbonne consented so that he could *prove the ineffectiveness* of such religious baubles. The baron also added that Ratisbonne must recite the Memorare once a day. He promised that he would, saying, "If it does me no good, at least it can do me no harm."

The baron and a close circle of aristocratic friends increased their prayers for the skeptical Jew. On January 20, 1842, while waiting for Bussières, he wandered through the church, admiring the beautiful artwork. But then he decided to turn to leave out the front door. A huge black dog suddenly appeared and blocked his path. The animal was vicious, baring his fangs. As Ratisbonne froze in his place, unable to move, the dog vanished, and a brilliant light began glowing from a side chapel directly in front of him. As he stood before the altar dedicated to St. Michael the Archangel, Our Lady suddenly appeared to him. She was wearing a crown and a simple long white tunic with a jeweled belt around her waist and blue-green mantle draped over her left shoulder. Her peaceful gaze reached deeply into his soul. Her hands were open, spreading rays of graces. The light coming from her was so brilliant that he had to look away from her enchanting face and captivating eyes. Her height and elegance gave the impression of a great lady, fully conscious of her own dignity. She transmitted both grandeur and mercy in an atmosphere of great peace. He said that her hands "expressed all the secrets of the Divine Pity." Ratisbonne understood that he was in the presence of the Mother of God. Although Mary never said a word to him, he felt that he "understood all." He fell to his knees, sobbing, and converted.

Alphonse Ratisbonne is stunned into conversion by Mary's unexpected appearance in Rome, Italy in 1842.
(painting hangs in the National Shrine of the Miraculous Medal, Perryville, Missouri)

The baron was surprised to find Ratisbonne praying fervently on his knees. Ratisbonne immediately asked to go to a confessor so that he could receive baptism. Eleven days later, he received baptism, confirmation, and his first Communion. The entire Catholic world became aware of this amazing conversion. Ratisbonne became a Jesuit priest and founded a religious group, the Daughters of Zion—*to help with the conversion of Jews*! (143)

BE NOT AFRAID TO FOLLOW THE FOOTPRINTS FROM HEAVEN

TRE FONTANE, ROME, ITALY (1947)

Bruno Cornacchiola, born in 1913, came from a poor background, joined the military, got married, and then decided to fight on the Nationalist side in the Spanish Civil War to earn some money. He deserted his wife in order to fight on the side of the anti-Catholic forces. He came under the influence of a German Protestant who managed to convince him that the papacy was the cause of all the world's ills. Bruno immediately conceived a hatred for the Catholic Church and vowed to kill Pope Pius XII—and bought a dagger in Spain for that purpose! He carved the words on it: "Death to the Pope."

Bruno returned to his wife, but he was far from a model husband. He frequently used blasphemous and obscene speech, committed adultery, beat his wife, and had forbidden her from going to a Catholic church or practicing her faith in any manner. He joined the Seventh Day Adventists and plotted to kill the pope on the Feast of the Nativity of the Blessed Virgin Mary, September 8, 1947.

On the Saturday after Easter Sunday, April 12, 1947, Bruno took his three children (Isola-ten, Carlo-seven, and Gianfranco-four) for a picnic to Tre Fontane (the area outside of Rome where the Romans beheaded St. Paul). On that lovely spring day, Bruno sat in a grove of eucalyptus trees, preparing a talk to ridicule the Immaculate Conception. Earlier that day, as if to manifest his bitter hatred for the Immaculate Mother, he had written on the base of a statue of the Holy Virgin, "You are neither virgin nor mother!"

One of his children lost his ball and interrupted Bruno's thoughts by asking for his help. He followed this child but saw his youngest child kneeling at the entrance to a cave. The child's face was radiantly joyful as he stared into the cave, repeating, "Beautiful lady, beautiful lady." His hands were folded as if engrossed in deep prayer. Bruno looked into the cave and could see nothing that would account for the boy's actions. He then turned toward his other two children, but by then, they too, had dropped to their knees with hands folded in prayer and their eyes transfixed on someone in the cave. The three children were mesmerized by something supernatural that he could not see. Seized with fright, Bruno tried to grab his children and carry them away, but he could not move them! It was as if they were glued to the ground. Then, in the midst of an intense perfume of flowers, Mary appeared to Bruno as well. An intense light filled his eyes for a moment, and then everything in front of him disappeared—his children and the cave. He felt himself becoming weightless.

After this momentary blindness, Bruno saw in the most illuminated part of the cave a woman of indescribable celestial beauty. She was dressed in a long, brilliantly white dress with a rose-colored sash. Over her black hair was a green mantle which extended to her bare feet. Her head was adorned by a halo of brilliant golden light. Her face had an expression of motherly kindness, although cloaked by sadness at times. She was holding a dark gray Bible close to her heart. At her bare feet lay a black cloth which had a smashed crucifix on it. Her hands were crossed at her breast, but she unfolded them once to point to the broken pieces of the crucifix.

> "I am the one who is of the Divine Trinity. I am Daughter of the Father, Mother of the Son, and Spouse and Temple of the Holy Spirit. I am the Virgin of Revelation.
>
> (Then she turned on Bruno.) **You persecute me. Enough of it now!** Enter into the true fold, God's Kingdom on Earth... You must be like the flowers which Isola picked. They make no protest—they are silent and do not rebel."

Mary then spoke with Bruno at length about many things that afternoon, including her Assumption into heaven. "**My body could not decay and did not decay. My Son came for me with His Angels.**" She revealed the sad condition of Bruno's soul to him. She was admonishing a return to God and a more literal living of the holy Gospel: "**Return to the pure source of the Gospel**." At this point, Mary taught him the sure means of salvation for him and all mankind—***which is prayer***, and in particular, the daily praying of the Holy Rosary.

> "Pray much and recite the Rosary for the conversion of sinners, of unbelievers and of all Christians. I want to give you absolute

proof of the divine reality which you are experiencing, so that you will exclude any other motive for this encounter—evil motivation included. This is the sign: Every time you meet a priest in church or in the street, approach him and address him with these words, 'Father, I must talk to you.' If he answers, 'Ave Maria! My son, what do you want?' Beg him to stop, because he is the chosen one. Tell him what your heart dictates and obey him. In fact, he will direct you to another priest by saying, 'He is the one for you.' Afterwards, you will go to the Holy Father, the Supreme Shepherd of all Christians, and give him My message personally. The one that I will point out to you will take you to the Pope. Some people will not believe, but let that not disturb you."

Having said that to Bruno, she turned and serenely moved in the direction of St. Peter's Basilica. Still transfixed in an ecstasy, he could not move for a few moments. Bruno's conversion took place immediately. Our Lady's predictions came true as Bruno was guided through certain priests to the pope. He gifted Pope Pius XII with the actual dagger that he had planned to kill him with. He also passed police interrogations and psychiatric examinations. Blessed Mary appeared to Bruno three more times. He repented his sinful life and became an outstanding Catholic. Like Paul, he dedicated his life to evangelizing and teaching the truths of the Catholic Faith (153).

Our Blessed Mother Mary has clearly demonstrated in these examples from history that she relentlessly pursued the development or restoration of countless churches worldwide. She also persuaded doubters, critics, atheists, troublemakers, and anti-Catholics to literally "see the light" and come back to Her Son, Jesus Christ. Whether she was subtle, clever, or directly confrontational, Mother Mary was indeed the Great Evangelist—and still is today!

However, she shared many other important messages with us as well.

Keep tracking these heavenly footprints through our history!

CHAPTER 9

ACCURATE HEAVENLY PREDICTIONS

"The only true prophet is the one whose prophecies actually come to pass."

A logical test for the reality of these reported encounters is whether what is promised or predicted actually comes true. With a delusional or fantasy prone person, they will make many claims and grand predictions—which, of course, **never** come true. The delusional person then always has an excuse or rationalization for why the predicted event did not take place. With a hoax or a scam, **nothing** will take place as foretold—and it won't matter to the sociopath because the tickets have been sold, the money collected, and scam already completed to steal your funds.

With alleged visits from the Virgin Mary, she may tell us of events to come, good or bad, with specific details. This could even include where and when she will appear next. And if Blessed Mary says that she will appear on a certain date at a certain time, *she has never failed to show for a predicted visit* yet! The visionaries provide that proof, not only by their words, but by our observing the changes in their appearance upon Our Lady's arrival when they visibly enter into her supernatural realm. And if the visionaries are deliberately delayed, detained, or even kidnapped, her presence is still felt at the appointed time as supernatural signs are given to others present.

For example, at Fatima on August 13, the three shepherd children were scheduled to meet with Blessed Mary at the usual time of

12:00 noon. But governmental officials had arranged to kidnap and detain the three children on purpose, threatening their lives if they did not reveal Our Lady's secrets to them. Although the children missed the rendezvous with the Virgin Mary, the crowd of eighteen thousand interested followers had their own experiences when Mary arrived as promised (detailed in Chapter 6). Mary actually then met with the children later on August 19 instead (29:169).

Similarly, in Medjugorje, in 1981, two social workers **from the government** deliberately tried to cause the six children to miss their expected meeting with Our Lady. On Tuesday, June 30, the two social workers took the children on a long day of treats and sightseeing, deliberately away from the site of the apparitions. As the rendezvous time of 6:30 p.m. approached, the children demanded to be let out of the car. They were on the opposite side of Crnica Hill while twenty thousand people awaited their arrival on the other hillside. A light began to illuminate the selected area where the crowds had gathered, but then the luminous cloud started moving toward the children who were several miles away. All six saw her clearly a moment later, gliding toward them through the air, her long veil streaming behind her. Ivanka asked the social workers if they saw the light—*and they did.* (Just moments before, the two workers had been making sarcastic remarks and jokes about Mary coming to see them.) The children knelt, and Mary appeared to them. They asked if she was upset that they were not at the regular location, and she indicated that it did not make a difference. Stunned at what the government workers had witnessed, the terrified social workers jumped back in their car and sped away. Later, they resigned their positions after the shock of that day (52:35–36) (8:99).

Another prediction involving Mary's own appearances happened in Lithuania in July 1962. After several visits, the Virgin told an eighteen-year-old girl where her next apparition site would be:

> "I will not appear here again. **I will appear in Egypt soon** with two angels. If anything goes wrong, come here to pray, and I will give you advice" (59:181).

Sure enough, the Virgin began appearing in Zeitoun, Egypt just six years later in 1968! She was actually returning to Egypt on a promise that she made back in 1920. At that time, Our Lady had asked a wealthy family to build a church in her honor on their land. If they did as she requested, she promised then to return in "about fifty years" to dedicate the church in some special way. She began appearing on the roof of that church for four years, beginning in 1968 (forty-eight to fifty-one years after her promise made in 1920)—to the delight of hundreds of thousands who watched her wave at them and bless them for hours at a time! (68:178)

Therefore, Blessed Mary keeps her promises regarding *her own* appearances. But can she really predict the future of world events—including disasters, diseases, wars, or politics?

VICENZA, ITALY (1426, 1428):
"Madonna of Mount Berico"

There was so much pestilence and sickness between 1404 and 1428 in the region of Vicenza, Italy, that the population declined drastically from death or fleeing the area. On March 7, 1426, at 9:00 a.m., Vincenza Passini, age seventy, encountered a beautiful woman on her path up the hill. Overcome by the beauty of the woman, she fell to the ground. The Virgin Mary spoke:

> "I beg you to go and say in my name to the people of Vicenza that they must build in this place a church in my honor if they want to recover their health. Otherwise, the plague will not cease. You will insist so that my people do my will, otherwise they will never be rid of the plague—and, until they obey, they will see My Son angry with them."

Vincenza immediately obeyed the beautiful woman and began telling everyone that she met. But she soon realized that nobody believed her! Even Bishop Pietro Emiliani gave little credence to her story. So, as Mary predicted, the plague raged on. On August 1, 1428, the Virgin Mary appeared again to Vincenza. She repeated her previous warning and recommendation for the health of the people.

Because of the horrific conditions of the ongoing plague, the people chose to believe her this time. The Hall of Government decided to build a church on Mount Berico, beginning construction just twenty-four hours after this last apparition! **As soon as the church was completed, the plague disappeared, and the region no longer suffered from it (3:10–11).**

QUITO, ECUADOR (1610): "Our Lady of Good Success"

The Virgin Mary is somber in predicting the future.
(statue from the National Shrine of Our Lady
of the Snows, Belleville, Illinois)

During the apparitions to Sister Mariana, the Blessed Mother confided several prophecies, some of which have already taken place, thus validating her words. Many predictions made around 1610 were designated for the twentieth century—and are indeed pertinent to the troubled times of our present day. Some of these prophecies include a warning that Masons and other secret sects would have an influence—even within the Church. She warned:

> "A worldwide campaign against the virtues of chastity and purity will succeed in corrupting the youth…evil will invade

childhood innocence. The clergy will leave much to be desired because priests will become careless in their sacred duties... Faithful priests upholding, the Faith will suffer greatly and will be overwhelmed with vexations in order to stop them from fulfilling their ministry. The precious light of Faith will be extinguished in souls by the almost total corruption of customs."

"The sacrament of Matrimony, which symbolizes the union of Christ with the Church, will be thoroughly attacked and profaned. Masonry, then reigning, will implement iniquitous laws aimed at extinguishing this sacrament. They will make it easy for all to live in sin, thus multiplying the birth of illegitimate children without the Church's blessing."

"The devil will work to persecute the ministers of the Lord in every way, working with baneful cunning to destroy the spirit of their vocation and corrupting many. Those who will thus scandalize the Christian flock will bring upon all priests the hatred of bad Christians and the enemies of the One, Holy, Roman Catholic, and Apostolic Church. This apparent triumph of Satan will cause enormous suffering to the good pastors of the Church..."

"In those times the atmosphere will be saturated with the spirit of impurity which, like a filthy sea, will engulf the streets and public places with incredible license...Innocence will scarcely be found in children, or modesty in women. There shall be scarcely any virgin souls in the world. The delicate flower of virginity will seek refuge in the cloisters...Without virginity, fire from heaven will be needed to purify these lands..."

"Sects, having permeated all social classes, will find ways of introducing themselves into the very heart of homes to corrupt the innocence of children. The children's hearts will be dainty morsels to regale the devil..."

"Religious communities will remain to sustain the Church and work with courage for the salvation of souls...The secular clergy will fall far short of what is expected of them because they will not pursue their sacred duty. Losing the divine compass, they will stray from the way of priestly ministry mapped out for them by God and will become devoted to money, seeking it too earnestly" (141).

LICHEN, POLAND (1850)

Our Lady appeared in 1850 to Mikolaj Sikatka who was pasturing his cattle. She called for people to come to conversion, penance, and prayer. She informed about the punishment which would come—predicting wars and **an epidemic of cholera**. But she gave hope and promised:

"When hard days will come, those people who will come in front of this picture and will pray and do penance, **will not die**. Whenever this nation will come to Me and ask for help, I will never leave this nation, and I will protect this nation, and I clasp this nation to My heart."

The Holy Virgin predicted the formation of the sanctuary and the monastery in Lichen from which her glory would flow. The shepherd Mikolaj started to expound Our Lady's message, but he was persecuted and imprisoned by Russian authorities. But just as the Virgin had predicted, two years later in 1852, the epidemic of cholera began. That same year, the picture was placed in the parish church in Lichen. People remembered the Virgin's prophecy and thronged to her portrait to kneel and pray. *Whoever prayed in front of this picture received graces and did not become ill or die. Those who were already ill or dying, recuperated* (125).

PARIS, FRANCE (1830)

In a surprising visit in the night at the Rue du Bac convent, the Virgin Mary tells Catherine Laboure many important details for about two hours—including these predictions:

"The times are very evil. Great misfortune will come to France. Her throne will be overthrown. There will also be victims among the clergy. The archbishop himself will die. The cross will be insulted; blood will flow in the streets. But come to the foot of this altar. Here, great graces will be poured upon all those who ask for them with confidence and fervor. Graces will be bestowed upon the great and the small."

Mary finally broke down in tears after revealing all the misfortunes and outrages that France would suffer. Within one week, Mary's sad predictions began to come true as riots broke out on the streets. Paris became a "bloodbath for three days," and then the king was deposed and fled the country. The revolutionary forces slaughtered priests and religious. But as Mary had promised, no harm came to the sisters of the Rue du Bac convent (1:96–97).

LA SALETTE, FRANCE (1846)

The basilica of La Salette was built high in the Alps after the appearance of the Virgin Mary there in 1846.

Two shepherd children encountered a weeping Virgin Mary high in the Alps:

> "God is being dishonored with swearing. The price for such abuse would be costly. If the harvest is spoiled, it is your fault. A great famine is coming. Many young children will die from a serious disease."

> "In the year 1864, Lucifer, together with a large number of demons, will be unloosed from hell. They will put an end to faith, little by little, even in those dedicated to God. Several religious institutions will lose all faith and will lose many

souls. Evil books will be abundant on earth, and the spirit of darkness will spread everywhere a universal slackening in all that concerns the service of God."

"The true faith of the Lord having been forgotten, they will abolish civil rights as well as ecclesiastical. All order and all justice will be trampled underfoot, and only homicides, hate, jealousy, lies, and dissension would be seen without love for country and family. All the civil governments will have one and the same plan—which will be to abolish and do away with every religious principle, to make way for materialism, atheism, spiritualism, and vice of all kinds."

"The earth will be struck with calamities of all kinds. There will be a series of wars until the last war. Before this comes to pass, there will be a time of false peace in the world. People will think of nothing but amusement. The wicked will give themselves to all kinds of sins" (10:85–90).

FATIMA, PORTUGAL (1917)

The three shepherd children are given these messages from Our Lady for mankind:

"God wishes to establish in the world a devotion to My Immaculate Heart. If what I say to you is done, many souls will be saved, and there will be peace. The war (World War I) is going to end; but if the people do not cease offending God, a worse one (World War II) will break out during the pontificate of Pius XI (whom nobody had heard of at that time). When you see a night, illuminated by an unknown light, know that this is the great sign given to you by God that He is about to punish the world for its crimes, by means of war, famine, and persecutions of the Church and of the Holy Father" (29:121).

Lucia adds details from a vision given to the children:

"And we saw a bishop dressed in white. We had the impression that it was the Holy Father. Other bishops, priests, men and women religious, were going up a steep mountain, at the top of which there was a big cross of rough-hewn trunks, as of a cork tree with the bark. Before reaching there, the Holy Father passed through a big city half in ruins, and half trembling with halting step—afflicted with pain and sorrow, he prayed for the souls of the corpses he met on his way. Having reached the top of the mountain, on his knees at the foot of the big cross, he was killed by a group of soldiers who fired bullets and arrows at him. And, in the same manner, there died, one after another, the other bishops, priests, men and women religious, and various lay people of different ranks and positions. Beneath the two arms of the cross, there were two angels—each with a crystal aspersorium in his hand, in which they gathered up the blood of the martyrs and with it sprinkled the souls that were making their way to God" (29:122).

The Virgin Mary finally appeared to Lucia in May 1952, and stated again:

"Make it known to the Holy Father that I am always awaiting the Consecration of Russia to My Immaculate Heart. Without the Consecration, Russia will not be able to convert, nor will the world have peace" (32:83).

On **May 13**, 1981, Pope John Paul II almost died from several gunshots from a would-be assassin. This happened on the anniversary date and exact hour of the first Fatima apparition. He traveled to meet Sister Lucia one year later on **May 13**, 1982 and thanked her for his being saved by Our Lady of Fatima. The third secret had described a holy man clothed in white falling to the ground as though dead from gunshots. Doctors said that the bullet should have killed him but had traveled an odd, zigzag path that missed vital organs. That bullet fit neatly and permanently into the crown of Our Lady of Fatima's statue when the pope visited the Fatima shrine.

Pope John Paul II meets with Fatima's Lucia
after his near fatal attack because the Virgin had
predicted this occurrence years earlier.

The pope had a statue of Fatima placed, facing Russia from his Poland, and on March 25, 1984, he consecrated the *world* to Mary's Immaculate Heart in a joint effort with the world's bishops in Rome. Just seven weeks later on **May 13**, 1984, a mysterious explosion devastated a Soviet Naval base, destroying two-thirds of their missiles for the northern fleet. Within five years, the Berlin Wall came down without a fight. Two years later, the Soviet Union disintegrated without a single battle and lost its power by dissolving into separate countries.

GHIAIE DI BONATE, ITALY (1944)

Adelaide Roncalli, the seven-year-old visionary, reports, "Many people had urged me to ask Our Lady to heal their children and to ask when peace would come. I reported everything to the Lady—who answered me: (May 15, 1944)

> "Tell them that if they want their children to be healed, they must repent, pray a lot, and avoid certain sins. If people repent soon, the war will finish **in two months**; otherwise, it will go on for two more years" *(110)*.

From the stream of people who arrived afterwards, it was assumed that all the prayers and repentance that Our Lady had asked for had been accomplished, and everybody thought that the war would now finish within two months' time. Instead, **two months** after that, on Thursday, the 20th of July, there was the attempt on Hitler's life, which caused the beginning of Germany's decline and its successive defeat. The war lasted until the end of Easter 1945, with the gradual cessation of hostilities.

AMSTERDAM, HOLLAND (1945–1959)

Ida Peerdeman was thirty-nine years old when the first apparition of Mary came to her in Amsterdam on March 25, 1945, on the Feast of the Annunciation—which was also Palm Sunday that year. According to Dr. Richard Russell, a CIA expert with seventeen years of experience,

> "This Dutch woman had more of an awareness of what was going to happen in the world—much more than the CIA and Russian KGB combined. *Where could she have gotten it from?* We've studied foreign affairs and world politics for years and never would have predicted some of the things that she did—that came true" (88:77).

Here are a few of the visions and predictions given to Ida by the Virgin Mary (13):

March 25, 1945:

(First apparition) Blessed Mary gives Ida the date "**May 5**," shows her a rosary and says, *"It is thanks to this."* Ida is given a vision in which she sees many Allied soldiers in front of her. Mary takes the crucifix of the Rosary and points at the soldiers, saying, *"These will soon go home."* Just a little over a month later, on **May 5**, 1945, the Allied forces liberated Holland from Nazi occupation—exactly as Our Lady had foretold.

October 7, 1945:

In a vision from Mary, Ida describes seeing "China with a red flag." Four years later in 1949, Chinese communist forces led by Mao Tse-tung defeated the nationalist forces and established the People's Republic of China—*with a red flag* flying over its new capital in Beijing. Also, in her message of that same date, Blessed Mary tells of the end of the Cold War some forty-four years later. Ida describes "swastikas beneath the cross. I see time fall, then stars—they fall away; sickles and hammers—everything falls beneath the cross." The cold war ended with the fall of the Berlin Wall in 1989. The flag of the Soviet Union contains a sickle and a hammer.

August 30, 1947:

Our Lady gave Ida visions which showed the close coordination between the United States and the Vatican that would happen decades later. Ida was told that at that time in the future "the pope is kept informed of everything." Ida was shown a large room in the Vatican with the pope seated there. Secret meetings are being held there. There is an envoy from the United States and "all sorts of papers are in front of the pope." Sure enough, decades later, President Reagan secretly made a decision to share U.S. intelligence with Pope John Paul II to keep the pontiff privy to events unfolding behind the eroding Iron Curtain. President Reagan dispatched key intelligence officials to brief the pope in Rome.

December 26, 1947:

Ida had a vision of conflict embroiling the Middle East. "All at once, I see Cairo clearly, and I get a strange feeling about it. Then I see various Eastern peoples: Persians (Iranians), Arabs, and so on. Mary tells her, *"The world is going to be torn in two… Great sorrow and misery will come."* Then Ida sees a great crack appearing, a break winding right over the world. Heavy clouds are hanging over it, and she feels great sorrow and misery.

The recent Egyptian revolution that started in 2011 might be the unfolding of Our Lady's prophecy about Cairo. This uprising is a watershed event similar to the Iranian revolution of 1979. Perhaps Our Lady was also referring to the Islamic world being ripped in half between the Arab Sunni and the Iran Shia groups.

On this same date, Our Lady warned of more conflict to come in the Middle East. Ida has another vision: "I see a round dome. I am given to understand that it is a dome in Jerusalem." The Dome of the Rock is a domineering and captivating feature of Jerusalem's skyline. Mary says, *"In and around Jerusalem heavy battles will be waged."* This could refer to a number of conflicts over the years.

Another message on this same date involved a foretelling of chemical and biological warfare. Ida describes her vision from Mary in great detail:

> "Then I see a very peculiar scene. I have to look at the sky, and something seems to be launched into it. There is something flying past me so rapidly that I can hardly see it. It is shaped like a cigar or torpedo, and its color is like that of aluminum. All of a sudden, I see something shooting off from the back. I feel about with my hand, and different terrible sensations come over me. At first, a total numbness. I live and yet I do not live. Then I see horrible images of people before me. I see faces, wide faces, covered with dreadful ulcers, something like leprosy. Then I feel terrible deadly diseases: cholera, leprosy—everything those people have to suffer.
>
> Then that is gone again, and I see tiny black things floating about me. I try to feel what it is, but that is not possible. It seems to be very fine matter. With my eyes I cannot discern what it is. It is as if I would have to look through something, and below I now see brilliant white fields. Upon those fields I see those little black things, but enlarged, and it is as if they are alive. I don't know how to describe this properly. I ask Mary, "Are these bacilli?" She answers,
>
> *"It is hellish…and that is what they are inventing…that Russia, but others as well. People be warned!"*

> "Then I feel my face and my whole body swelling. It feels like my face gets very bloated, and everything is stiff and swollen. I cannot move."

Despite more than one hundred countries signing an international ban on chemical and biological weapons at the 1972 Biological and Toxin Weapons Convention, two Russian scientists revealed that Russia had employed as many as thirty thousand people to secretly work on such weapons by the late 1980s.

October 1, 1949:

Ida sees a conflict in the Balkans, forty-two years before it happens. "There is a war there; there is much fighting." Mary tells her, ***"Child there will be a severe fight. Economic disasters will come."*** As predicted, the former Yugoslavia in the Balkans was ripped apart between 1991 and 1995 which led to the creation of three separate nation-states: Croatia, Serbia, and Bosnia.

Our Lady made emphatic warnings about Russia's future experimentation and development of chemical and biological weapons. She showed Ida a vision:

> "The Lady takes me along to glass buildings, underground, too—all kinds of people are working there. These seem to be Germans, Frenchmen, Poles, but others, too. I hear them speaking different languages. It seems to be deep in Russia, somewhere in the great uninhabited plains of northern Russia. Mary says,"
>
> ***"They are making chemicals there. America, be warned! Intervene, do intervene! Not only human lives are at issue here, but higher powers."***

December 16, 1949:

During a visit from Our Lady, Ida is given a vision of "a sign on which is written 50-51-53." Mary tells her that during this period, there will be a fight and disasters. These were the years (1950–1953) of the Korean War which started one year after her vision from Mary. Later, Our Blessed Mary tells Ida more details:

"The fighting in Korea is a sham and the start of a great misery. By this I mean that there will be periods of apparent tranquility. But this will not last long. The Eastern peoples have been roused by a type of humanity which does not believe in My Son."

Ida then, in 1950, saw "demarcations being made at intervals" with "barbed wire and walls"—three years *before* the demilitarized zone (DMZ) was formed. The so-called truce between North and South Korea has been a false one or "sham" as violent skirmishes continue to this day with recent attacks and fifty deaths in 2010.

August 15, 1950 (Feast of the Assumption):

Ida envisions Taiwan and another island nearby, feeling that something big would happen there. Taiwan is where the Chinese nationalists fled when the communist Chinese revolution occurred in 1949. China would love to claim these islands. In this message, Mary exclaims, **"America, take warning here!"** Four years later, President Dwight Eisenhower used veiled threats of nuclear weapons to hold off communist China's attempts to invade in 1954, 1955, and 1958.

December 10, 1950:

Ida is given a vision from Mary in which she sees "a glaring light, a blinding light in Russia. It is as if it explodes from the ground upward. It is a horrible sight."

Mary tells her that she *"will no longer see anything"* because she would *"be blinded by that light."* Ida then felt something very disgusting come over her…

"I saw a scorched plain. It is a ghastly sight, just as if death had gone over it."

Three years later in 1953, Russia detonated its most powerful hydrogen bomb.

Also on December 10, Our Lady again foretells the end of the cold war. Mary describes a ***"thick line in Germany…Europe is divided in two. I will remove that line with one sweep of the hand."*** Thirty-nine years later, the Berlin Wall that divided Germany for decades came down quickly without any resistance.

May 31, 1955: Our Lady instructs Ida to repeat these words:

> "A time of great inventions is to come. There will be alarming inventions, such that even your shepherds will be astonished and say, 'We are at a loss.' I just said: alarming inventions will be made. God allows this; but you peoples, you can see to it that it does not result in disaster. You peoples, I beg you…the Lady begs you; hear this well. Never has the Mother of God begged you…So that you do not arrive at alarming things, nations, the Lady begs you now, today; ask the Father, the Son, and the Holy Spirit to protect His people, to bring His people to unity once again. People have to attain unity, to be one, and over them, the Lady of All Nations. One community, peoples; here I am stressing these words: one community."

She may have been referring to such alarming inventions as what scientists achieved in May 2010. For the first time, scientists made a chain of DNA of some one thousand genes from off-the-shelf laboratory chemicals and created the first creature which had no ancestor that could reproduce on its own, marking the age of artificial life.

Ida was very conscientious about these messages, making sure to always transmit everything as faithfully as possible. But she, herself, just wanted to disappear, to remain unknown—to not play a role in the forefront. Finally, on May 31, 1996, Ida was delighted in that both Bishop Bomers and Bishop Punt of Haarlem authorized public devotion and ***approval of the messages.***

GARABANDAL, SPAIN (1965)

Blessed Mary told the four girls that they would contradict each other and doubt that they had even seen the apparitions—even deny seeing Mary—in the future! The girls were stunned that she could suggest that they would ever do that! But years later, under great pressure, stress, and death threats, all four girls did deny these events with three of them moving to the United States to feel safe (and eventually marry husbands there). Of course, the three that moved away felt safe enough later to reaffirm their beliefs (34:28–29).

KIBEHO, RWANDA (1981–1989)

With Mary promising to appear on August 15, 1982 for the Feast of the Assumption, there was much festivity, anticipation, and excitement. More than twenty thousand people turned out—some hoping for cures for their sick relatives. But when Blessed Mary appeared, the visionaries' efforts to sing to her were cut short unexpectedly by Mary's tears of pain and grief. Mary indicated that her efforts were not appreciated, and then one horrifying vision after another came to Alphonsine, causing her to scream in terror. There were images of destruction, trees exploding into flames, torture, human carnage, severed human heads gushing blood, and a vast valley piled high with the remains of a million rotting, headless corpses with not a single soul left alive to bury the dead. Every visionary received the same horrific images from the weeping Virgin that day. For hours, their horrified cries echoed through the hills, all of them describing "rivers of blood, savage murders, and the rotting remains of hundreds of thousands of people."

The visions lasted anywhere from several months to a year for the seven youth, ending in 1989. Our Lady said that if her warning came to pass, not to cry for those who would die because the gates of heaven would be open for them as they will have died innocently.

> "Cry for those who will remain alive because many will be tempted to violence and revenge. Others will not be able to bear to live with the wrong they have done to others. There will

be some who will be left; they will be left to tell of the goodness of God, because there is nothing else that could console then after the pain they would have experienced" (36:47).

Then, as horribly predicted by the Virgin Mary, a terrible genocide came to Rwanda in the spring of 1994 with more than a million innocent souls murdered and chopped to pieces by the rival tribal party in an effort to exterminate all those who belonged to the Tutsi tribe. Thousands upon thousands of decapitated bodies were dumped into rivers that then ran thick with human blood. Three visionaries, Marie-Claire, Stephanie, and the boy, Segatashya, all died in the holocaust. The amazing and detailed accuracy of the Virgin Mary's predictions convinced everybody of her authentic messages. Finally, in 2001, after twenty long years of investigation and seven years after the genocide, Bishop Augustin Misago declared with overwhelming evidence the apparitions to be authentic (39:145–151).

The aftermath of the Rwandan genocide, predicted by Blessed Mary ten years earlier.

HRUSHIV, UKRAINE (1914)

The first incident actually occurred two weeks ***before*** World War I, on May 12, 1914, in the village of Hrushiv. Twenty-two people, who were mowing fields near the local church of the Holy Trinity, all witnessed an apparition of the Virgin Mary. She said to them:

> "There will be a war. Russia will become a godless country. The Ukraine, as a nation, will suffer terribly for **eighty years**—and will have to live **through the world wars**, but it will be free afterwards."

Then, on April 27, 1987, seventy-three years later after 1914 and exactly one year after the Chernobyl nuclear reactor disaster, a bright light covered this church of the Holy Trinity and the surrounding area. A television program even recorded part of this light phenomenon. From within this "impressive silver dazzle" over the church, the Virgin Mary appeared and floated above the cupola of the church.

She first appeared privately to Marina Kizyn, age twelve, who immediately called her mother and a few neighbors—who then came, and all saw her there too. Soon, hundreds and then thousands came from all over Russia to see the apparitions which continued every day until August 15, 1987. It is estimated that a total of five hundred thousand people had seen her by the time these apparitions ended. On most days, the crowd might reach as many as forty-five thousand to seventy thousand people at one time.

> "I have come on purpose to thank the Ukrainian people because you have suffered most for the church of Christ in the last seventy years. I have come to comfort you and to tell you that your suffering will soon come to an end. Ukraine will become an independent state."

Our Lady predicted that the Ukraine would "suffer terribly for eighty years" before gaining independence; she was extremely close in her prediction! The Ukraine had its declaration of independence ratified in Kiev on August 24, 1991—some seventy-seven years after Blessed Mary's prediction in 1914 (1:142) (118).

Has heaven ever *deliberately* intervened in our world events, essentially guiding the course of history?

Historic "footprints" ahead…

CHAPTER 10

ALTERING HISTORY

"The power of the Rosary is beyond description."

—Archbishop Fulton Sheen

Has heaven ever directly intervened in human events to alter the course of history? And if so, why doesn't heaven intervene more often? The answer may have more to do with prayer—especially the Rosary. Heavenly interventions appear to be more frequently the direct result of intense and timely prayers. Here are some historical examples that suggest a connection.

PONTMAIN, FRANCE (1871)

On January 17, 1871, Eugene Barbadette (twelve) and brother Joseph (ten) heard the priest pray through Blessed Mary at Mass for mercy to come to the area. Paris was already besieged by Prussian forces, and war-torn France was in complete disarray. The little town of Laval nearby would be the next to fall to the invading Prussians.

That wintry night, looking outside the family's barn at 6:00 p.m., Eugene noticed in the cold starry night that a section of the sky was without stars. Suddenly, in that very area, a young woman of eighteen years old appeared to be hovering in the sky and smiling down at him. She was strikingly beautiful and wearing a dark blue dress covered with stars and a black veil with a golden crown on top. He gasped a yell of surprise, and brother Joseph came to him and stared up at the apparition as well. Their parents then came to see what was going on but could not see what the boys continued to marvel at. The mother boxed their ears, scolded them, and then forced them to come in and eat dinner.

But when a local nun heard the startled mother's story, she reminded her that Blessed Mary often comes to young children. Going on the theory that *maybe only children could see the Virgin Mary*, she brought two young girls Francoise Richer and Jeanne-Marie Lebosse (ages nine and eleven) from the convent school to the family's farm. The nun made certain to not tell the young girls anything. Although not having heard what the two brothers had seen, the two young girls immediately became excited and began describing the *exact same image* of the Virgin Mary down to the last precise detail.

Clusters of people began to gather within twenty minutes after this vision had begun—yet, none of the adults could see anything. Three more small children began pointing at the sky and describing the same apparition of Mary. Even a two year old in her mother's arms started clapping with joy, looking up into the sky, and holding out her arms as if wanting Our Blessed Mother to come pick her up. A total of about sixty villagers gathered before the barn and knelt in the snow to begin praying. Sister Mary Edward began leading the **Rosary**. The children reported that Our Lady smiled throughout the **Rosary**, appearing very much alive and showing the dazzling whiteness of her teeth. The dreadful news arrived that the Prussians were now at nearby Laval and heading soon toward Pontmain. Words appeared in the sky beneath Our Lady

> "God will hear you in a little while. My Son permits Himself to be moved."

So she was telling them that God had heard their prayers and their fears about the invasion of soldiers, and that he would answer their needs shortly. He would answer because he is a God who allows himself to be touched by pleading and prayers. The visions in the sky ended about 9:00 p.m.; the experience had lasted a total of three hours!

By the next morning, the town learned that the Prussian soldiers had witnessed a vision of the Virgin Mary on the outskirts of their town. The startled and frightened soldiers had told their Prussian superiors,

> "Madonna is guarding the country and *forbidding us to advance*! We can go no further—Madonna is barring the way."

Within eleven days, the Prussian soldiers had mysteriously retreated and abandoned the country they had planned to invade and occupy. A truce was signed, and the war ended (11:117–124).

DONG LU, CHINA (1900)

Dong Lu (or Tong Lu) was a very poor village, formerly called the place of beggars. It was probably the poorest place in the whole region near Peiping, China. The Vincentian Fathers started a Poor Mission in Dong Lu. By 1900, there were about seven hundred to one thousand Christians gathered about the little hamlet.

Suddenly, the Boxer Rebellion swept through China and grew to such proportions that even small places like Dong Lu could not escape its fury. In April 1900, a force of ten thousand hostile rebels were about to attack Dong Lu. The Chinese priest of the village, Father Wu, fervently prayed to Mary, asking for her help and protection. Suddenly, a "woman in a white robe surrounded by light" appeared in the sky. It was the beautiful glowing image of the Virgin Mary. The soldiers, in a senseless rage, started to fire their bullets into the sky at her. But the apparition was not harmed and would not fade.

When the apparition did not fade, the attackers did not have any time to reorganize because a "fiery horseman," probably St. Michael, came charging toward them, surrounded by "blazing flames of fire." The strange horseman put fear into the ten thousand rebels, and they scattered and fled like rats—never to return. After they disappeared over the horizon, Father Wu then confessed to his flock that he had invoked the help of Mary (106) (1:84).

JOHN S. CARPENTER

MANILA, PHILIPPINES (1986)

As urged by the cardinal in Manila, the Catholic faithful jam the streets to slow the advance of President Marcos' tanks and their murderous mission.

The events in the Philippines began in February 1986, as the virtual twenty-year dictatorship of Ferdinand Marcos came to an abrupt and unexpected end through a series of strange events. President Marcos had actually called for an election to put an end to the efforts by the opposition, but it backfired! Corazon Aquino, the widow and reluctant political replacement of slain opposition leader, Ninoy Aquino, had won the presidential election in a stunning upset by an overwhelming margin. However, through illegal actions and total control of the media, Marcos, instead, flagrantly lied and declared himself as the winner.

The rigged election results were blatant and obvious to everyone, sending millions into the streets to protest and triggering an unexpected coup attempt by a dissatisfied faction of the military. The saga of EDSA (Epifanio de los Santos Avenue) culminated in a four-day, tension-filled event when the rebel group in the Armed Forces of the Philippines was discovered by the Marcos troops and was ordered to be arrested. The archbishop of Manila, Cardinal Jaime Sin, enjoined the people to go out in the streets to protect the rebel leaders. The Catholic faithful heeded the call and massed along EDSA.

BE NOT AFRAID TO FOLLOW THE FOOTPRINTS FROM HEAVEN

The non-violent Catholic crowd in Manila
carries statues of Blessed Mary and rosaries while
singing and praying to God for help.

The people milled around the rebel leaders, bringing nothing with them but **rosary** beads, flowers, food, and images of the Blessed Virgin. Hundreds and thousands of religious priests and sisters, parish priests, and their parishioners including onlookers and curiosity seekers stayed on the streets, immobilizing the tanks sent out to crush the rebel leaders and, according to reports, even the people. The masses of people in the streets continued to **pray the Rosary** endlessly. Some offered garlands of flowers to the soldiers who stood guard. Some brave nuns climbed up on the tanks that were approaching. Those who stayed in their homes sent supplies of food and drinks to the streets.

As the soldiers tried to advance, they saw up in the sky what appeared to be a crosslike image, but this did not hinder them from pursuing their goal, and they continued to press on toward the crowd. The **Rosary** was recited continuously; the melody of *Ave Maria* sounded after every ten Hail Marys.

All of a sudden, the soldiers were awestruck, stopping dead in their tracks. A "beautiful woman encased in immense bright light and dressed as a nun" became clearly visible, standing in front of the tanks. The light was dazzling as the crowds saw her appear. According to these soldiers, a beautiful woman dressed in blue with heavenly eyes appeared in front of them, extended her arms outward and spoke in a voice that was clearly audible to everyone:

> "Dear soldiers, stop! Do not proceed. Do not harm my children. I am the queen of this land."

Stunned by the Virgin Mary's sudden appearance and demand for peace, the soldiers abandon their mission to the delight of the crowd in the Philippines.

The soldiers then dropped their weapons, withdrew from pressing forward and joined the throngs of people to turn and fight *with them* against the Marcos regime. The soldiers claimed that the woman who appeared to them was the Virgin Mary. A television station was covering the event which prompted thousands of residents of the Philippines to run out of their homes in celebration: "*Mother Mary is with us!*"

President Marcos and his family left for exile in Hawaii that night (164) (2:191–192).

Cardinal Jaime Sin vouches for the veracity of the apparition. The cardinal stated that he did not know the soldiers—but that they came to him in tears, awestruck by the "beautiful heavenly lady," telling him that it had been, without a doubt, the Virgin Mary. The cardinal added:

> "Yes, my heart was telling me that this was indeed Mary. And since they obeyed this woman who appeared to them—and did not follow orders to fire upon the people, then President Marcos had nobody to give him any power or support. This is when he fled from the Philippines. That was the end of him."

A statue of Mary is created and placed on the site of her Manila appearance to honor her help in bringing down the dictatorship of Marcos with her 1986 intervention.

The cardinal also revealed that he met with Sister Lucia, the only living visionary from Fatima, just before he was to travel to the United States to first tell of the Virgin's visit at a surprised international press conference in New York City. Although Sister Lucia had no access to newspapers, radio, television, or magazines, he was amazed that ***she knew and recounted every detail to him of what had happened*** (47:171–172).

GENOA, ITALY (1490)

On August 29, 1490, Benedict Pareto was grazing his flock on Mount Figogna when his attention was drawn to a brilliant movement of light. Within this heavenly glow was the image of a woman holding a child on her arm. Although he did not know who she was, he felt compelled to kneel as she approached him. Standing before him, the "beautiful lady" assured him with these words:

> "Do not be afraid. I am the Queen of Heaven and have come to you with My Divine Son for this reason: You are to arrange for a church to be built on this spot, to be dedicated in My name. Trust me, Benedict. The money will not be lacking. Only your good will is needed. With My aid, all will be easy."

Then Benedict watched as the apparition slowly faded. After he recovered from the sweetness and beauty of the apparition, he felt a great urgency to tell others. He ran back down the hill toward his home and met his wife on the way. But she mocked him, disbelieving, and said that he must be suffering from sunstroke. He continued running, excitedly, down the mountain path to tell the parish priest. The priest and Benedict's neighbors were all skeptical upon hearing his story.

The following day, Benedict climbed a fig tree to pick fruit, but the branch to which he was clinging snapped off, and he fell. Friends carried him home where it was learned that he had broken a number of bones and suffered severe internal injuries. Due to his serious condition, he was given the last sacraments or last rites by the priest. Now he feared that he would be unable to spread Our Lady's request to the proper individuals. Grieving these circumstances, he promised that if the Blessed Virgin would help save his life, he would make certain that the church would be built.

Blessed Mary appeared to him again and repeated her request for a church to be built at the place of her first appearance on the mountain. She scolded him for his lack of faith and indicated that his fall from the tree was punishment for allowing his wife to persuade him that his vision had only been an illusion. Our Lady stretched out her hand toward him and then vanished. When she left, he was instantly cured!

When his neighbors, who knew the severity of his injuries, observed his immediate cure, they replaced their doubts and skepticism with wholehearted belief. With approval from the priest, they began collecting money for the building of a small chapel on Mount Figogna. The church became popular so quickly that it had to be extended—and by 1530, it needed to be completely replaced by a bigger church.

Of all the miracles attributed to "Our Lady of the Guard," the most famous is that which took place in 1625. Charles Emmanuel, Duke of Savoy, marched on Genoa with an army of fourteen thousand men. Knowing that they were outnumbered, a saintly Capuchin lay brother, Fra Tomaso da Trebbiano, urged the people to **pray the Rosary** to "Our Lady of the Guard" for protection. The next day, when Charles's huge army marched confidently toward the city, it was repulsed by a few hundred, poorly armed, local peasants who had been sent into battle with mostly religious fervor and the blessing of their priest. It was seen as a miracle! (3:15–17)

CHAMPION, WISCONSIN (1859–1871)

In 1859, in the settlements near Green Bay, Wisconsin, Adele Brice, age twenty-eight, was stunned to encounter the glowing, beautiful presence of the Virgin Mary along a peaceful trail in the woods. Amazed and confused, she asked her local priest if it could be a lost spirit. He told her to ask the lady who she was and what she wanted. On third encounter, with two friends present, Adele asked the beautiful lady those questions.

- A: "In God's name, who are you, and what do you desire of me?"
- VM: "I am the Queen of Heaven, who prays for the conversion of sinners, and I wish you to do the same." (She spoke in a soft, sweet voice.)
- VM: "You have done well, but I wish you to do more. Pray for nine days. Go and make a general confession and offer

your Holy Communion for the conversion of sinners. If they do not convert themselves and do penance, **My Son will be obliged to punish them.**"

A: (crying) "What more can I do, dear Lady?"
VM: "Teach the children."
A: "How can I teach them when I know so little, myself?"
VM: "I do not mean the science of the world. Teach them their catechism, how to sign themselves with the sign of the cross, and how to approach the sacraments, that they may know and love My Son; otherwise, the people here will lose their faith."
A: "With God's grace, and the help of your intercession, I promise, dear Lady, to be faithful to what you bid me."
VM: "Go and fear nothing. I will help you."

Adele took her mission seriously and began teaching the children in the area, eventually having a school built, a convent established, and five acres of land donated toward her goals. She always seemed to receive heavenly help whenever she had difficult times.

On Sunday, October 8, 1871, a most deadly fire was created by a gale force wind that turned the prairies and forests of Wisconsin into a raging inferno. Fire tornadoes ripped through the area causing death and destruction everywhere. Flames jumped rivers, embers rained down, and small fires were whipped up into a giant fireball that destroyed homes, buildings, farms, factories, and entire towns. It was described as "a wall of flame a mile high, five miles wide, traveling 90–100 m.p.h., hotter than a crematorium, turning sand into glass." The heat was so strong that it killed people before the fire ever got to them. Approximately 2,500 people died, twelve towns destroyed, and 1.2 million acres devastated—the deadliest fire in American history. This was the same fire that swept into Chicago, causing that famous disaster. The ground was burned to a depth of two feet deep in some places. Hiding in brick homes or underground basements did not help. Only those hiding in rivers had the best chance of survival.

The five acres dedicated to Blessed Mary were directly in the path of this deadly firestorm. Sister Adele decided it was impossible to flee the fire, so the sisters, schoolchildren, and frantic neighbors gathered in the chapel on the five-acre grounds and prayed to Mary for help. Then Adele led a prayerful procession around the perimeter of the chapel grounds, carrying a statue of Mary. The procession continued all night, **praying the Rosary**, all around the grounds.

The fires stopped right at the fence line surrounding the five acres. The outside of the fence posts were charred; the inside surfaces were untouched. The wind cooled; a heavy downpour drenched the remaining flames. Everything surrounding their five acres—including the lush green forest, farm buildings, and homes—was blackened, obliterated, and gone. Only the people and animals that had come to these grounds survived. *The five-acre grounds that had been dedicated to Mary were green and untouched like a green emerald island in a sea of black ash*—"a glorious sight." Exhausted from their night-long processions of **praying the Rosary**, the people praised God and retired to sleep. Twelve years earlier, ***on this exact date***, Mother Mary had warned of this potential punishment.

Just recently in 2010, the Bishop of Green Bay declared that the apparitions involving Adele Brice were authentic and worthy of belief, thus becoming the first church-approved Marian apparitions in the United States (20:11–12, 19–21, 26–27, 48).

HIROSHIMA, JAPAN (1945)

The Jesuit missionaries (lower right corner) walk the deadly radioactive streets unharmed after the 1945 atomic blast in Hiroshima, Japan. Their two-story frame house is also untouched in the devastation (upper right corner).

On August 6, 1945, an American B-29 bomber dropped the first atomic bomb on Hiroshima, Japan, at 8:15 a.m. Half a million people were instantly annihilated. The bomb exploded *just eight city blocks* from the Jesuit Church of Our Lady's Assumption in Hiroshima. This church was reduced to skeletal remains, but the associated home nearby where eight German missionaries **prayed the Rosary faithfully every day**, miraculously survived.

Missionary Father Schiffer had just finished Mass and had sat down at the breakfast table, sliced a grapefruit, and had just put his spoon into the grapefruit when there was a flash of light.

> "Suddenly, a terrific explosion filled the air with one bursting thunder stroke. An invisible force lifted me from the chair, hurled me through the air, shook me, battered me, whirled me round and round like a leaf in a gust of autumn wind."

The next thing he remembered was that he opened his eyes and was lying on the ground. He looked around, and there was NOTHING in any direction. The railroad station and buildings in all directions were leveled to the ground. The only physical harm to himself was that he could feel a few pieces of glass in the back of his neck. As far as he could tell, there was nothing else physically wrong with himself. Many thousands were killed or maimed by the explosion. Doctors and scientists explained to him that his body would begin to deteriorate because of the radiation. To the doctors' amazement, Father Schiffer's body contained no radiation or ill effects from the bomb—**EVER**. Father Schiffer attributes his devotion to the Blessed Mother and his **daily praying of the Rosary** as a heavenly shield provided by the Blessed Mother, protecting him also from all radiation and ill-effects.

Not only did *all* eight missionaries survive with relatively minor injuries, but they *all* lived well past that awful day with no radiation sickness, no loss of hearing, nor any other visible, long-term defects, or maladies. Naturally, they were interviewed numerous times by scientists and health care professionals about their remarkable experience. The Jesuits say:

> "We believe that we survived because we were living the Message of Fatima. **We lived and prayed the Rosary daily in that home.**"

Of course, the secular scientists are speechless at this explanation. They are certain that there must be some "real" explanation. But at the same time, over seventy years later, the scientists are still *absolutely baffled* when it comes to finding a plausible scenario to explain the missionaries' unique escape from the hellish power of that deadly bomb. According to the experts, they "ought to be dead," being within a one-mile radius of the explosion.

Dr. Stephen Rinehart, a professional with impressive scientific credentials from the U.S. Department of Defense, states:

> "At one kilometer the bulk temperature was in excess of 30,000 degrees—perhaps as high as 1,000,000 degrees F within this one kilometer. The blast wave would have hit at a sonic velocity with pressures on buildings greater than 600 psi. Buildings were demolished over a mile from the epicenter. The fireball diameter is probably on the order of two to four kilometers. There is no way that any human could have survived. There were a few badly burned survivors out at ten to fifteen kilometers, but all of them died within fifteen years from some form of cancer. All cotton clothes would be on fire at 350 F, and your lungs would be inoperative within seconds of breathing the air at these temperatures."

There are no physical laws to explain why the Jesuits were untouched in the Hiroshima air blast. All who were at this range from the epicenter should have received enough radiation to be dead within a matter of minutes—even if they had no other injuries. **A panoramic photograph from the epicenter after the blast does show a two-story house totally intact with the windows still in place—as well as the Jesuits walking down the street toward the church!**

It must be concluded that some other external force was present whose power to transform energy and matter as it relates to humans is beyond current comprehension. An enormous external force field was present which precisely cancelled the weapon's effects over the totally irregular geometry of the residential house—including the total protection of the occupants. Either way, it is a plausible argument for the existence of God who demonstrated His own divine powers at Hiroshima (116).

THE RUSSIAN NUCLEAR THREAT (1961)

In early October 1960, Nikita Khrushchev, the president of Russia, made a terrifying speech at the United Nations, pounding his shoe on the desk and threatening to bury the United States with his nuclear power. Immediately, Pope John XXIII and the bishop of Fatima responded, issuing letters to all the bishops of the world and requesting a massive prayer vigil for PEACE for the night of October 12 and into the day of the 13th, the anniversary of the Miracle of the Sun at Fatima. **One million pilgrims prayed the Rosary** in the chilling rain at Fatima along with three hundred other dioceses around the world.

On that very night, Khrushchev suddenly flew back to Russia. A final testing of a nuclear missile was about to launch. Mysteriously, the rocket did not launch. After waiting cautiously for fifteen minutes, the three hundred scientists, engineers, researchers, and the finest minds in the program stepped outside to investigate. Without warning the nuclear missile suddenly exploded, killing all three hundred Russian specialists and setting back Russia's nuclear program for an estimated twenty years! (25)

Then, on **May 13**, 1984, about seven weeks after Pope John Paul II consecrated the world to Mary's Immaculate Heart, the largest crowd that had ever assembled in Fatima **prayed the Rosary for World Peace**. Later that same day of **May 13** in Russia, a mysterious and massive explosion occurred at a Soviet Naval Base. It destroyed two-thirds of the missiles that had been stockpiled for Russia's northern fleet. It was considered the worst naval disaster in recent Russian history (25). Once again, the power of many prayers seems to be halting evil plans. Five years later, the Berlin Wall came down peacefully. Two years after that, the Soviet Union dissolved and split into multiple countries—without a single battle ever fought.

Are these just coincidences?

Or is the power of many prayers having a direct impact on the outcome of history?

Heaven seems to be very aware of our issues and needs. Heaven appears to be responding well to many fervent and sincere prayers. But if we don't pray and don't ask for help, how can we really expect to be heard and assisted?

In her appearances, the Blessed Virgin commented on the power of praying the Rosary as revealed in these following excerpts from various, historically documented visits of the Blessed Mother.

SOUTHERN SPAIN (1206)

When St. Dominic was agonizing over how to convert the sinful pagans, Blessed Mary appeared to him in a forest near Toulouse and said:

> "Dear Dominic, do you know which weapon the Blessed Trinity wants to use to reform the world?...I want you to know that, in this kind of warfare, **the principal weapon has always been the Angelic Psalter**, which is the foundation-stone of the New Testament. Therefore, if you want to reach these hardened souls and win them over to God, preach my Psalter" (163).

The Angelic Psalter was the foundation for the formation of the Rosary.

FATIMA, PORTUGAL (1917)

The Blessed Mother Mary appeared to three young children in Fatima, Portugal in 1917, asking them to *pray the Rosary every day* in order to obtain world peace and the end of the war. She called herself "Our Lady of the Rosary" and suggested that they make a change to the Rosary:

"When you pray the Rosary, say, after each mystery: O my Jesus, forgive us, save us from the fires of hell. Lead all souls to heaven, especially those who are most in need" (1:113).

Our Lady of the Rosary also told the children that if Russia did not become consecrated to her Immaculate Heart, then Russia would cause many problems for the world in the future.

KIBEHO, RWANDA (1981–1989)

"The **Rosary is the most powerful** tool of prayer and conversion **to fight evil** and receive God's love."

EL ESCORIAL, SPAIN (1986)

"The Holy Rosary is my favorite prayer. **We could save the all of mankind with it**. We could end a war with it if we wanted. You must meditate every mystery a little while praying it. It is important that you say the fifteen mysteries. I promise to assist anybody who prays the Rosary when that person dies" (107).

MEDJUGORJE, BOSNIA (1986)

"Do not be afraid. If you pray, Satan cannot injure you, not even a little, because you are God's children, and He is watching over you. Pray, and **let the Rosary always be in your hands**" (48:78).

"Dear children! I am calling you to begin to pray the rosary with a living faith. Only in that way will I be able to help you. You wish to receive many graces but you do not pray. **I cannot help you if you do not undertake the task of prayer seriously.** Dear children, **I am calling you to pray the Rosary.** This prayer is a must, and you should pray it with joy" (52:174).

SAN NICOLAS, ARGENTINA (1986)

"What value prayer has for the Lord, you cannot imagine! My children, that is why I ask for so much prayer! **Say the Holy Rosary** meditating! I assure you that your prayers will rise like a true song of love to the Lord" (149:3).

HRUSHIV, UKRAINE (1987)

"Russia rejects real life and continues to live in darkness. If there is not a return to Christianity in Russia, there will be a Third World War; the whole world will face ruin. Teach the children to pray. Teach them to live in truth and live yourselves in truth. **Say the Rosary. It is the weapon against Satan**. He fears the Rosary. Recite the Rosary at any gathering of people" (117) (1:143).

CUENCA, ECUADOR (1988)

"Rejoice in experiencing the love of God in your hearts. **The Rosary is the most complete prayer.** Do not ask yourself why you pray it. **Let it be your shield against the evil one** who is at work. Do not detach yourselves of it. The Spirit of God descends upon you. Feel the warmth which enters your heart" (23:21).

NAJU, KOREA (1990)

"Pray fervently, especially **the Rosary, to defeat the devil**."

AGOO, PHILIPPINES (1992)

"**Pray the Holy Rosary**—Satan will be defeated because he hates hearing the name of My Son and my name. Teach your children how to pray the Holy Rosary…My children, listen. Satan works to take away peace and unity, to stir up trouble all over the universe. **We have to launch a counterattack—which can only be through the Holy Rosary**. So pray the whole mysteries of the rosary daily, because this is the most evangelical prayer" (July 4, 1992) (98:4).

According to these remarks by Mary from a number of historical accounts around the world, heaven *is telling us* which prayer is most effective against evil in the world.

Prayers have also been effective in seeking help from heaven in other miraculous ways.

The "footprints" from heaven are becoming numerous and leading us in many directions!

CHAPTER 11

UNDENIABLE MIRACLES

There are many accounts of miraculous healings that defy medical or scientific explanation. Doctors often refuse to discuss them because they cannot even begin to explain how such remarkable changes could happen. Others believe that the power of suggestion and strong beliefs can produce such "mind over matter" transformations. But what if the person was not even praying? What if they did not have any strong belief? What if they were unconscious and unable to pray? What if they were totally unaware of anyone else praying for them?

One such event was actually reported on the national CNN news and NBC's *Today Show*. This report was taken more seriously because a photo of "an angel" or supernatural light that was witnessed accompanied the miraculous healing. The story was presented as this:

Angelic supernatural light caught on film
at time of a hospital miracle.

"In September of 2008, 14-year-old Chelsea Banton lay dying of pneumonia in a hospital room in Charlotte, North Carolina. She had been born prematurely with developmental disabilities and had battled serious health problems all of her life. Doctors had exhausted all treatment; the family had told her their goodbyes. All they could do now was pray for her as her life support was removed. Mother Colleen waited for her dying daughter to take her last breath. It was at that moment that a bright light appeared in the room—but only seen by people on the television screen of the room monitor. Quickly, a picture was taken of the supernatural light on the TV screen—and immediately the young girl began making a full and miraculous recovery. The doctors and nurses could not begin to explain her amazing improvement. The medical staff on duty at that time agreed that the three vertical shafts of light that suddenly appeared were not a reflection or glare from within the room. Everybody felt that an angel had appeared and saved her life" (61).

It must be stated here for the record that the Virgin Mary is ***not*** the one who does the healing. People may pray to her for help from her son Jesus, but the Virgin Mary cannot perform the healing. The Blessed Virgin has stated that Jesus is with her during every appearance that she has made throughout history. Our Heavenly Mother has even announced the time when some miracles will happen (because God has affirmed it)—and they *have always* come to pass.

Sometimes, the healings become necessary in order for Our Lady's mission to succeed. Here are a few excerpts from historical accounts.

VAILANKANNI, INDIA (1580)

A lame boy had been helping his mother in Vailankanni by selling her daily pot of buttermilk to travelers along the main road. Buttermilk was a real treat, and he had no problem selling all of it by the end of each day. One day, as he sat along the side of the road, a strange and brilliant light surrounded him. A beautiful lady appeared in the light, holding an infant in her arms. She asked if she could have some buttermilk for her child. Without hesitation, he poured her a cup, and she gave it to her child. Then she asked the lame boy if he would deliver a message for her to a certain Catholic gentleman in nearby Nagapattinam. The boy replied that he wanted to do her the favor but could not because of being so lame. She smiled and told him to stand up. **Immediately, he was surprised that he could walk, jump, and run—for the first time in his life!** She again commanded the boy to contact the Catholic gentleman in the nearby town of Nagapattinam to build a church in her honor. He was so excited that he ran down the road, thrilling the villagers who knew he had been unable to walk. The gentleman had no trouble believing the young boy because he had had a dream in which Blessed Mary had also told him to do the same thing. He asked the boy to take him to the spot of this apparition. The first thatched church was built on that very spot by this Catholic gentleman (1:77–78).

QUERRIEN, LA PRENESSAYE, FRANCE (1652)

Querrien is a small village in the northwestern part of France known as Brittany. On August 15, 1652, Jeanne Courtel, age twelve, was a poor shepherdess tending her father's flock of sheep. She had been both deaf and mute ever since her birth. She was mentally reciting her prayers when she was surprised by the sudden appearance of the Blessed Virgin. Our Lady was holding the Child Jesus on one arm and holding a stalk of lilies in the other. Blessed Mary had only spoken a few words when **Jeanne suddenly realized that she could actually hear her! The twelve year old had been miraculously healed.** Our Lady spoke in a sweet voice:

> "I choose this place to be honored. Build for me a chapel in the middle of this village and many people will come" (3:73–74).

The little girl returned to her parents quickly—and they were *astonished* to hear her speak!

JOHN S. CARPENTER

GUAITARA CANYON, COLOMBIA
(1754): "Our Lady of Las Lajas"

María Mueses de Quiñones was making the six-mile walk with her daughter Rosa when they approached the place called Las Lajas (the Rocks), where the trail passes through a deep gorge of the Guaitara River. Maria never liked this part of the trail because there were rumors that a cave in Las Lajas was haunted. Maria was carrying her **deaf-mute** daughter, Rosa, on her back. By the time she had climbed to Las Lajas, she was weary and sat on a rock to rest. The child got down from her back to play. The next thing that Maria knew was that Rosa was at the cave *shouting*:

"Mommy, there is a woman in here with a boy in her arms!"

Maria became very frightened. ***This was the first time she had ever heard her daughter speak!*** She didn't see the figures that the girl was talking about, nor did she want to. She grabbed the child and ran on to Ipiales. When she told people what happened, nobody at first took her seriously. However, as the news spread, some asked if maybe it was true. *After all, the child was now able to speak!*

A few days later, Rosa disappeared from home. After looking everywhere, the anguished Maria realized that her daughter must have gone to the cave. Little Rosa often said that the woman was calling her. Maria ran to Las Lajas and found her daughter, kneeling in front of a splendid woman and playing affectionately with a child who had come down from His mother's arms to let the girl enjoy His divine tenderness. Maria fell to her knees before this beautiful spectacle in reverence and admiration. She knew now that she was seeing the Blessed Virgin and Jesus. Fearful of ridicule, Maria kept quiet about the event. But frequently, she and Rosa went to the cave to place wild flowers and candles in the cracks of the rocks.

The months went by with María and Rosa keeping their secret. However, one day, the girl fell gravely ill—and actually died. A distraught Maria decided to take her daughter's body to Las Lajas to ask Our Lady to restore Rosa to life. Pressed by the sadness of Maria's unrelenting supplications, the Blessed Virgin obtained Rosa's resurrection from Her Divine Son. **Young Rosa awoke in perfect health.** Overflowing with joy, Maria went home. It didn't take long for a crowd to gather. Friends and neighbors *who had seen the child without life* were now overwhelmed with awe at this latest miracle (3:84–85).

POMPEII, ITALY (1884)

The new shrine of Our Lady of the Rosary was completed in 1883. Within the month, miraculous events began to take place at the shrine. Four healings were recorded, including the following:

Fortuna Agrelli, a very ill young girl suffering **three incurable diseases** that most doctors had given up on, was joined by her family in saying a novena of Rosaries starting on February 16, 1884. The *Virgin Mary then appeared to her* on March 3, sitting upon a high throne, profusely decorated with flowers. She held the Divine Child on her lap and a rosary in her hand; both were clad in gold-embroidered garments. St. Dominic and St. Catherine of Siena accompanied them. Fortuna asked Mary—as "the Queen of the Rosary"—for a cure for herself.

> "You have invoked me by various titles and have always obtained favors from me. Now, since you have called me by the title so pleasing to me, *Queen of the Holy Rosary*, I can no longer refuse the favor that you petition—for this name is most precious and dear to me. Make three novenas, and you will obtain all" (9).

Fortuna did as Mary said and was *completely cured* from her three incurable diseases. Many healings are attributed to Our Lady of Pompeii. Between 1891 and 1894, *hundreds of miracles* have been officially recorded at the sanctuary.

AKITA, JAPAN (1973–1981)

Born in 1931, Agnes Katsuko Sasagawa was always a frail child. She had her appendix removed at age nineteen, but due to a hospital error with the anesthesia, she became paralyzed. After ten years of immobility while being cared for by a Catholic nun, she made a spontaneous and miraculous recovery. In May 1973, she entered the convent of the Handmaids of the Eucharist in Yuzawadai, a suburb of Akita. One month earlier, she had been suddenly afflicted with total deafness.

On July 5, Sister Agnes approached a tall statue of Mary and knelt before her. Suddenly, the statue became instantly ablaze and bathed in a brilliant light—as if the statue was coming to life! Though deaf, she heard the statue speak to her:

> "My daughter, my novice, you have obeyed me well in abandoning all to follow me. Do you suffer much because of the handicap which deafness causes you? You will be assuredly healed. Be patient, it is the last trial…"

On October 13, the fifty-seventh anniversary of the last apparition at Fatima, Sister Agnes was **_healed from deafness_** during the benediction of that church service and was delighted at hearing the church bells ring! She telephoned Bishop Ito to report that Mary's promise of restoring her hearing had come true (11:192–200).

MEXICO CITY, MEXICO (1531)

Juan Diego was overjoyed at meeting the Virgin Mary and to receive her promise that she would help him with the local bishop's disbelief. But that was short-lived as he found his uncle—his only living relative—gravely ill upon returning home. As he could not leave his uncle's side the next day, he was forced to not show up for Mary to receive the sign of proof she had promised. He felt horrible, but when he did manage to get out on the following day, he took a different route, hoping to not run into her. However, he suddenly ran into the Virgin, face-to-face. He begged her forgiveness and told her about his sick uncle. She reassured him with these words:

> "Listen and be sure, my dear son, that I will protect you. Do not be frightened or grieved or let your heart be dismayed however great the illness may be that you speak of. Am I not here, I who am your Mother, and is not my help a refuge?

> Am I not of your kind? Are you not under my shadow and protection? Do not be concerned about your uncle's illness, for he is not going to die. Be assured, he is already well."

When Juan Diego returned home, he found his uncle completely healed and telling of a visit that he, too, had had with the Virgin Mary.

> "I, too, have seen her. She came to me in this very house and spoke to me. She told me that she wanted a temple to be built at Tepeyac Hill. She said that her image should be called 'Holy Mary of Guadalupe,' though she did not explain why."

The uncle had no idea yet what image she was talking about (11:44–48).

SILUVA, LITHUANIA (1608)

Word spread rapidly, and the next day, a large number of people went to the place where Blessed Mary had appeared, impressed by the children's tearful insistence that they were telling the truth. When the children were questioned, either separately or together, each told the same identical story, even to the smallest detail. The Calvinist catechist was also present, along with the rector of the Calvinist seminary. The Catechist dismissed the events as nothing but the work of the devil. But as he was speaking, the woman again appeared on the rock, very sorrowful with tears in her eyes, holding a child in her arms. The assembled people became very frightened and did not dare to say a word. The Catechist finally got enough courage to ask, "Why are you crying?" Blessed Mary replied,

> "Formerly in this place, My Son was honored and adored, but now, all that the people do is seed and cultivate the land."

Then she disappeared in front of everyone present. They were confused, dumbfounded, and stunned. They did not really believe that it was the work of the devil as the Calvinists had insisted.

A blind man, more than a hundred years old, heard about the apparitions from a nearby village. He recalled a night, eighty years ago, during which he had helped Father Holubka bury an ironclad chest, filled with church treasures, next to a large rock. The villagers led the blind man to the field where Mary had appeared to see if he might be able to locate the place where the treasures had been buried. **No sooner had he reached the spot, when his sight was miraculously restored.** Falling to his knees with joy and gratitude, he pointed to the exact spot where the chest had been buried. The ironclad chest was dug out of the ground, and when it was opened, there—perfectly preserved—was the large painting of the Madonna and Child, several gold chalices, vestments, church deeds, and other documents (151:3).

BETANIA, VENEZUELA (1984)

At age twelve, Maria Esperanza developed such a severe case of pneumonia that doctors only gave her a day or two to live. The young Maria prayed to the Virgin Mary about dying, and Mary appeared to her, assuring her that she would survive in order to serve God, and then told her what medications she needed. The doctors heeded the heavenly advice, got the medications, and Maria Esperanza recovered. She went on to receive over thirty appearances and countless messages from the Blessed Virgin from 1976 through 1990. Hundreds of others witnessed many supernatural events during those appearances, including the famous church picnic in 1984 when over one hundred participants witnessed Our Lady for themselves (11:267).

MEDJUGORJE, BOSNIA-HERZEGOVINA (2003)

A most remarkable healing comes with the story of Colleen Willard from Chicago, Illinois in September 2003. Besides having an inoperable brain tumor which threatened to end her life, Colleen had fifteen other major ailments—like critical adrenal insufficiency and Hashimoto's thyroiditis. No airline wanted to accept the responsibility of flying her to Medjugorje. She was so weak from her infirmities that she could barely talk and hold her head upright. Medical clearance was somehow, miraculously obtained, and she accompanied the tour group to Vicka's house (one of the six visionaries) upon arriving in Medjugorje.

It was so crowded there that the jostling, pushing, and tight quarters became a dangerous situation for this frail woman in her wheelchair. Just being touched could cause searing pain; a bang to her head could kill her. Her head dropped, and the tour leader was fearful that she had died. But her husband pushed his way to give her some medicine, and she revived. Vicka saw what was happening while she was talking. When she finished, Vicka pushed her way through the crowd and pulled Colleen from her wheelchair into a loving embrace. Placing her left hand on Colleen's head, Vicka prayed over her.

Colleen felt a strong heat throughout her body. Many witnessed what looked like a "golden globe coming from Vicka's hand." Colleen felt like her head was burning. Vicka stopped the loving prayers and embrace after ten minutes. Colleen was wheeled away to prepare for Mass and was positioned at the very front of the packed church. As the priest began to consecrate the Host, Colleen heard Our Blessed Mother say,

> "My daughter, will you surrender to God the Father? Will you surrender to my Spouse, the Holy Spirit? Will you surrender to My Son Jesus? Will you surrender now?"

Colleen agreed and began to feel her legs tingle. As she received the Eucharist, she could feel the heat and pain leaving her body. To the shock of everyone, Colleen stood up and left her wheelchair. After Mass, she was soon laughing and moving about freely. Everyone had tears of joy. That night, Colleen danced with her husband in the joyous celebration that ensued. The next day, Colleen climbed rocky Mount Krizevac without any trouble! Upon returning home to Chicago, she stunned the medical personnel of her doctor's office with her inexplicable, healthy, vibrant presence (45:154–159).

Healing waters have been closely associated with the appearances of the Virgin Mary. And often, the miraculous spring did not even exist prior to her visitation. Here are some excerpts from history:

TLAXCALA, MEXICO (1541)

To help Juan Bernardino's relatives who had been stricken with smallpox in the village of Xiloxostla, Juan walked to the River Zahuapan to collect water that was thought to have medicinal properties. After filling his jug with water, he made his way to the village through a thick grove of ocote trees. He abruptly halted at the sight of a "beautiful woman" of regal bearing standing among the trees. The reassuring smile of the Lady gave him the courage to draw closer to her. With a heavenly voice, she greeted him,

> "May God preserve you, my son. Where are you going?"

Overcome by the woman's beauty and surprised at seeing her among the trees, Juan hesitated before he was able to reply,

> "I was taking water from the river to my sick ones who are dying."

> "Come with me," the Lady said, "and I will give you water to cure the disease. It will cure not only your family, but all who will drink of it. My heart is ever ready to help those who are ill, for I cannot bear to see their misfortune."

Anxious to obtain miraculous water that would cure his relatives, Juan followed the lady with happy anticipation. When they came to a depression in the ground, the lady indicated a new spring of fresh water. In her soft, almost musical voice, she told Juan,

> "Take as much of this water as you wish, and know that those who are touched by even the smallest drop will obtain, not merely relief from their illness, but perfect health."

Juan emptied his jug of the river water and filled it with the clear water of the spring. When the Lady disappeared among the trees, Juan hurried to the village with his precious water. Upon reaching the bedside of his afflicted relatives, he told them about the Lady and the miraculous spring, as well as her promise of health through use of the water. Juan watched in amazement as the Lady's word was realized when each relative was restored to health after drinking the miraculous water (3:37–38).

RAPALLO, ITALY (1557)

On July 2, 1557, a farmer named Giovanni Chichizola was walking on a donkey trail on a wooded hill overlooking the city of Rapallo. Coming upon a cool, shady spot, he paused for his noonday rest. The sound of a sweet voice calling his name startled him to alertness. There, standing close beside him, was a beautiful lady surrounded by an intense light. The Blessed Virgin Mary appeared to him and reassured him by saying,

> "Do not fear, Giovanni. I am the Mother of God. I have chosen you to be a messenger of my motherly will. Visit the ecclesiastics of Rapallo and let them know that the Mother of God has chosen this place as her perpetual dwelling place and would like a church to be erected here. I leave here a pledge of my love."

Much to his surprise, a spring had begun flowing from the dry ground by the rock—the exact spot where the Blessed Virgin had appeared. He went to the village and told the people what had happened. The priests to whom he told his story were skeptical, but because of Giovanni's excitement, they reluctantly followed him to the place of the apparition. There they saw the spring which had mysteriously appeared. Today, a white marble trough with a faucet is provided for those who want to drink the miraculous water or collect it in bottles (3:43–44).

LA SALETTE, FRANCE (1846)

About a week after the apparition had occurred, a spring gushed forth beside the rock upon which the Virgin Mary had sat. This place had only collected water previously whenever snows melted or after heavy rains. But now, the spring flowed steadily, incessantly, and fully—even in dry weather conditions. And it has *never* stopped since that time. Numerous miraculous cures have been attributed to the water (10:86) (68:265).

LOURDES, FRANCE (1858)

On February 25, with hundreds of curious people watching her silent interactions with the Virgin Mary, Bernadette performed some very strange actions.

> "She told me to go drink at the spring and to wash in it. Not seeing any spring, I headed toward the river to drink, but she beckoned with her finger for me to go under the rock. I went and found a little muddy water, almost too little for me to hold in the hollow of my hand. Three times I threw it away— it was so dirty. The fourth time I succeeded to drink some and then spit it out" (42:9).

Onlookers feared that she had gone mad, digging in the mud, drinking it, and smearing some on her face. The crowd gasped at each odd behavior, but they were later told that she had been instructed to do so "for sinners." Nevertheless, the crowd left confused and dismissing her; her embarrassed aunts took her home. But later that same day, clear water started flowing from that muddy place. On February 26, there was now a clear pool of fresh water where she had dug into the mud.

On March 1, 1858, Catherine Latapie and her two toddlers came to the water. She had broken her arm, paralyzing two fingers the year before, but when she placed her arm into that clear pool of running spring water, her hand was perfectly healed.

Today, approximately 14,500 gallons of water are generated daily from the spring which started as a mudhole that Bernadette had dug with her fingers. During the next 150 years, seven thousand authenticated medical cures were documented by the International Medical Bureau of Lourdes (11:113). The medical commission at Lourdes does not use the word "miracle" in its reports. It declares that the healing under investigation "cannot be explained by any of the laws and knowledge of medical science." Also of immense scientific interest is the claim that the water of the spring at Lourdes has a unique quality: **Bacteria cannot live in it** (68:109).

Of those miraculous healings, the Catholic Church has conservatively accepted sixty-seven of them as clearly from the hand of God **with no other possible explanation**. Here is a sampling of the miraculous healings from the waters of Lourdes (42:15–20):

Louis Bouriette (fifty-four), a quarryman, had lost complete vision in his right eye during a mine explosion. He bathed his eye several times with water from the spring, and his sight was totally restored.

Henri Busquet (sixteen) begged his parents to take him to Lourdes because his suffering from tuberculosis was unbearable. A neighbor brought him water from Lourdes, and within two days, his tuberculin ulcers had healed and infections were gone.

Justin Bouhort (two) had never walked and was so sick from various illnesses that he was close to death. His mother plunged her baby into the cold waters of the spring, ignoring the fears of bystanders. The next day, young Justin walked for the first time—and lived to attend the canonization ceremonies for Bernadette in 1933 at the age of seventy-seven.

Bedridden for over twenty years, Madeleine Rizan (fifty-eight) was paralyzed on her left side. Her daughter gave her a few sips of the Lourdes water and applied some to her face and body. She was instantly healed!

Marie Moreau (seventeen) had a bad infection that had nearly robbed her of most of her eyesight. A compress soaked in Lourdes water was placed over her eyes. The next morning, after removing the compress, her vision was completely restored!

A fallen tree had crushed the left leg of Pierre de Rudder (fifty-two). Infection had prevented the compound fracture from healing. Hobbling on crutches for eight years, he faced amputation soon. He prayed to the Blessed Virgin in front of a replica of the Lourdes grotto in Belgium. Within minutes, his bones fused back together, and he was able to walk away without any crutches. He was quite active until he eventually died at the age of seventy-five.

In 1963, Vittorio Micheli of Italy (twenty-three) was suffering from a cancerous tumor on his hip bone. Lowered into the Lourdes bath waters on a stretcher, his tumor vanished as well as all of his pain. He resumed an active, healthy life again.

Serge Perrin (forty-one) suffered from a blocked carotid artery which caused paralysis, blackouts, and vision issues. In 1970, he visited Lourdes and was completely cured.

Delizia Cirolli (twelve) suffered from a potentially fatal tumor in her knee and faced amputation soon. After a trip to Lourdes and praying to Our Lady, she was 100 percent healed.

Jean-Pierre Bely, a nurse, was diagnosed with multiple sclerosis in 1972. By 1987, he was bedridden and 100 percent disabled. After the Anointing of the Sick at Lourdes, he felt a great sense of peace; he regained his mobility and sense of touch again.

Anna Santaniello (forty-one) suffered from severe heart disease, labored breathing, and low oxygen levels. Carried to the Lourdes baths on a stretcher, she walked out on her own. Doctors confirmed her good health, regular heart rhythm, and breathing without restrictions.

CHAMPION, WISCONSIN (1859–1871)

Statue of the Virgin Mary on the exact location of her appearances in Champion, Wisconsin where miraculous healings continue to occur (photo by author).

Blessed Mary's five acres of land that had miraculously survived the great fire of 1871 had other miracles as well. One had to do with the chapel well. The weather had been extremely dry all summer with the deepest of wells in the region barely containing any water at all. The chapel well was only a few feet deep, and yet, *it was always providing plenty of water.* All the neighbors, their surviving livestock which they had brought to the grounds, and everyone else living on Mary's five acres had plenty of water from this shallow well. There was no explanation or logic for this small well to serve so many for so long under the dry conditions. People started taking some of the well water home as it was believed to have led to some miraculous healings (20:28).

Many other miracles were documented. A seventeen-year-old boy developed pleurisy from double pneumonia. Despite his lungs becoming extremely weak, he said a novena at the chapel, and he was completely healed. Another boy, Michael Fonde, age nine, fell from a barn and was crippled. Four years later, a group of women prayed a novena with him at the chapel, and he walked out healed, leaving his crutches behind. A little girl with bleeding sores, who had been treated by doctors for years, was completely healed after she and her mom made the pilgrimage to this chapel. Another small girl had become blind from a severe case of measles. When her mother brought her to this chapel to pray, she was instantaneously healed. And a deaf boy brought by his mom to the chapel completely regained his hearing (20:44–45).

CASTELPETROSO, ITALY (1888)

The apparitions were accompanied by another phenomenon; in May 1888, the body of water at the foot of the mountain began bestowing miracles. Soon, believers from other countries came in masses to behold and experience the extraordinary events and the fountain of miracles. Angelo Verna, a six-year-old mute boy, was given a drink of this water by his father and was completely healed by receiving the gift of speech (9).

BANNEUX, BELGIUM (1933)

They found Mariette leaving the garden area and entering the road, drawn down the road as if in a trance. Mariette said, "She is calling me." They watched in amazement as she was thrown to her knees twice on the pavement in the cold, twelve-degree air and started praying earnestly. It sounded like her knees cracked on the frozen ground. They followed her to a stream where Mary had led her and stated,

> "Plunge your hand into the water. This spring is to be dedicated to me."

The next evening, at 7:00 p.m., Mariette saw the Blessed Virgin again. Now as many as twenty others were observing her visitations. Mariette asked her, "Who are you, Madame?"

"I am the Virgin of the Poor."

Again, she was led to the icy-cold stream. Mary explained to her, **"This small brook is to be reserved for all nations to relieve the sick."** The stream began providing amazing cases of miraculous healings: a fractured skull, deafness, broken jaw, cerebrospinal meningitis, paralysis, and many more. Benito Garcia from Spain had a badly injured right arm. His wife had heard stories of the healing waters and insisted that they walk from Barcelona to Banneux. Benito thrust his injured arm into the spring and felt it to be boiling hot. He exclaimed,

> "I have come all the way from Spain. If you are indeed the Virgin of the Poor, then prove it to me!"

He withdrew the drain-tube from his arm, and the *wound healed immediately* in front of many witnesses! Bishop Kerkhof documented at least twenty miraculous cures between 1933 and 1938 (4:33–34).

SAN DAMIANO, ITALY (1964)

On October 16, Our Lady requested that a well to be dug in the location next to the miraculously blooming pear tree on the apparition site. *Miraculous water began flowing* which led to the documented cures of blindness, deafness, paralysis, and other ailments (58:7).

FONTANELLE, ITALY (1966)

On April 17, 1966, the Sunday after Easter in Fontanelle, a small settlement just outside of Montichiari. The Blessed Virgin said to visionary Pierina Gilli,

> "My Divine Son is total Love, and *He is sending me to give miraculous powers to this spring*. The sick and all my children must kiss the crucifix and ask my Divine Son for forgiveness before they take the water or drink from it. (She approaches the spring.) Take mud into your hands. Wash yourself with water! This is to teach the sinners that sin makes the soul dirty, yet the soul will be cleansed again through the water of grace."

Our Lady bowed down and touched the water of the spring in two places. She repeated her wish for the sick to come to this miraculous spring along with many of her children.

Second Apparition (May 13, 1966): In the presence of about twenty people Blessed Mary again appeared at the spring. She wanted her appearance to be made known. She suggested that "**the world is walking the road to perdition,**" but She has obtained mercy. She insisted again on prayer, sacrifice, and penance "**to save mankind.**" She pointed to the right side of the spring and insisted that a comfortable basin be constructed to immerse the sick, while on the left side, the water there would be for drinking. It would be named the Spring of Grace (134:5–6).

HRUSHIV, UKRAINE (1987)

The people of Hrushiv had planted a weeping willow tree at the site many years ago, commemorating an appearance of the Blessed

Mother some 350 years earlier. Later, *a spring suddenly appeared* beneath the tree. During the severe cholera epidemic of 1855, a local person dreamed that the Virgin had instructed the residents to clear and reclaim the ancient spring and hold Mass. **Not one cholera death was reported afterwards (165).**

AGOO, PHILIPPINES (1989)

Then Our Blessed Mother stood up over a guava tree on a rise, high, overlooking the spring, and spoke. Her Immaculate Heart was visible on her chest, and light radiated outward toward the spring of water—which the infant Jesus then waded in. Scores of miraculous cures have been attributed to the water spring at this apparition site (98).

ITAPIRANGA, BRAZIL (1994–1998)

Many spiritual fruits of conversion and life changes are attributed to these apparitions. Thousands of people come every day to Itapiranga to drink the water from the healing fountain. Some doctors have studied the reported healings there and sent their findings to the Apostolic Prefecture of Itacoatiara. At one point, Blessed Mary requested that the visionary, Edson Glauber, bring the healing waters that were flowing at the site of the apparitions to the sick who could not go there for themselves (121).

Although there are countless other miracles that could be listed, there is little doubt that many amazing healings have occurred in association with the appearances and visits of the Virgin Mary. Here is a brief scan of the kinds of numbers of miraculous healings that have been carefully documented in various places around the world.

VAILANKANNI, INDIA

Pope John XXIII officially recognized this pilgrimage site as the "Lourdes of the East" due to the healing waters of the pond. Adjacent to this basilica is a museum of "offerings" left behind by hundreds of pilgrims—often with their personal stories of miraculous healings (1:79–80).

KEVELAER, GERMANY

Reinier and Margaretha van Volbroek traveled with their invalid son, Peter, who had been paralyzed for five years—unable to walk or stand. Although his case had been declared hopeless by physicians, just two days after their visit to Our Lady of Luxembourg, Peter was totally cured and able to walk again without any difficulty. A woman suffering open wounds on her legs that no treatments had helped for years was healed miraculously after just two visits. Her healing was so dramatic and profound that it was reported by the mayor of Huissen, Holland for official documentation on August 13, 1643. Many other miraculous cures were documented at the shrine (122:2) (3:65).

VINAY, FRANCE

Prayers said before this altar have led to more than one hundred miraculous cures. These miraculous healings are said to "undoubtedly genuine" due to the sworn testimonies of reliable witnesses (3:71).

LAUS, FRANCE

As news of the continuing apparitions spread, the number of visitors to Laus increased in 1664–1665. Graces and blessings poured down upon souls; people came by the hundreds and then thousands to pray in the poor little chapel. Cures of all kinds abounded, and sinners were converted in great numbers (123:4).

LICHEN, POLAND

Just as the Virgin had predicted, two years later in 1852, the epidemic of cholera began. That same year, her religious portrait was placed in the parish church in Lichen. People remembered the Virgin's prophecy and thronged to her portrait to kneel and pray. *Whoever prayed in front of this picture received graces and did not become ill or die.* Those who were already ill or dying recuperated. A special Episcopal committee of the Roman Catholic Church investigated these claims and by 1939 had documented around three thousand recorded acts of grace, including many miraculous recoveries and cures (3:92) (125).

PARIS, FRANCE

The "Miraculous Medal" -- known to be involved in numerous healings and conversions (photo by author).

Imagery provided by Blessed Mary to Catherine Laboure was depicted on the medal struck in 1832. This was originally called the Medal of the Immaculate Conception. But what was to follow led to the popular change in its name to the "Miraculous Medal." Reports started pouring in from those who wore the new medal: physical cures, conversions, and miracles of every sort. Even the archbishop of Paris, who had finally authorized the medal's production, was one of the first to wear it and experience a miracle. Reports came in of miraculous healings of those who had been hopelessly incurable. Some of the worst enemies of the church experienced unlikely and amazing conversions. Billions of medals are spread worldwide today (1:96) (5:57).

CHAMPION, WISCONSIN, USA

When doubters began to give visionary Adele Brice a hard time, miracle healings began occurring in the chapel when Adele asked for divine assistance. Blind visitors regained their sight, deaf people regained their hearing, the desperately sick were healed, and cripples would walk again, leaving their canes and crutches behind as evidence. Word spread across the Midwest in the 1860s of these divine healings near Robinsonville (later renamed Champion) (20:15).

KNOCK, IRELAND

Miracles began as early as ten days after the apparition. A young girl, Delia Gordon, had experienced deafness and pain in her left ear. While visiting the apparition site, her mother put a small piece of cement from the wall of the church into her ear. Afterward, during Mass, Delia experienced an excruciating pain in her ear, followed by a complete healing of her deafness and no further pain. Jane O'Neill was suffering serious spinal troubles when she was carried to the church on a couch. On September 8, 1880, she was cured and left her spinal plaster jacket with iron rod attached hanging on the gable. A lad brought from England had suffered a serious injury to his spine from an accident in a coal mine. He was carried to the apparition site and laid on the ground. He had barely touched the ground when he bounded up to his feet, having been instantaneously cured. Father Tom Neary reports that 687 miraculous cures were documented in that first year from 1879–1880. People were using the cement or grout from that church wall which had been directly behind the apparitions. Crutches and canes were left there. Eventually, wooden planks had to be placed over the wall to preserve it (40:63–66).

BEAURAING, BELGIUM

Within a few weeks of the last visit from Blessed Mary, reports of miracle healings began. A young girl, Pauline Dereppe, was healed of a severe bone disease after praying at Beauraing. A middle-aged woman, Madame Van Laer, was cured of her tuberculosis. As this news spread, two and a half million pilgrims traveled to Beauraing in 1933! (4:39)

GHIAIE DI BONATE, ITALY

Monday, May 29, 1944, a stream of people flowed to the place of the apparitions. The influx of sick and invalid people was so impressive at Ghiaie di Bonate that a special service of volunteers, Red Cross nurses, doctors, and ambulances had to be on hand. There were many miraculous recoveries in the field—so much so that Bergamo's Curia established a special office for the customary investigations. At 6:32 p.m., Adelaide saw the Virgin Mary with angels. Again, three hundred thousand people were in attendance!

Wednesday, May 31, 1944, at 8:00 p.m., the flow of pilgrims from everywhere carried on incessantly from the night before. The authorities were worried for the public order. It is believed that more than ninety thousand people arrived from Piedmont, many of whom were on foot. ***About 350,000 people*** were in attendance for the last apparition. A solar phenomenon was again seen at Ghiaie and from other locations. Many healings occurred on this day and soon afterwards—about three hundred documented complete recoveries (110).

TRE FONTANE, ROME, ITALY (1980)

The solar phenomenon lasted about thirty minutes. Meanwhile, the Mass that had been in progress was halted so that the people could calm down and return their attention to the service. There were many physical cures. A medical center was set up; after extensive research, it was confirmed that the cures were indeed miraculous and beyond any medical or scientific explanation. True to Mary's promise, the dirt from the Grotto of Tre Fontane has proven to be miraculous. It has worked wonders for the welfare of both bodies and souls. There have been so many bodily cures and conversions that no one disputes that these graces have been received through the intercession of the Virgin (57).

BE NOT AFRAID TO FOLLOW THE FOOTPRINTS FROM HEAVEN

LIPA, PHILIPPINES

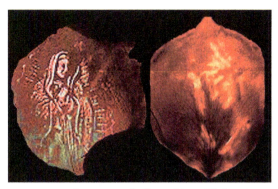

The supernatural rose petals from Lipa, Philippines with
miraculous images and healing powers
(left: Virgin Mary; right: Jesus on cross with Mary profile).

Many cures have been reported using the rose petals that have fallen from the sky—*both indoors and outdoors*, associated with the Virgin's appearances. A baby, Soccorro Dichoso, was born with a hole in her skull. The parents applied rose petals from one of the "showers" to the baby's skull on January 28, 1949. X-rays confirmed that the hole closed up, and the brain receded, curing the child. On December 24, 1950, a girl was receiving the last rites, dying from a cerebral hemorrhage, when the priest placed one of those "heavenly rose petals" on her forehead. Upon the ringing of the Angelus bell, the girl suddenly awakened as if nothing was wrong—and she was completely healed. Another child, Menania Sungo, age nine, had been born with a severely deformed right foot. It was curled so much that she could not wear a shoe; her leg had atrophied, shortened, and wasted away. Her uncle brought a bottle of water that had been placed by Mary's statue overnight. The mother rubbed this water on her foot every evening for a week, and then the child awoke one morning to a perfectly healed foot and leg! Neighbors reported a strong fragrance of flowers around the child's home. The Sungo family was shocked when a shower of rose petals fell *inside* their own home (126:2).

GARABANDAL, SPAIN

Blessed Mary explained that Jesus would perform miracles through objects kissed by her. Mary added that God bestows special graces upon those who believe and have faith. Many physical cures (**hundreds** associated with Garabandal) and conversions have been obtained by simply touching the objects kissed by Mary (34:17–19).

ZEITOUN, EGYPT

During the Virgin's four years of appearances to thousands, numerous miraculous healings have been documented. Two girls, blind since birth, studying at a school for the blind, fully regained their sight. A 34-year-old mute, Adel Abdel Malek, unable to speak since birth, was cured and now able to speak. A Muslim girl with a malignant tumor on the side of her head visited a public apparition of Mary at the church the night before her surgery and showed up the next day completely free of her tumor. Miss Madiha Mohammed Said, age twenty, had lost her sight and speech and had failed all medical efforts to improve her condition. On June 4, 1968, her two brothers took her to the church, asking the priest to pray for her. Suddenly, she cried out in a loud voice, "I see the apparition of the Blessed Virgin!" In that instant, she regained both her eyesight and her power of speech. Cases of paralysis were also cured—one woman arrived in her wheelchair at the church, felt burning electrical sensations, and then walked away (59:127–133).

KIBEHO, RWANDA, AFRICA

The messages given during Mary's visits were accompanied by extraordinary signs seen in the sky. Several times people saw a cross or crown of thorns in the sky near the sun. Anathalie related that Our Lady knew that so many had traveled great distances and suffered much to be there with Her. When the Virgin asked Anathalie to "water her flowers," that meant to sprinkle holy water on them. Because there was such a large crowd, it would take such a long time to sprinkle them all, so she asked Blessed Mary, "Oh, Mother, there are so many of them that I can't water them all. Won't you help me?" At that moment, a refreshing rain fell on all the hot and weary pilgrims, washing and cooling them while the **surrounding countryside remained dry**. The shower also *actually healed cuts, sores, and wounds* from the pilgrims' long trek to get there. The sun then returned and dried all of their clothes (39:91).

DAMASCUS, SYRIA

When oil flowed from the hands of Myrna, the clergy and civil authorities all investigated for any evidence of a fraud or trick. When they asked Myrna to pray in front of them, having washed her hands well, the oil would flow from her palms again. A priest saw a "brilliant liquid" flowing abundantly from her palms. A bishop who was also present in the room noted that the oil had the scent of myron—or holy oil. Medical doctors and scientists gathered to decipher the origin of the healing oil that continued to exude from Myrna's hands when she prayed. Thousands of people began to visit her home. The sick gathered in her courtyard, asking to be anointed with the healing oil. Phenomenal cures resulted for many of them. On December 19, 1982, a man carried his paralyzed nine-year-old son into Myrna's bedroom. Oil poured from Myrna's hands while she and the boy's father prayed over him. As she anointed his legs, the twisted limbs straightened out, and the boy stated excitedly that he could feel his legs for the first time in his life! The father screamed praises for the miracle, and his son ran and jumped and danced with great joy and many tears. On January 5, 1983, a Muslim woman, who was completely blind, was healed and recovered her eyesight completely. It is estimated that one hundred thousand people have witnessed these miracle healings from the oil with their own eyes. It is also estimated that over a million people have seen filmed documentation of these miracles (2:250, 254).

BETANIA, VENEZUELA

On one occasion, Dr. Arrieta, stricken with prostate cancer which had metastasized to his spine, was in attendance. In the morning, thousands saw the sun lose its light, turn green in its center. Then, like at Fatima, the sun seemed to come down toward the screaming, fearful crowds. Dr. Arrieta felt an infusion of heat throughout his body and believed he was being healed at that very moment. Medical tests confirmed he was now completely free of cancer. By 1987, **five hundred** cures had been documented at Betania. The church deemed these events to be authentic (11:283).

AGOO, PHILIPPINES

On February 11, 1993, reported by cloistered nuns, a six-year-old boy—who had been born blind—had his sight miraculously restored during the apparition on this date. This was the first documented healing associated with the apparitions. The weeping statue was also attributed to two unexpected healings of a high official's critically ill wife. Scores of miraculous cures have been attributed to the water spring at the apparition site (98:7) (129).

Can these miracles possibly be the effect of suggestion during an intense religious experience? But how do mental suggestions cure twisted, deformed limbs, lifelong blindness, or hopeless terminal illnesses? A baby does not have that kind of mental ability. A person not present or one unconscious in a coma would not even have any awareness of such prayers or be able to practice any form of suggestion to heal oneself.

When the Virgin Mary said a cure would take place by way of her Son, it always did. Miracles were plentiful in the days of the Bible—*but they have never stopped...*

The "footprints" are everywhere! But are they *really* "footprints" *from heaven*?

Science will now examine the physical evidence. Let's put those "footprints" under the microscope and take a closer look...

CHAPTER 12

EVIDENCE LEFT BEHIND

Supernatural occurrences leave us wondering…
What did we just experience?
Was it real?
Could we have imagined it?
Would anyone *ever* believe us?
Why would anyone ever believe us?
But what if we have some kind of tangible evidence? What if it could be studied scientifically? And what if science agrees that it has no reasonable or natural explanation?

WEEPING STATUES

AGOO, PHILIPPINES (1993)

On January 23, 1993, Blessed Mary said, **"On February 6, I will give a great and special sign to the people coming to Agoo."** And on February 6, 1993, the statue of Our Lady cried tears of blood after an apparition at Apparition Hill. Later that night, the statue was brought to the bishop's palace in San Fernando. Bishop Lazo reported that he witnessed with his own eyes the statue shedding tears of blood. He said that the room filled with the strong fragrance of roses, "and we knelt and prayed." He even placed his own fingers in the blood that was on the face of the statue—and tasted the blood. It was salty. A photograph captured the moment, showing the smeared bloody face of the statue after he placed his fingers on it. The National Bureau of Investigation tested the blood and determined that **it was human blood, type O** (98:7).

AKITA, JAPAN (1973)

The weeping statue of the Virgin Mary
in Akita, Japan, 1973-1981.

On June 28, Sister Agnes experienced a sharp pain in the palm of her left hand. A small, rose-colored cross was etched across her palm and remained, painfully, for three days. But on July 5, the pain returned in her left hand, and it bled more than she could conceal from others. Tears flowed from her eyes as she let another nun help bandage her hand. This was no illusion! That night, she rose to pray at 3:00 a.m., and a voice came to her *despite her deafness* and said,

> "Be not afraid. Pray with fervor, not only because of your sins, but in reparation for those of all people. The world today wounds the most Sacred Heart of Our Lord by its ingratitude and injuries. The wounds of Mary are much deeper and more sorrowful than yours. Let us go to pray in the chapel together."

Sister Agnes approached a tall statue of Mary and knelt before her. Suddenly, the statue became instantly ablaze and bathed in a brilliant light—as if the statue was coming to life! The next morning,

Sister Agnes asked Sister Kotake to inspect the statue. She found a cross-shaped wound, bleeding, in the right hand of the wooden statue of Mary. Sometimes, it gushed blood profusely. Sister Agnes' hand continued to have bouts of intense pain as well. Sister Agnes's wound appeared on Thursday evenings, grew worse on Fridays, and disappeared each Sunday—as if commemorating the passion and death of Jesus.

On July 26, the Feast of St. Anne, the Mother of the Virgin Mary, the wound on Sister Agnes became more painful than ever. At the same time, the statue in the chapel began to bleed more profusely. She went to Bishop Ito to reveal her pain and suffering; he advised going to a doctor. But she went to the chapel, first, to pray for strength. There, she suddenly heard the voice of the angel again:

> "Our pain will come to an end today. Pray to the Sacred Heart and the Precious Blood. Pray for the sins of the whole world. Tell the Bishop that the blood is shed today for the last time."

At once the pain left, and the wound in her hand was healed. The statue also ceased its bleeding at the same time—though the imprint of the wound remained in the wood.

On September 29, with another nun at her side, Sister Agnes saw the statue of Mary ablaze with light again. *For the first time, the companion with her was able to see the unearthly light and gasped with excitement.* The statue's hands glowed brightly, and the wound was healed finally. But later that night, when the statue glowed again, **tears began flowing** from the statue's eyes. The tears had a wonderful *fragrance of flowers* that persisted for seventeen days! The Virgin explained her own tears to Sister Agnes:

> "I am weeping because humanity is not accepting my motherly invitation to conversion. The (public) signs of my immense sorrow…are not believed in. Man is becoming ever more corrupt, godless, wicked, and cruel…I am weeping because the Church is continuing along the road of division, of loss of the true faith…I am weeping because, in great numbers, the souls of my children are being lost and going to hell…"

On January 4, 1975, one of the nuns ran to the office of their chaplain, Father Yasuda, to tell him that the statue had begun to shed tears again. The weeping was extraordinarily lifelike. The church documented a total of 101 incidents of the statue shedding tears over the next six years, finally ending on September 15, 1981, the Feast of Our Lady of Sorrows. Professor Eiji Okuhara, a doctor and biochemist, analyzed three fluids coming from the statue: blood, tears, and perspiration. A colleague, Dr. Kaoru Sagisaka, was given the samples without any history or details and blindly made his conclusions:

> "The matter adhering to the gauze is human blood. The sweat and tears absorbed in the pieces of cotton are also of human origin."

Repeated independent analyses revealed human blood of type B, tears and perspiration both of type AB (11:192–210).

CUENCA, ECUADOR (1989)

From the beginning, Patricia had made a small altar or shrine in her bedroom where she had arranged pictures and statues along with blessed candles. On January 15, 1989, these pictures and statues began exuding oil and tears. Droplets of blood formed on the crucifix. Regarding this phenomena, Blessed Mary revealed to Patricia on February 1, 1989 that the oil was an oil of salvation for those with strong faith—and that the sick should be blessed with this oil.

> "The Father has allowed the grace of the holy oil, and my tears have been shed for the ingratitude of my little children due to the lack of unity, lack of love, and because each nation opens its doors to evil and to its own destruction. Love one another, children, and do not hurt the Father. I am the Guardian of the Faith."

Patricia's boyfriend, Andres, had been out of the country for much of this time and was not sure what he believed. Taking a dry picture of the Holy Shroud of Christ, he held it in his own hands while the group prayed. He was amazed to see oil coming from the eyes in the picture and droplets of liquid forming from around the crown of thorns. All of his doubts about the apparitions vanished with this stunning event.

A doctor took samples of the blood droplets and oil from the holy objects. The blood had red blood cells; the oil had human cells in it, but the type of oil could not be identified. In March, Blessed Mary explained that the tears were from her sadness because so many of her children were still so far away from God (23:31–33).

DAMASCUS, SYRIA (1982)

The traveling, weeping, pilgrim statue of the Virgin Mary

A small, three-inch tall icon of Mary with the Christ child in Myrna's bedroom began oozing enough oil to fill a saucer! Confused, family members were summoned—and they all began praying. Within one hour, four more dishes of oil came from the small image. Suddenly, Myrna could not hear any sounds around her—as if mysteriously blocked by some presence. Then a most beautiful voice said to her,

> "Mary (Myrna), do not be frightened. I am with you. Open the doors and do not deprive anyone from seeing me. Light a candle for me."

Then she could hear sounds around her again. The icon poured forth oil for the next four days. The clergy and civil authorities all investigated for any evidence of a fraud or trick. They could only conclude that oil was indeed coming from the picture. When they asked Myrna to pray in front of them, having washed her hands well, the oil would flow from her palms again. One day, a priest was kneeling near Myrna while she was praying, and he heard her say, "Father, I feel like the Virgin has entered into me!" Then he saw a "brilliant liquid" flowing abundantly from her palms. A bishop who was also present in the room noted that the oil had the scent of myron—or holy oil. Medical doctors and scientists gathered to decipher the origin of the healing oil that continued to exude from Myrna's hands when she prayed.

On June 18, 1990, the Roman Catholic archbishop of Damascus attested to being an eyewitness on several occasions to oil exuding from Myrna and her little icon. Myrna has also bore the stigmata on the Fridays preceding Easter. One video clearly shows the bloody outline of an unseen crown of thorns on her forehead. Her hands exhibit gaping wounds in each palm. She is seen in the video, writhing in pain, on her bed.

Although Myrna has no idea why she was chosen for these spiritual gifts, she treasures them and accepts her "assignment." It is not known if the oil ever stopped flowing from her palms, so she may be still offering the healing oil to this present day (2:249–256).

MONTICHIARI, ITALY (1947)

Third Apparition (October 22) - Our Lady again appeared to Pierina Gilli in the hospital chapel in the presence of many staff members, doctors, and religious from the town. *A statue of Mary came to life, and blood started dripping from the side of Christ.* Pierina took a purificator and wiped the drops of blood. Blessed Mary said,

> "I have placed myself as the Mediatrix between my Divine Son and mankind, especially for the soul consecrated to God. Tired of the continuous offenses, He already wants to dispense His justice....Live out of Love! For the last time, I come to

ask for the devotion already registered at other times. **My Divine Son wanted to leave traces of his blood** to witness how great is his love for the people from whom he is countered with serious offenses. Get the purificator and show it to those present. Here are the drops of the blood of the Lord!" (134:3)

UNEXPLAINED PHYSICAL IMAGES

MEXICO CITY, MEXICO (1531): "Our Lady of Guadalupe"

The miraculous image of "Our Lady of Guadalupe" on cactus cloth from 1531 (photo by author).

Juan Diego was shocked and humbled by the sudden appearances of the Virgin Mary. She wanted a church built on Tepyac Hill and asked him to request this from the local bishop. However, the bishop was skeptical and wanted "proof" that this was truly the Virgin Mary! Blessed Mary agreed to provide such proof to Juan Diego. She directed him to climb to the top of the barren Tepeyac Hill where he would find roses growing miraculously among the thistles and thorny brush in the winter. There appeared a lush abundance of every color of rose. He picked them and carried them to the Blessed Mother, and *she arranged them in his cloak*, which he then folded shut for his journey to the bishop's house.

> "My little son, this is the sign I am sending to the Bishop. Tell him that with this sign I request his greatest efforts to complete the church I desire in this place. Show these flowers to no one else but the Bishop. You are my trusted Ambassador. This time the Bishop will believe all that you tell him" (2:54).

This was the fourth and last time he would see her. The bishop was actually eager to see what miracle had been brought to him, but not even Juan Diego was prepared for what was about to happen. As he unfolded his cloak to dump the multicolored winter roses before the bishop, they were all stunned to see a beautiful image of the Virgin Mary imprinted on the rough cactus fiber of his cloak! The bishop fell to his knees in reverence and from that moment forth, all followers worshipped and adored this treasure.

Ordinarily, the cloth of Juan Diego's tilma or cloak should have deteriorated in twenty to thirty years. It is made from the maguey cactus plant and is something like burlap, rough and latticelike. The material is called *ayate* and is ill suited for use as a canvas for painting. It is actually made up of two pieces sewn together lengthwise and held together by a single cotton thread (35:16). An effort to make a replica of the cloth and image to test its true durability failed miserably—as it deteriorated badly within fifteen years. The original cloth and image will be nearly five hundred years old soon! And the image is as fresh as ever as it hangs near the altar in the great basilica of Mexico City today.

Miguel Cabrera, a famous Mexican artist, was commissioned along with six other artists to examine it in 1750. After a very careful examination in great detail, they concluded that it had been created in a "miraculous" fashion—*not by any human artist*! (35:16)

In 1754, Pope Benedict XIV wrote,

> "In it everything is miraculous: an Image emanating from flowers gathered on completely barren soil on which only prickly shrubs can grow; an Image entrusted to a fabric so thin that through it the nave and the people can be seen as easily as

through a trellis; an Image in no matter deteriorated, neither in her supreme loveliness, nor in its sparkling colors, by the niter or the neighboring lake, which however, corrodes silver, gold, and brass…God has not done likewise to any other nation" (72:47).

For the first 116 years, it was unprotected by glass. People freely kissed it, rubbed it, and touched objects to it. Afterwards, it went under glass. In 1753, it was removed from its glass protection for just two hours. But at least five hundred people filed by and touched the frail cloth with many objects like sharp-edged crosses, medals, swords, and rosaries—yet no harm came to it (35:17).

On November 14, 1922, a bomb was secretly planted in a bouquet of flowers that was placed on the altar—just beneath the divine image hanging above it. The bomb exploded with such force that it blew out windows in the old Basilica, shattered the marble altar, and twisted a large bronze crucifix. Yet, the image of Our Lady and the glass enclosing this sacred treasure were completely unharmed and safe—*despite its location right above the bomb* (72:48).

Father James Meehan and Dr. Charles Wahlig examined the sacred image in 1975. They reported that the image does not impregnate the threads of the cloth but lies on top—something like the emulsion of a photographic print. They state, "The picture defies human explanation. Its artistic source is outside human capabilities. It is a miracle" (35:18).

In 1979—448 years later—Dr. Philip Callahan, an infrared specialist and biophysicist, scientifically analyzed the Guadalupe image. He found the pigments to be authentic for that period in time but amazingly well preserved, whereas later-added embellishments were fading, cracking, and deteriorating while the original image appears to have never aged at all. There were no preliminary sketched lines underneath the painting as could be expected in a hoax. Careful examination with a magnifying glass revealed NO brush marks and no deterioration or cracks in the coloring material. His greatest discovery came with the enlarged photos of her eyes, *revealing the reflection of a man's image—that resembling the image of Juan Diego!* (11:51)

An esteemed ophthalmologist, Dr. Javier Torella-Bueno, noted that this image is located and distorted in the precise position that such a real reflection would have occurred on the curvature of an eyeball. Dr. Rafael Torija-Lavoignet adds,

> "It is impossible to attribute to chance, to a textile accident or the pictorial matter this extraordinary coincidence between the localization of the reflections in the Virgin's eyes and the most elaborate and up-to-date laws of optical physiology…" (72:58)

It was also discovered that all of the stars on her gown matched the exact constellations visible in the night sky of that day, December 12, 1531. However, it was a "mirror image" of the night sky; it was not the view from an earthly perspective but exactly reversed—as if from a heavenly perspective instead (71). Over the years, many healing miracles have been documented regarding those who came before her image. The image has also been observed to weep tears.

GUAITARA CANYON, COLOMBIA (1754)

In the previous chapter on Undeniable Miracles, we described the story of the mother, Maria, and her deaf-mute daughter, Rosa, who journeyed past a "haunted cave" on their six-mile walks through the Guaitara Canyon. One day, her daughter was immediately healed from her deaf-mute condition after seeing a "beautiful woman holding a child." Rosa often felt "summoned" to that cave—where her mother finally saw for herself the divine images of Jesus and His Mother playing with her daughter. When Rosa became very ill and died, Maria pleaded to and begged the Virgin for Jesus to bring her back to life—and her heartfelt prayers were miraculously answered.

Friends and neighbors who had seen the child without life were now overwhelmed with awe at this latest miracle. Early the next morning, everyone went to the cave—each one wanting to check the details for themselves. That was when the marvelous picture of Our Lady on the wall of the grotto was discovered. Maria could not recall ever noticing it until then. The Virgin's delicate and regal features are those of a Latin American, perhaps an Indian. Her eyes sparkle with a pure and friendly glow. She looks about fourteen years old. The Indians had no doubt: this was their Queen (3:85).

BE NOT AFRAID TO FOLLOW THE FOOTPRINTS FROM HEAVEN

Not a painting! Actual cave wall rock colors formed miraculously after two other miracles associated with the appearances of Blessed Mary and child Jesus in Guaitara Canyon, Colombia. Metallic crowns were added later.

The child Jesus is in Our Lady's arms. On the right side of Our Lady is Saint Francis; on the left side is Saint Dominic. St. Dominic is receiving a rosary from Our Lady; St. Francis is receiving the Franciscan cord from the Child Jesus. These two Orders, the Franciscans and the Dominicans, were the founding two Orders that first evangelized Colombia, South America.

The ensemble of colors in the picture gives an undeniable ambience of majesty. The burgundy of her dress is a warm, rich, red, embroidered with a golden flower pattern, giving the impression of the garment of a Queen. Her long hair flows freely in such a way that it appears to be a royal mantle. She has the royal countenance of a person who imposes respect with confident strength. In contrast, the Divine Infant is very amiable and turned toward the supplicant. One could say that He is distributing the gifts while she appears as a Queen. This image is a masterpiece reflecting both the majesty and the maternity of Our Lady.

Intricate detail of the miraculous image in the Guaitara Canyon cave in Colombia.

Tests done show how incredible this image actually is. Geologists from Germany bored core samples from several spots in the image. ***There is no paint, no dye, nor any other pigment on the surface of the rock.*** No brush strokes are visible despite meticulous inspections. **The colors are the colors of the rock itself.** Even more incredible, the rock is perfectly colored to a depth of several feet! The picture penetrates the rock miraculously. It is not painted, but mysteriously imprinted deeply into the rock. The colors are not applied in a surface layer of paint or other material but, instead, *penetrate the cave wall up to two feet deep*. Certainly, it has no natural geological cause. There is no known place in the world where nature has reproduced human faces with such perfection. These circumstances seem to indicate that it is an "akeropita" image; "akeropita" in Greek means "not made by human hands," i.e., **made by the angels**. This miraculous image has been nicely preserved as the backdrop for the altar in a breathtaking Gothic church that was constructed around it and extends out over the Guaitara Canyon on massive pillars (161).

The stunning basilica built on pillars in the Guaitara Canyon, extending outward from the cave wall with the miraculous image.

PHOTOGRAPHIC IMAGES

Anyone claiming to have a photo of the Virgin Mary would certainly be initially doubted, and such a photo would be placed under cautious examination and meticulous scrutiny. However, the following examples just may have passed those rigorous tests.

ZEITOUN, EGYPT (1968–1971)

In the early hours of April 13, Wagih Rizk Matta, a photographer, succeeded in photographing the appearance of the Blessed Mother for the first time—overcoming an inexplicable sensation of immobility which prevented the vast majority of people from operating their cameras. Having taken the pictures, he then became aware of being completely healed from an old injury to his arm! (Doctors confirmed his miraculous healing.) In two photos, the Blessed Virgin appears as a glowing figure, floating in front of one of the church towers with one of the luminous doves flying above. Another photo shows her standing on the roof of the church, hands folded in prayer with a glowing halo behind her head. Two young boys are looking up at her from the street. Closer examination of her image reveals a tall crown on her head and a rosary hanging in front of her. One photo shows the luminous doves flying in the formation of a cross. Other photos show images of Mary and Jesus in the sky just over the domes and also with a cloud of mysterious incense that appeared occasionally (59:21–22, 80).

Enlarged image of the Virgin Mary in 1968 on the roof of St. Mary's Church in Zeitoun, Egypt (computer enhancement by author).

What is significant about these photographs is that the photographers had at least one hundred thousand witnesses on each occasion who were observing exactly the same images that they were photographing. That rules out a photography hoax or any trick photography. Within a few weeks, the crowds reached an estimated 250,000 people every night! These differing religions had all come together, praying together, singing together in praise to Blessed Mary. She would acknowledge the massive crowds below, waving at them, holding out an olive branch—which would generate an ecstatic cheer from the masses. Those who saw her features the clearest report a youthful, healthy looking, beautiful lady with beautiful eyes, hair, and hands. At the time of her visits, most people became transfixed in wonder, amazement, or a state of ecstasy to the degree that all actions became impossible. Arms and fingers could not move to adjust cameras or take pictures (59:80–81, 88).

Authorities wanted to rule out any pranks, hoaxes, or clever light shows. Police searched an area up to fifteen miles out from the church, extensively, for any kind of device that might create such an effect. At one point, they initiated a power blackout in the area so that nothing electrical could be possibly utilized to create these images. And the radiant Virgin Mary, her flying luminous doves, and the eerie heavenly lights continued to materialize just as brilliantly as ever during the power outage—much to the delight of thousands in the dark (59:25).

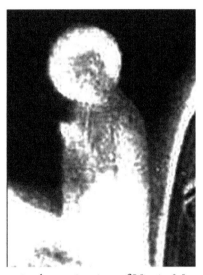

Computerized examination of Virgin Mary image on roof of Zeitoun church. Note tips of a crown on her head (photographic analysis by author).

Laser light shows were not in existence yet—and certainly could not have produced moving, three-dimensional images. Holography was in its infancy and could only produce a one-foot by one-foot, stationary, two-tone image at the distance of a half mile at the cost of $500,000. Mary was life-size and even larger at other times, moving from one side of the church to the other, and in many different colors—reddish, yellowish, golden, blue, and white. **Even careful scrutiny and computer enhancement of the photos taken indicate no trick photography whatsoever** (59:104). This was *before* digital cameras, digital manipulations, cell phone cameras, and Photoshop were ever invented. In fact, color-print film had just come out about four years earlier. Therefore, these visits of the Virgin Mary were authenticated by the Church on May 5, 1968—just one month after she began appearing.

GARABANDAL, SPAIN (1961–1965)

Another series of photos actually came from a movie film that was shot at the moment of the anticipated and predicted miracle in Garabandal. On various occasions, St. Michael the Archangel had appeared and told the girls to prepare for Communion by praying the "I Confess to God." Then he would administer Communion to them. **Villagers would observe them stick their tongues out to receive the Host but could never see the Host (because it was invisible).** The girls never realized that the Host was actually invisible because they could feel it and swallow it quite naturally. After Communion, St. Michael taught them to give thanks to God through the prayer of St. Ignatius Loyola. On June 22, 1962, he told Conchita **that he would give her a visible Host** during Communion—which was when she first learned that the Host had NOT been visible. The Virgin Mary told Conchita that the date for this public miracle would be July 18, 1962. Word of this spread like fire, and there was a joyous celebration and much anticipation on that day. However, as the day wore on, many people became disappointed and went home. Finally, at 1:40 a.m., Conchita left her home in ecstasy, and the lingering crowd eagerly accompanied her. Several eyewitnesses reported seeing this miracle (34:45–49):

BE NOT AFRAID TO FOLLOW THE FOOTPRINTS FROM HEAVEN

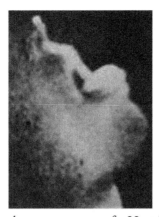

The miraculous appearance of a Host becoming visible on Conchita's tongue in Garabandal, Spain- caught by the movie camera of a witness.

Benjamin Gomez: "I was so close…inches from her face…I looked in her mouth…nothing…I turned my head just for an instant. When I looked back, the Host was on her tongue. It was white—out of this world…like snow, a snowflake upon which the sun's rays were striking…"

Pepe Diez: "I was scarcely 18 inches away from her face…She kept her tongue out like that for about a minute. As I stood there—my eyes riveted to her, something incredible happened! Without moving my eyes for a fraction of a second, suddenly a neat, precise, and well-formed Host appeared miraculously on Conchita's tongue…Her tongue was out and bare, and then all of a sudden the Host was there! I did not see how it came. It was instantaneous!…It was just there!"

Alejandro Damians: "There was a great deal of confusion— crowding, pushing, people trying to see…I crouched over, and Conchita was on her knees. I took the (movie) camera out of the bag and looked through the lens without making any adjustments…I was sure I could see her head and shot. I caught the last seconds of the miracle (on movie film). I would not exchange the bliss which I felt in those moments for anything in this world. It was a joy, deep and intense, which I cannot explain."

This was the evidence that so many people were looking for! Because church law states that one can partake in Communion only one time per day, St. Michael had waited until the early hours of the next morning because Conchita had already been to Mass earlier on the anticipated day with all of its celebrations. But *the pictures served as proof* for those who had given up and left earlier that evening. Multiple witnesses and movie film footage documented this predicted miracle (33).

SANTA MARIA, CALIFORNIA (1990)

In May 1990, author Janice Connell was invited to visit Santa Maria, California, where a housewife was allegedly receiving messages from the Virgin Mary. The Blessed Mother desired that a huge cross be erected on a hill overlooking the town. Driving out to that hill, she was amazed to find as many as twenty thousand people—mostly of Spanish descent—assembled on the hill. They were all dressed in their Sunday best clothing—the men in suits, the women in beautiful attire as if attending a wedding, and the children exquisitely dressed in white clothing, dresses, white shoes, and white veils. They were praying the Rosary and singing hymns. It was very hot with no room to sit as everyone was standing on the hill. There was an air of expectation and a spirit of joy in the air.

Suddenly, people began to exclaim, "Look at the sun!" It was spinning and pulsating. Great rays of light of every possible color streaked from the center of the sun across the sky like lightning. Some people wept; others tried to film the phenomenon; others just gazed in wonder. A little girl about seven years old, standing near Janice, suddenly fell to her knees and stretched her arms toward the sun, crying, "Madre de Dios!" (Mother of God). Two little boys, probably two and three years old, also fell to their knees. Great tears of joy fell to the ground from their little cheeks as they, too, cried out, "Madre de Dios!" Their little arms reached up to a figure only they could see.

Some people claiming to see her were trying to take Polaroid pictures. Walking up to one woman, Janice asked to see her developing Polaroid photograph. In about three minutes, the photo was fully developed, and there was a clear white image of the traditional figure of the Blessed Virgin! (2:313–314)

ARTIFACTS GIVEN TO VISIONARIES

ZARAGOZA, SPAIN (40 AD)

On January 2, while the apostle James was deep in prayer by the banks of the Ebro, the Mother of God appeared to him and gave him a small statue of her image holding Jesus and also a six-foot column of jasper. She instructed him to build a church in her honor.

"This place is to be my house, and this image and column shall be the title and altar of the temple that you shall build. The faith of the people will become as strong as this pillar."

The pillar of jasper and small statue given to St. James by Blessed Mary in 40 A.D., still protected today by the people of Zaragoza, Spain.

About a year after the apparition, James arranged to build a small chapel in Mary's honor—the first church ever dedicated to the honor of the Virgin Mary. After James returned to Jerusalem, he was executed by Herod Agrippa in about 44 AD—the first apostle to be martyred for his faith. Several of his disciples took his body and returned it for final burial in Spain (1:70).

Although this first chapel was eventually destroyed along with various other Christian shrines, the statue and pillar stayed intact under the protection of the people of Zaragoza, Spain. Today, a Baroque-style church, completed in 1686, exists on this site **and still houses the precious items given to James by the Virgin Mary in 40 AD**. During the Spanish Civil War of 1936–1939, three bombs were dropped on the church, but *none of them exploded*. Two of them are on display in the basilica today (160).

TLAXCALA, MEXICO (1541)

Our Lady had appeared to Juan Bernardino to show him where to obtain healing waters for his sick family. Wanting to express his gratitude, he turned to the Lady, who then entrusted him with a message for the Franciscans at the Monastery of San Lorenzo where Juan was employed.

> "Tell the religious for me that in this place (among the ocote trees) they will find my image. It will not only manifest my perfections, but through it I shall generously bestow favors and kindness. When they find the image, they are to place it in the chapel of San Lorenzo."

When the Lady disappeared among the trees, Juan hurried to the village with his precious water. The next day, Juan returned to the monastery and told the friars of his experience. After questioning him during the day, they decided that his story had merit and planned on visiting the place with Juan at night so as to avoid the curious. Before reaching the place, they noticed a glow in the distance; and when they arrived, the grove of ocote trees was on fire. The largest tree in the grove—and ONLY this one—was burning along its entire length. Since nothing could be done, they left but planned on returning after Holy Mass the next morning.

With the addition of some of the parishioners, they set out and found a puzzling situation. The fire had destroyed only the lower branches of the surrounding trees. The tallest tree, which had burned its entire length, was indeed blackened. Why the dry summer heat had not destroyed the other trees in a similar manner remained a mystery. One of the friars had fortunately brought an ax with him and was instructed by the abbot to chop down the trunk of the large tree. A Mexican writer of that time left this report:

> "A new marvel met their eyes. Within the trunk of the fallen tree was visible the image (statue) of the Holy Mother of God, representing the mystery of her Immaculate Conception—which can be seen today in the temple lovingly erected later by her children…" (3:39)

The actual statue of the Virgin Mary retrieved from inside of the burned Ocotlan tree near Tlaxcala, Mexico in 1541.

Thus, the apparitions of Juan Bernardino were validated in the presence of many witnesses. With the singing of hymns, the statue was brought to the chapel in a grand procession. The abbot removed the present statue of San Lorenzo and replaced it with the miraculous image of the Mother of God. Today, the original fifty-eight-inch tall statue of Our Lady is now found in a magnificent niche or Camarin above and behind the altar in the Basilica of the Virgin of

Ocotlan. From the earliest days, the statue was called Nuestra Senora de Ocatlatia—which means Our Lady of the Burning Ocote (tree). Now, it is simply called Our Lady of Ocotlan—Ocotlan being the Nahuatl word for "place of the pine tree." The beautiful statue of Our Lady is always dressed in costly vestments. She wears a splendid golden crown which is surrounded by a halo of stars. The crown represents Our Lady's coronation by the pope in the year 1906 (3:40).

MEDJUGORJE, BOSNIA-HERZEGOVINA (1981–present)

Just two months **before** the first apparition, Franjo, the youngest brother of Vicka Ivankovic (one of the visionaries) was preparing to take the family's little tractor and trailer out to collect wood at 6:00 a.m. one morning. As he was gathering tools to place in the trailer, he discovered two sets of rosary beads lying in the back of the trailer. One had a beautifully carved crucifix in ivory, depicting the scenes of all fourteen Stations of the Cross. Franjo took them to his mother and grandmother, joking with them that this must be a sign from Mary, suggesting that "you need to pray more!" Nobody in the village claimed the beads or had ever seen them before. But when the apparitions began just two months later—and his sister Vicka became one of the visionaries, the mother asked Vicka to ask Blessed Mary where the Rosary beads had come from. And the Virgin Mary replied,

> **"They were a special gift from me to your family..."** (48:21–22)

Later, the Virgin indicated that "things will turn golden" as evidence of her presence in Medjugorje. Numerous rosaries have "turned golden" as pilgrims pray there. One army medic, Donald Hartley, witnessed as many as twenty rosary chains change color in his presence, capturing one on videotape in the process of transition from silver to gold (83).

In the early months of the apparitions, **Blessed Mary presented a strange parchment** to Mirjana that contained all ten secrets

written in an unknown language. The parchment was neither cloth nor paper, but of a material "unknown" on earth. It could be balled and wrinkled but not torn. Mirjana was to select a priest, Father Petar Ljubicic, who is to be given the parchment ten days before the first secret is to be revealed. He will only be able to read the first one. After seven days of fasting and prayer and three days before the event, he *must* announce it to the world in whatever means he chooses (45:207).

INCORRUPT BODIES

This is one phenomenon that science has not even attempted to explain. Normally, when one dies, the body begins to decay within days. Two processes called autolysis and putrefaction are typical types of decay. With autolysis, there is a process of self-digestion where the body's enzymes begin to go into a post-death meltdown. Putrefaction is when bacteria is released into the body from the intestinal tract and begin the process of melting the body down. Within just thirty-six hours, the neck, abdomen, shoulders, and head begin to turn a discolored green. Bloating happens next, distorting the face, and then the skin blisters, hair falls out, and fingernails sink back into the fingers. The skin develops a "marbled" appearance before finally turning a black-green color as fluids drain from the corpse (120).

The incorrupt body of St. Bernadette
Soubirous today, deceased since 1879.

The incorrupt body of St. Vincent De Paul today, deceased since 1660.

A number of visionaries and Catholic Saints **DO NOT** go through this process when they die. There are at least three hundred "incorrupt bodies" that have been documented. A number of them have been photographed. **That's right—they DO NOT DECAY**. How is that even possible? Science cannot even begin to explain this phenomenon. Most are discovered by accident—sometimes many years later—but no efforts had ever been made to try to preserve these bodies. Many look exactly like they did on the day that they died. The skin and hair are often intact, down to the fingernails and eyelashes. The muscles are often soft and flexible and can be moved with little effort. Not only do they not decay, but their skin appears fresh—even moist—and may have a sweet fragrance like roses. The lingering sweet fragrance could be transferred to other objects that were touched to them. In some cases, oil could be found weeping from the body, often containing special healing properties. In a few cases, fresh blood has been known to flow from incorruptible many years after their death (75) (69:35). Here are a few examples:

QUITO, ECUADOR (1634, 1635)

During the eighth apparition of the Blessed Mother, the Child Jesus made this comment:

> "I know…that the preservation of the incorrupt bodies of some of My servants is beyond comprehension to human beings…" (56:73)

Visionary Mother Mariana of Jesus Torres died on January 16, 1635, after receiving the Holy Eucharist and the Sacraments of the Church. Three hundred years later in 1906, when the church was being remodeled, her tomb was opened. They were stunned to find her body perfectly intact with no decay after three hundred years! This divinely incorrupt body is now kept in a small chapel under glass in the lower level of the cloistered convent (3:57).

PARIS, FRANCE (1876)

Visionary Catherine Laboure quietly died on December 31, 1876. On May 28, 1933, she was beatified in St. Peter's Basilica in Rome. As part of the Canonization process, the body of the saint had to be identified. In a solemn procession, her coffin was removed from the vault under the convent's chapel and brought to the motherhouse at Rue du Bac. In the presence of the archbishop of Paris, civil officials, and various doctors, the coffin was opened. They were stunned at what they witnessed. The body of Catherine Laboure had been in this coffin for fifty-seven years—*and yet, she had not decayed in the slightest and appears more youthful than at the time of death*. It was as if she were still alive and simply sleeping peacefully. The medical examiner studying her exhumed remains concluded,

> "The body is in a perfect state of preservation, and its joints are still supple."

Today, some 140 years later, she is still perfectly preserved by supernatural means as a "totally incorrupt" body—and can be viewed, enclosed by glass, in the little chapel at 140 Rue du Bac in Paris, France (54:20).

LOURDES, FRANCE (1879)

During Holy Week of 1879, Bernadette's pains and ailments worsened. "I wouldn't have thought it took so much suffering to die." On Easter Wednesday, April 16, she stretched out her arms like a cross and said, "My God!...Holy Mary, Mother of God, pray for me, a poor sinner." Then she died at the age of thirty-five due to her poor health. Yet, her body lies under glass *without any decomposition over 137 years later* in the chapel of the Convent of the Sisters of Charity in Nevers! She appears to be sleeping peacefully. Her facial features remain clean with healthy skin tones—and even her fingernails appear perfect. She was beatified on June 14, 1925 and canonized on December 8, 1933 in Rome—*on the Feast of the Immaculate Conception*! (42:130)

The incorrupt body of St. Padre Pio today in Italy, deceased since 1968.

FATIMA, PORTUGAL (1920)

Visionary Jacinta died at 10:30 p.m., alone, in her hospital bed on February 20, 1920. A nun swore that tears of dried blood were on her face, suggesting that she shared something of her Savior's agony. Doctors were amazed that after three days, her body smelled "as sweet as a bouquet of roses." This was a surprising and drastic change in fragrance from the horrible, repulsive stench of her illness. She still looked alive in her coffin with cheeks and lips of a beautiful pink color. A number of witnesses testified to the extraordinary sweet odor emanating from her body. It was clearly the fragrance of flowers! (29:265–268)

On September 12, 1935, her body was transferred to a memorial where people could honor her life. When the coffin was opened for positive identification, her parents, medics, clerics, and a few others were stunned that her body had not yet decayed in fifteen years! During her transfer to the final resting place in the great basilica in 1951, her coffin was opened again—and her body was *still incorrupt with very little decay after thirty-one years* (29:271–274).

There is absolutely no logical or natural reason for these bodies to not decompose. Nothing special has been done to preserve them. Most are found by accident years later. They are simply miracles—preserved by the will of God. Believe it or not, they continue to exist today without any medical or scientific explanation. However, in a religious sense, they were all passionately devoted to God as visionaries with the Virgin Mary or those approved as saints because they were inspirational, dedicated followers of God.

Science has carefully investigated other religious miracles as well—which will be the "footprints from heaven" analyzed in the next chapter…as further "proof!"

CHAPTER 13

SCIENCE VALIDATES THE SUPERNATURAL

Skeptics and disbelievers demand undeniable proof of anything which is claimed to be "supernatural." Yet, even when they are provided with convincing evidence, they may still deny the facts or doubt the possibility of something extraordinary because it would challenge their whole way of thinking. "Be not afraid," I say to them, "to examine these amazing truths which *do challenge* our beliefs." After all, science should be the investigation of the unexplained—not the explanation of the uninvestigated.

Officials were afraid to look through Galileo's telescope for fear of seeing something unexplainable—perhaps demonic—and punished him for tempting them. Esteemed scientists a few centuries ago swore that it was *impossible* for rocks to fall from the sky. Yet, a few decades later, it was determined that meteors do impact the Earth from outer space. Just eleven years prior to the historic Apollo moon landing, a top scientist stated that there was no way that man could ever travel to the moon and be able to return as well. Yet, it was achieved six times within four years (1969–1972) with a total of twelve men walking on the lunar surface. So remarkable were those achievements that younger generations who were not alive in those days are now proposing that the moon trips were cleverly faked! This demonstrates how amazing yet genuine events can be totally disbelieved—**despite the facts.**

This chapter will provide incredible facts that may challenge your present beliefs. But it has the exciting potential to awaken your spirit and strengthen your faith in new ways. Here are more excerpts from scientific research into the supernatural realm of religious events.

CUENCA, ECUADOR (1990)

Over 115,000 people gathered for the final apparition of the Virgin Mary on March 3, 1990. Once inside the designated, sacred "Garden" area, Patricia's body arched backward as she looked up to the sky and went into the usual ecstasy. She stared at a single spot in the sky, became unaware of anyone around her, and was unaffected by the sudden drenching downpour of rain. She spoke Mary's message without any conscious recollection afterwards. Because there were television cameras and radio microphones present on this last apparition, the message was broadcast over the entire area as it was being given by Our Lady. People began to weep. Broadcasts repeated the messages over and over for several days throughout the country of Ecuador. The Holy Virgin also gave her instructions for building a sanctuary high in the mountains at El Cajas—complete with dimensions and descriptive details.

Patricia also asked her why the statues and pictures on the altar in her bedroom were weeping again. Our Lady replied,

> "My tears are poured out for the evil that exists in the world, through atheism and materialism, through adoring false gods, through ignoring the Word of God and the Sacraments. I have not come in order that they recognize me without recognizing My Son Jesus in their heart. I am the Mother of all who believe and who do not believe in me. The pain from having told you what is coming to the world fills my heart with sadness. I also was a Mother, and I felt the pain of saying goodbye to My Son. In the same way, today, I feel the pain of saying goodbye to you, because I am your mother. You should go out into the world, evangelizing, with the Word of God in one hand and my messages in the other."

A geological team had been performing experiments before, during, and after these apparitions. They had two fascinating discoveries: (1) the temperature was clearly measured as warmer *only within* the sacred, roped-off, "Garden" area of El Cajas, (2) a compass needle shifted ninety degrees during the apparition, pointing in the direction of where the Virgin was said to have appeared. Sister Isabel Bettwy replicated this experiment with her own compass, watching it suddenly shift from its normal position during the apparition to wildly rotating 360 degrees one direction and then the other without any obvious cause—other than the Virgin's invisible presence at that moment (23:61–64, 100–101).

KIBEHO, RWANDA, AFRICA (1981–1989)

Three of the visionaries took mystical journeys with the Virgin Mary. Before Alphonsine went on her journey, Mary instructed her to inform the school director "not to bury her—even if she appears dead." The stunned director knew by now to take Alphonsine seriously. She told them that she would be away with the Virgin for the whole weekend. Failing to show for the Friday evening meal, a nun went to check on her on Saturday morning. She was stunned to find Alphonsine lying unresponsive on her bed—unable to be awakened or even budged an inch. The director grabbed the school nurse and summoned Abbot Augustin Misago, a leading member of the Commission of Enquiry. Soon, there were many concerned officials, priests, and others in attendance as Alphonsine truly appeared dead. Medical experts concluded that she was still alive, but that her pulse rate was impossibly slow and her blood pressure too low with breathing almost nonexistent—a shallow breath just once a minute. As many as six men tried with all their might to roll her over, separate her clasped hands, or lift her from the bed, but without any success! Eighteen hours later, Alphonsine awoke, livelier than ever -- with sparkling eyes, relaxed muscles, and a glowing face. (Details of her journey will be described in another chapter) She seemed perfectly fine now! (39:131–135)

Another of the visionaries, Anathalie, also had a mystical journey which began on the podium in front of the crowds after a five-hour apparition. She collapsed into the same "frozen-limbs" state of near death with the same officials and doctors vigilant and testing her. Seven hours later, she awoke and was carried to her bed where she did not speak for two days. Then she spoke the details of her mystical journey with Mary (it will be described later) (39:136).

Vestine's trip was largely a test of faith—as Jesus asked her to die for Him on Good Friday, have her soul go to heaven, but be resurrected and returned on Sunday—like he had. She trusted that He would keep His promise, so she begged others to not bury her if she appeared dead. Investigators, journalists, doctors, officials, and members of the Commission of Enquiry tensely awaited Easter weekend, wondering how she was going to die.

At 3:00 p.m. on Friday, Vestine was seized with a sudden pain and fell back on her bed, closed her eyes and "died." Doctors were dumbfounded—her blood pressure had dropped to zero; no heartbeat or pulse could be detected. For hours, they pondered what to do, wanting to trust that what she had said would happen—but staring at cold science that indicated she was truly dead. Vestine would take a deep breath *every hour or two*, so everybody sat tight and waited for the next forty hours. Just after dawn on Easter Sunday, Vestine woke up, rubbed her eyes, stretched her arms, yawned, and exclaimed cheerfully, "Good morning, everyone! Happy Easter!" Doctors checked her and found her body to be back to complete and normal functioning again. However, a cross had formed on the center of her forehead—which doctors said was some kind of mysterious change in the pigmentation of her skin—not caused by injury, bruising, or burning (details of her journey will come later) (39:138 –143).

SCIENCE TESTS THE VISIONARIES

MEDJUGORJE: A team of physicians from the University of Montpellier conducted the most complete scientific study of an alleged supernatural event in the history of Catholicism when they traveled to Medjugorje in Bosnia-Herzegovina in 1984. The leader of the French doctors was Dr. Henri Joyeux, an internationally renowned cancer researcher. Six months earlier, he had already been videotaping the six visionaries with an electronics engineer to investigate whether their synchronized movements were in any fashion orchestrated. Close scrutiny of those films greatly impressed this medical researcher, leading to the call for his whole team of experts.

The most eminent of these specialists was Dr. Francois Rouquerol, an ear, nose, and throat specialist. He was able to demonstrate a clear "disconnection of the auditory pathways during the ecstasy" of each visionary. He proved, most convincingly, that no visionary reacted to the blaring of ninety decibels of engine noise into their ears *during their apparitions.* Sensations travelled in a normal manner to the brain of the Medjugorje seers, but the findings of evoked auditory potential tests and screening tests showed that the cerebral cortex did not perceive the transmission of the auditory and visual neuronal stimuli received from the surrounding environment. This indicates a disconnection located somewhere in the cortex, and it can be thought of as functional dualism, comparable to a motorcar being functionally divided into two by pressing the clutch.

Dr. Rouquerol also reported that his instruments indicated their voices had become completely silent during their supernatural experience, but their tongues, lips, and facial muscles had continued to function exactly as when speech is audible. The larynx or voicebox of each visionary had somehow ceased to operate—*an inexplicable condition unknown to medical science*, according to Dr. Rouquerol. With an impedanceometer, the medical team carefully studied the visionaries' uncommon voice activity, distinguished by unmistakable axiomatic articulation without phonation. Their tests revealed a number of exciting findings. The instrument's needle showed extensive movements of larynx muscles while the seers recited the Rosary before the apparitions, but as soon as the apparitional episode began and the voices became inaudible, the larynx stopped moving, and the needle was still. During the conversation with the apparition, the seers' lips moved without phonation. As the voices returned in the middle of the apparition to recite the Our Father, which, according to the visionaries, had been initiated by the Virgin, the needle moved again. Articulation without phonation occurred once more during the final phase of the apparitional experience, as the visionaries voice was replaced by silence, although their lips were moving. As the seers began to speak, at the end of the apparition, the movements of the larynx resumed, showing that the vocal extinction experienced at the beginning of the apparitional experience is linked to the absence of movement of the larynx, and although the lips were moving quite normally, the act of exhaling did not vibrate the vocal cords. The visionaries themselves have admitted to hearing their own voices of verbal communication as normal during the apparitional experience and are surprised that others cannot hear them. This observation itself rules out manipulation and psychogenic aphonia.

The team's opthalmologist, Dr. Jacques Philippot, confirmed a profound inhibition of eyelid reflexes to brilliant dazzling lights in all visionaries. He also discovered that the gaze of all six children during their experience remained fixed on exactly the same fixed point in space several feet above their heads. Dr. Philipott's tests demonstrated that Ivanka and Marija's eyelid movements during the apparitional experience were two times slower than before and after. Even when he blocked their vision with an opaque screen, none of their eyes reacted or shifted at all. What he considered most impressive was that he had measured a simultaneity of eyeball movement among the visionaries of less than one-fifth of a second using electrooculogram readings at both the beginning *and* the end of their shared apparition. This is so far beyond the capacity of normal human functioning that no form of collusion or manipulation could account for it. After the apparition, however, eye and muscular movements resumed at exactly the same time. Electrooculographic recording demonstrated that their eyes converged at the same point. During the apparitional experience, blinking reflex was absent but was normal before and after.

Heart specialist, Dr. Bernard Hoarau reported that electrocardiogram, blood pressure, and heart rhythm examinations of the visionaries during their ecstasies "allow us to exclude totally the existence of dreaming, sleep, or epilepsy." Neurologist Dr. Jean Cadhilac added that his tests "formally eliminate all clinical signs comparable to those observed during individual or collective hallucinations, hysteria, neurosis, or pathological ecstasy."

Dr. Joyeux was most impressed by the electroencephalogram tests that had measured activity in eight distinct areas of the brains of these six children. All states of consciousness known to neuroscience involve some mix ratio of alpha and beta impulses. Dr. Joyeux found these ratios to be normal in all the children prior to their apparition experiences. Going into a sleep or trance state would have increased beta cycles while decreasing alpha cycles. But *exactly the opposite actually occurred*: their beta impulses stopped completely! They were considered to be "hyper-awake" in a state of *pure meditation*—an extremely rare condition only observed in a few Buddhist monks while deeply in prayer. Dr. Joyeux and his team concludes,

"The ecstasies are not pathological, nor is there any element of deceit. No scientific discipline seems able to describe these phenomena. The apparitions at Medjugorje cannot be explained scientifically. In one word, these young people are healthy, and there is no sign of epilepsy, nor is it a sleep, dream, or trance state. It is neither a case of pathological hallucination nor hallucination in the hearing or sight facilities...It cannot be a cataleptic state, for during the ecstasy the facial muscles are operating in a normal way...It is more like a state of deep, active prayer, in which they are partially disconnected from the physical world, in a state of contemplation and sane *encounter with a person whom they alone can see, hear, and touch.* We cannot reach the transmitter, but we can ascertain that the receivers are in a state of sane and good working order" (8:201–204).

The assembly of seventeen renowned natural scientists, doctors, psychiatrists and theologians in their research came to a twelve-point conclusion on January 14, 1986 in Paina near Milan (131a).

1. *On the basis of the psychological tests, for all and each of the visionaries, it is possible with certainty to exclude fraud and deception.*
2. *On the basis of the medical examinations, tests and clinical observations, etc., for all and each of the visionaries, it is possible to exclude pathological hallucinations.*
3. *On the basis of the results of previous researches for all and each of the visionaries, it is possible to exclude a purely natural interpretation of these manifestations.*

4. *On the basis of information and observations that can be documented, for all and each of the visionaries, it is possible to exclude that these manifestations are of the preternatural order, i.e., under demonic influence.*
5. *On the basis of information and observations that can be documented, there is a correspondence between these manifestations and those that are usually described in mystical theology.*
6. *On the basis of information and observations that can be documented, it is possible to speak of spiritual advances and advances in the theological and moral virtues of the visionaries, from the beginning of these manifestations until today.*
7. *On the basis of information and observations that can be documented, it is possible to exclude teaching or behavior of the visionaries that would be in clear contradiction to Christian faith and morals.*
8. *On the basis of information or observations that can be documented, it is possible to speak of good spiritual fruits in people drawn into the supernatural activity of these manifestations and in people favorable to them.*
9. *After more than four years, the tendencies and different movements that have been generated through Medjugorje, in consequence of these manifestations, influence the people of God in the Church in complete harmony with Christian doctrine and morals.*
10. *After more than four years, it is possible to speak of permanent and objective spiritual fruits of movements generated through Medjugorje.*
11. *It is possible to affirm that all good and spiritual undertakings of the Church, which are in complete harmony with the authentic magisterium of the Church, find support in the events in Medjugorje.*
12. *Accordingly, one can conclude that after a deeper examination of the protagonists, facts, and their effects, not only in the local framework, but also in regard to the responsive chords of the Church in general, it is well for the Church to recognize the*

supernatural origin and, thereby, the purpose of the events in Medjugorje.

Shortly after Dr. Joyeux left Medjugorje in 1985, the Italians dispatched their own all-star team of medical specialists from Milan's Mangiagalli Clinic. Dr. Michael Sabatini, a psychopharmacologist specializing in pain research, applied his algometer to the six visionaries. This device measures the intensity of pain created by applying pressure to particularly sensitive areas of the body. The results showed that the six visionaries entered a state of "complete analgesis" during their apparition ecstasies—that *they could feel no pain*. This proved, beyond any doubt, according to Dr. Sabatini, that the visionaries "do not fake and do not deceive." The head of their medical team, Dr. Luigi Frigero, added that the visionaries "were not simply awake, but hyper-awake during their ecstasies. This cannot be explained naturally and thus can be only preternatural or supernatural" (8:204).

Dr. Enzo Gabrici, a neuropsychiatrist, spent four days examining Ivan, Jakov, Marija, and Vicka. In his report, he excluded any possibility of "hallucinatory phenomena, epilepsy, or posthypnotic suggestion." He saw no indication of neurosis or psychosis. Unlike spirit mediums, the visionaries retain "perfect consciousness of their identity." He also noted,

> "The apparition does not tire Vicka as is the case with hysterical trances; on the contrary, she feels more invigorated. Jakov would run outside to play soccer immediately after his apparition; such normal behavior simply is not an aspect of hysterical or hallucinatory visions" (8:162–163).

Dr. Lucia Capello, a neurologist, was not only impressed but deeply shaken by the "three synchronizations" in the visionaries' behavior. First, the visionaries dropped to their knees and their voices became inaudible in the same instant—without even a split second of separation. Second, without any observable awareness of one another, their voices again became audible at exactly the same moment—on the third word of the Our Father prayer. Finally, the head and eyes of each visionary were raised simultaneously in the same instant at the end of the apparition (when the Virgin ascended), as all five uttered the word "Ode."("There she goes.") They justify this movement by explaining that "the Virgin Mary disappears upward." Their eye movements reflect those of a person looking at a real moving object—which is different from those of a person looking at an imaginary moving object. The eyeballs of the visionaries are converging toward an external point indicating true objectivity and do not follow the established eye movement patterns associated with remembering or visualizing. He concludes that there is *no natural explanation* that could account for such perfect simultaneity (8:163).

Heart surgeon Dr. Mario Botta's electrocardiogram of Ivan's heart rate revealed that he maintained a perfect rhythm without any fluctuations before, during, and after the apparition. Given the extraordinary level of activity indicated by Ivan's brain waves at the same time, Dr. Botta concluded that the visionary's experience "transcends normal physiology" (8:163).

Dott Santini, the Italian investigator, used an estesiometer to confirm the absence of corneal reflex; the hundred-watt bulb used during his tests failed to make the seers blink. The most aggressive tests performed on the visionaries were conducted by Dr. M. Frederica Magatti, who tried shouting at, jabbing, and pinching them during an apparition—without obtaining any observable reactions. After noting that the eyes of each child had become "hugely dilated," Dr. Magatti used a film projector with a one thousand-watt bulb to blast their pupils with light. None of them reacted; not only did their pupils remain unusually dilated, but the eyelids of each child continued to blink at a normal rate. There was no change in alpha rhythm in the brain to the one thousand-watt light. This is *scientifically inexplicable and never seen before.* FOR THE PUPIL TO RESPOND, THE BRAIN MUST REGISTER THE LIGHT—BUT NO BRAIN WAVE CHANGE TOOK PLACE. Additionally, such intense stimulation normally causes a significant cortical response, but none occurred during the apparition period (131a). Dr. Magatti asserted that the Medjugorje visionaries "were demonstrating the most complete suspension of consciousness of their relationship with the exterior world" that she had ever observed (8:163). The medical observations and synchronisms suggest that the Medjugorje visionaries are responding to an outside power and not to internal stimuli. The dual modes of perception also suggest that there is a "nonphysical agent in front of the visionaries."

Dr. Giorgio Sanguinetti, a prominent psychiatrist, makes the following report:

> "The 'visionaries' sit down on little stools, and recite the Rosary in a thoughtful, recollected manner. Suddenly, at exactly the same time, which is amazing, the young people stand up and line up in front of one of the walls of the room. All of them gaze upward at the same time, without ever looking at each other, and they seem to stare intensely at something that is outside the room and very far away. They keep their hands joined in prayer, and some of them move their lips, but their voice cannot be heard. After approximately one minute of time, on the occasion I was there, and again, amazingly all together, they give signs of a fleeting bodily tremor, and all withdraw from the place where they were standing. The expression on their faces becomes like ours. Behaving quite normally and with no haste—but deliberately, they go toward a table, do not speak to each other and each taking a pen and a notebook wherein their names are written, they sit down, and again without talking to each other, write down quickly, without pausing, the message which was given to them during the 'vision.' The length of the text differs from one to another. When they have finished, they leave the notebook and the pen, and with a quick handshake they greet us and leave the room, each going about his or her own business. I know that this description of the 'vision' has already been given by other witnesses; however, I considered it useful to describe it after I had sketched pathological mystical behavior so that the reader can compare these and take account of the psychic normality of the young 'visionaries.' Something unusual, extra-ordinary exists but it seems to be strictly limited to the short period of the 'vision.' However, nothing authorizes us to say that the visionaries, because of this experience, manifest any personality disorders. They seem to be in a world beyond the perception of others and, for what concerns them, to have left our sphere of perception" (131a).

Fresh medical teams from Poland, Austria, England, Italy, and America continued to replicate and validate these scientific findings. Father Rene Laurentin, who closely watched over these efforts, concluded:

> "The best explanation is that the visionaries are in living, personal, and normal contact with a person from another world" (8:204).

Further testing on June 25, 2005 by Dr. Philippe Loron, a colleague of Dr. Henri Joyeux, indicated that the visionaries were *not* transcending into an altered state, but rather that they transcend into a **deeper state of reality**. The apparition and any views of "eternal life" are seen by them as *more real* than what they would experience in everyday life. This depth of reality which they perceive is superior to any known reality of life on earth. Afterwards, they return to a lesser state of reality or "ordinary level" that the rest of us in the human race are accustomed to. Through science, we now can say, empirically, that what they are seeing is *not of this world*. We cannot confirm *what* they are seeing—only that they are able to do so with how their brains are functioning. With three visionaries as subjects on this day, electroencephalograms recorded alpha rhythms on the whole brain during ecstasies. These examinations capture on the surface of the scalp minimal electricity produced by the activity of brain cells. The alpha rhythm (between eight and thirteen Hertz) is a normal rhythm of wakefulness, mainly of rest. It occurs essentially in the posterior regions of the brain when the eyes are closed. Similar results are usually obtained when listening to soothing music or when one is in a state of contemplation, meditation or prayer, especially with eyes closed. It also corresponds to the intermediate state between wakefulness and the first stage of sleep: when one relaxes with the light off but is not yet asleep. *Therefore, in Medjugorje, the results are remarkable since the alpha rhythm occurs preferentially at the moment of ecstasy with a tendency to spread to anterior regions of the brain, while the eyes remain open and oriented toward the apparition.* **Of course, science can't demonstrate that these are apparitions of the Virgin Mary, but it can support the** *absence of* **deception** (131a).

GARABANDAL: Dr. Celestino Ortiz Perez of Santander, a pediatrician specializing in child psychology, examined the four girls when they were in a state of ecstasy during the apparitions. He concluded,

> "In this state of ecstasy they gave proof that they are beyond the explanation of medical science and all natural laws. They showed no reaction to pain, pin pricks, et cetera. Once out of their trances, however, they reacted immediately. From a pediatric and psychiatric point of view, the four little girls have always been and continue to be normal. The trances in which we have observed these young girls do not fit into the framework of any psychic or any psychological pathology presently known. Our conceit falls apart when we are faced with this kind of dilemma which God bestows on us in order to point out our own medical limitations" (68:249).

Dr. Ricardo Puncernai, a neuropsychiatrist and director of Neurological Services at the university clinic in Barcelona has also examined the visionaries during their ecstasies. He concluded,

> "Even though we try to explain only part of these extraordinary phenomena, the truth is that we do not find any natural scientific explanation which could explain the whole affair" (68:250).

EUCHARISTIC MIRACLES

Christians generally practice the ritual of Communion in various ways depending upon their particular church. About four times per year, Protestants often partake in the eating of bread and grape juice as a symbolic ritual of eating Christ's body and blood as initiated at the Last Supper. Catholics state that when a priest consecrates the bread and wine, it is no longer a symbolic practice but rather the true blood and body of Christ that is consumed. This is because the Catholic faith believes that the priests have been divinely granted the gift of transforming the wine and bread into true blood and true body in a consecration process at every Mass. Yet, many Catholics probably *still see this as only symbolic.*

BE NOT AFRAID TO FOLLOW THE FOOTPRINTS FROM HEAVEN

Has the priest *actually* facilitated and invited through God a genuine transformation? Again, many Catholics would tend to doubt an actual transformation has occurred because it still looks and tastes like bread and wine. Yet, God has a way of showing us the truth when we doubt and lose faith. The conservative Catholic Church has documented and received Vatican approval for at least 126 historic examples of these miraculous transformations: bread actually becomes human tissue and can bleed; wine truly becomes blood. Here are a few examples—along with careful scientific examination.

LANCIANO, ITALY (750 AD)

The ring of supernatural flesh that appeared around the Host at the moment of consecration during Mass in Lanciano, Italy in the 8th century.

The large pellets of blood that miraculously formed at the moment of consecration during Mass in Lanciano, Italy. There is still fresh blood within them 1,200 years later!

A Eucharistic miracle occurred during the eighth century in Lanciano, Italy. At that time, the priest was having personal difficulty *truly believing* that the bread and wine could be changed into the actual body and blood of Jesus Christ. During a Mass, as the priest was lifting the Host at the moment of consecration, the round, white wafer was instantly surrounded by a ring of visible flesh. At the same moment, the consecrated wine in the chalice on the altar formed into five jellylike pellets of human blood. The astonished priest and congregation at once begged God to forgive them for their weak faith.

The miraculous flesh and blood were carefully enshrined—but without preservatives or an airtight container. They should have deteriorated over the centuries, but only the white wafer disintegrated, leaving the ring of flesh behind. The five pellets of blood had hardened on the outside but were still fluid on the inside! The five unequal portions of blood weigh the same altogether *as each pellet weighs separately* (15.85 grams) (74:122–124).

In 1971, Professor Edoardo Linoli, an expert in anatomy and pathological histology, received permission to examine the substances in Italy. The blood was determined to be **human blood, type AB**—both in the blood and flesh samples. The blood was shown to contain the same minerals, chemicals, and proteins as *fresh human blood* taken the same day—even though this blood was 1,250 years old! Professor Linoli discovered that this tissue was actually from the *muscle of the heart*. The tissue is neither dead nor mummified but considered to *still be living tissue* because the commission determined that it responded rapidly to all the clinical reactions distinctive of living beings. These miraculous samples remain in the same condition as one would expect to find flesh and blood *taken the same day from a living human being* (78:74–77).

BETANIA, VENEZUELA (1992)

A great miracle occurred on December 8, 1992, during a midnight Mass on the vigil of the feast of the Immaculate Conception. Several thousand people saw a bright light over the Host (Communion wafer). Father Otty Aristizabal, the chaplain of Betania, broke the

Host in half, placing a small piece in the chalice. But the remaining piece of the Host began to bleed. Miraculously, the blood on this wafer-thin Host did not seep through to the other side. Examination revealed it to be **human blood of AB type**. This miracle has been preserved in the Convent of Los Teques by the Recollect Augustinian Sisters (68:204).

AGOO, PHILIPPINES (1992)

December 13, 1992: A Eucharistic miracle was witnessed by Father Cortez and nuns at the convent. A statue of Mary, carved according to Judiel's description of her, was brought to the convent and shed tears to the amazement of the nuns and Father Cortez. When Father Cortez placed a Host on Judiel's tongue, witnesses reported that they saw it "turn into flesh and blood." When Judiel went back to his pew after Communion, he felt liquid dripping from his mouth. Then the Host swelled in his mouth, and the person next to him alerted Father Cortez, who urged him to spit it out. The Communion Host had transformed into pulsating flesh and blood. Father Cortez wanted to preserve this Eucharistic miracle, but Our Lady intervened and said that Judiel must swallow it. As a concession, however, the nuns were allowed to press and imprint the bloody Host onto their white handkerchiefs. Each nun did receive an imprint on each handkerchief. Then Judiel put the Host back on his tongue—at which time it slowly turned back into a white Host—just before he swallowed it, according to witnesses. When Father Cortez asked him to open his mouth afterwards, there was no trace now of blood, flesh, or the Host (98:6).

NAJU, KOREA (1985–2010)

Pope John Paul II witnesses a Eucharistic miracle on the tongue of Korea's Julia Kim while she was a guest at his private Mass in the Vatican.

The Blessed Virgin Mary began weeping through her statue owned by Julia Kim in Naju, Korea, on June 30, 1985. Two and a half weeks later, on July 18, Julia received the first message from Our Lady. On October 19, 1986, the statue's clear tears turned into bloody tears. Julia has continued receiving messages and suffering pains. Other miracles have also continued—fragrant oil from Our Lady's statue, the heavenly fragrance of roses, the healing of incurable illnesses, and at least thirteen Eucharistic miracles.

A SUMMARY OF THE SUPERNATURAL SIGNS IN NAJU

For a total of seven hundred days between June 30, 1985 and January 14, 1992, both regular and bloody tears flowed from the statue of the Virgin Mary. Samples of the bloody tears were tested in a medical laboratory and were **found to be human blood**.

For seven hundred consecutive days from November 24, 1992 to October 23, 1994, fragrant oil exuded from the statue of Blessed Mary.

Twelve times between May 1988 and October 1996, the bread in the Holy Eucharist changed into visible flesh and blood on Julia's tongue with many clear photographs documenting the transformations in front of witnesses. The miracle on October 31, 1995 was **witnessed by Pope John Paul II** during a Mass in the pope's private chapel in the Vatican. Bishop Roman Danylak from Toronto, Canada, and Bishop Dominic Su of Sibu, Malaysia, also witnessed the miracles in Naju and Sibu, respectively, and wrote their testimonies expressing their belief in the authenticity of these miracles.

Seven times between November 24, 1994 and August 27, 1997, the Sacred Host *descended from above out of thin air* to the chapel in Naju. The first two miracles were witnessed by the Apostolic Pro-Nuncio in Korea during his visit to Naju.

On July 1, 1995, seven Sacred Hosts descended from above. They were consumed by two priests and five lay people, including Julia Kim, according to the local Archbishop's instruction. The external appearance of the Sacred Host that Julia received changed into visible flesh and blood on her tongue. A sample of this blood was tested in the medical laboratory at Seoul National University and was **found to be human blood**.

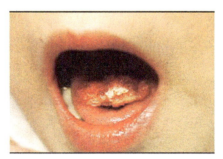

One of thirteen occasions when the Host in Julia Kim's mouth miraculously transformed into living flesh and blood during Communion.

The descent of the Eucharist bread out of the air from above on June 12, 1997 was witnessed by Bishop Paul Kim of the Cheju Diocese in Korea. The Host again descended on August 27, 1997 during Fr. Raymond Spies' visit to Naju. An intense fragrance of roses is continuing (as of May 1998) from the spot on the floor in the chapel where the Host landed.

Bleeding occurred on Julia's two hands and two feet during her sufferings. Doctors examined Julia's stigmata and stated that her wounds and bleeding had **no medical explanation** (135).

Eyewitness Testimonies

Archbishop Giovanni Bulaitis, the Apostolic Nuncio to Korea (1991–1997), and Fr. Chang celebrated Mass in the archbishop's chapel on February 28, 2010.

"Suddenly, it became noisy in the front of the chapel. When I opened my eyes, I saw Archbishop Bulaitis and a volunteer worker standing before Julia and intensely looking at something. I stood up and went to the front. Julia was keeping her mouth open. When I looked—without knowing what was going on—I saw a lump of flesh instead of the white Eucharist Host on Julia's tongue. The white wafer that Julia received in her mouth just a few minutes ago changed into a lump of red flesh covered with many tiny blood vessels. Some parts of the Eucharist were still white, and scarlet-color blood was exuding from the Host. As I was observing the Host, which had been white a moment ago, changing into visible flesh and blood, I became totally shaken up and had difficulty controlling myself. I was really stunned."

"*What's going on before my eyes? How can such a mysterious phenomenon occur now?* An indescribable shudder penetrated deeply into my whole body. I immediately knelt on the floor. Then, with an immense feeling of awe and shock that totally conquered me before this unexpected, astonishing, and mysterious miracle, I burst into tears and cried. I prostrated very low on the floor as a very little person before the Lord. Others in the chapel also cried."

"The time was about 10:50 a.m. on February 28, 2010. I later learned that the Blessed Mother told Julia that the miracle this time was the **thirty-third** and last Eucharistic miracle for Naju. It was also the **thirteenth** Eucharistic miracle that occurred on Julia's tongue. I returned to my pew, still trembling with intense emotion and weeping, and was about to do some meditation on the Lord's Real Presence in the Eucharist, but someone screamed loudly, and I went to Julia again to see what was happening. I saw on Julia's tongue the Host in the form of flesh and blood swelling to a thickness of five to seven centimeters like a dough mixed with yeast and in the shape of a heart. The Host also continued moving like a living organ. I could still see some white spots on the Host. Scarlet-color blood continued flowing from the rear top of the Host.

I had heard about the Eucharistic miracles before and seen them in photographs and DVDs, but I never imagined that I was going to be an eyewitness of such an amazing and great miracle. That was why I was so shocked and was feeling an enormous emotion. From the deepest bottom of my heart, I thought, *"This Eucharistic miracle tells us how great the Lord's love for human beings is…"* (anonymous witness from Germany) (135)

Naju, Korea: September 22, 1995

"As we continued to distribute Holy Communion to the others present, we heard the sudden sobbing of one of the women assisting at Mass. The Sacred Host received by Julia Kim was changed to living flesh and blood. Fr. Joseph Finn, who had remained at the altar during the Communion of the faithful, was observing Julia. He noted that at the moment he turned to observe Julia, he saw the white edge of the Host disappearing and changing into the substance of living flesh.

Fr. Chang and I returned to Julia. The Host had changed to dark red, living flesh and blood was flowing from it. After Mass, Julia shared with us that she experienced the Divine Flesh as a thick consistency and a copious flowing of blood, more so than on the occasion of previous miracles of the changing of the Host into bleeding flesh. We remained in silence and prayer; all present had the opportunity of viewing and venerating the miraculous Host. After some moments, I asked Julia to swallow and consume the Host. And, after the Mass, Julia explained that the Host had become large and fleshy; and that she consumed it with some difficulty. In testimony of this, I append my signature, together with the signatures of all the witnesses present" (135). (Roman Danylak, titular bishop of Nyssa, apostolic administrator, eparchy of Toronto, Canada)

What is God trying to tell us? That His Son's body and blood are alive for us today?

Or would you like some more scientific investigation before allowing your faith to grow?

BLOOD ANALYSIS AND DNA TESTING

Ron Tesoriero, a lawyer and author, teamed up with Mike Willesee, an investigative journalist, to investigate supernatural religious claims. They usually expect to expose a fraud—and often did so. So, when Ron invited Mike to join him in South America to investigate a bleeding plaster statue of Jesus in Bolivia, Mike fully expected the plaster statue to be a clever hoax. After all, how could a plaster statue of Jesus weep real tears and bleed real blood?

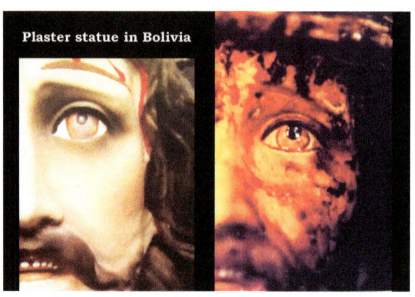

Chilling transformation of a plaster statue of Jesus into one with bleeding scabs, weeping tears, and tortured tissue. Note watering of eye and enlarged pupil (thanks to the wonderful research by Ron Tesoreiro and Mike Willesee).

Arriving in Cochabamba, Bolivia, they began to carefully examine the ten-inch, plaster, head-and-shoulders bust of Christ, obviously in the pain of his crucifixion. An investigative TV station had a camera continuously filming the statue for hours—as well as anybody who might go near it. The camera caught a tear forming in the eye and finally rolling down his cheek. Ron touched his finger to the plaster eye and felt the eye begin to water and moisten his finger. Then he watched as another tear formed and rolled down the statue's cheek. The face appeared to be bloody from "wounds," so samples of the "blood" were obtained. While the "blood" samples were being analyzed, it was important to fully examine the statue for hidden mechanisms that might secretly produce these fluids. The statue was placed in an X-ray scanning machine which scanned the object in consecutive layers. It revealed a hollow statue with nothing unusual hidden within. There was absolutely no evidence of a hoax (73) (78:179–186).

One blood sample was taken to Gen Test Labs in the United States where Dr. Anne Montgomery subjected the sample to high-quality genetics testing. She determined that it was ***definitely human blood***. However, she could not get the sample to yield a genetic profile or DNA code. Puzzled by this, more efforts by this lab still **could not produce any DNA profile** (73) (78:186–187). More samples were taken to a distinguished lab in Australia. They determined that it was definitely human blood—but strangely ***missing a genetic profile***! They stated that if the blood had been placed there by somebody, that person's DNA would definitely have been present. More samples were taken to the Gemelli Hospital in Rome, where Dr. Angelo Fiori, a highly respected professor of legal medicine, examined them carefully—not knowing the source nor the history of the blood samples. His conclusion was:

> "It is human blood, but I **could not obtain a genetic code**. I have *no explanation* for this unusual phenomenon" (73) (78:188).

The genetic profile in DNA is handed down from generation to generation, becoming an accumulation of all the possible genetics from previous generations. This is why dark-headed parents could give birth to a blonde-headed baby—resembling the blonde hair of a great-grandmother rather than the dark hair of either parent. To have *no genetic profile* means that there was *nobody before you* to give you any. You would have to be the first source of life or, logically, the Creator. According to the Bible, Jesus was "consubstantial" with God or "of the same substance as God."

Science then pursued analyzing several scabs of dried blood from this plaster statue. Ron Tesoriero and Mike Willesee continued to carefully oversee this scientific investigation. They watched as a scab was carefully peeled from the plaster face of Jesus which would then be analyzed by two different pathologists. Neither of these pathology experts would be given any information about where the scabs had come from or what they would be likely to find. What they said was *even a bigger surprise* for the researchers! Dr. Robert Lawrence, a forensic pathologist from the United States, concluded (78:189):

> "This scab was pulled from the face of a person, because it has epidermal cells mixed in. A process of healing was occurring as white blood cells are present that help the scab form" (73).

When informed that this sample had been peeled from the face of a plaster statue, Dr. Lawrence adamantly claimed, "No! It's ***not*** from any statue!"

Dr. Richard Haskell, a histopathologist and cytopathologist, was next to examine the scabs in "blind fashion" without any history or source information. He concluded:

> "This looks to me like a blood sample that has traumatized tissue mixed with it. This person's tissue was subjected to a severe beating, traumatizing the skin—which is intermixed in this blood sample" (73) (78:189–190).

So, now, we have a plaster statue in Bolivia that cries tears, bleeds human blood, and develops scabs from a healing process. Furthermore, there is no DNA genetic profile and the tissues show evidence that the person was subjected to trauma as in torture or beatings. Science states that it has *no explanation* for these findings coming from a plaster statue.

Theologians feel that they may have an answer—coming from the very man that this statue represents. On Palm Sunday, as Jesus was praised as a king by jubilant crowds, the Pharisees asked him to silence his disciples. Jesus replied, "If these will keep silent, the stones themselves will cry out." Does this mean that if religion or a belief in God is suppressed or rebuked, inanimate objects could actually cry out, weep, or bleed?

Microscopic examination also revealed the tip of a thorn embedded in that tissue sample from a scab on the statue's forehead—the type that grows in an arid region and most likely used in the crown of thorns that Christ had worn (73).

Ron Tesoreiro and Mike Willesee began looking for other blood samples possibly related to Jesus for scientific comparison. There have been a number of Eucharistic or Communion "miracles" documented over the centuries in which the symbolic bread and wine actually turned into flesh and blood. These stories sound too fantastic and improbable until one realizes that evidence of these miraculous transformations has been carefully preserved.

Ron and Mike heard a story, coming from Buenos Aires, Argentina, about a Communion Host that had been left over—and the priest could not just throw it away. The practice is to place it in a bowl of water, let it dissolve, and then store it reverently in the locked tabernacle. However, within days, a bloodlike substance had begun to ooze from the Host. Over the next several weeks, that bloody substance had tripled in quantity!

Cardinal Jorge M. Bergoglio (now Pope Francis) gave permission for scientific analysis in 1999. It was determined to be human blood, **but the human DNA would not yield a genetic profile**. Because flesh was discovered in the sample, this tissue was passed on to another expert, Dr. Frederick Zugibe, a forensic pathologist and heart specialist. Without being given any details or source information, his "blind" microscopic examination revealed the following details (78:48–52):

"I can tell you exactly what this is. This flesh is part of the muscle of the heart. It's the muscle that gives the heart its beat and the body its life. I can see white blood cells infiltrated through this tissue, which tells me two things. **This heart *was* alive at the moment this sample was taken**, and the white blood cells are addressing an injury. So, this heart has suffered. This is the sort of thing that I see in people who have been beaten severely about the chest" (73).

Once again, we have human blood coming from an inanimate object with no genetic profile. Once again, we have tissue and white blood cells that indicate the person was beaten severely. But now we know that this is heart tissue—yet from a *recently living heart*!

In 1971, Professor Edoardo Linoli, an expert in anatomy and pathological histology, received permission to examine the blood and tissue samples from the Eucharistic miracle in Lanciano, Italy. The blood was determined to be human blood, type AB—both in the blood and flesh samples. The blood was shown to contain the same minerals, chemicals, and proteins as *fresh human blood*—even though this blood was 1,250 years old! Professor Linoli discovered that this tissue was from the *same muscle of the heart* that Dr. Zugibe had just described in the tissue sample from Argentina (70:6) (73).

A fourth opportunity for analysis arose recently with a Eucharistic miracle that occurred in Sokolka, Poland on October 12, 2008. A young assistant priest, Fr. Jacek Ingielewicz, accidentally dropped a consecrated Host in the Church of St. Anthony. He did what he was trained to do and placed it in a special liturgical vessel called a vasculum, adding some water, and then locking it in the tabernacle. Fr. Stanislaw Gniedziejko, the parish priest, noted it in the tabernacle the same day and asked the sacristan, Sister Julia, to empty the vasculum into a glass bowl and lock it in the safe in the sacristy behind the main altar. Seven days later, on October 19, 2008, Fr. Stanislaw asked Sister Julia to check the Host to see if it had dissolved yet. But it had remained whole with an apparent bloodstain visible upon it now. The priest was stunned by its appearance and requested Archbishop Edward Ozorowski and Chancellor Fr. Andrew Kakareko to investigate. The stained Host was removed from the water and laid on a linen cloth before being locked back in the tabernacle again (78:62–63).

The archbishop appointed a special commission to investigate the unusual transformation. Two highly respected pathomorphologists from the University of Bialystok were formally requested on January 5, 2009 to conduct an independent analysis of the material. Both were specialists in histopathology dynamics for over thirty years with international recognition. Professor Sobianic-Lotowska started with a centimeter square-size sample and reported her findings (78:63):

> "What is most important is that the material analyzed consists entirely of cardiac tissue. This sample is cardiac muscle—just **before** death. It is in agony caused by great stress. This is proved by the presentation of a very strong phenomenon of segmentation or damage to myocardial fibres at the site of the intercalated discs, which does not occur after death. Such changes can be observed only in living tissues. They show evidence of rapid spasms of the heart muscle in the period *just before* death" (78:64).

> "Noteworthy is the surprising absence of autolysis, the process whereby a cell is destroyed by the action of its own enzymes. This occurs in injured or dying tissue due to the cessation of active processes in the cell. The fact that this process is absent astonishes me. It is my opinion that, according to the current state of knowledge in biology, *we cannot explain this phenomenon scientifically*" (78:65).

The other scientist, Professor Sulkowski, adds another startling revelation:

> "What is even more difficult to comprehend is that the tissue which appeared in the Host is closely bound to it—penetrating the base on which it appeared. If someone intended to tamper with the sample, it would be impossible to bind the two pieces of matter (heart tissue and Host) in such a dissoluble way. This extraordinary phenomenon of inter-absorption of the heart muscle with the communion Host, observed under the

microscope, and also by an electron microscope, proves to me that there could not be any human interference with the sample" (78:65).

What they witnessed under the sophisticated electron microscope was the inextricable interweaving of human tissue with the material components of the Communion Host. Professor Sobaniac-Lotowska adds another amazing conclusion:

> "The heart was alive, just before death. The sample analyzed was not from a dead person. **The person was alive** (78:66). No bacteria known to science can actually produce matter with the characteristics of heart-muscle tissue, and this is what we have found in the Host. If someone doesn't want to believe it, even if he sees it, he will close his eyes" (78:71).

TIXTLA, MEXICO (2006)

On October 21, 2006, a reddish substance began oozing from a consecrated Host during Mass in Tixtla in the Diocese of Chilpancingo-Chilapa. Bishop Alejo Zavala Castro convened a Theological Commission of Investigation and asked Dr. Ricardo Castanon Gomez to lead the scientific research, which was conducted between 2009 and 2012. Research conclusions were presented at an International Symposium held in that diocese:

1. The reddish substance was determined to be human blood with hemoglobin and DNA of human origin. Yet, *no genetic profile could be extracted* from the DNA.
2. Two studies conducted by eminent forensic experts with different methodologies have determined that the substance *originates from the interior*, excluding the hypothesis that someone could have placed it on the exterior surface. Blood flowed from the interior to the exterior as the same occurs with a wound.
3. The blood type is AB, matching the samples from Lanciano and the Shroud of Turin.

4. A microscopic analysis of magnification and penetration reveals that the blood nearest the surface has been coagulated since 2006 whereas the innermost layers still reveal the presence of fresh blood as of February 2010.
5. They also found intact white blood cells, red blood cells, and active macrophages that engulf lipids. The tissue appears lacerated with recovery mechanisms—exactly as occurs in living tissue.
6. A further histopathological analysis determined the presence of protein structures in a state of deterioration, suggesting mesenchymal cells characterized by an elevated biophysiological dynamism.
7. The immunohistochemical studies reveal that the tissue found corresponds to the *muscle of the heart* (myocardium). This heart tissue was *alive*—which normally could not last more than forty-eight hours. But the tissue was not examined until three months had passed—and yet, it was still living heart muscle tissue!

Bishop Alejo Castro and his commission finally concluded on October 12, 2013 that there was neither fraud nor any natural explanation. "I declare the case as a Divine Sign…" (166)

2006 Tixtla, Mexico miracle: Host bleeds
from inside toward outer layers.

Science cannot explain these findings. However, religion offers the only explanation thus far: "The Sacred **Heart** of Jesus is in the Eucharist." Evolution cannot explain living tissue and fresh blood coming into inanimate objects. But Catholic Faith believes that a priest can invoke God's intervention to bring life into lifeless objects, changing bread and wine into actual body tissue and fresh blood. **Science CAN verify now that these miraculous changes have truly occurred.** Therefore, science has validated Faith. Yet, science does not offer a clue as to WHY or HOW this can happen! This also goes a long way toward giving credibility to the Creation Theory—*that life CAN be divinely started by God with an inanimate object and not necessarily required by a process of evolution.*

THE SHROUD OF TURIN

This very fine linen is allegedly the burial cloth that was wrapped around the dead body of Jesus Christ. It has been studied intensely by many scientists since 1978. There has been much controversy and many misunderstandings. So why is this artifact so important? First of all, it would validate the biblical account of Jesus being scourged, tortured, beaten, and finally crucified—giving much credibility to the biblical story with physical evidence. Secondly, it also would provide physical evidence toward validating a supernatural event—the resurrection of his body and how he mysteriously disappeared from his tomb. It strengthens the faith for many people when we actually have physical evidence to confirm the details of such biblical stories.

Luke 23:50–53 describes the body of Jesus being wrapped in a fine linen shroud from the wealthy Joseph of Arimathea—who had also donated a wonderful tomb for the body. This exquisite "dining table cloth" measures 14.3 inches long by 3.7 inches wide—or exactly four cubits by one cubit in the ancient method of measurement for that time period. It was considered a table cloth because of its dimensions and the drip patterns found on one side. Jewish custom had people recline at the table on one side as they were to be served from the other side (as pictured in the *Last Supper* painting). Textile experts established that its distinct "triple herringbone weave" is consistent with fine, first century weaving (77:10). Some researchers even theorize that since the drip patterns of sauce or wine had not been cleaned from it yet, that, perhaps, this was the dining cloth from the Last Supper. In any case, it was definitely one of the finest and most expensive linens of its day (76).

Researchers reveal that the man's image on the cloth indicates that he was five foot eleven tall, about 175 lbs., and approximately thirty to thirty-five years old. Due to the publicized carbon-14 dating test performed in 1988, many began to believe instead that this was some kind of medieval artistic creation—since the test suggested that the shroud was no older than 1290–1360 AD. However, that carbon-dating analysis failed to pass peer review of fellow scientists and was never published in any scientific journals due to serious flaws in the testing procedure (the results were actually published, instead, in *Nature Magazine*). Here are the reasons that scientists listed for questioning, challenging, and rejecting this carbon-14 testing (76):

1. Proper sampling of the material was to have three postage-stamp-size pieces removed from three different areas of the shroud. This protocol was violated as all three pieces were taken from a single site—a site that was later found to be a rewoven and repaired section of the shroud not typical of the rest (76).
2. On January 20, 2005, a paper by Ray Rogers, published in "Thermochimicaacta," a highly respected, peer-reviewed, scientific journal concluded: "The combined evidence from chemical kinetics, analytical chemistry, cotton content, and pyrolysis/mass spectrometry proves that the material from the radiocarbon testing area of the shroud is significantly different from that of the main cloth. The radiocarbon sample was thus not part of the original cloth and is invalid for determining the age of the shroud" (77:22).
3. In August 2008, Robert Villarreal and a team of eight researchers from Los Alamos National Laboratory analyzed Roger's samples and corroborated all of Roger's conclusions (77:23).

4. The shroud survived three fires over the centuries. The most intense fire in 1532 reached 920 degrees centigrade and melted the silver casket that contained the shroud. The melting silver burned holes in the linen. Since intense heat could affect the results of a carbon-dating process, Russian scientists set out to determine how much it could throw off test results. Simulating the heat intensity from that 1532 fire, the Russians determined that carbon-dating tests could be in error by as much as 700 to 1,300 years!
5. Studies examining the burial linens of mummies found a strange anomaly. Despite being the same age as the mummy, carbon-dating suggested that the linens were anywhere from three hundred to six hundred years *younger*.
6. Microorganisms, bacteria, and fungi found on the shroud could also throw off the carbon testing results by as much as three hundred years.
7. Because the image appears to be oxidized or "burned into" the fibers, this, too, would affect the linen and subsequent carbon-dating tests (76).

It is important to understand those serious flaws and potential contaminations for any carbon-dating test. **That was the only scientific test in over thirty years that cast any doubt upon the shroud's authenticity.** Sadly, it seems to be the most publicized because it suggests a hoax and gave skeptics and atheists the "evidence" they desired. However, the above facts are certainly more than enough reasons to discard the infamous 1988 carbon-dating tests—and thus eliminate the only known challenge presently to the shroud's authenticity.

On May 28, 1898, Secondo Pia photographed the shroud and was stunned to see a positive, three-dimensional image on the negative plate in his darkroom. Until the technology of photography had reached this level, nobody knew that this was a negative image. In the 1960s, Leo Vala, a professional London photographer, was also impressed by the three-dimensional, negative image:

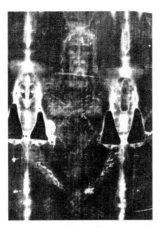

Negative image of the famous Shroud of Turin that science has yet to explain.

"I have been involved in the invention of many complicated visual processes, and I can tell you that nobody could have faked that image. Nobody could do it today with all the technology we have. It's a perfect negative. It has a photographic quality that is extremely precise" (78:198).

In the late 1970s, an electronics engineer, Peter Schumacher, developed a sophisticated topographical device for NASA's space program called the Interpretation Systems VP-8 Image Analyzer. It translated a monochromatic tonal scale of the photographed surfaces of planets into layers of vertical relief. In other words, it could examine a flat photograph of a three-dimensional object and convert it into a three-dimensional image. When a regular photograph is analyzed, it "collapses and distorts." But when Dr. John Jackson analyzed the shroud image with the VP-8 device, it was consistently and uniquely three dimensional:

"The results are unlike anything I have processed through the VP-8 Analyzer before or since. Only the Shroud of Turin has ever produced these results. One must consider how and why an artist would embed three-dimensional information in the grey shading of an image when no means of viewing this property of the image would be available for at least 650 years. Would an artist produce this work before the device to show the results was even invented? No method, no style, and no artistic skills are known to exist that can produce images that will induce the same photogrammatic results as the shroud does…" (78:199)

Other details validate this image as truly being the image of Jesus Christ: (76)

1. Max Frey, a Swiss criminologist, found fifty-eight species of pollens on the shroud. Forty-five of them could have come from the Jerusalem area; eighteen of them could ONLY come from the Holy Land and from flowers blooming in early April—around Passover/Easter!
2. Scientists have found no pigments, paints, dyes, stains, or brush marks to suggest an artist's creation. The image color would not dissolve with the twenty-five solvents tested.
3. Ultraviolet light tests reveal blood serum halos for each scourge mark and the wound in his side from when a spear lanced his side after death. These "invisible" details are further proof that a hoax is unlikely; what artist would add invisible attributes?
4. A visible wound in his side between the ribs correlates with the scripture's reporting of a Roman guard's lancing his dead body to verify death. The bloodstains from this wound confirm that the wound was inflicted postmortem. Present also are stains from a clear bodily fluid such as pericardial fluid or fluid from the pleural sac or pleural cavity. These findings indicate that the man was stabbed near his heart after he died.
5. Common to crucifixions are the breaking of legs to hasten death. Jesus reportedly died too quickly for that to happen, and the shroud image indeed shows that no leg bones had been broken.
6. From the angles of the bloodstains, the forensic experts have determined that this blood flowed while the man was upright with his arms angled like the hands of a clock at ten and two—as in a crucifixion on a cross.

7. Fifteen puncture wounds encircling the top of the head correlate with the crown of thorns reportedly jammed onto the head of Jesus Christ. Thorns in that region were most likely from two to four inches long. No other crucified men were known to have worn a crown of thorns.
8. The visible shoulder abrasions are consistent with injuries sustained while carrying the crosspiece of the cross. The tip of his nose as well as his knees were scraped badly. These injuries would be consistent with falling face first while carrying the cross.
9. The soldiers had struck blows on Jesus's face; the shroud reflects blows to the forehead, brow, right cheek (swollen), right upper lip, jaw, and nose.
10. We believe that the reported scourging of Jesus was horrible. Jewish law only allows thirty-nine lashes, but it was the Romans who did the torture. Approximately 120 scourge marks are present on the shroud's image of his body, indicating that two Romans were striking him, one on each side, according to the directionality of the lash marks.
11. The shroud depicts clear nail holes in his wrists and one through his feet. The wrist holes would have severed the median nerve, causing the thumbs to draw inward. The shroud depicts the thumbs as drawn in, hidden behind the other fingers.
12. The wound in his side is between the fifth and sixth ribs and measured on the shroud as one and a half inches long and three-fourth of an inch wide—the exact size and dimensions of a Roman lance. There was no swelling—which is consistent with a postmortem wound.
13. Dr. Frederick T. Zugibe noted that travertine aragonite dust taken from the bloody foot area of the shroud was a very high and significant match to Jerusalem dirt samples when using a scanning ion microprobe of high resolution (77:18).
14. As there are no signs of decomposition or decay with the shroud image, the body was still in a state of rigor mortis—

which lasts only for about forty-eight hours. All bodies would be expected to be still wrapped at that time, but the body of Jesus departed in some fashion on Sunday morning about forty hours after his death. The image depicts his feet still angled downward as if still nailed to the cross. He "left" the shroud before his body could begin decaying.

15. The 3-D imaging analysis also revealed other images on the shroud. Hundreds of flower petals and leaves are evident around his body—and match the blooming flowers of springtime in the Holy Land. Coins had been placed on his eyes. Through computer analysis, polarized image overlays of ancient coins found an exact match—the Lepton, produced around 29 AD under Tiberius Caesar and Pontius Pilate!

Were the bloodstains *real* human blood or added later by artists? Pathologists and scientists all agree with the following summary:

> "Microchemical, fluorescence, and spectrographic tests reveal that **the stains are human blood, type AB.** They resulted from real bleeding from real wounds of a real body that came into contact with the linen. The distinctive forensic signature of clotting (red corpuscles around the edge of the clot and a clear yellowish halo of serum) is clearly present. Some of the blood flow was venous and some was arterial. Most of the blood flowed while the man was alive, and it remained on his body. Some, however, clearly oozed from a dead body" (78:200) (77).

All of these scientific and medical facts present overwhelming evidence to suggest that this is indeed the burial cloth of Jesus Christ. But the Shroud of Turin also documents a supernatural event that confirms the foundation of the Christian faith—the Resurrection of the Son of God. If the Bible story is valid, then the Shroud MUST provide clues to this supernatural event. Here are what the scientists discovered (76):

1. They cannot determine, despite all of their scientific studies, exactly how the image was created on the linen cloth.

Efforts to recreate such an image with chemistry and physics on old linen cloths have all failed. **Science cannot explain how the image exists.**

2. It is not burned as there is no evidence of scorch marks—as if the linen was subjected to a heated, three-dimensional statue. The material does not fluoresce under ultraviolet illumination.
3. Scientists have determined that the top layer of linen fibrils have been oxidized to a depth of only six microns—half the thickness of a human hair. They theorize that a brief blast of energy like radiation could cause such a reaction. When the atomic bomb was dropped on Hiroshima, the shadows of the vaporized residents were imprinted on the side of any building left standing—as if a dark image on negative film had been created from this burst of radiation.
4. In the 1980s, a chemist at Michigan University, Dr. Giles Carter, discovered that the shroud displayed properties shared with long wave X-rays. A skeletal structure of bones, hands, and two rows of teeth were uncovered. Even the thumbs which were drawn in from the piercing of the median nerve in the wrist can be seen *through* the other parts of the hand. What kind of energy would produce a negative image with X-ray quality on this cloth?
5. This was **not** just a contact phenomenon between the body and the shroud. Parts of the body ***not*** in contact with the linen (and as far away from contact as several inches) *still show up in the imprinted image.* **It is like the body has *passed through* the cloth.**
6. The lack of any blood smears on the shroud suggests that the body made a very strange exit from within the shroud. Lifting the shroud off the body would have smeared the blood in areas where it had collected, possibly reopening wounds. To state it simply, ***the man disappeared from within the wrapped linen***. The apostles Peter and John found the burial cloth "flattened"—and "they saw and believed." The current theory is that His glorified body

passed through the cloth, and it collapsed on to itself—which would have been an incredible sight to behold afterwards. The apostles would have seen the linen still in a wrapped position, but now emptied. Luke 24:12: "he saw the linen cloths positioned alone, and he went away, wondering to himself about what had happened." Like a magic trick, the body vanished from within the shroud without the linen being unwrapped from the body. Remember that it was reported later in the scriptures that Jesus's glorified body also passed through solid walls and doors to meet with his apostles.

7. Another bizarre finding that scientists determined was that the image depicts "a weightless body" because there are no marks of pressure on certain parts of the shroud when the image was made. If the body had had weight at the time of the light burst, then the image would have appeared differently with pressure points. Instead, the image is "evenly photographed" by the flash without obvious pressure points.

8. It was also determined that at the time of the light burst, the man was in an upright position with his long hair falling straight down due to gravity. If he had been lying down, his shoulder-length hair would have fallen back and away from his shoulders.

9. Many tests were run to precisely determine what direction this light source was coming from that illuminated his body in a totally dark tomb. Assuming from the evidence that he was upright and probably suspended slightly above the ground, the light would have been coming from directly overhead. This was confirmed by numerous photographic tests to determine the direction of the light source that created this image blast onto the shroud like a photo negative (76).

What kind of supernatural light appears in a totally pitch-black tomb? How does anybody disappear from within a wrapped linen without unfolding it and smearing blood everywhere?

Matthew 28:2–4: "For an Angel of the Lord descended from heaven, and as he approached, he rolled back the stone and sat down on it. Now his appearance was like lightning, and his vestment like snow. Then, out of fear of him, the guards were terrified, and they became (immobilized) like dead men."

The majority of the scientists involved with all of the testing and analyses with the Shroud of Turin were generally atheists or agnostics. According to Father Francis Peffley, by the time their research ended, 95 percent of them had become Christians (76). And yet, there is still *another* artifact that validates the authenticity of the Shroud of Turin…

SUDARIUM DOMINI

The Sudarium Domini or "sweat cloth of the Lord" has been secretly stored in Oviedo, Spain for well over a thousand years (since 630 AD) after its well-documented passage from Palestine. It was the other burial cloth that had been wrapped around the head of Jesus immediately after his death on the cross. It is clearly referenced in the scriptures:

John 20:6–7: "Then Simon Peter arrived, following him (John), and he entered the tomb, and he saw the linen cloths lying there, and the separate cloth which had been over his head, not placed with the linen cloths, but in a separate place, wrapped up by itself."

The Sudarium bears no image like the Shroud. But it does show what appear to be bloodstains of varying color densities. A team of forty scientists and experts began studying this artifact in 1989. The Spanish forensic team established that this cloth had covered the head of a male who was already dead. He had died in an upright position with his head tilted 20 percent to the right, 70 percent forward, and with outstretched arms—a position maintained for forty-five minutes after death. The victim died of asphyxiation as shown by the 5:1 ratio of pulmonary edema on the cloth (78:204–205).

Dr. Alan Whanger applied a polarized image overlay technique on both the Shroud and the Sudarium. Comparisons of the type and positions of bloodstains and comparisons of the facial features reveal over **seventy points of coincidence** on the front of the image and **fifty points of correlation** between the two artifacts on the back of the image. This is an extremely high rate of alignment and significance. For example, the nose is exactly the same length, swollen and displaced to the exact degree in both cloths. Puncture wounds from sharp objects (crown of thorns) on the head coincide perfectly. Blood and lymph densities match perfectly as well (78:205–206).

Even fingerprint analysis or facial recognition software require less than thirty points of correlation to be considered a very close or identical match. According to microscopic forensic analysis, **both cloths covered the same victim.** If this were the elaborate trickery of some skillful prankster, then he would have to have faked both this cloth and the Shroud in precisely the same perfect manner—which would have been virtually IMPOSSIBLE (78:206).

Science has clearly validated supernatural events and artifacts that defy explanation.

I did not state that science could *explain* these matters. It is the fact that they *cannot explain* them which becomes important in our journey. It is time to examine your faith in what you cannot always see or immediately comprehend. Do you *really need* more proof or physical evidence?

We have been analyzing those "footprints" from…heaven.

Want to hear what heaven may be like?

CHAPTER 14

HEAVEN IS FOR REAL... BUT SO IS HELL

For centuries, man has pondered the existence of an afterlife. Is there really a heaven? Are there pearly gates, streets paved with gold, angels playing harps, and eternal happiness?

Is there actually a hell? Is it truly governed by Satan and filled with fire and misery? Are there any other realms that exist between these two extremes?

People who have described near-death experiences report glimpses of these realms in the precious minutes during which they were declared clinically dead. One of the more recent and intriguing accounts was publicized in the book *Heaven Is for Real*. As an assertive, matter-of-fact, no-nonsense, four-year-old Colton Burpo confidently described seeing beautiful views of heaven:

Visions of heaven as described by various sources (Photo-Art created by author).

"Heaven is more amazing than you can imagine. I could hear beautiful music and see lots of colors. Big, bright rainbows are everywhere you look. The streets are gold, the gates are made of pearl, and shiny jewels are on the walls" (64:9).

Are these the fanciful wishes of a four year old's imagination? Perhaps—that is, until you read **Revelation 21:19, 21:**

"The foundation stones of the city walls had every kind of jewel in them…The twelve gates were twelve pearls. Each gate was made from a single pearl. The street of the city was made of pure gold. The gold was clear as glass."

Don Piper was on his way home from a conference when his car was crushed by a semitruck that crossed into his lane. Medical personnel said he died instantly. While his body lay lifeless inside the ruins of his car, Piper experienced the glories of heaven, awed by its beauty and music. *Ninety minutes after the wreck*, while a minister prayed for him, *Piper miraculously returned to life* on earth with only the memory of inexpressible heavenly bliss. He describes the gates and walls of heaven as well as the streets within—and the glorious music:

"Looming just over the heads of the loved ones who had come to greet me stood an awesome gate interrupting a wall that faded out of sight in both directions. It struck me that the actual entrance was small in comparison to the massive gate itself. I stared, but I couldn't see the end of the walls in either direction…The gate wasn't made of pearls, but was pearlescent—perhaps iridescent…To me it looked as if someone had spread pearl icing on a cake. The gate glowed and shimmered" (65:50–51).

"I paused just outside the gate, and I could see inside. It was like a city with paved streets. To my amazement, they had been constructed of literal gold. If you imagine a street paved with gold bricks, that's as close as I can come to describing what lay inside the gate. Everything I saw was bright—the brightest colors my eyes had ever beheld—so powerful that no earthly human could take in this brilliance" (65:51).

BE NOT AFRAID TO FOLLOW THE FOOTPRINTS FROM HEAVEN

"It was the most beautiful and pleasant sound I've ever heard…I felt awestruck, wanting only to listen…It seemed like I was part of the music—and it played in and through my body…I felt embraced by the sounds…As I became aware of the joyous sounds and melodies that filled the air…I felt as if the heavenly concert permeated every part of my being…I call it music, but it differed from anything I had ever heard or ever expect to hear on the earth. The melodies of praise filled the atmosphere…the praise was unending…Praise was everywhere, and all of it was musical, yet comprised of melodies and tones I'd never experienced before" (65:46–47).

Four-year-old Colton also describes,

"Heaven is not scary—ever! There is no sun, but it never gets dark in heaven because the light of God is so bright. No one ever cries or is afraid in heaven. No one ever gets sad or mad. Everyone is happy there!" (64:10)

Don Piper adds his impression of the light in heaven:

"Coming out from the gate—a short distance ahead—was a brilliance that was brighter than the light that surrounded me, utterly luminous…Everything I saw glowed with intense brightness…as far ahead as I could see, there was absolutely nothing but intense, radiant light…The light engulfed me, and I had the sense that I was being ushered into the presence of God" (65:44).

Revelation 21: 23–24 —

"The city does not need the sun or the moon to shine on it. The glory of God is its light, and the Lamb is the city's lamp. By its light the people of the world will walk."

If we can accept that the visionaries who have encountered the Virgin Mary are credible, honest, and genuine witnesses to supernatural visits, can we also believe their accounts of visiting or seeing heaven, hell, and other realms? Hesitate before you answer that question—because first you need to hear what they are actually reporting. Here are some excerpts from their testimonies:

FATIMA, PORTUGAL (1917)

Again the doubts, ridicule, and abrasive comments by skeptical adults soured the children's desire to return in July, but at the last moment, they all decided to keep their rendezvous with the Lady. Two to three thousand people were already waiting for them there! Blessed Mary again insisted that they pray the Rosary fervently. The Virgin Mary called herself the Lady of the Rosary. Then, Our Lady did something entirely different—the rays of light from her outstretched hands poured through the children into the earth below them, opening up a view of hell:

> "The rays of light seemed to penetrate the earth, and we saw, as it were, a sea of fire. Plunged in this fire were demons and souls in human form, like transparent burning embers, all blackened or burnished bronze, floating about in the conflagration, now raised into the air by the flames that issued from within themselves, together with great clouds of smoke, now falling back on every side like sparks in huge fires, without weight or equilibrium, amid shrieks and groans of pain and despair, which horrified us and made us tremble with fear. The demons could be distinguished by their terrifying and repellent likeness to frightful and unknown animals, black and transparent like burning coals" (29:120).

Then Our Lady commented upon what they had witnessed,

> "You have seen Hell where the souls of poor sinners go. To save them, God wishes to establish in the world a devotion to my Immaculate Heart. If what I say to you is done, many souls will be saved, and there will be peace."

CUAPA, NICARAGUA (1980)

On June 8, 1980, Mary appeared again, giving Bernardo four visions—"which were like movies in the sky." The first vision was of the first Christians, singing and marching toward heaven. They were dressed in white—their bodies glowing with light. The second vision was of another group of people also dressed in white. They held illuminated rosaries in their hands. The leader read from a book, and after meditating on the reading, they prayed one Our Father and ten Hail Marys. Mary explained that they were the first ones to whom she had given the Rosary. She wanted everyone to pray the Rosary like they were doing. In the third vision, Bernardo saw a group of men dressed in brown robes. Mary explained that these were the Franciscans. "They received the Rosary from the hands of the first ones." In the fourth vision, he saw a large group, as big as an army, of people in normal dress, all holding rosaries. Light radiated from their bodies, and they were beautiful. He wanted to join them and go with them even though he was not illuminated, himself. The Virgin replied,

> "No! You are still lacking. You have to tell the people what you have seen and heard. I have shown you the glory of Our Lord, and you people will acquire this if you are obedient to Our Lord, to the Lord's Word—if you persevere in praying the Holy Rosary and put into practice the Lord's Word."

Bernardo only shared these visions with the priest, knowing that the church must approve them first. The priest gave Bernardo approval and permission to spread the visions (2:159–161).

MEDJUGORJE, BOSNIA-HERZEGOVINA (1981–present)

In early October 1981, Vicka received a surprise while visiting Jakov at his home. The Virgin Mary suddenly appeared and announced that she was going to take them to see heaven. Jakov became frightened, thinking that they would not return and said, "Why don't you just take Vicka? She has many brothers and sisters, but I am the only child of my mother." The Virgin just smiled sweetly and took the two of them by their hands. Vicka describes the experience:

> "I was wondering how many days we would be traveling (to get to heaven), and whether we would go through the sky or the ground. Our Lady took my right hand and Jakov's left

hand and took us with her. We saw the ceiling opening, giving us just enough space to go through, and within the wink of an eye, we found ourselves in heaven. Heaven is one huge endless space. It has a brilliant light which does not leave it. There is a special kind of life that does not exist on the earth at all. We saw people dressed in pink, yellow, and gray gowns. **Nobody was older than thirty-three years old.** They were walking, praying, and singing, and there were small angels circling around. We saw people praying and singing, together in groups, but we could not understand what they were saying. It must have been some heavenly language. We experienced a special indescribable joy. Our Lady told us to have a good look at how overjoyed all those who were in heaven were. It was a special kind of joy that cannot be experienced on earth. Everything is definitely so much more beautiful. When you are entering heaven, you experience an enormous feeling of separation from this life and enter a special new life" (48:65–66) (45:135).

Mary: "**All those who are faithful to God will have that. I did this so you could see the happiness which awaits those who love God**" (45:135).

Then Our Lady took them through purgatory; they described it as "dark and gloomy" and filled with "a gray-brown mist" and "something like ashes." They did not actually see anybody but "felt anguish," a sense of suffering, and a "strong yearning for peace." The Blessed Mother indicated that the souls in purgatory are extremely lonely. The only time they can see us on earth is during those moments we pray for them (48:66) (45:135).

Mary: "**These people are waiting for your prayers and sacrifices**" (52:61).

The vision of hell was so upsetting that Jakov refuses to describe it—even today! Vicka is reluctant to do so, but she does give us the following account:

"In the center of this place is a great fire—like an ocean of raging flames. Fire…demons…awful. We literally saw a teenage blonde girl going into the flames and coming out as a horrendously disfigured, animal-like creature. The more they are against the Will of God, the deeper they enter into the fire, and the deeper they go, the more they rage against Him. When they come out of the fire, they don't have a human shape any more. They are more like grotesque animals, but unlike anything on earth. It is as if they were never human beings before. They were horrible, ugly, angry! And each was different—no two looked alike. When they came out (of the flames), they were raging and smashing everything around—hissing and gnashing and screeching" (51:67–68) (45:134–135).

Mary: "**Do not be afraid! I have shown you hell so that you may know the state of those who are there. Keep the faith, fast, and pray. The devil is trying to conquer us. Do not permit him. I will be with you at every step**" (45:135).

The children were not dreaming this, nor were they just given visions. They were **physically absent** from Jakov's house for exactly twenty minutes. Jakov's mother saw them in the home right before they departed. When she couldn't find them a moment later, she frantically searched everywhere for them, inside and outside of the house for twenty minutes. She was becoming very fearful when they suddenly reappeared within the home, telling her where Blessed Mary had just taken them (45:135) (52:61).

Visions of hell as described by various sources
(Photo-Art created by author).

BIBLICAL CORRELATION: Matthew 13:37–43

> **37** He answered, "He who sows the good seed is the Son of man; **38** the field is the world, and the good seed means the sons of the kingdom; the weeds are the sons of the evil one, **39** and the enemy who sowed them is the devil; the harvest is the close of the age, and the reapers are angels. **40** Just as the weeds are gathered and burned with fire, so will it be at the close of the age. **41** The Son of Man will send his angels, and they will gather out of his kingdom all causes of sin and all evildoers, **42** and throw them into the furnace of fire, where there will be weeping and gnashing of teeth. **43** Then the righteous will shine like the sun in the kingdom of their Father. He who has ears, let him hear."

Vicka adds this bit of awareness, many years later:

> "We all know that there are persons on this earth who simply don't admit that God exists, even though He helps them. He tries to nudge them onto the path of holiness. But they say that they don't believe, and they deny Him. They deny Him even when it is time to die. They continue to deny Him after they are dead. It is their choice. It is their will that they go to hell. They choose hell. When the illumination of the soul occurs in each individual (at death), they immediately have full knowledge of God and of all truths. Thus, they *know* where they are to go" (also confirmed later in a message from Mary) (45:225).

Speaking of heaven, Ivanka was granted a special request by Our Lady on May 7, 1985.

> "I never saw Mary so beautiful as on this evening. She wore the most beautiful gown I have ever seen in my life. Her gown, veil, and crown had gold and silver sequins of light. There were two angels with her—I don't have words to describe this! Our Lady asked me if I had some wish. I told her I would like to see my earthly mother (recently deceased). She smiled, nodded her head, and my mother immediately appeared. She was smiling. Our Lady told me to stand up. I did, and my

mother embraced and kissed me, and said, 'My child, I am so proud of you.' Then she kissed me and disappeared. After this, I asked Our Lady if I could kiss Her. She nodded her head, and I kissed Our Lady. She blessed me, smiled, and said, 'Go in God's peace'" (52:234).

Ivanka said later that her mother looked the same but much prettier with no evidence of the suffering that she had gone through in the last years. But her body was no longer like our earthly bodies. Ivanka added that touching Our Lady's body was different than that—and that her dress had a "metallic" feel to it (52:33). Ivanka adds,

> "Many people do not believe there is life after this life. But I am here as a living witness, and I can say there is life after life because I was able to see my Mom. This witnessing was not just for me, but for all mankind" (45:127).

Vicka said that "nobody is older than thirty-three years old" in heaven. Colton Burpo validates her perception as he further describes his views of heaven from his four-year-old perspective:

> "One of the most wonderful things about heaven is that no one ever gets sick or hurt there. No one ever has bumps or bruises or skinned knees. No one needs glasses or wheelchairs. In heaven, **no one is old; everyone is young and healthy**. And no one dies in heaven. In heaven, you live forever with God!" (64:20)

Young Colton had never met or seen a picture of his great-grandfather, "Pop," who had died years before Colton was born. Yet, he reports that this great-grandfather came up to him and greeted him while he was in heaven. When Colton's parents showed him a recent picture of "Pop" before he died, Colton did not recognize him. Then his parents remembered that Colton had said that everyone was young in heaven. They found a picture of the great-grandfather at **age twenty-nine** in 1943 (that Colton had never seen), and he *immediately recognized* him this time (63).

Colton also described a young girl about age seven running up to him and hugging him. He did not recognize her either, but she said that she was his older sister. She knew about Colton and was so glad to finally meet him in person. Colton says,

> "My big sister was so excited to see me that she wouldn't stop hugging me!" (64:13)

Later, Colton confronted his mother on not telling him that he had had an older sister. His mother was stunned and in tears; she had never revealed that she had had a miscarriage of a female fetus several years before Colton was born. How could he possibly have known about this? When shown a picture of his mother as a young girl, Colton stated that she looked just like that older sister in heaven! (63)

Visionary Geraldine from Australia had a very similar experience in November 1989.

> "Many things had been going wrong…I needed my grandmother who had partly raised me and was missing her very much. I needed advice, and I was still grieving for her (she had died in 1982). With tears streaming down my face, I was thinking of how we used to talk—and of her loving ways—my heart breaking as I wished she was still here."

> "Then, to my surprise, I heard a woman's voice speaking inside of me clearly. She said, '**I am your Blessed Mother. I am speaking to you from within. Your earthly mother is not here with you right now so I have come to comfort you during your trials. However, your other mother (grandmother) is here with Me. Would you like to speak to her?**' At that moment I thought I was losing my mind…but yet…I felt peaceful and calm and very comforted and loved by this voice. So, I said, 'Yes, I would.'"

> "The next thing I knew, somehow, I was flying in spirit through the sky. By my left side was an Angel guiding me, and I felt it was my Guardian Angel—and it was nighttime. I saw in the distance a city. As we approached this city, it was like a warm and peaceful Sunday afternoon because there was

a holiness about it. I saw white stone houses with flat roofs and park bench seats outside. There were people sitting on the seats. As we got closer, I recognized some of the people. My grandmother was sitting on the right side and my (deceased) sister, Karen, opposite her. My grandmother **looked younger**, and there was a beautiful glow about her. I could see she was looking forward to my being with her."

"Then I found myself looking toward my sister. It was like looking through a camera as the focus moved from place to place. **My sister looked about thirty years old now**; she was twelve years old when she had died. Yet, her features were the same. She was beaming and so happy and smiling. She said, 'I have someone very, very special here who is really looking forward to meeting you. Don't worry, I am looking after her for you.' At that moment my view shifted down to see that she was holding the hand of a little girl about nine years old. She had long hair tied back in a ponytail, and she wore a **plain gray** dress. I didn't know who she was."

"Then my sister said, 'This is Geraldine Margaret.' At that moment I nearly fainted with shock. I felt the hair stand up on the back of my head, and I felt hot, then cold, as I realized it was the little baby I had miscarried nine years earlier, and it was a girl. I was going to call her Margaret Geraldine after my grandmother, but instead, they called her after me. Then this experience ended. As I came out of the room, my husband said, 'What's the matter?' as he could see by the look on my face that something had happened."

"I cried continuously at the thought of having a daughter and not knowing her. Again, I was so upset—not knowing what to make of all this. Again, I heard this beautiful, soft, loving woman's voice: **'Do not be sad at what you have seen. Rejoice, rejoice, for your Father in Heaven has given you a wonderful gift.'** I stopped crying and was comforted, feeling a great peace" (14:29–30).

The last three examples have suggested that everyone appears younger in heaven, perhaps no older than thirty-three, the age at which Jesus Christ died. Maybe nobody is allowed to appear older than Jesus? In any case, the last two examples suggest that miscarried babies continue to grow up in heaven, consistent with the age that each would have been if still living on earth.

KIBEHO, RWANDA, AFRICA (1981–1989)

Remember when Alphonsine appeared "dead" for eighteen hours while officials watched apprehensively and waited hopefully for her to "return" from her alleged journey with the Virgin Mary? Here, finally, is her report of her experience during that eighteen-hour journey. Alphonsine awoke, livelier than ever—with sparkling eyes, relaxed muscles, and a glowing face.

> "The first place Mary took me was dark and very frightening, filled with shadows and groans of sadness and pain. She called it the Place of Despair, where the road leading away from God's light ends. Another place was filled with the golden light of happiness and laughter and songs sung by so many joyous voices. Mary explained that I could not see them while I was still living below. But one called out my name and said that she had been a visionary, too, and had been persecuted for her visions. But she joyfully urged me to have faith and confidence in the Blessed Mother, for she would protect me" (39:135–136).

Anathalie also had a mystical journey which began on the podium in front of the crowds after a five-hour apparition. She collapsed into the same "frozen-limbs" state of near death with the same officials and doctors vigilant and testing her. Seven hours later, she awoke and was carried to her bed where she did not speak for two days.

She finally described her journey with Mary. The first landscape was comprised of varying shades of vivid color and light, and people there traveled by "sliding through the light." Another strange land was illuminated only by white light. She saw seven handsome men (angels) wearing white cloaks, standing in a circle, and creating the most beautiful music without any instruments. Mary called it a place of Communion where angels praise God, watch over Earth, and aid humanity when they are needed or called upon. The third place contained millions of people dressed in white, who seemed overwhelmingly happy, but not as blissful as the angels had been. Mary called this a place of purification. The last place they visited was "a land of twilight"—illuminated only by an unpleasant shade of red, and stifling dry and hot. She couldn't look at the countless people there because of their misery and anguish. She knew it must be hell. Mary said,

> "Spend two days reflecting in silence on what you have seen. Do not meditate on the angels you saw; they are not of this world. The first place, the happy world of the cherished of God, was reserved for people whose hearts are good, who pray regularly, and who strive always to follow God's will. Our second visit was to the place of purification—for those who called on God only during times of trouble, turning away from Him when their troubles were over. The last place of heat and no name was for those who never paid God any attention at all" (39:136–138).

Visionary Vestine's trip was largely a test of faith—as Jesus asked her to die for Him on Good Friday, have her soul go to heaven, but be resurrected and returned on Sunday—like he had. But she trusted that he would keep his promise, so she begged others to not bury her if she appeared dead. After collapsing into "death" at 3:00 p.m. on Friday, stunned officials and medical personnel remained vigilant for forty tense hours until she awakened on Sunday morning, full of life and healthy energy again. She said that heaven was difficult to describe:

> "There are just no words for it. **There were colors I'd never seen before, and they sounded like music. And there was music I'd never heard before that sounded like color.** I just don't know how to explain the feeling of being there. I begged Jesus from the bottom of my soul to let me stay there. He said that it wasn't my time, so I must leave" (39:142–143).

CUENCA, ECUADOR (1989)

Eighteen more apparitions occurred in chapels in Quito, Guayaquil, and Paute. At one point, Blessed Mary gave her visions of hell, heaven, and purgatory; Patricia Talbot describes:

> "Hell is a terrible place, like a big volcano where you see souls that hate each other. There are skulls, and they don't have faces, but they hate and insult God. I saw some of those bishop 'hats' in hell also. Purgatory was like a bunch of hands reaching out and crying, trying to get out of that volcano. While I was there, I heard a voice telling me to pray for them because they couldn't do anything without our help. I didn't go into heaven because I didn't feel that I deserved to. There were two choirs of angels at each side of the door. The Rosary (prayer) is the door, and the cross of the Rosary is the key to open the door to go into heaven. Prayer takes us to Jesus, who is the way, the truth, and the life; the cross that we carry over our back—our sufferings—is the key to open the door into heaven" (23:98–99).

Visions of a lower level of purgatory as described by various sources (Photo-Art created by author).

NAJU, KOREA (1988)

From the journal of visionary Julia Kim (135:27–28):

July 24, 1988: "At about 9:00 p.m., I suddenly lost energy in my whole body and fell down. I barely went upstairs to my room, supported by others, but I still struggled with excruciating pains. A while later, I entered into an ecstasy and saw heaven, purgatory, and hell."

"In the secular world, people often use the expression: *the difference between the heaven and the earth*. Yes. That was what I saw. It was an unconceivable difference! The saved children were sharing peace, joy, and love in the flower garden, whereas the condemned ones were burning in the intense flames with resentment and hatred."

Heaven (according to visionary Julia Kim)

"Countless angels are performing a beautiful and majestic symphony and chorus to welcome the souls who are entering heaven. Also, numerous saints are welcoming them with loud cheers. Jesus is waiting for them with open arms and the Blessed Mother is stretching out her hands to hold them. God the Father is smiling, expressing a welcome with His eyes. St. Joseph is also greeting them joyfully."

"It is a place where there is no jealousy or envy. All are practicing love with one another. It is overflowing with love, peace, and joy. It is a place of heavenly banquet where one never becomes hungry even without eating."

"The Blessed Mother prepared crowns of flowers and is putting them on everyone. They are dancing holding each other's hands. In the flower garden, Jesus and the Blessed Mother are together holding up her mantle and all are entering the inside of the mantle. All are humble to each other and are keeping order to avoid inconveniencing others. Their faces are full of smiles and are beautiful."

Purgatory

"It is a place where one must walk into the terrible flames of fire. There, one does the unfinished penances of this world and becomes purified. It is a place where those who died in the grace of God but still have unfinished reparations must walk by themselves to complete the atonement. When they are completely purified, they are lifted into heaven by the Blessed Mother's help and the angels' support. The process can be expedited, if we in this world pray for them. When we help them with sacrifices and penances for them, they can enter heaven faster. It will be too late to regret not having done penances in this world. So, while living in this world, one must offer love constantly through sacrifices for others."

Hell

"When angels tie the hands of the condemned souls and drop them, devils snatch them violently. Then, they fall into the flames of fire. It is a place of perdition from which one cannot come out forever. It is useless, no matter how hard one may regret and struggle. It is a sea of fire, full of hatred. Who will grab their hands? Nobody."

"People struggle like a person drowning and trying to grasp even a straw, but only run around in the fire that becomes hotter and hotter, tearing and scratching each other, and trying to take food away from each other but all the food burns in the fire and nobody can eat anything, which make them snarling more angrily at each other. With their protruded eyes, they become horrible devils. It was a terrible scene I could not look at with open eyes."

ZAKARPATTYA, UKRAINE (2002)

In a dream at night, the Virgin Mary took the visionary, Olenka Kuruts, on a cloud, riding to paradise, purgatory, and hell. She was surprised to see bishops and priests in all three places. Mary explained that they were in hell because they did not really believe in God. Some priests were in purgatory because they did not listen to the righteous bishops as they should have (159:4).

MEDJUGORJE, BOSNIA-HERZEGOVINA (1981–present)

Other visionaries comment on their own experiences and perceptions.

Mirjana Dragicevic:

"I have seen purgatory and heaven, but I have not seen hell because I did not want to see it. I saw heaven as if it were a movie. The first thing I noticed was the faces of the people there. They were radiating a type of inner light which showed how immensely happy they were. Heaven is an actual place. The trees, the meadows, the sky are totally different from anything we know on earth. And the light is much more brilliant. Heaven is beautiful beyond any possible comparison with anything I know of on the earth. Their bodies were different from what we are like now. **Perhaps they were all around thirty years of age.** They were walking in a beautiful park. They have everything. They need or want nothing. They are totally fulfilled. They were dressed in the types of clothing that Jesus wore" (51:28–29).

"There are several levels in purgatory. The more you pray on earth, the higher your level in purgatory will be. The lowest level is closest to hell, where suffering is the most intense. The highest level is closest to heaven, and there the suffering is the least. What level you are on depends on the state of purity of your soul. The lower the people are in purgatory and the less they are able to pray, the more they suffer. The higher a person is in purgatory and the easier it is for him to pray, the more he enjoys praying, and the less he suffers. The Blessed Mother has asked us to pray for the souls in purgatory. They are helpless to pray for themselves. Through prayer, we on earth can do much to help them. The Blessed Mother told me that when souls leave purgatory and go to heaven, most go on Christmas Day" (51:29).

"The Virgin described purgatory as a series of 'levels' that stretched all the way from the gates of hell to the portal of paradise. Souls in purgatory who prayed frequently were permitted occasionally to communicate with the living, the Madonna said, because the dead no longer have free will. They cannot atone for their sins and are completely dependent upon the prayers of those still living" (8:156).

"There are in purgatory souls who pray ardently to God, but for whom no relative or friend prays on earth. God makes them benefit from the prayers of other people. It happens that **God permits them to manifest themselves in different ways, close to their relatives on earth,** in order to remind men of the existence of purgatory and to solicit their prayers to come close to God, who is just, but good. The majority of people go to purgatory. Many go to hell. A small number go to heaven" (45:172).

Ivanka Ivankovic:

"I told the Blessed Mother I did not want to see hell. Heaven is a place that is very, very beautiful. Most beautiful. I saw only people in gray robes. Everyone I saw was filled with a happiness I can't explain—and I can't forget! The gray clothes didn't matter. They were not a part of the happiness. Purgatory was only darkness. The Blessed Mother showed me these things because she wants to remind her children of the results of their choices here on earth" (51:40–41).

Ivan Dragicevic:

"I have seen heaven already. Heaven is worth any cost!... People in heaven are happy. They live in the fullness of God. It is better than anything you can imagine! The Blessed Mother told me that those who go to purgatory are those who only prayed occasionally. They were filled with doubt—they were not certain that God exists. They did not know how to pray on earth, or if they did know how, they did not pray. Souls in purgatory suffer. If no one prays for them, they can suffer even more. I prefer not to discuss hell" (51:93–94).

Marija Pavlovic:

"Purgatory is a large place. It is foggy. It is ash gray. It is misty. You cannot see people there. It is as if they are immersed in deep clouds. They can pray for us but not for themselves. They are desperately in need of our prayers. With our prayers, we can send them to heaven. The biggest suffering that souls in purgatory have is that they see that there is a God, but they did not accept Him here on earth. Now they long so much to come close to God. Now they suffer so intensely because they recognize how much they have hurt God, how many chances they had on earth, and how many times they disregarded God" (51:129).

"Hell is a large space with a big sea of fire in the middle. There are many people there. I particularly noticed a beautiful young girl. When she came near the fire, she was no longer beautiful. She came out of the fire like an animal; she was no longer human. The Blessed Mother told me that God gives us all choices…In the moment of death, God gives us the light to see ourselves as we really are. The one who lives in sin on earth can see what he has done and recognize himself as he really is. He chooses hell because that is what he is. That is where he fits. It is his own wish. God does not make the choice. God condemns no one. We condemn ourselves. Every individual chooses for himself what he personally deserves for all eternity…" (51:130–131)

Blessed Virgin Mary:

"You go to heaven in full conscience—that which you have now. At the moment of death, you are conscious of the separation of the body and soul. It is false to teach people that you are reborn many times and that you pass to different bodies. One is born only once. The body, drawn from the earth, decomposes after death. It never comes back to life again. Man receives a transfigured body (in heaven)…" (July 24, 1982) (45:169)

> "Dear children! Today, I would like to invite you to pray every day for the souls in purgatory. Every soul needs prayer and grace in order to reach God and His love. By praying for these souls, you will gain intercessors for yourselves who will be able to help you recognize in this life that earthly things hold no importance; that heaven is the only goal worth aspiring to. For this reason, dear children, pray without interruption so that you may help yourselves and those to whom your prayers bring joy" (Nov. 6, 1986) (52:179).

The similarities and correlations are intriguing. But, *is it as real as it sounds?*

Could a disbelieving, scientific-minded, medical professional ever report such "fantasies" or spiritual visions? Doubtful. Unlikely?

Dr. Eben Alexander, an academic neurosurgeon for over twenty-five years, summarizes his skeptical mind-set—just prior to an extraordinary, life-changing experience:

> "As much as I'd grown up wanting to believe in God and heaven and an afterlife, my decades in the rigorous scientific world of academic neurosurgery had profoundly called into question how such things could exist. Modern neuroscience dictates that the brain gives rise to consciousness—to the mind, to the soul, to the spirit, to whatever you choose to call that invisible, intangible part of us that truly makes us who we are—and I had little doubt that it was correct. Like most health-care workers who deal directly with dying patients and their families, I had heard about—and even seen—some pretty inexplicable events over the years. I filed these occurrences under "unknown" and let them be, figuring a commonsense answer of one kind or another lay at the heart of it all." Over the years, my scientific worldview gently but steadily undermined my ability to believe in something larger. Science seemed to be providing a steady onslaught of evidence that pushed our significance in the universe ever closer to zero. Belief would have been nice. But science is not concerned with what would be nice. It's concerned with what is" (66:34–35).

Then Dr. Alexander became deathly sick with a rare and dangerous illness, lying in a coma at death's doorstep for seven days with doctors ready to give up on him. However, Dr. Alexander—the skeptical, disbelieving, but brilliant neurosurgeon—was now having his own inexplicable experience.

"Darkness…but a visible darkness—like being submerged in mud yet being able to see through it. Or maybe dirty Jell-O describes it better. Transparent, but in a bleary, blurry, claustrophobic, suffocating kind of way. There were sounds…a deep, rhythmic pounding, distant yet strong, so that each pulse goes right through you…like the sound of metal against metal, as if a giant subterranean blacksmith is pounding an anvil somewhere off in the distance…pounding it so hard…I didn't have a body—I was simply…*there*…in this place of pulsing, pounding darkness. My consciousness wasn't foggy or distorted when I was there. It was just…*limited*. I was simply a lone point of awareness in a timeless red-brown sea" (66:29–31).

"The longer I stayed in this place, the less comfortable I became. It was a feeling like I wasn't really part of this subterranean world at all, but *trapped* in it. **Grotesque animal faces bubbled out of the muck, groaned or screeched, and then were gone again.** I heard an occasional dull roar. Sometimes, these roars changed to dim, rhythmic chants—chants that were both terrifying and weirdly familiar. The more that I began to feel like a "*me*"—like something separate from the cold and wet and dark around me, the more the faces that bubbled up out of the darkness became ugly and threatening. The movement around me became less visual and more tactile, as if reptilian, wormlike creatures were crowding past, occasionally rubbing up against me with their smooth or spiky skins. As my awareness sharpened more and more, I edged ever closer to panic. I did not belong here. I needed to get out…" (66:31–32)

"Something new emerged from the darkness above. If I tried for the rest of my life, I would never be able to do justice to this entity that now approached me…to come anywhere close to describing how beautiful it was. Something had appeared in the darkness. Turning slowly, it radiated fine filaments of white-gold light, and as it did so the darkness around me began to splinter and break apart. Then I heard a new sound—like the richest, most complex, most beautiful piece of music you've ever heard. Growing in volume as a pure white light descended, it obliterated the monotonous mechanical pounding that, seemingly for eons, had been my only company up until then" (66:32, 38).

"The light got closer and closer, spinning around and around and generating those filaments of pure white light that I now saw were tinged, here and there, with hints of gold. Then, at the very center of the light, something else appeared. I focused my awareness hard, trying to figure out what it was. An opening…I was no longer looking at the slowly spinning light at all, but *through* it. The moment I understood this, I began to move up. Fast. There was a whooshing sound, and in a flash I went through the opening and found myself in a completely new world. The strangest, most beautiful world I had ever seen" (66:38).

"Brilliant, vibrant, ecstatic, stunning…I could heap on one adjective after another to describe what this world looked and felt like, but they'd all fall short. I felt like I was being born. Not reborn or born again. Just born……Below me there was countryside. It was green, lush, and earthlike. I was flying, passing over trees and fields, streams and waterfalls, and here and there, people. There were children, too, laughing and playing. The people sang and danced around in circles, and sometimes I'd see a dog, running and jumping among them— as full of joy as the people were. They wore simple yet beautiful clothes, and it seemed to me that the colors of these clothes had the same kind of living warmth as the trees and the flowers that bloomed and blossomed in the countryside around them. A beautiful, incredible dream world…**except that it wasn't a dream!** Though I didn't know where I was or even *what* I was, **I was absolutely sure of one thing: This place I'd suddenly found myself in was** *completely real*" (66:38–39).

"Someone was next to me—a beautiful girl with high cheekbones and deep blue eyes. She was wearing the same kind of peasantlike clothes that the people in the village down below wore. Golden-brown tresses framed her lovely face. We were riding along together on an intricately patterned surface, alive with indescribable and vivid colors—the wing of a butterfly. In fact, millions of butterflies were all around us—vast fluttering waves of them, dipping down into the greenery and coming back up around us again. Without using any words, she spoke to me. The message went through me like a wind, and I instantly understood that it was true. I knew so in the same way that **I knew that the world around us was real—was not some fantasy**, passing and insubstantial. The message had three parts, and if I had to translate them into earthly language, I'd say that it was something like this: (1) 'You are loved and cherished, dearly, forever,' (2) 'You have nothing to fear,' and (3) 'There is nothing you can do wrong' (66:40–41).

"I know the difference between fantasy and reality, and I know that the experience I'm struggling to give you…was the single most REAL experience of my life" (66:41).

"Meanwhile, I was in a place of clouds. Big, puffy, pink-white ones that showed up sharply against the deep blue-black sky. Higher than the clouds—immeasurably higher—flocks of transparent orbs, shimmering beings arced across the sky, leaving long, streamer-like lines behind them. Birds? Angels? They were more advanced. Higher…A sound, huge and booming like a glorious chant, came down from above, and I wondered if the winged beings were producing it. The sound was palpable and almost material, like a rain that you can feel on your skin but that doesn't get you wet" (66:45).

"Seeing and hearing were not separate in this place where I now was. **I could *hear* the visual beauty of the silvery bodies of those scintillating beings above, and I could *see* the surging, joyful perfection of what they sang.** It seemed that you could not look at or listen to anything in this world without becoming a part of it—without joining into it in some mysterious way. A divine breeze—like a warm wind—blew through. It changed everything, shifting the world into an even higher octave, a higher vibration. I began wordlessly putting questions to this wind—and to the divine being that I sensed at work behind or within it."

"Where is this place? Who am I? Why am I here?"

"Each time I silently posed one of these questions, the answer came instantly in an explosion of light, color, love, and beauty that blew through me like a crashing wave. They answered, but in a way that bypassed language. Thoughts entered me directly. These thoughts were solid and immediate—hotter than fire and wetter than water—and as I received them I was able to instantly and effortlessly understand concepts that would have taken me years to fully grasp in my earthly life" (66:45–46).

"I continued moving forward and found myself entering an immense void, completely dark, infinite in size, yet also infinitely comforting. Pitch-black as it was, it was also brimming over with light—a light that seemed to come from a brilliant orb that I now sensed near me. The orb was a kind of "interpreter" between me and this extraordinary presence surrounding me. It was an inky darkness that was also full to brimming with light. The Creator told me that there is not one universe but many—in fact, more than I could conceive—but that **love** lay at the center of them all. Evil was present in all the other universes as well, but only in the tiniest trace amounts. Evil was necessary because without it free will was impossible. Without free will, there could be no growth—no forward movement. In the larger picture, love was overwhelmingly dominant, and it would be ultimately triumphant" (66:46–48).

"I saw the abundance of life throughout the countless universes, including some whose intelligence was advanced far beyond that of humanity. I saw that there are countless higher dimensions, but that the only way to know these dimensions is to enter and experience them directly. They cannot be known or understood from lower dimensional space. Cause and effect exist in these higher realms, but outside of our earthly conception of them. The world of time and space in which we move in this terrestrial realm is tightly and intricately meshed within these higher worlds. In other words, these worlds aren't totally apart from us because all worlds are part of the same overarching divine Reality. From those higher worlds one could access any time or place in our world" (66:48–49).

"I was going back, away from the Core. Its inky-bright darkness faded into the green dazzling landscape. Looking down, I saw the villagers again, the trees and sparkling streams and the waterfalls—as well as the arcing angel-beings above. My companion was there, too. She had been there the whole time, all through my journey—even transforming into that orb-like ball of light. She said, **'We will show you many things, but you will be going back.'** This whole adventure, it began to occur to me, was some kind of tour—**some grand overview of the invisible, spiritual side of existence**. And like all good tours, it included all floors and all levels" (66:68–69).

"**Love is, without a doubt, the basis of everything**. In its purest and most powerful form, this love is not jealous or selfish, but *unconditional*. This is the reality of realities, the incomprehensibly glorious truth of truths that lives and breathes at the core of everything that exists or that ever will exist. Not much of a scientific insight? Well, I beg to differ. I'm back from that place, and **nothing could convince me that this is not only the single most important emotional truth in the universe, but also the single most important *scientific* truth as well.** Science does not contradict what I learned up there. But certain members of the scientific community, who are pledged to the materialist worldview, have insisted again and again that science and spirituality cannot coexist. **They are mistaken**" (66:71–73).

Could this *still* just be a vivid imagination—even though it comes from an objective scientist? One further revelation does tend to validate his experience as genuine reality. As a child, Eben Alexander was given up for adoption. The family that put him up for adoption shared a picture of his deceased sister (of whom he was unaware), and **he recognized her as the woman from his experience who had served as his "guide!"** Therefore, a doubting scientist and dedicated medical doctor could be dramatically transformed by such an experience—rich in otherworldly spirituality and visions that our present science cannot understand or explain.

Yet, it exists. Heaven—a glorious and happy place illuminated by Divine Light; hell—darkness with a fiery sea and screeching beasts; and the many dimensions of purgatory—may truly be **REAL** places after all. We may not be certain of any of this until we arrive there, but the important question now should be—**"Which place are we headed?"**

We have followed the "footprints" back to heaven, but there were other "footprints" travelling along beside us while we were in heaven—and now following us again as we head back home.

Who are these beings of light?

They are the angels.

Let's follow their "footprints" next...

CHAPTER 15

THE ROLE OF ANGELS

Beings of light have been witnessed within many of these supernatural encounters. What exactly are they? Are these angels? If so, what are they doing? Why are they present? What is their purpose? Why are they around? Through the historical eyewitness accounts presented in this chapter, many of these questions may be answered.

When four-year-old Colton Burpo described his unexpected visit to heaven during his deadly illness, he clearly saw these angelic beings and was impressed by them:

> "Angels are everywhere! God's angels are mighty and amazing! Michael and Gabriel are the biggest—they are as tall as giants. Michael carries a sword that is about as big as my dad. His sword is covered in flames and is really powerful. The angels do lots of things in heaven. They help God and sing praises to Him. They also deliver messages and protect people on earth. Angels are very busy!" (64:16)

The Bible makes references to angels numerous times. The church states, "Angels are spiritual persons created without bodies. They are pure spirits created by God out of nothing as part of the wonder of divine creation"(62). Some theologians would claim that they are the connecting bridge between humanity and divinity. Nine "choirs" or groups of angels are mentioned throughout the Bible. Theological scholars have carefully categorized these nine levels of angels with their heavenly duties into three hierarchies of a sacred order.

"Song of the Angels" - a painting by
William Adolphe Bouguereau, 1881.

The highest hierarchy which focuses on the adoration of God contains the *Seraphim, Cherubim*, and *Thrones*. The middle hierarchy deals with receiving illumination, knowledge, and truth from the first hierarchy in order to govern the material world, nature, and the universe. This hierarchy contains the *Dominions, Virtues, and Powers*. The lowest and third hierarchy receives the illumination from the second level with the purpose of carrying things out as it relates to serving and directing mankind. This hierarchy is comprised of the *Principalities, Archangels, and Angels* (which includes *Guardian Angels*). Here is a summary of the roles of each choir (62).

SERAPHIM (Isaiah 6): They have three pairs of wings—the first pair cover their face out of humility and reverence for God; the second pair cover their feet in modesty and respect for the divine presence; the third pair is for flying—as in a messenger role. Their primary role is the endless praise of, burning love for, and unceasing adoration of God.

CHERUBIM (Genesis 3:24, Exodus 25:18): They excel in *truth* and *knowledge* about God. They know the divine secrets of God and therefore have great *wisdom*.

THRONES (Colossians 1:16): They represent the firmness and permanence of God's presence. They pass on illumination and what is needed to the second hierarchy.

DOMINIONS (Colossians 1:16): They have the role of heavenly government. They preside over the actions of the Virtues and Powers. They appoint things that are to be done by the lower choirs, making known the commands of God.

VIRTUES (Ephesians 1:21, 1 Peter 3:22): They move the heavens with godlike energy. They are responsible for miracles and miraculous signs. They preserve us from evil.

POWERS (Ephesians 3:10, 6:12): They order HOW what has been commanded from above is to be done by lower angels. The chastisements from God are executed by the *Powers*. They are also the "warrior angels" who protect the world from evil spirits.

PRINCIPALITIES (Jude 1:6): They are the princes, the leaders or "generals" of this lower hierarchy. They are responsible for shifts of power among nations or kingdoms. Most defections came from this choir and went to the dark side of evil because they did not want to serve man who is so far beneath them.

ARCHANGELS (1 Thessalonians 4:16, Jude 1:9): These are the "officers" who lead the many angels beneath them and deliver the most important messages to humanity. Michael is the archangel for God the Father and is in command of the heavenly warriors, often protecting the Virgin Mary in her missions. Gabriel is the archangel for God the Son (Jesus) and His Mother. And Rafael is the archangel for the God the Healer or the Holy Spirit.

ANGELS (Matthew 18:10, Catechism: 336): These include the vast numbers of guardian angels. They are to guard, comfort, and support man. They are to protect us toward eternal life. Each human being has his own guardian angel. One should acknowledge them and show love and appreciation.

Therefore, divinely inspired scholars and biblical experts have attempted to categorize and describe the appearance, duties, and activity of these spiritual beings. But does history record further appearances of these choirs of angels ***beyond*** the days of the Bible? Are they showing up in conjunction with the alleged appearances of the Virgin Mary? Do their actions reflect the "angel theology" that was just described? Taking a look at historical accounts might just answer those questions. Spiritual beings are being witnessed in *at least one third* of the appearances of the Virgin Mary according to a review of eighty-nine of the documented visitations by Our Lady. Let's take a careful look at how they are appearing and the roles that they perform.

MESSENGERS

The Bible has many examples of angels delivering heavenly announcements in order to enlighten, proclaim, give direction, or warn of danger. Here are some historical excerpts for consideration *beyond the Bible* from recent Marian apparitions.

FATIMA, PORTUGAL (1916)

Lucia Santos (nine) and her two cousins, Francisco Marto (eight) and Jacinta Marto (six), were herding sheep when what they thought was an early summer rainstorm caused them to seek shelter in a cave. A sudden stiff breeze whipped the tree branches and caused them to be afraid. Suddenly, in front of them, appeared a shining, young, incredibly handsome man who was "more brilliant than a crystal penetrated by rays of the sun." He began walking toward them over the tops of the olive trees as if following the sun's rays to the ground at the entrance of the cave. He told them he was the Angel of Peace and taught them a prayer of adoration.

> "My God, I believe, I adore, I hope, and I love You! I ask pardon of You for all those who do not believe, do not adore, do not hope, and do not love You. Pray thus; the Hearts of Jesus and Mary are attentive to the voice of your supplication" (32:5).

He saw them again later that summer and also in the autumn of 1916. They learned about praying frequently and sacrifices. He interrupted their play:

> "What are you doing? Pray! Pray a great deal! The most Holy Hearts of Jesus and Mary have merciful designs for you. Offer prayers and sacrifices constantly to the Most High. This will draw peace upon your country. I am its guardian angel, the Angel of Portugal. Above all, accept and endure with submission the suffering which the Lord will send you" (32:6).

As the Virgin Mary would start appearing in May 1917, this angel was preparing the children ahead of that time for her arrival by acclimating them to supernatural visits and teaching them about the importance of prayers and sacrifices.

MARIENFRIED, GERMANY (1946)

The first supernatural event took place in Marienfried, near Paffenhofen, Germany on April 25, 1946. Barbara Reuss, age twelve, was amazed when an angel appeared to her. The angel announced that he was "the Angel of the Great Mediatrix of Graces." He instructed Barbara to kneel while he introduced a prayer to be addressed to the Blessed Virgin Mary. This was his prayer:

> "Act as the Mother of Grace; act as the thrice miraculous Mother; the thrice admirable Mother of Grace, Thou Great Mediatrix of Graces!"

> As the angel recited this prayer, the Blessed Virgin appeared in a brilliant light.

> "She was unspeakably beautiful, brilliant, a blinding vision of the most pure light and radiance…Above her head were brilliant rays forming a three-tiered crown."

The third appearance of Our Lady occurred on June 25, exactly two months later, with many others in attendance. After the Blessed Virgin ceased speaking, she was suddenly surrounded by an immense number of angels wearing long white garments. Kneeling on the earth, they bowed deeply and recited a homage to the Holy Trinity. On its completion, the angel asked Barbara to repeat the prayer. This was the same angel who had been present during the first apparition on April 25 (3:199–201) (130).

ROME CITY, INDIANA, USA (1954–1955)

In the autumn of 1954, Sister Mildred Neuzil was graced with an appearance of St. Michael, the Angel of Peace, who offered her a sword (to conquer the world, the self, and the devil), a palm (for victory), and a cross (for the suffering she would be asked to endure in union with Jesus' passion). Sister was suspicious of the offer of a palm of victory—for she could think of no victory of hers deserving of such a reward. So then, St. Michael asked her if she would accept the cross. When she agreed to accept the cross, St. Michael replied,

> "Then you will accept the palm and the sword. With the sword the saints conquered themselves, the world, and the devil. I am the Angel of Peace; I come to those whose hearts are attuned to the Voice of God. To such as these I remain a perpetual light through blinding darkness. I was sent by Him who said, 'I am the Light of the world.'"

November 20, 1955 (the appearance of St. Gabriel)

> "I knelt down and asked him, 'Who are you?' He replied, 'I am the Angel Gabriel. I have come to tell you that Our Lord is pleased with your effort to do good. He asks that you go to His Mother and learn great purity of heart.'"

Following the visits of these two archangels, the apparitions of Our Lady began (1956–1958), and the favor and the responsibility to her children in America were made very clear (144: Part II).

GARABANDAL, SPAIN (1961–1965)

On Sunday, June 18, 1961, the people of the small town of Garabandal often congregated in the village square following Mass at their little church. Two girls, Conchita Gonzalez, age twelve, and Mari Cruz Gonzalez, (a second cousin) age eleven, decided to sneak away to a nearby apple tree in the yard of their schoolteacher while their parents caught up on gossip. Two other friends, Mari Loli Mazon, age twelve, and Jacinta Gonzalez, age twelve, had seen them sneak away and followed them. At first, they accused the first two girls of stealing—with threats of telling on them, but soon, they were all laughing and eating apples. They all fled when they heard their teacher's loud voice inside her home. They began to feel guilty for their actions and started throwing stones at an imagined location for the devil so as to please their saddened guardian angels. They grew weary of that play and were startled by a loud clap of thunder.

The Virgin Mary accompanied by angels in a brilliant supernatural light (Photo-Art created by author).

Suddenly, in the rocky lane, Conchita saw a very bright beautiful figure surrounded by a brilliant light. Stunned and speechless, she pointed to the apparition. The girls were first worried about Conchita's actions until they looked and saw the apparition also—and exclaimed, "An angel!" The angel looked at them but said nothing and disappeared. Frightened, the four girls ran back to the village square, hid behind the church and cried. Their teacher knew them well and could tell they had definitely seen something. They described the angel as a small, nine-year-old, childlike figure—but of great strength. He wore a long, blue, seamless robe. He had large, pinkish wings. His eyes were black. The teacher was convinced by their consistent description and strong emotions, but when each girl went home, their families were full of doubt and disbelief (34:1–3).

On Wednesday, June 21, 1961, they returned to the rocky lane to pray—accompanied now by several adults. After their prayers, the angel appeared. Conchita asked the angel what the priest had suggested (Who are you? Why are you here?), but the angel just smiled and disappeared. The adults were amazed by the physical transformation that the girls had gone into—an "ecstasy"—faces became "pale, transparentlike, and glowing with beautiful expressions." They radiated an indescribable beauty which impressed the villagers (34:7–8).

On Saturday, June 24, the angel said a word which meant "it is necessary that" and held a sign that contained Roman numerals on it. When the girls responded that they did not understand, the angel just smiled at them. Because the girls were in the light of the angel and oblivious to anything else around them, they were often surprised at how dark the day had become when the enveloping light of the angel had gone. From June 28–30 the angel reappeared, would not answer questions, and just smiled back at them.

But on Saturday, July 1, 1961, the angel finally revealed why he had come. He announced that the Virgin Mary will appear on the next day, Sunday, as Our Lady of Mount Carmel and would explain more to them. The girls were so excited and talked for two hours with the angel while the villagers could tell that something very special was happening! (34:9–11)

Sunday, July 2, 1961, was greatly anticipated as word spread like wildfire that Mary was expected to appear in Garabandal. The Spanish Civil Guard escorted and protected the four little girls. Many priests and doctors were present. Soon, after 6:00 p.m. in the rocky lane, the Virgin Mary suddenly appeared before them. There was light all around her with two angels standing on either side of her. The angel that they had been seeing was now recognized as St. Michael. When Mary confirmed St. Michael's identity, Jacinta giggled and said that she had a brother named Michael—"but without the saint part!" (34:12–14)

AGOO, PHILIPPINES (1989)

Our Blessed Mother instructed the visionary to go with some of his friends up to the small spring of water in the hills above Agoo, the site of San Antonio. This is where the first public apparition took place on March 31, 1989. First, there was a bright flash of light. Then he heard voices and the sounds of trumpets while angels descended from heaven toward him, singing "Alleluia" and "Salve Regina." The angels formed an inverted V with three angels on both sides and St. Michael at the apex with a white dove above his head. The Holy Family appeared on a cloud—St. Joseph with a shepherd's staff, and Our Lady was sitting on a rock, holding baby Jesus on her lap. Then Our Blessed Mother stood up over a guava tree on a rise, high, overlooking the spring, and spoke. Her Immaculate Heart was visible on her chest, and light radiated outward toward the spring of water (97:1).

ESCORTS / GUARDIAN ANGELS

PARIS, FRANCE (1830)

Catherine Laboure meets the Blessed Mother in 1830 after a glowing "child-angel" escorts her to the chapel (stained glass window in the National Shrine of the Miraculous Medal in Perryville, Missouri / photo by author).

On April 21, 1830, Catherine Laboure entered the convent of the Sisters of Charity at 140 Rue du Bac in Paris. On the eve of the Feast of St. Vincent de Paul, Catherine worked hard to prepare the chapel and convent for the next day's events. Exhausted, she fell into a deep sleep on this night of July 18, 1830.

> "At 11:30 in the evening, I heard someone calling me, 'Sister, Sister, Sister.' I awoke and looked in the direction that I heard the voice coming from. I saw a little child dressed in white who appeared to be about four or five years old. The child said to me, 'Let us go to the chapel. Get up quickly and go to the chapel. The Blessed Virgin is waiting for you.' The thought came to me 'but someone will hear me.' The child told me, 'Do not worry, it is 11:30 in the evening, and everyone is asleep. Come, I am waiting for you."

> "I arose and dressed quickly while the child waited for me at the foot of the bed. I followed him; he was always on my left. He shone brightly and illuminated the path we were taking. This astonished me greatly. But I was even more surprised as I entered the chapel and found that the door opened at the child's touch. My amazement was made complete when I saw that all the candles and lights in the chapel were illuminated as if for midnight mass. I did not yet see the Blessed Virgin. The child led me into the sanctuary to the chair where the sisters' director always sat."

> "I fell to my knees, and the child remained with me. I thought a long time had passed and looked to see if the sisters on the night watch passed by. Finally, the time had come. The child sensed this and told me, 'Here is the Blessed Virgin. She is here.' I heard a rustling like the sound of a silk dress. This sound was coming from the Gospel side of the altar...I doubted at first that this was the Blessed Virgin. After this, it was impossible for me to describe what I was feeling or what was going on around me. It seemed that I still could not recognize the Blessed Virgin...Now the child no longer spoke to me in a child's voice *but in a man's strong voice*."

Catherine's heart pounded furiously. From out of nowhere, the most beautiful lady she had ever seen appeared before her. Mary appeared so young and exuberant. The Blessed Virgin sat in the priest's chair. A wave of emotion swept through Catherine. She paused, then rushed forward, kneeling and placing her hands on Mary's knees.

> "I do not know how long I stayed there. All I know is that when she left, she suddenly was gone in the same way that she arrived. I found myself on the steps of the altar, and I saw that the child was where I had last seen him. He told me, 'She is gone.' We returned the same way we had come with the path illuminated before us. The child was always on my left. I believe that this child was my guardian angel who had become visible to guide me to the Blessed Virgin. Because I had prayed so hard he obtained this grace for me. He was dressed in white and was miraculously illuminated. I returned to my bed. I heard the clock sound the time; it was 2:00 a.m. I could not get back to sleep."

Catherine pondered all that had been said, wondering what her mission was to be. The "angel boy" faded away as she got back into bed. She was so excited that she could not fall back asleep (54:11–12).

GARABANDAL, SPAIN (1961–1965)

Father George Costigan, both a priest and a retired U.S. Army colonel, had lost all vision in one eye due to cancer. He was drawn to Mary's messages in Garabandal that emphasized *prayer, penance,* and *sacrifice*. He decided to visit Garabandal, unannounced in everyday clothing, and was greeted much to his surprise by a five-year-old girl *who spoke perfect English*. She asked him if he would like for visionary Jacinta to put her hand on his forehead. He asked the child why she would want to do that. The little child replied,

> "Aren't you the priest who has cancer?"

He was speechless. **How could this tiny child possibly know him or his condition and speak to him in perfect English?** He decided that *this must be an angel.* Minutes later, without any greeting, introduction, or identification, Jacinta arrived (in ecstasy) and promptly placed her hand on Father Costigan's forehead. A short time later, during Mass, his eyesight was fully restored, perfectly, with the last Hail Mary of the Rosary. His healing story is a powerful testimony today (33).

AKITA, JAPAN (1973)

On the night of July 5, 1973, Sister Agnes rose to pray at 3:00 a.m., and a voice came to her despite her deafness and said,

> "Be not afraid. Pray with fervor, not only because of your sins, but in reparation for those of all people. The world today wounds the most Sacred Heart of Our Lord by its ingratitude and injuries. The wounds of Mary are much deeper and more sorrowful than yours. Let us go to pray in the chapel together."

A beautiful figure suddenly stood next to her right shoulder. "I am the one who is with you and watches over you." The angel (her guardian angel) led her to the chapel and then disappeared. Sister Agnes then approached a tall statue of Mary and knelt before her to pray (11:193).

DAMASCUS, SYRIA (1982)

On December 15, 1982, at 11:37 p.m., while a huge crowd of people were praying in front of Myrna's little statue, Myrna Al Akharas felt an **invisible being tug at her arm and firmly escort her** to the roof garden. She was afraid and knelt on the tile floor. When she looked up, she saw the Virgin Mary in front of her! "She shined as if she were covered with diamonds. I was afraid, and I ran away screaming." Her husband and family were overwhelmed and confused. What was going on? On December 18, 1982, Myrna was once again mysteriously escorted by an invisible being to the roof garden. But this time, her husband and nine others followed. Myrna then had a beautiful experience with the Blessed Mother in the roof garden (2:250–251).

ZAKARPATTYA, UKRAINE (2002)

On August 27, 2002, two girls from the village of Nyzhne-Bolotne (in Western Ukraine) went to a grove to get some water from the spring there. Olenka Kuruts was ten years old and her friend, Mar'yanka Kobal, was nine years old. Olenka looked up to see a "beautiful lady" standing at some distance behind Mar'yanka. When Mar'yanka first turned around to look, she did not see her. But after she filled her bucket with water and looked around again, she did also see the "beautiful lady," standing quietly several paces away. Because the lady did not say anything, they became frightened, thinking she might be a witch. The lady was standing on a small cloud adorned with all kinds of flowers, just above the ground. Mary was wearing a white dress with a blue belt and a white headscarf. As the girls took their filled buckets and headed back to the village, the lady on the cloud glided along behind them, escorting them home.

Later that same day, the girls headed to pick up Olenka's younger sister from kindergarten when they saw the lady on the little cloud again. When they made the sign of the cross to protect themselves, the lady was quite pleased and smiled radiantly. Mary then made the sign of the cross in return with her folded fingers. When the girls asked who she was, they were told that she was "the Most Pure Virgin." On their way home from the kindergarten, the lady appeared again—this time with "two angels" with her. One "angel" was taller than the other. They later learned that these were "guardian angels." A third angel which appeared in later encounters was identified as St. Michael (159).

GIVING COMMUNION

FATIMA, PORTUGAL (1916)

On another day, while pasturing their sheep, the children decided to pray near the cave as the angel had urged them to do. They became aware of an extraordinary light shining on them. When they looked up, the angel was standing over them. In his left hand, he held a chalice with a Host suspended above it. Drops of blood fell from the Host into the chalice. Leaving the chalice suspended in midair, the angel knelt down and made them repeat three times:

> "Most Holy Trinity, Father, Son, and Holy Spirit, I offer you the most precious Body and Blood, Soul and Divinity of Jesus Christ, present in all the tabernacles of the world, in reparation for all the outrages, sacrileges, and indifference with which He, Himself, is offended. And through the infinite merits of His most Sacred Heart and of the Immaculate Heart of Mary, I beg of You the conversion of poor sinners."

Then he took the chalice and Host with both hands, giving the Host to Lucia and sharing the chalice between Jacinta and Francisco.

> "Take and drink the Body and Blood of Jesus Christ, horribly outraged by ungrateful men. Make reparations for their crimes and console your God" (29:56, 60).

But wait a minute—only priests can convert the bread and wine into the Body and Blood. How can an angel do this? This question was raised in later apparitions, and the answer from heaven was this: Yes, only priests can do this; Angels are borrowing the consecrated Host and wine from tabernacles of parishes. So, was any parish nearby missing anything? Not well known until now is the fact that a local parish miles away had their Host strangely missing *from within the locked tabernacle* about that same time. The chalice was present, but *it had been moved* to a different position inside the tabernacle. The priest was so dumbfounded—as he held the only key—that he never told anybody other than his bishop. It bothered him for years as he could not explain the disappearance of these precious items entrusted to his care and protection. Several months before he died, he confessed this inexplicable incident to others (29:61–62).

LIPA, PHILIPPINES (1948)

On an occasion, Sister Teresita Castillo was too ill to attend Mass, so *an angel brought her communion, placing a Host on her tongue* (126).

GARABANDAL, SPAIN (1961–1965)

On various occasions, St. Michael appeared and would administer Communion to the four girls (visionaries). Villagers would observe them stick their tongues out to receive the Host but could never see the Host. The girls never realized that the Host was actually invisible as they could feel it and swallow it quite naturally. On June 22, 1962, he told Conchita that he would give her a visible Host during Communion—*which was when she first learned that the Host had NOT been visible*. The Virgin Mary told Conchita that the date for this miracle would be July 18, 1962. This was the night that the miraculous Host appeared "out of thin air" and was witnessed by many people at close range as well as captured on film by a movie camera (see chapter 12) (33) (34:45–46).

CUENCA, ECUADOR (1989)

On November 8, 1989, Patricia Talbot was trying to study in her bedroom when she sensed Mary's presence just before she appeared to her. Our Lady told Patricia to look in the little box that the little Fatima statue had been placed on; "There is My Sacred Son." Patricia removed the statue and opened the box; there was a Sacred Host inside! As she dropped to her knees immediately in adoration, Mary told her that **St. Michael had placed it there**—and that she should pray before it every day, telling very few people. After several months of dedicated adoration and cautious disclosure, Jesus told her that a priest should distribute it to the inhabitants of the house. On March 4, 1990, after the last apparition of Mary, Father Teran celebrated that special Mass in their home (23:52–53).

AGOO, PHILIPPINES (1992)

August 1, 1992: An angel appeared and gave Judiel Nieva Holy Communion from a Host and a chalice suspended in midair (97:2).

CONDUCTING MISSIONS

"Thy will be done, on earth as it is in heaven." If God's will shall prevail, then man's efforts shall often be frustrated and confused by his own inability to have *his* will succeed. The following historic accounts seem to illustrate how heaven does prevail whenever it chooses. And angels are the invisible agents conducting those secret missions...

TLAXCALA, MEXICO (1541)

When the abbot removed the present statue of San Lorenzo from the chapel and replaced it with the miraculous image/statue of the Mother of God that had been discovered in the burned-out Ocotlan tree (see chapter 12), not everyone was happy about the change. The Indian sacristan resented the removal of the statue of San Lorenzo and secretly transferred Our Lady's statue to another location in the middle of the night. But the next morning, the statue of the Virgin Mary was found back on the altar where the abbot had originally placed it. Determined to not be stopped, the sacristan again removed the statue of Mary the next night—and actually took it home with him. But to his shock, the statue disappeared from his home and reappeared back on the altar in the church by the next morning. Stubbornly, the sacristan was even more determined to stop this mischief. On a third night, he hid the statue of Mary at the church in a cabinet with vestments—and then slept in front of it in order to catch the mischievous ones! Once again, the beautiful God-given image of Our Lady escaped through supernatural means and appeared back on the altar where Blessed Mary had desired it to be placed. The sacristan was now convinced that Our Lady's wish to be placed on the altar should be respected (3:40) (9).

RAPALLO, ITALY (1557)

On July 2, 1557, a farmer named Giovanni Chichizola was walking on a donkey trail on a wooded hill overlooking the city of Rapallo.

Coming upon a cool, shady spot, he paused for his noonday rest. The sound of a sweet voice calling his name startled him to alertness. There, standing close beside him, was a beautiful lady surrounded by an intense light. The Blessed Virgin Mary appeared to him and reassured him by saying,

> "Do not fear, Giovanni. I am the Mother of God. I have chosen you to be a messenger of my motherly will. Visit the ecclesiastics of Rapallo and let them know that the Mother of God has chosen this place as her perpetual dwelling place and would like a church to be erected here. I leave here a pledge of my love."

The vision then directed his attention to a small picture propped against one of the rocks where he had been resting.

> "Tell the people that **this picture was brought here from Greece by the angels**. I leave it here as a token of my love for them. Fast on Saturday."

The vision then disappeared as if carried away in a cloud. The farmer Giovanni studied the icon on the rock. The picture depicts Our Blessed Mary lying on a bier at the time of her passing from this world on to the heavenly kingdom. The Holy Trinity is represented by the figures in the central part of the icon. Surrounding the Virgin in a mournful attitude are several saints and two angels. Giovanni attempted to pick the icon up off the rock, but he could not budge it at all.

Later, when others arrived to investigate his amazing story, one of the priests raised the portrait without difficulty and carried it in procession to the parish church, where it was carefully locked up pending further investigation. But the next morning, the icon had disappeared from the church—only to be found back up on the rock on the wooded hill.

Once again, the villagers brought the icon back down the hill and to the church where it was displayed all day to the veneration of many. The people were impressed with the details of Giovanni's experience. At the end of that day, the icon was locked away for safekeeping. But they were surprised the next morning to find that it had disappeared again! After a long search, the icon was discovered to be back up on the rock on the hill overlooking Rapallo. All agreed that these supernatural journeys of the icon were a clear sign and indication that the Blessed Mother wished for the icon to remain in that particular place. They believed that they should build her requested church on that spot so that it could house and protect the treasured icon. The very next year in 1558, the archbishop of Turin authorized the building of a church on the "Hill of Joy" where Mary's visit had taken place. Construction began immediately, and during the following year, the church opened and was dedicated to Our Blessed Mother. For seventeen quiet years, the precious icon was loved and venerated on the Hill of Joy.

In 1574, a group of Greek sailors, sailing from Ragusa, experienced a bad storm while crossing the Gulf of Tigullio. The ship's captain, Nicholas de Allegretis, together with the crew, prayed to and promised Our Lady that if they were saved, they would make a pilgrimage to the nearest sanctuary dedicated to her. Upon safely reaching land, they climbed the hill to the sanctuary to fulfill their vow of thanksgiving. It was then that they noticed the treasured icon, recognizing it and declaring that it was formerly venerated in Ragusa—**but that it had mysteriously disappeared from there in 1557.** The Greeks claimed ownership, which resulted in court proceedings before the magistrate of Genoa. Eventually, the icon was given back to the Greeks for safe transport to its original location in Ragusa.

The icon was taken to the port, boarded on the ship, and placed in a secure location. The ship was well out to sea when **the icon suddenly disappeared**! Eventually, the captain and his crew learned that the icon had reappeared back in the church on the hill **where Our Lady had wanted it to stay.** All agreed this time that it should remain there out of respect for Blessed Mary's wishes (3:43–45).

SCUTARI, ALBANIA / GENAZZANO, ITALY (1467)

With the death of the last great Albanian leader in January 1467, the Turkish army poured into Albania, occupying all its fortresses, cities, and provinces with the exception of Scutari in the north of the country. However, the city's capacity to resist was limited, and its capture was expected at any moment. With its fall, Christian Albania would be defeated. Faced with this prospect, those who wished to practice their faith in Christian lands began a sad exodus. Two men named Giorgio and De Sclavis also studied the possibility of fleeing, but something kept them in Scutari, near the church with the miraculous painting. In this church, the faithful Christians venerated an eggshell-thin fresco of Our Lady **which had mysteriously descended from the heavens two hundred years before**. According to tradition, it had come from the east. Having poured out innumerable graces over the whole population, its church became the principal center of pilgrimage in Albania. Their great Albanian leader himself had visited this shrine more than once to ardently ask Our Lady for victory in battle. Now the shrine was threatened with imminent destruction and profanation.

The two Albanians were torn by the idea of leaving the great treasure of Albania in the hands of the enemy in order to flee the Turkish terror. In their perplexity, they went to the old church to ask their Blessed Mother for the good counsel they needed. That night, the Virgin Mary inspired **both of them** in their sleep. She commanded them to prepare to leave their country, adding that the miraculous fresco was also going to leave Scutari for another country to escape profanation at the hands of the Turks. Finally, she ordered them to follow the painting *wherever it went.*

The next morning, the two friends went to the shrine. Suddenly, they saw the picture detach itself from the wall on which it had hung. Leaving its niche, it hovered for a moment and was then suddenly wrapped in a white cloud through which the image continued to be visible. The painting left the church and floated out of Scutari. It traveled slowly through the air at a considerable altitude and advanced in the direction of the Adriatic Sea at a speed that allowed the two walkers to follow. After covering some twenty-four miles, they reached the coast.

Without stopping, the picture left the land and advanced over the waters of the Adriatic Sea while the faithful Giorgio and De

Sclavis continued to follow, *walking on the waves*. When night would fall, the mysterious cloud, which had protected them with its shade from the heat of the sun during the day, guided them by night with light, like the column of fire in the desert that guided the Jews in their exodus from Egypt.

They traveled day and night until they reached the Italian coast. There, they continued following the miraculous picture, climbing mountains, fording rivers, and passing through valleys. Finally, they reached the vast plain of Lazio from where they could see the towers and domes of Rome. Upon reaching the gates of the city, the cloud suddenly disappeared before their disappointed eyes. Giorgio and De Sclavis began to search the city, going from church to church, asking if the painting had descended there. All their attempts to find the painting failed, and the Romans disregarded these two foreigners with their strange and incredible tale.

Transported miraculously by the angels, a fresco flies from Albania to Italy with two men following it- as requested by the Virgin Mary.

Meanwhile, in Genazzano, a charming medieval town about thirty miles south of Rome, financial difficulties had prevented the necessary and urgent restoration of the ancient temple there. Petruccia de Nocera had been left a modest fortune following the death of her husband in 1436. Living alone, she dedicated most of her time to prayer and services in the church of the Mother of Good Counsel. It grieved her to see the deplorable state of the sacred premises of the attached ancient chapel, and she prayed fervently that they would be restored. Finally, she resolved to take the initiative. After obtaining permission from the friars, she donated her goods to initiate the restoration in the hope that others would help complete it once it was commenced.

Petruccia, who was already eighty years old, found that her generous offering was scarcely enough to complete the first phase of the new construction of the chapel. To make matters worse, no one came forth to help. To her dismay, the building had hardly risen three feet when construction came to a halt due to lack of resources.

On April 25, 1467, the feast day of the city's patron, Saint Mark, a solemn celebration began with Mass. It was Saturday, and the crowd began to gather in front of the church of the Mother of Good Counsel. The only discrepant note in the celebration was the unfinished work of Petruccia's ancient chapel. At about four in the afternoon, everyone heard the chords of a beautiful melody that seemed to come from heaven. The people looked up toward the towers of the churches and saw a white cloud that shone with a thousand luminous rays; it gradually neared the stupefied crowd to the sound of an exceptionally beautiful melody. The cloud descended on the church of the Mother of Good Counsel and poised over the wall of the unfinished chapel of Saint Biagio, which Petruccia had started.

Suddenly, the bells of the old tower began to ring by themselves, and the other bells of the town rang miraculously in unison. The rays that emanated from the little cloud faded away, and the cloud itself gradually vanished, revealing a beautiful object to the enchanted gaze of the spectators. It was a painting that represented Our Lady tenderly holding her Divine Son in her arms. Almost immediately, the Virgin Mary began to cure the sick and grant countless consolations, the memory of which was recorded for posterity by the local ecclesiastical authority.

Shortly thereafter, amazing news came to Rome: **a picture of Our Lady had appeared in the skies of Genazzano to the sound of beautiful music and had come to rest over the wall of a church that was being rebuilt.** The two Albanians rushed to find their country's beloved treasure miraculously suspended in the air next to the wall of the chapel where it remains to this day. Although some inhabitants found the strangers' story difficult to believe, careful investigation later proved that the two were telling the truth, and that the image was indeed the same one that had graced the shrine in Scutari for two hundred years. This miraculous painting had made the incredible journey, *carried by the angels*, upon the request and direction of the Blessed Virgin as foretold to these two devoted gentlemen (108).

LORETO, ITALY (1291)

In Loreto, Italy, a small house enclosed in a grand basilica is believed to be the house where the Virgin Mary lived and raised Jesus. On May 12, 1291, ***the angels moved the house*** to a small town named Tersatto in Croatia. Very early in the morning, the neighbors discovered it, and they were astonished to see this house without a foundation. They could not explain how it arrived there. Some days later, the Virgin Mary appeared to a priest of that place and explained to him where the house came from. She said,

> "You should know that the house that was recently brought to your land is the same house in which I was born and grew up. Here, in the Annunciation of the Archangel Gabriel, I conceived the Creator of all things. Here, the Word became flesh. The altar that was moved with the house was consecrated by Peter, the Prince of the Apostles. This house has come from Nazareth to your land by the power of God for whom nothing is impossible. Now, so that you can give a testimony of this, be healed. Your unexpected and sudden healing will confirm the truth that I have declared to you today."

The priest who had been sick for a long time was healed immediately and announced to the people about the miracle that had occurred. Pilgrimages to the Holy House began. The residents of this small town built a simple building over the Holy House to protect it from the elements of nature.

After the three years and seven months, the house disappeared from Tersatto on the night of December 10, 1294—never to return again. On that same day of December 10, **some shepherds in the region of Loreto, Italy reported to have seen a house flying over the ocean, *held by angels*.** There was an angel dressed with a red cape (St. Michael) who directed the others; the Virgin Mary with the Child Jesus were seated on the house. The angels lowered the house on the place named Banderuola. Many arrived to visit this holy house, but there were also some who went to mug the pilgrims. For this reason, people stopped going there, and the house was **again moved by the angels** to a hill in the middle of a farm. The Holy House would not remain there for much longer either. The farm belonged to two brothers who began to argue over who was the owner of the house.

For a third time, the house was moved to another hill, placing it in the middle of the path. This is the place that it has occupied for seven hundred years. The residents of Recanati and Loreto truly did not know the story of the Holy House; they only knew of the miracles that took place there. Two years later, the Virgin Mary appeared to a hermit named Paul, and she told him the origin and the history of the Holy House:

> "It was kept in the city of Nazareth until—with the permission of God—those who honored this house were thrown out by the enemies. Since it was no longer honored and it was in danger of being profaned, My Son wanted to transfer it from Nazareth to Yugoslavia and from there to your land."

Paul then told this story to the townspeople, and they began a process to verify the authenticity of the house. They first went to Tersatto and later to Nazareth. All of the descriptions of the interior elements and other details correlated. In Nazareth, they discovered that it truly was the house of the Virgin Mary. The measurements of its foundation (left behind) were exactly the same as those of the little house in Loreto.

A story recounts that the bishop of Portugal visited the Holy House and wanted to take a stone to build a church in honor of the Virgin of Loreto. The pope gave him permission, so the bishop sent his secretary to remove the stone and take it back with him. The bishop suddenly became sick—and when his secretary arrived, the bishop was almost dead. The bishop asked a few religious sisters to pray for him, and some days later, he received this message, "Our Lady says, **'If the bishop wants to recover, he should return to the Virgin Mary what he has taken from her.'**" The secretary and bishop were astonished about this since no one had known about the stone being taken from the Holy House. The secretary departed immediately to Loreto with the stone. When the secretary returned, the bishop had been completely healed. For this reason, over the centuries, the popes have prohibited the removal of any part of the Holy House under threat of ex-communication (127) (128).

In 1920, Pope Benedict XV declared Our Lady of Loreto as patroness of pilots. Seven years later, her medal hung on board Charles Lindbergh's plane on his famous flight across the Atlantic Ocean. He stated that the medal's rapping against the control panel woke him when he fell asleep at the controls—thus saving his life (67:20).

ARTISTS AND CRAFTSMEN

A beautiful and miraculous creation like the Our Lady of Guadalupe image on Juan Diego's cactus cloth in 1531 (chapter 12) was not likely due to any artistic talents of the Virgin Mary. Instead, this would have been a divine task assigned to the elite spiritual beings—the angels. "Angel theology" states that the Virtues are responsible for miraculous signs and miracles. Likewise, the Virgin Mary would not have been able to change the natural color of the cave wall rock in Guaitara Canyon, Colombia (chapter 12) into the brilliant colors of the artistic masterpiece that miraculously appeared there overnight in 1754. We can *assume* that the angels were responsible for that amazing image also. But do we have any absolute proof or eyewitnesses to angels creating or crafting items? Here is some evidence from historical encounters.

WALSINGHAM, ENGLAND (1061)

In a small village in North Norfolk, England, in 1061, lived a devout young widow, Richeldis de Faverches, Lady of the Manor of Walsingham. The Blessed Virgin appeared to her three times in a vision, and each time showed her the house in which the Holy Family had dwelt in Nazareth. Mary led Richeldis "in spirit" to Nazareth to show her the place where the Archangel Gabriel had greeted her and directed the widow to take measurements of the house so that she could build one like it at Walsingham. In this spot, the Virgin Mary explained, the people would celebrate the Annunciation, "the root of mankind's gracious redemption."

> "Do all this unto my special praise and honor. And all who are in any way distressed or in need, let them seek me here in that little house you have made at Walsingham. To all that seek me, there shall be given succor. And there at Walsingham in this little house shall be held in remembrance the great joy of my salutation when Saint Gabriel told me I should through humility become the Mother of God's Son."

Three times Richeldis experienced this vision and request. This confirmed her desire to have the replica constructed, but the directions about the exact location were unclear to both her and the carpenters. Richeldis gave instructions for the building to commence but nothing seemed to go right. When the carpenters could make no progress in building, Richeldis found it difficult to go to sleep. She spent the night in prayer, asking for guidance. There was an energy in the air that "made the night seem almost alive." She heard singing that seemed "not of this world" and went out into her garden to investigate. She noted that the "heavenly singing" was coming from the direction of the unfinished construction. As she approached the site, she was amazed to see that the little house had been completed—but had been moved about two hundred yards from the site of the original construction! **She then saw what appeared to be angels leaving the now completed house.** When the carpenters returned to the site, they, too, reported hearing strange sounds and were amazed to see that the house had been moved and completed. They pronounced the craftsmanship of the completed construction to be *far superior to their own*. The Holy House had been miraculously built, and very soon pilgrims began to arrive (4:63) (155-b).

LICHEN, POLAND (1850)

Our Lady appeared in 1850 to Mikolaj Sikatka, who was pasturing his cattle. She called for people to come to conversion, penance, and prayer. She informed about the punishment which would come—predicting wars and an epidemic of cholera. She asked for her painting to be hung in a new church:

> "When hard days will come, those people who will come in front of this picture and will pray and do penance will not die. Whenever this nation will come to Me and ask for help, I will never leave this nation, and I will protect this nation. The pilgrims from all of Poland will come to this picture, and they will find consolation in their distresses. I reign for My nation forever. On this place will be built a magnificent church for My veneration. **If people will not build this church,** *the angels will build it*." (125)

QUITO, ECUADOR (1610)

The statue of Mary in Quito, Ecuador that was miraculously completed by the angels in the 1600's while Mother Mariana watched.

BE NOT AFRAID TO FOLLOW THE FOOTPRINTS FROM HEAVEN

Mother Mariana of the Royal Convent of the Immaculate Conception had been having visits from the Virgin Mary for some time when she received a special request from Our Lady on January 21, 1610:

> "It is now necessary that you have my holy statue made promptly, just as you see me, and that you make haste to place it in the place which I indicated to you."

Mother Mariana responded with great humility:

> "Beloved Mother of my soul, the tiny ant that thou hast before you will be unable to relate any of thy beautiful features… or thy height. It will be necessary that the three archangels who accompany thee…would come to sculpt thy statue which thou askest me to have made, so that the work may be as thou wilt…"

Blessed Mary replied, in a calming manner,

> "Do not be worried about any of this, dear daughter. *The perfection of the work is my concern. Gabriel, Michael, and Raphael, with the whole Heavenly Court, will secretly take care of the making of the statue*…Regarding my height, bring the cord here that you wear and measure me without fear, since to a Mother like me, the confidence, respect, and humility of her daughters pleases her. Beloved daughter, put into my hands one of the ends of your cord, and I will place it upon my forehead, and you will apply the other end to my right foot."

The three archangels lifted the crown of the Queen of Heaven while she was placing the end of the cord on her head. But the cord was too short to reach to the ground. But the Child Jesus reached out from his Mother's arms and miraculously stretched it to reach. Then Mother Mariana came out of her ecstasy and now had the exact measurements for the statue.

On February 5, 1610, she contacted a Spanish sculptor, Francisco del Castillo, and honored him with this special project that would be due for consecration on February 2, 1611. The bishop routinely inspected the work going on in the choir loft. On January 10, 1611, he noted that the statue only needed a final coat of paint before completion. The sculptor indicated that he must travel far to Pasto, Colombia to get the fine paints required, and so he left town.

At midnight, the first hour of January 16 (the day the sculptor was to return), Mother Mariana witnessed the choir loft, and the entire church illuminated with a supernatural light. The tabernacle opened by itself, and the three archangels—Michael, Gabriel, and Raphael—placed themselves before the throne of God, and something was given to them. Choirs of angels united their voices in singing, "Blessed Mary, temple and tabernacle of the Blessed Trinity." In the next instant, Mother Mariana saw the three archangels in the choir loft, illuminating the statue with their divine light. St. Francis of Assisi appeared and joined the three archangels as they approached the unfinished statue. The statue was transformed so rapidly that Mother Mariana could not perceive how it happened. St. Francis took the cord from around his waist and placed it around the statue's waist. Then he and the archangels disappeared as the Blessed Virgin appeared and entered the statue herself while angels continued to sing the Latin hymn, *Salva Sancta Parens*.

At 3:30 a.m. Mother Mariana came out of her ecstasy and saw the statue still illuminated by Divine Light. When all of the convent sisters came to see the miraculous completion of the statue, they heard the angels still singing and saw the supernatural light still present. Later that day, when the sculptor returned, the nuns watched quietly as he approached the choir loft. As he approached the statue, he dropped to his knees and cried out, "This exquisite statue is not my work!" He wept as he realized that a miracle had been performed. He immediately composed a written statement testifying to the beautiful changes in the sculpting and painting that "were not of my hands." The bishop was notified, and he, too, knelt and wept before the beautiful masterpiece, verifying the miraculous changes *performed by angels* that had completed the wooden statue in the sculptor's absence (56:43–44, 50–56).

If you can accept even *just one* of the historical accounts presented in this chapter as genuine and true, then angels are indeed among us. And even though "angelic footprints" appear to be all around us, there is still more evidence ahead in our next consideration…

Did you ever imagine that there would be so many "footprints" from heaven to consider?

CHAPTER 16

ANGELIC PROTECTION

"He will order His angels to protect you wherever you go. They will hold you up with their hands so you won't even hurt your foot on a stone." (**Psalms 91:11–12**)

The first thing that you should understand by now is that you should never attack or assault the Mother of Jesus—should you ever happen to encounter her. Remember what happened in Dong Lu, China in 1900? (See chapter 10.) When the barbaric warriors of the Boxer Rebellion saw the Virgin Mary in the sky, they fired their guns at her! This brought the fiery archangel Michael out of the sky on his flaming horse to swoop down and terrorize the ten thousand rebels to scatter like rats, never to return and threaten the village of Dong Lu ever again (1:84). Here are excerpts from other accounts throughout history.

ZARAGOZA, SPAIN (1936–1939)

Although this first chapel was eventually destroyed along with various other Christian shrines, the statue and pillar gifted by the Virgin Mary stayed intact under the protection of the people of Zaragoza, Spain. Today, a baroque-style church, completed in 1686, exists on this site and houses the precious items given to James by the Virgin Mary in 40 A.D. During the Spanish Civil War of 1936–1939, three bombs were dropped on the church, but ***none of them exploded***. Two of them are on display in the basilica today (160:3).

MEDJUGORJE, BOSNIA-HERZEGOVINA (1981–present)

During Bosnia's bloody war, the conflict came to within five miles of Medjugorje. All the surrounding villages were destroyed by the enemy and most of their people massacred. But Medjugorje seemed protected—as if in a safe bubble from all evil, maintaining a tranquil, peaceful atmosphere. Even when bombs were directed at the village, they would explode safely high in the air or **lie unexploded** in nearby fields. More than four thousand Serbian artillery shells had been fired at Medjugorje with the war's battlefront just two miles away. But the only casualties were one cow, two chickens, and a dog. Father Slavko called it a miracle (8:260).

Finally, on a clear, blue-sky morning, two Russian-made MIG fighter jets approached Medjugorje to destroy it. On this cloudless morning, a dense "strange silver fog" suddenly appeared, mysteriously covering the entire town and obstructing their vision. They were unable to drop their bombs, and for some reason, one of the jets went down, killing the pilot. The other jet returned safely to base. Apparently, the surviving pilot was so unnerved by the bizarre incident that he defected from his military unit. The peacefulness of Medjugorje continues to only be disturbed by the church bells ringing and roosters crowing! (8:261) (131a)

MANAOAG, PANGASINAN, PHILIPPINES (1610)

When the villagers heard of the vision, they hastily journeyed there and soon built a small church over the place of the apparition. A town soon flourished near it and was named "Manaoag"—which means "to call." The Blessed Virgin seems to have protected this region ever since then from numerous threats. There was a time in which mountain tribes were accustomed to burning Christian villages. One day, when Manaoag was destined to be torched, flaming arrows were shot into the little church. Not a single flame set it on fire.

In 1698, huge swarms of locusts began to ravage the rice fields. They came in swarms so vast that the sky was darkened. An image of the Blessed Virgin (that had been brought to the Philippines by Padre Juan de San Jacinto of Spain in the early seventeenth century) was taken out to the fields. Desperate for help, they placed the small image on the ground and then watched in amazement as the locusts **began to destroy each other** in a totally unexpected manner that had never been witnessed before. The carnage continued until not a single locust could be found alive.

On an even greater scale, during World War II, four bombs were dropped. Three landed on the patio and only damaged the facade of the church. One bomb crashed through the roof of the church, but it **failed to explode** inside. The church was miraculously saved.

Another spectacular miracle was documented in 1698. It was on Easter Sunday when a fire of unknown origin devoured the whole town and crept steadily toward the church. The parish priest was notified of the danger and rushed to the scene. He grabbed the statue of Our Lady from inside the church and took it out to protect it from harm. He prayed and pleaded with Blessed Mary, saying,

"Dear Lady, if you do not spare the church from fire, I will hurl myself into the flames with you so that the two of us may be consumed by it."

After he pleaded with Our Lady of Manaoag, the flames immediately died down and were extinguished. Once again, the church was miraculously saved (3:59–61).

MEXICO CITY, MEXICO (1921)

In November 1921, a bomb was secretly planted in a bouquet of flowers that was placed on the altar—just beneath the divine image of Our Lady of Guadalupe hanging above it. The bomb exploded with such force that it blew out windows in the old Basilica, shattered the marble altar, and twisted a large bronze crucifix. Yet, the image of Our Lady of Guadalupe and the glass enclosing this sacred treasure were **completely unharmed** and safe—*despite its location right above the bomb* (4:130).

FATIMA, PORTUGAL (1922)

After these two young visionaries, Jacinta and Francisco, died, a small chapel was built at the site of the apparitions in the Cova da Iria. But on March 6, 1922, two bombs were placed at the site—one in the chapel and one by the holm oak tree. The bomb in the chapel blew the roof off, but the one by the tree, where Mary had appeared, **failed to explode.** This attack enraged people, leading to a rebuilding of the chapel, and a grand procession of sixty thousand faithful followers on May 13, 1923 to return the preserved statue of Our Lady to its home in the chapel (32:75).

ROME, ITALY (around 600 AD)

Pope Liberius provided a special painting of Madonna and Child from St. Helen, mother of Emperor Constantine, to be housed in this new basilica that had been inspired by Our Lady of the Snows. Many miracles are attributed to this wonderful painting. When Gregory I was pope (590–604 AD), Rome was ravaged by a plague. Pope Gregory carried the image of the Holy Mother in a procession from the basilica as far as Hadrian's Mausoleum. When the procession arrived, **they heard an invisible heavenly choir** singing *Regina Coeli*. When the pope asked the Virgin to pray for the city, **he saw an apparition of St. Michael** replacing the sword of vengeance into its scabbard. *And then the plague ended* (4:117).

St. Michael the Archangel (Photo-Art created by author)

FATIMA, PORTUGAL (1917)

The publicity toward the children was endless on every day. Lucia later reported the details of one of these visions:

"At the left of Our Lady and a little above, we saw an angel with a flaming sword in his left hand. Flashing, it gave out flames that looked as though they would set the world on fire—but they died in contact with the splendor that Our Lady radiated toward him from her right hand. Pointing to the earth with his right hand, the angel cried out in a loud voice, 'Penance! Penance! Penance!'…" (29:121–122)

SEREDNE, UKRAINE (1954–1955)

Anna saw the Virgin Mary on fifteen further occasions, teaching her to pray with her heart and other important things. Many of these apparitions were accompanied by phenomena such as a spinning sun, shooting stars, powerful winds, and unusual cloud formations. Shortly thereafter, on May 15, 1955, St. Michael the Archangel appeared to the young girl in the grotto. Anna described him as "shining like the sun with a flaming sword which he brandished three times in a swooping gesture, leaving a trail of fire blazing through the heavens to eternity." As Anna gazed at the flaming heavens, the Blessed Mother appeared in the center of immense rays of brilliant light (2:270).

L'ILE-BOUCHARD, FRANCE (1947)

Halfway through praying a decade of the Rosary in front of the altar, they looked up and were astonished to see a "beautiful lady" with her hands joined in prayer. A white rosary hung from her right arm. To the left of the lady was an angel, holding a lily while his eyes were fixed in contemplation of the lady. The angel was kneeling on his right knee, surrounded by an intense white light. He wore a robe of a soft rose color. He, too, had blue eyes and long blonde curly hair. In his left hand, he held a lily stalk while his right hand was placed over his heart. His white wings were trimmed in gold while his feathers moved slightly in a breeze that the children could not feel. He seemed to be in profound contemplation of Our Lady. He stated that his name was Gabriel. This area of the church was strangely lit with colors that the girls had never seen before. Eventually, the apparition disappeared into what appeared to be a "cloud of silvery dust" (3:204–205).

KNOCK, IRELAND (1879)

"The entire back wall of the church was bathed in a brilliant light, which could be seen from quite a distance away. Everything was raised about two feet off the ground. There was an altar, on top of which stood a lamb with a cross. The altar and lamb were surrounded by angels, hovering above. Around them were golden stars or small brilliant lights, glittering like glass balls…I also saw the wings of the angels fluttering!" (3:148–150)

BARCELONA / MADRID, SPAIN (1998)

When Father Joshua Waltz was only eighteen years old, he had travelled to Rome with other students and two priests. He was fortunate to meet Pope John Paul II and talk with him as part of a select group. The pope gave him a blessed rosary before he departed. Prior to this, he had balked at becoming a priest because he had other dreams and romantic visions typical of many young men. He also had the invincible mind-set and naïve attitude typical of a young adult. As he left his group and set out for Barcelona on his own to meet his mother who was arriving there shortly, he began having many misfortunes: catching a slow train that went on strike for six hours, arriving Nice, France in the early hours of the morning and running for his life to avoid being robbed and beaten by a gang of five young men and becoming penniless and hungry.

When he finally arrived to rendezvous with his mother in Barcelona—36 hours later than planned—he learned that her flights had been cancelled, so she would be late also! But he was penniless and hungry. With his last dollar, he bought a loaf of bread and a bottle of water and wondered how he would possibly survive. As he prayed with the Rosary that Pope John Paul II had given him, a stranger approached him. He was a six-foot, five-inch tall, 280-lb. black man. The kind stranger asked how he was doing, and Joshua related all of his recent troubles. The tall stranger offered to buy him a full meal, and Joshua was stunned by his kindness. After Joshua ate and they talked, the stranger parted—never having mentioned his name.

Joshua felt uplifted and hopeful again and started strolling down one of the main streets of Barcelona. A young lady approached him on the street and suggested that he pay for sex with her. When he told her that he was not interested and turned to leave, he ran right into her five pimps, blocking his path. They challenged and confronted him, insisting that he cooperate with having sex with her and pay the price. When they started getting physical, he turned and screamed at them, "LEAVE ME ALONE!"

Much to his surprise, they halted, backed off, and said, "Okay." Puzzled by their reaction, he turned around and ran directly into the towering, six foot five, 280-lb. stranger again, standing directly behind him! "Hey, man, looks like you were getting roughed up and needed my help." Joshua was stunned how he had suddenly appeared to help him out. After thanking him, they parted again, but he still did not know the stranger's name.

Joshua connected with his mother soon afterwards, and two weeks later, they journeyed on to Madrid, some 315 miles away. While shopping, they got separated in this city of three million people. Suddenly, Joshua ran right into the same towering stranger once again. How could this possibly happen, he thought, two weeks later, over three hundred miles away, in such a large city? This time, grateful Joshua had some money and offered to buy the stranger a meal. They sat together on the outdoor patio of a restaurant to eat their pizza and talk. When Joshua caught sight of his mother passing by, he told the kind stranger that he wanted to have his mother meet him—and ran to grab her. This outdoor patio was fenced so that the *only access is from within the restaurant*. Yet, as Joshua returned a moment later with his mother, the towering stranger had magically vanished *without having exited the patio*. On the table, written on a piece of paper, was this parting message, "**God Bless - Michael**." It was *then* that Father Joshua Waltz finally *knew* who had actually been watching over him and protecting him (60).

KOREA (1950)

This is a true story of a marine wounded in Korea in 1950. Father Walter Muldy, a navy chaplain who spoke to the young marine, his mother, and also the outfit commander, always affirmed the veracity of this narrative. Someone who read the original letter retells the story here in all its details—and in the first person narrative to better convey the impact it must have had when first told by the son to his mother.

"Dear Mom,

I am writing to you from a hospital bed. Don't worry, Mom, I am okay. I was wounded, but the doctor says that I will be up in no time. But that's not what I have to tell you, Mom. Something happened to me that I don't dare tell anyone else for fear of their disbelief. But I have to tell you, the one person I can confide in, though even you may find it hard to believe. You remember the prayer to Saint Michael that you taught me to pray when I was little: 'Michael, Michael of the morning?' Before I left home for Korea, you urged me to remember this prayer before any confrontation with the enemy. But you really didn't have to remind me, Mom. I have always prayed it; and when I got to Korea, I sometimes said it a couple of times a day while marching or resting."

"Well, one day, we were told to move forward to scout for Commies. It was a really cold day. As I was walking along, I perceived another fellow walking beside me, and I looked to see who it was. He was a big fellow, a marine about 6'4" and built proportionally. Funny, but I didn't know him, and I thought I knew everyone in my unit. I was glad to have the company and broke the silence between us. 'Chilly today, isn't it?' Then I chuckled because suddenly, it seemed absurd to talk about the weather when we were advancing to meet the enemy. He chuckled too, softly.

"I thought I knew everyone in my outfit," I continued, "but I have never seen you before."

"No," he agreed, "I have just joined. The name is Michael."

"Really?! That's mine, too."

"I know," the marine said, "Michael, Michael of the morning…"

"Mom, I was really surprised that he knew about my prayer, but I had taught it to many of the other guys, so I supposed that the newcomer must have picked it up from someone else. As a matter of fact, it had gotten around to the extent that some of the fellows were calling me Saint Michael. Then, out of the blue, Michael said, "There's going to be trouble ahead."

I wondered how he could know that. I was breathing hard from the march, and my breath hit the cold air like dense clouds of fog. Michael seemed to be in top shape because I couldn't see his breath at all. Just then, it started to snow heavily, and soon, it was so dense I could no longer hear or see the rest of my outfit. I got a little scared and yelled, "Michael!" Then I felt his strong hand on my shoulder and heard his voice in my ear, "It's going to clear up soon."

"It did clear up, suddenly. And then, just a short distance ahead of us, like so many dreadful realities, were seven Commies, looking rather comical in their funny hats. But there was nothing funny about them now; their guns were steady and pointed straight in our direction.

"Down, Michael!" I yelled as I dove for cover. Even as I was hitting the ground, I looked up and saw Michael still standing, as if paralyzed by fear, or so I thought at the time. Bullets were spurting all over the place, and Mom, there was no way those Commies could have missed at that short distance. I jumped up to pull him down, and then I was hit. The pain was like a hot fire in my chest, and as I fell, my head swooned and I remember thinking, "I must be dying…"

"Someone was laying me down; strong arms were holding me and laying me gently on the snow. Through the daze, I opened my eyes, and the sun seemed to blaze in my eyes. Michael was standing still, and there was a terrible splendor in his face. Suddenly, he seemed to grow, like the sun, the splendor increasing intensely around him like the wings of an angel. As I slipped into unconsciousness, I saw that Michael held a sword in his hand, and it flashed like a million lights."

"Later on, when I woke up, the rest of the guys came to see me with the sergeant.

"How did you do it, son?" he asked me. "Where's Michael?" I asked in reply.

"Michael who?" The sergeant seemed puzzled. "Michael, the big marine walking with me, right up to the last moment. I saw him there as I fell."

"Son," the sergeant said gravely, "you're the only Michael in my unit. I handpicked all you fellows, and there's only one Michael. You. And, son, you weren't walking with anyone. I was watching you because you were too far off from us, and I was worried."

"Now tell me, son," he repeated, "how did you do it?"

It was the second time he had asked me that, and I found it irritating. "How did I do what?"

"How did you kill those seven Commies? There wasn't a single bullet fired from your rifle."

"What?"

"Come on, son. They were strewn all around you, **each one killed by a sword stroke**."

And that, Mom, is the end of my story. It may have been the pain, or the blazing sun, or the chilling cold. I don't know, Mom, but there is one thing I am sure about. **It happened**.

Love,
Your son, Michael" (133)

Angelic protection? You decide. But if it is there, and you don't pray for it, you might be really missing out. Want to take that chance? Free will gives us that choice—and therefore, that chance to ignore perhaps one of the greatest forms of heavenly love. Remember: comfortable denial or feeling safer in disbelief could leave you out in the cold.

Is it really so hard to have faith and believe? The rewards are *truly heavenly*.

Now we shall listen to what these "footprints" are saying to us. We all have ears, but few of us have been ready to listen. Do you dare to hear what heaven is trying to tell us? Do you dare NOT to hear the messages for mankind?

"Be not afraid…"

CHAPTER 17

MESSAGES FOR MANKIND

> Now, as he journeyed, he approached Damascus, and suddenly a light from heaven flashed about him. And he fell to the ground and heard a voice saying to him, "Saul, Saul, why do you persecute me?" And he said, "Who are you, Lord?" And he said, "I am Jesus, whom you are persecuting; but rise and enter the city, and you will be told what you are to do." The men who were traveling with him stood speechless, hearing the voice but seeing no one. (**Acts 9:3–7**)

Thousands of messages have been given to visionaries and prophets over hundreds of years. Most of the time, they were face-to-face with the Blessed Virgin or Jesus. Remember that these visionaries have been established as sane and normal in their lives—not psychotic or delusional. Having worked in the psychiatric field for over thirty-six years, I can assure you that these inspiring messages are not typical of any auditory hallucinations or psychotic delusions. Moreover, they reveal a *great consistency* with each other—despite the fact that they are shared from different personalities from vastly different cultures and countries around the world—as well as hundreds of years apart in time! As even bewildered scientists have proclaimed, "These individuals are in contact with a supernatural and unseen presence."

Mirjana Dragicevic of Medjugorje asked the Blessed Virgin, "Why are you appearing to us? We are no better than others." The Virgin smiled, paused, and then answered,

"I do not necessarily choose the best" (**June 26, 1981**) (45:33).

"Pray! Pray a great deal and make sacrifices for sinners, for many souls go to hell for not having someone to pray and make sacrifices for them" **(Mary to Lucia [9], Jacinta [6], and Francisco [8], Fatima, Portugal, August 19, 1917)** (32:41).

"Today, I am calling you to prayer. You know, dear children, that God grants special graces in prayer…I call you, dear children, to prayer with the heart. Without unceasing prayer, you cannot experience the beauty and greatness of the grace which God is offering you. May prayer reign in the whole world. You know that I love you and am coming here out of love, so I could show you the path of peace and salvation for your souls. I want you to not permit Satan to seduce you. Dear children, Satan is strong enough! Therefore, I ask you to dedicate your prayers so that those under his (Satan's) influence may be saved. Give witness by your life; sacrifice your lives for the salvation of the world…Therefore, **do not be afraid**. If you pray, Satan cannot injure you, not even a little, because you are God's children, and He is watching over you. Pray, and let the Rosary always be in your hands" **(Mary to teenagers in Medjugorje, Bosnia-Herzegovina, 1981–present)** (48:77–78).

"You must begin your prayers by offering God all that you conceal in your soul. God sees your every action and knows your every thought. You can hide nothing from Him. Hold back nothing. Admit all your bad deeds and thoughts. Then you must ask for God's forgiveness from the bottom of your heart. Then your sins will not distract you from praying sincerely.…Then pray to forgive all of those who have trespassed against you.…Pray for the spiritual and physical welfare of your relatives.…You must ask God for strength to do His will. Pray for courage and wisdom to stay on the right path" **(Mary to Valentine Nyiramukiza, Kibeho, Rwanda, Africa, May, 1982)** (39:121–122).

"Have them believe and pray; I cannot help him who does not pray and does not sacrifice. The more you believe firmly, the more you pray and fast for the same intention, the greater is the grace and mercy of God" **(Mary to teenagers in Medjugorje, Bosnia-Herzegovina, August 18, 1982)** (45:170).

"I don't want it (Rosary) prayed only in the month of May. I want it to be prayed permanently, within the family, including the children old enough to understand—to be prayed at a set hour when there are no problems with the work in the home. Love each other. Fulfill your obligations. Make peace. Don't ask our Lord for peace, because if you do not make it, there will be no peace. Renew the Five First Saturdays. You received many graces when all of you did this" **(Mary to Bernardo Martinez [50], Cuapa, Nicaragua, May 8, 1980)** (102).

"Jesus prefers that you address yourselves directly to Him rather than through an intermediary. In the meantime, if you wish to give yourselves completely to God, and if you wish that I be your protector, then confide to me all your intentions, your fasts, and your sacrifices so that I can dispose of them according to the will of God. I beseech you, pray to Jesus! I am His Mother, and I intercede for you with Him. But all prayers go to Jesus. I will help, but everything does not depend solely on me, but also your strength, and the strength of those who pray" **(Mary to teenagers in Medjugorje, Bosnia-Herzegovina, September 4, 1982)** (45:171).

"Teach the children to pray. Teach them to live in truth and live yourselves in truth. Say the Rosary. It is the weapon against Satan. He fears the Rosary. Recite the Rosary at any gathering of people" **(Mary to Marina Kizyn [12], Hrushiv, Ukraine, 1987)** (2:275).

"The Rosary is the most powerful tool of prayer and conversion to fight evil and receive God's Love" **(Mary to teenagers in Kibeho, Rwanda, 1981–1989)** (39-CD).

"Dear children! I am calling you to begin to pray the Rosary with a living faith. Only in that way will I be able to help you. You wish to receive many graces, but you do not pray. I cannot help you if you do not undertake the task of prayer seriously. Dear children, I am calling you to pray the Rosary. This prayer is a must, and you should pray it with joy. Only then will you begin to understand why I am with you for such a long time. I wish to teach you how to pray" **(Mary to teenagers in Medjugorje, Bosnia-Herzegovina, June 12, 1986)** (52:174).

"Pray the Holy Rosary—Satan will be defeated because he hates hearing the name of My Son and my name. Teach your children how to pray the Holy Rosary…" **(Mary to Judiel Nieva [15], Agoo, Philippines, July 4, 1992)** (98:4).

"**Do not be afraid**. Satan cannot harm you as you have My motherly protection. But you must still arm yourself with prayer, especially My Holy Rosary. My daughter, please be guided by Me. Do not be deceived by the world…Oh, My daughter, why do they not listen to My words? I want only to save them from eternal perdition…Thank you, My child, for listening. Go in peace!" **(Mary to Geraldine, Australia, April 24, 1992)** (14:55)

"The most beautiful thing is to believe. All prayers are good if they are said with faith" **(Mary to teenagers in Medjugorje, Bosnia-Herzegovina, 1981–present)** (45:174).

"You have forgotten that with prayer and fasting, *you can ward off war and suspend natural laws*" **(Mary to teens in Medjugorje, Bosnia-Herzegovina, 1981–present)** (52:201).

"As a good mother I come here each and every month to encourage you, to guide you in wisdom and truth. Learn the true faith of the Church. God will never fail you. God is in control of all things, and He knows all things. He sees the hearts and minds and souls of all of you. God sees good here. If you saw what your prayers are doing—and the power of your prayers, you would never cease praying" **(Mary to Neal [42], Perryville, Missouri, USA, May 13, 2013)** (84).

"Dear children! You are not aware of the importance of the messages which God is sending you through me. He is giving you great graces and you don't realize it. Pray to the Holy Spirit for enlightenment. If you only knew how many graces God is giving you, you would pray without ceasing" **(Mary to** teenagers in Medjugorje, Bosnia-Herzegovina, November 8, 1984)** (52:157).

"I have come to prepare the way for Him for your own good—and yet, you do not want to accept. You do not want to understand. There is so little time remaining, yet you still allow yourselves to be distracted by earthly goods and desires—which will soon all pass away. I see so many of My children going astray. And so I come to plead with them and to show them the correct way" **(Mary to teenagers in Kibeho, Rwanda, 1981–1989)** (39-CD).

"If you want to pray better, you always need to *pray more*. Time is not a problem. The problem is love. Because, if you love something and care about something, you will always find the time for it" **(Mary to Ivan Dragicevic, Medjugorje, Bosnia-Herzegovina, 1981–present)** (48:214).

"You must renounce your preoccupations and be ready so that the Spirit can lead and guide you interiorly. Only in this way can you advance spiritually. When you do this, you will discover that you have the time to complete all your duties and also have time left over" **(Mary to teenagers in Medjugorje, 1984)** (52:99).

"Praying for your departed loved ones is of great comfort to them and of great help for the souls in purgatory, but people still must work to earn a place in heaven" **(Mary to Marie-Claire Mukangango, Kibeho, Rwanda, Africa, 1982)** (39:64).

"There are many souls in purgatory. Pray for their intentions… There is a large number of souls who have been in purgatory for a long time because no one prays for them. These persons wait for your prayers and your sacrifices" **(Mary to teenagers in Medjugorje, Bosnia-Herzegovina, 1981–present)** (45:168).

"The one who turns to God in this world and lives according to God's Will, can, through Divine Mercy, shorten and even avoid his time in purgatory" **(Mary to teenagers in Kibeho, Rwanda, 1981–1989)** (39-CD).

"Do not work on Sundays. Blessed is he who believes and unhappy the man who does not believe" **(Mary to Auguste Arnaud [30], Herault, France, July 8, 1873)** (3:135).

"Why do you gladly accept the worldly material privileges which God grants you? And yet you won't accept the trials which lead you to God. Which of these ways, do you reckon, will lead you to God? You, who carry the cross without even knowing that you are doing so, accept the cross and the one for whom you are carrying it" **(Mary to teenagers in Kibeho, Rwanda, 1981–1989)** (39-CD).

"Jesus gives you His graces in the Mass. Let the Holy Mass be your life. Mass is the greatest prayer of God. You will never be able to understand its greatness. That is why you must be perfect and humble at Mass, and you should prepare yourselves for it…for an hour at least. May the Mass, the most exalted and most powerful act of your prayer, be the center of your spiritual life. Receive Holy Communion with an open and pure heart…" **(Mary to teenagers in Medjugorje, Bosnia-Herzegovina, 1981–present)** (48:82)

"It saddens me the most to see that people have no respect for My Son in the Eucharist, and the way people pray whilst their minds are on other things. I say this to those who pretend to be pious" **(Mary to Estelle Faguette [33], Pellevoisin, France, February 18, 1876)** (137).

"Do not walk indifferently near churches. I am waiting for you in the Blessed Sacrament. I ease every suffering. I console every dejected heart, if the heart turns to me with the trust and confidence" **(Jesus to Wladyslawa Papis [12], Sierkierki, Poland, September 26, 1943)** (150).

"I am waiting for you, hidden in the tabernacle. Kneel before the altar and pray" **(Jesus to Wladyslawa Papis [12], Sierkierki, Poland, January 19, 1944)** (150).

Jesus awaits you in all the tabernacles of the world (Photo-Art created by author).

"I am wounded by those who insult me. Make amends for them" **(Jesus to Wladyslawa Papis [12], Sierkierki, Poland, September 8, 1949)** (150).

"I am with you, but I am leaving now. Pray to My Holy Mother. She listens to your prayers. She hears you" **(Jesus to Wladyslawa Papis [12], Sierkierki, Poland, September 15, 1949)** (150).

"I do not dispose all graces. I receive from God what I obtain through prayer. God has placed His complete trust in me. I particularly protect those who have been consecrated to me" **(Mary to teenagers in Medjugorje, Bosnia-Herzegovina, 1981–present)** (45:171).

"Bring many sacrifices and offerings to me. Offer your prayers to me as sacrifices. Be not seekers of self. That honor be shown to the eternal and atonement be made to Him is required of these times. If you consecrate yourselves without reserve, I shall take care of all the rest. Crosses weighty and deep as the sea I shall lay upon my children, because I love them in my Sacrificed Son. I beseech you, be prepared to carry the cross that peace may soon be achieved" **(Mary to Barbara Reuss [12], Marienfried, Germany, June 25, 1946)** (130).

"Man is chasing the wind. Some people do not believe in the existence of heaven. They say that the only heaven is on this earth. Yet, on this earth, all are poor, and all need the gifts of God. Poverty is not a lack of money, nor is it a lack of food to eat. The only real poverty is the lack of the grace that leads to the Lord. Possessions of this world are only ashes, while the only real riches are the riches of the heart" **(Jesus to teenagers in Kibeho, Rwanda, 1981–1989)** (39-CD).

"**Wherever I appear, My Son is with me—but Satan also follows.** You have unwittingly allowed him to take charge of you and rule over you. Sometimes, you understand that some of your deeds are not allowed by God—but you soon suppress those thoughts. Do not give in, dear children. Wipe away from my face the tears which I shed as I watch what you do. Look around you. Take the time to come to God in the church. Come into your Father's house. Take the time to meet for family prayer and ask for God's grace. Remember your deceased; make them happy by offering Mass. Do not look down your nose at the poor man who is begging for a crust of bread. Do not send him away from your rich table. Help him and God will help you.…Do not fool yourself into thinking, 'I am good—but my brother who lives next to me is not good.' You will be mistaken" **(Mary to the world through Mirjana Dragicevic [22], Sarajevo, Bosnia-Herzegovina, January 28, 1987)** (52:231).

"Your every action must be born of kindness, your every word spoken with love. Live as God would have you live, and others will be inspired to do the same. By walking the world as a shepherd, you will show My earthly children that the walk to heaven is a long and narrow road that is not easy to travel. But the road leading to Satan is wide and easy to follow because the devil puts no obstacles on the road to darkness" **(Mary to teenagers in Kibeho, Rwanda, 1981–1989)** (39-CD).

"In other places where I have appeared, the Lord has been present. My children, without the hand of God, nothing is possible. I make you listen to things that you had listened to before, but did not practice. Now the Lord gives you a new chance. The answer is in you" **(Mary to Gladys Quiroga de Motta [47], San Nicolas, Argentina, April 12, 1984)** (149:2).

"Make your peace with God and among yourselves. If confession does not mean anything for you, really, you will be converted with great difficulty. Pray, pray! It is necessary to believe firmly, to go to confession regularly, and likewise, to receive Holy Communion. It is the only salvation. One must invite people to go to confession each month, especially on the first Saturday...Do not go to confession through habit. Confession should give an impulse to your faith. It should stimulate you and bring you closer to Jesus" **(Mary to teenagers in Medjugorje, Bosnia-Herzegovina, 1981–present)** (48:81).

"Daughter, children, here I am as I announced before; some will feel Me...others will see Me between the shrubs...others will perceive the perfumed roses of My garden from heaven... and even more, some, who are sick, drinking from the water of My grotto of prayer, will be relieved; others, will be healed, attaining health and peace...! Daughter, wherever I place My Feet, it is as sowing the seed...and behold, the Doctrine and the Gospel are enacted through the faith that comes forth from the heart of those who seek Me! And I tell you, all of you will be saved...for the church renews and calls to a burning faith... when her children draw close to the flock of My Divine Son... to nourish themselves with His Mystical Body...and daughter, today many will be nourished!" **(Mary to Maria Esperanza [57], Betania, Venezuela, 11:00 a.m., December 8, 1986)** (9)

"Take mud into your hands. Wash yourself with water! This is to teach the sinners that sin makes the soul dirty, yet the soul will be cleansed again through the water of grace" **(Mary to Pierina Gilli [40s], Fontanelle, Italy, April 17, 1966)** (134:6).

"Fast strictly on Wednesdays and Fridays. The best fast is on bread and water. *Through fasting and prayer, one can stop wars, one can suspend the natural laws of nature...*Works of charity cannot replace fasting…Everyone except the sick has to fast… There is only one path—prayer, strong faith, and fasting…" **(Mary to teenagers in Medjugorje, Bosnia-Herzegovina, 1981–present)** (48:79)

Father De Marchi lists a number of teachings from Blessed Mary that Jacinta (from Fatima) shared with Mother Godinho during Jacinta's hospital stay in 1919:

"The sins which cause most souls to go to hell are the sins of the flesh."

"The world is perishing because the people do not meditate."

"Many marriages are not of God and do not please Our Lord."

"Wars are punishment for sin."

"Priests must be very, very pure."

"Confession is a Sacrament of Mercy, and we must confess with joy and trust. There can be no salvation without confession."

"The Mother of God wants more virgin souls bound by a vow of chastity" **(Mary to Jacinta Marto [8], Fatima, Portugal, 1919)** (29:260).

"My little white dove, do you know what I find most lacking in the world today? It is Faith. There are so few souls that believe in Me and My love. They profess their belief and their love, but they do not *live* this belief. Their hearts are cold, for without faith there can be no love. Pray and sacrifice yourself, My Child, that faith may once again find entrance into the hearts of man" **(Jesus to Sister Mildred Neuzil [38], midwest USA, May 29, 1954)** (144: Part II).

"There are many lights in the world to follow, but there is only one True Light—that of God. Live with your Faith throughout your life. Don't wear it like a coat that you put on and take off, since this won't save you when you die" **(Mary to teenagers in Kibeho, Rwanda, 1981–1989)** (39-CD).

"I know that many will not believe you, and that many who have an impassioned faith will cool off. You remain firm, and motivate people to instant prayer, penance, and conversion. At the end, you will be happier. When you suffer difficulties and need something, come to me" **(Mary to teenagers in Medjugorje, Bosnia-Herzegovina, 1981–present)** (45:173).

"The first and greatest commandment is Love. One who possesses love will honor one's Lord and Creator in His creation. One who possesses love will do nothing dishonorable toward one's neighbor. That is what this world lacks: Love of God, Love of neighbor" **(Mary to Ida Peerdman [45], Amsterdam, Holland, July 2, 1951)** (13:40).

Blessed Mary among the flowers, promoting love and peace (photo by author).

When a Croatian Catholic priest doubted the healing of a Serbian gypsy child, he asked one of the Medjugorje visionaries how the Mother of God could intercede for the healing of a child of the Orthodox faith of the despised ethnic enemy, the Serbians? The visionary stated that Mother Mary gazed at the priest for a long time "with long-suffering tolerance" before answering:

"Tell this priest; tell everyone, that it is **you** who are divided on earth. The Muslims and the Orthodox, for the same reason as Catholics, are equal before My Son and me. *You are **all** my children*. Certainly, all religions are not equal, but all men are equal before God, as St. Paul says. It does not suffice to belong to the Catholic Church to be saved, but it is necessary to respect the commandments of God in following one's conscience" **(January 1985)** (45:23–24).

"My little white dove, if the world is dying, it is because it will not let Me give it life. I am the resurrection and the life, and unless souls seek their life in Me, they will find only death and destruction. They fear man-made destroyers of life, yet destruction is in themselves. Man destroys himself through the evil that is in himself. Implements of war kill only that which is without. Man kills that within himself which none but he can kill. God *is* light; man is darkness, and unless he comes into the light, he will be forever darkness. The Voice of My Heart *is* the Voice of Mercy. If man will not listen, there is no more I can do, for he ties My hands" **(Jesus to Sister Mildred Neuzil [38], midwest USA, May 22, 1954)** (144: Part II).

"You should love your enemies. You should not judge, nor bear rancor, nor curse anyone, but bless and pray for them. I know that you are not able to love your enemies, but I beg you to pray every day at least five minutes to the Sacred Heart and to My Heart and we will give you the divine love with which you will be able to love even your enemies" **(Mary to teenagers in Medjugorje, 1984)** (52:98).

"You must love each other and not hold on to anger. Many in this country have hatred in their hearts. You must cleanse your own heart with My Son's love. Pray, children! Pray to me, and I will help you. A small seed of anger can grow into a great tree of hatred that can block God's light and cast you into darkness" **(Mary to teenagers in Kibeho, Rwanda, 1981– 1989)** (39-CD).

"Many souls err, are lost, waiting for somebody to save them. The sin of impurity greatly offends Our Lord. A big part of the clergy—that is priests, bishops, and cardinals—are stepping on paths of perdition, and it is because of them that many souls are condemned" **(Mary to Luz Amparo Cuevas, El Escorial, Spain, 1980–1992)** (107).

"Dear children! I wish to call you to grow in love. A flower cannot grow without water. Neither can you grow without God's blessing. You should pray for His blessing from day to day so that you can grow normally and carry out your activities with God" **(Mary to teenagers in Medjugorje, Bosnia-Herzegovina, April 10, 1986)** (52:172).

"I do not ask you to give money to churches. I ask you to love. **Those who give money to the poor and to the churches but yet have not love, have lives of no value**. I will visit the homes of my children more frequently, because those who go to church do not always go there to pray. Give. Do not deprive anyone who asks for help. Be humble, my children. Do not insult the proud. Forgive them. Then you will be forgiven" **(Mary to Myrna Al Akharas [18], Damascus, Syria, December 18, 1982)** (2:252).

"For the world is not saved by force. The world will be saved by the Spirit. For it is nothing other than ideas which rule the world" **(Mary to Ida Peerdman [45], Amsterdam, Holland, April 29, 1951)** (13:41).

"Pride leads to every other sin in the world. You must be humble and answer with humbleness every possible offense. With humbleness, you can achieve anything and be less likely to fall into temptation" **(Mary to Luz Amparo Cuevas, El Escorial, Spain, 1980–1992)** (107).

"Don't cover the soul with a mask of hatred, resentment, and pride. Remove the cancer of pride because it is killing your souls" **(Mary to Patricia Talbot [17], Cuenca, Ecuador, December 12, 1989)** (23:55).

"Great events and painful riots are growing around the world; countries and nations are being shaken by bad times! Men have lessened their potential, in regard to their spirituality… behold they are navigating against the divine current of peace, love, and brotherly unity! That is why, I am letting you feel Me and My Divine Son…so My children feel in their hearts Our soft touch and so they may listen to the announcement that: 'The time of their freedom has arrived'…may they make themselves present through sanctifying love…and may they continue their way seeking the light…and thus, their thoughts may receive the grace of the Holy Spirit, so they may be worthy of that light and music of the universe! Think that it is sufficient to enter into the constitution of men's structure, to find an immense forge…with the mission to fulfill an inevitable duty, that is to say, to build love in each deed which represents divinity! Much willpower is needed! That is why, humbly obey the teachings of the Commandments of My Beloved Son, so men may ascend to the stage of the great truth of God meeting with His children!" He comes to give life again! Anyone, regardless of his race, caste, religion for Him all are the same…the only existing truth should be to practice what is good…and to lead a generous life! I keep you here in My Heart!" **(Mary to Maria Esperanza [61], Betania, Venezuela, 6:00 p.m., January 5, 1990)** (9)

"Dear children! You are now preoccupied with material things, and in the material things, you lose everything that God wants to give you. I invite you, dear children, to pray for the gifts of the Holy Spirit that you need now, in order that you may give witness to my presence here and to everything I am giving you. Dear children abandon yourselves to me so that I can lead you totally. Do not be preoccupied with the material things of this world. Thank you for your response to my call" **(Mary to teenagers in Medjugorje, Bosnia-Herzegovina, April 17, 1986)** (52:172).

"Do not work for the things of this world, since they do not belong to you. And you won't be here forever. You are only temporary travelers" **(Mary to teenagers in Kibeho, Rwanda, 1981–1989)** (39-CD).

"My dear daughter, how sadly lost youth is! Drug addiction and easy life is the picture the evil one has set for the young! Sin, committed in very different ways, makes them stray further and further from God! If only they turn their eyes toward the Mother of God, the Mother will make them find God again. If only they penetrate the Mother's Heart will they be able to hear the Lord's voice" (**Mary to Gladys Quiroga de Motta [50], San Nicolas, Argentina, September 21, 1987**) (149:3).

"I have already given many signs and spoken often to the world, but people have not taken them seriously. On account of these outward signs, the greater multitude do not even grasp the essential things. Outward signs only succeed in distracting many, who do not draw the necessary conclusions from them" (**Mary to Barbara Reuss [12], Marienfried, Germany, June 25, 1946**) (130).

"Why do you insist on miracles? There are miracles every day, but you do not believe in them. Rather, ask for the light because you are blind...Happy is he who believes without waiting for miracles, since those who wait for miracles will have difficulties in believing when the miracles no longer take place. Their faith will disappear" (**Mary to teenagers in Kibeho, Rwanda, 1981–1989**) (39-CD).

"Children are not taught to love Me because those who have charge over them have no time or patience to do so. My Heart grieves over My children in the world. Their hearts are being driven farther and farther away from Me. They will not even listen to My Mother because *they have never been taught to listen* (to Her)" (**Jesus to Sister Mildred Neuzil [38], midwest USA, July 11, 1954**) (144: Part II).

Jesus had decided to save Estelle Faguette from death with a miraculous healing, but she humbly admitted to the Virgin Mary that it was okay if she died. An astonished Mary said, smiling:

"Ungrateful, if My Son gives you life, it is because you need it. What other more precious thing can He give the people on Earth other than life? Don't think that you will be free from suffering. No! You will suffer and not be free from troubles. This is what life brings. You have touched My Son's heart by your self-denial and patience. Don't lose those fruits by making the wrong choice" (**Mary to Estelle Faguette [33], Pellevoisin, France, February 15, 1876**) (137).

BE NOT AFRAID TO FOLLOW THE FOOTPRINTS FROM HEAVEN

> "My children, in truth, I am not staying as long as I used to do as I have told you all that was necessary...I am happy with the fruits that were born in Rwanda since I came here. Don't worry about the difficulties you have. Nothing is better than having God. My dear children, problems exist everywhere, but the most important thing is to have an accepting heart without complaining" **(Mary to Alphonsine Mumureke [24], Kibeho, Rwanda, Africa, November 28, 1989)** (36:98).

Mother Mary also told the visionaries that suffering is "a part of our daily bread while still on earth." She taught them how to accept and suffer well—and that suffering leads to heaven. Suffering teaches us many things that we would not otherwise learn. "Each person carries a cross, but what is important is to offer our sufferings to God and live through them without complaining" **(Mary to teenagers in Kibeho, Rwanda, Africa, 1981–1989)** (36:44).

> "It is not mankind who is abandoned by God, but God who is abandoned by mankind!" **(Mary to Gladys Quiroga de Motta [51], San Nicolas, Argentina, December 10, 1988)** (149:3)

At a time when AIDS was becoming an epidemic in Africa, Jesus told Agnes,

> "They should not use their bodies as an instrument of pleasure. They are using all means to love and be loved, and they forget that the true love comes from God. Instead of being at the service of God, they are at the service of money. They must make of their body an instrument destined to the glory of God and not an object of pleasure at the service of men. *Young men must seek to satisfy the hunger of their spirit, not feed the desires of their flesh.* They should pray to Mary to show them the right way to God" **(Jesus to Agnes Kamagaju [21], Kibeho, Rwanda, Africa, August 18, 1982)** (39:118).

> "Do not expect everything from God if you do nothing for Him. Awaken and return to the Lord" **(Mary to Gladys Quiroga de Motta [50], San Nicolas, Argentina, May 10, 1987)** (149:3).

"The sick who want to be healed must trust me more and sanctify their suffering if they want to earn Paradise. If they do not do this, they will not be awarded and will be severely punished instead. I hope that all those who get to know my words will make every kind of effort to earn Paradise. Those who suffer without complaining will obtain anything they ask from My Son and me. Pray a lot for those who have a sick soul; My Son Jesus died on the cross to save them. Many people do not understand these words of mine—that is why I suffer so much" **(Mary to Adelaide Roncalli [7], Ghiaie di Bonate, Italy, May 29, 1944)** (110).

"All of you who are sick with incurable diseases, a good heart surpasses all; there are no riches that are beyond a clean heart. All of you who have had difficulties of all kinds, there are difficulties everywhere, in all walks of life. When they don't go away, offer them to God. Every good Christian is requested to offer a sacrifice. All of you who have problems in your families, think of the Holy Family, who lived in poverty, and who lived among those who didn't like them nor understood them, and with the problems you have, come close to them" **(Mary to Alphonsine Mumureke [24], Kibeho, Rwanda, Africa, November 28, 1989)** (36:97).

"Dear Lady, the people told me to ask you whether their sick children must be carried here for being healed," stated Adelaide. In a heavenly voice, the Blessed Virgin answered,

"No, it is not necessary for everybody to come here; those who can afford it may come, and they will be healed or remain sick according to their sacrifices, but they must not commit great sins anymore" **(Mary to Adelaide Roncalli [7], Ghiaie di Bonate, Italy, May 19, 1944)** (110).

"After my ascension into heaven, I have always acted as Mediatrix between My Son Jesus and the whole of mankind. How many graces I have been able to obtain in all these centuries! How many graces were shown. How much punishment was prevented. How many dialogues did I hold with souls. How often have I visited Earth to bring my messages to the people—but people continue to offend Our Lord. I have chosen this place of Montichiari because there is still the humility of poor Bethlehem among my sons who till the soil. Because so many prayers are said continuously, this place will be transformed into a source of rich blessings" **(Mary to Pierina Gilli (40s), Fontanelle, Italy, August 6, 1966)** (134:8).

"Dear children! Give thanks with me to the Most High for my presence with you. My heart is joyful watching the love and joy in the living of my messages. Many of you have responded, but I wait for, and seek, all the hearts that have fallen asleep to awaken from the sleep of unbelief. Little children, draw even closer to my Immaculate Heart so that I can lead all of you toward eternity. Thank you for having responded to my call" **(Mary to teenagers in Medjugorje, June 25, 2011—the thirtieth anniversary)** (45:11).

"My children, be mindful of God because God is with us. You know much, but you really know nothing. Your knowledge is incomplete. One day you will know everything as God knows me. Do good to evildoers. Do not mistreat anyone. Repent and believe! Be mindful of me in your joy. Announce My Son Emmanuel. He who announces Him is saved. He who does not…his faith is in vain. Love one another" **(Mary to Myrna Al Akharas [18], Damascus, Syria, December 18, 1982)** (2:252).

"My little daughter, tell my children of all races, of all nations, of all religions, that I love them. All of my children are *the same*. There do not exist rich ones or poor ones, ugly ones or beautiful ones, black or white. I come to gather all of them to help them so that they can be saved. I love *all* of them…to the youth I am directing myself so that they will really serve me and make me happy…to save the world. Little daughter, you are beholding me with my hands outstretched with graces and wrapped in the splendor of light to call all my children to conversion" **(Mary to Maria Esperanza [47], Betania, Venezuela, March 25, 1976)** (9).

When asked about Protestants praying the Rosary, Blessed Mary replied,

"I do not look at religion. All people are My children regardless of their beliefs. Pray the Rosary—not as Catholics—but as My children" **(Mary to teenagers in Kibeho, Rwanda, 1981–1989)** (39-CD).

> "Before, the world was saved by means of Noah's Ark; today the ark is My Mother. Through Her, souls will be saved, because She will bring them toward Me. *He who rejects My Mother rejects Me!* Many are letting the grace of God pass by in these days" **(Jesus to Gladys Quiroga de Motta [52], San Nicolas, Argentina, December 30, 1989)** (149:3).

> "Children, today you have truly come to discern My message and at the same time, you have heard at daybreak, the song of the birds…in order to see My Image at the foot of a tree at My grotto…you saw the water of My spring flow over the stones, singing to the Lord…O children! My mystical eye has observed each one of your faces and has been able to see in the bottom of your hearts the desire of an inner renewal, to analyze and contemplate all the beautiful things this temple of nature holds, temple I have chosen to receive all of My children! Thus, sons and daughters, henceforth you will be enabled to understand the wonderful and heavenly gamut that exists here…and with will power you will be able to take part in the banquet of love My Divine Son and this Mother offer you…so you may lead a life, singing to the Lord His psalm of love!" **(Mary to Maria Esperanza [60], Betania, Venezuela, 9:30 p.m., June 21, 1989)** (9)

> "You, who rely on your intelligence, stop and take time to ponder—that this intelligence comes from nowhere but from the kindness of God. God has proved His Mercy by giving you the possibility of using His creation as you wish. If he had deprived you of your own free will, he would have created all of you equal. No one would have been able to think or understand. You would have perceived but not been able to distinguish between good and bad. Thus God has granted you freedom so that each man may choose. God shows you what is

good, and He shows you the true road. Choose then, with His help, the road that you wish to follow" **(Mary to teenagers in Kibeho, Rwanda, December 24, 1983)** (39-CD).

"My daughter, how beautiful is the earth. In this place, I shall establish my Kingdom and My peace. I shall give you My Heart in order to have yours. Your sins are forgiven because you are looking for Me. He who looks for Me, I shall imprint My image in him. Tell My children to come for Me, for I am with them at all times" **(Jesus to Myrna Al Akharas [22], Damascus, Syria, October 15, 1986)** (2:256).

"Dear children, if you knew how much I love you, you would cry without ceasing!" **(Mary to teenagers in Medjugorje, Bosnia-Herzegovina, 1981–present)** (45:176)

"Children, I speak to all of you who have seen Me seconds ago…ascending into heaven with My Arms opened, with a rain of roses…and you have had the proof in those petals, red fire, which represent the Heart of My Divine Jesus…He, as Christ Redeemer and Savior…renewing and purifying all men on earth! Sons and daughters, all this seems like a dream to you…but it is a lively truth, and unique in these times of great calamity for men! On this day when My Assumption into heaven is recalled…I want to leave you My roses of love… so keeping them in your hearts, you will have Me present with My Beloved Son! I keep you here in My Heart!" **(Mary to Maria Esperanza [60], Betania, Venezuela, 5:00 p.m., August 15, 1989)** (9)

"Dear daughter, I am sorry I must leave you, but my time has passed. Do not lose heart if you do not see me for a while. Think of what I have told you; I will come back in your hour (of death). You will be a little martyr in this valley of real sorrows. Do not get discouraged, I wish my triumph to happen soon. Pray for the Pope and tell him to act quickly because I want to be solicitous to everyone in this place. If anything is required from me, I will intercede with My Son for it. I will be your award if your martyrdom is cheerful. These words of mine will be of great comfort to you in your trials.

> Endure everything patiently and then you will reach me in Paradise. Those who make you suffer intentionally will not come to heaven if they do not make amends for their wrongs and do not repent deeply. Cheer up, because we will meet again, my dear little martyr." *I felt a sweet and gentle kiss on my forehead* **(Mary to Adelaide Roncalli [7], Ghiaie di Bonate, Italy, May 31, 1944)** (110).

And finally, here is one more example of a clear message coming from the Virgin Mary while miraculous and supernatural signs were occurring simultaneously for all who were present. These corresponding occurrences are unlikely to be coincidental—but rather a validation of the real presence of a divine being, accompanied by supernatural and inexplicable events. On this particular occasion, March 25, 1978, on this farm in Betania, Venezuela, many saw a radiant mist coming from the woods. As the mist settled on top of a large tree, visionary Maria Esperanza—with fifteen others—saw Our Lady materialize with hands on her chest.

Maria heard, "**Little daughter, this is not a dream. My presence among you is real**."

> "Then her hands opened up, and I saw what appeared to be rays coming from her hands. They came directly toward us, bathing us with light—and one man cried out, 'Everything is burning up!' The whole area appeared to be on fire. It was beautiful. The sun began to gyrate, and everyone was shouting with emotion" **(Maria Esperanza [49], Betania, Venezuela, March 25, 1978)** (11:276–277) (68:201–202).

These messages reveal teachings, inspiration, and great meaning from *seemingly the same source*—despite such differences among these visionaries in age, culture, life experiences, personalities, and time frames in history.

Many other heavenly messages yet to be read in this work have a stern warning—one which mankind needs to hear and carefully consider. Our tragic world can no longer remain deaf. *Be not afraid*, PLEASE, to read the next two chapters. The trail of "footprints" remains strong…Don't stop now…

CHAPTER 18

"JUST WAIT TILL YOUR FATHER COMES HOME"

"In the Old Covenant I sent prophets wielding thunderbolts to My people. Today I am sending you with My mercy to the people of the whole world. I do not want to punish aching mankind, but I desire to heal it, pressing it to My Merciful Heart. I use punishment when they themselves force Me to do so; My hand is reluctant to take hold of the sword of justice. Before the Day of Justice I am sending the Day of Mercy" (Jesus to St. Faustina) (96:563, 1588).

This chapter may be troubling to many readers due to its disturbing content. The purpose is not to create anxiety, worry, fear, or despair. The presentation of repeating patterns of information from around the world over hundreds of years has been a method of establishing reality and credibility with data of such a supernatural nature. ***The content is whatever it is***—with no conclusions or opinions attached—simply for your review and enlightenment. If it creates fearful concerns, please be reminded that YOU are in control of your destiny and still have the free will to choose a better religious path in your life and avoid certain implied consequences.

Just like many earthly mothers, our Heavenly Mother reflects upon our behavior and warns us that if we don't behave better, the Father may set forth a punishment when He "comes home." The Blessed Virgin often weeps over how sinful we have become. She fears how many souls of Her children could be lost forever. She worries about the punishment that the Father could deliver if we don't "shape up" soon. Here are some of the "bad behaviors" detailed in various messages.

> "A worldwide campaign against the virtues of chastity and purity will succeed in corrupting the youth…evil will invade childhood innocence. The clergy will leave much to be desired because priests will become careless in their sacred duties… Faithful priests upholding, the Faith will suffer greatly and will be overwhelmed with vexations in order to stop them from fulfilling their ministry. The precious light of Faith will be extinguished in souls by the almost total corruption of customs" **(Mary to Mother Mariana de Jesus Torres y Berriochaoa, Quito, Ecuador, 1610)** (3:56–57).

> "The true faith of the Lord having been forgotten, they will abolish civil rights as well as ecclesiastical. All order and all justice will be trampled underfoot, and only homicides, hate, jealousy, lies, and dissension would be seen without love for country and family. All the civil governments will have one and the same plan—which will be to abolish and do away with every religious principle, to make way for materialism, atheism, spiritualism, and vice of all kinds" **(Mary to Maximin Giraud [11], Melanie Mathieu [14], La Salette, France, September 19, 1846)** (10:89).

> "Put to death, therefore, whatever belongs to your earthly nature: sexual immorality, impurity, lust, evil desires and greed, which is idolatry. Because of these, the wrath of God is coming" **(Colossians 3:5–6).**

> "Those who continually sin ignore the fact that they depend on God. Few people seek heavenly treasures, while those desiring the riches of this world are so many. There is but one door that opens to heaven, but the doors to the abyss are many. The roads that lead to Satan are numerous. So many evils are caused by money" **(Jesus to teenagers in Kibeho, Rwanda, 1981–1989)** (39-CD).

> "How many times have I urged you to walk along the road of sanctification of the senses, of modesty, of good example, of purity, and of holiness? But humanity has not accepted my

urging and has continued to disobey...On the contrary, it has sought to exalt such a transgression and put it forward as the acquisition of a human value and a new way of exercising one's own personal freedom. Thus today, it has reached the point of legitimizing all the sins of impurity as good. It has begun to corrupt the consciences of little children and of youth, bringing them to the conviction that impure acts committed by oneself are no longer sins; that relations before marriage between those engaged is licit and good; that families may behave as they please and may also make use of the various means of birth control. And they have come to the justification and the exaltation of impure acts against nature—and even to the proposing of laws which put homosexual cohabitation on a par with marriage" **(Mary to Father Don Stefano Gobbi, Milan, Italy, 1997)** (86:10) (94:412).

"The sacrament of Matrimony, which symbolizes the union of Christ with the Church, will be thoroughly attacked and profaned. Masonry, then reigning, will implement iniquitous laws aimed at extinguishing this sacrament. They will make it easy for all to live in sin, thus multiplying the birth of illegitimate children without the church's blessing...Secular education will contribute to a scarcity of priestly and religious vocations" **(Mary to Mother Mariana de Jesus Torres y Berriochaoa, Quito, Ecuador, 1610)** (141).

"Today the blood of innocent children (abortions) has filled heaven. Their number is too great, too great. The wrath of the Eternal Father is about to fall on mankind...Their blood disturbs My Agonizing Heart..." **(Jesus to Barnabas Nwoye, Nigeria, 1998)** (86:8)

Jesus weeps over babies sent to heaven too soon (Photo-Art created by author).

"In the year 1864, Lucifer, together with a large number of demons, will be unloosed from hell. They will put an end to faith, little by little, even in those dedicated to God. Several religious institutions will lose all faith and will lose many souls. Evil books will be abundant on earth, and the spirit of darkness will spread everywhere a universal slackening in all that concerns the service of God" **(Mary to Maximin Giraud [11], Melanie Mathieu [14], La Salette, France, September 19, 1846)** (10:88).

"Unhappy, the children of those times (for the years after 2000)! Seldom will they receive the sacraments of baptism and confirmation. As for the sacrament of penance, they will confess only while attending Catholic schools, which the devil will do his utmost to destroy by means of persons in authority. The same will occur with Holy Communion. Oh, how it hurts me to tell you that there will be many and enormous public and hidden sacrileges!" **(Mary to Mother Mariana de Jesus Torres y Berriochaoa, Quito, Ecuador, 1610)** (141)

"My tears are poured out for the evil that exists in the world, through atheism and materialism, through adoring false gods, through ignoring the Word of God and the Sacraments. I have not come in order that they recognize me *without recognizing My Son Jesus* in their heart. I am the Mother of all who believe and who do not believe in me. The pain from having told you what is coming to the world fills my heart with sadness. You should go out into the world, evangelizing, with the Word of God in one hand and My messages in the other" **(Mary to Patricia Talbot (18), Cuenca, Ecuador, March 3, 1990)** (23:64).

"Unbridled passions will give way to a total corruption of customs because Satan will reign through the Masonic sects, targeting the children in particular to insure general corruption" **(Mary to Mother Mariana de Jesus Torres y Berriochaoa, Quito, Ecuador, 1610)** (141).

"Dear children! My motherly heart suffers tremendously as I look at my children who persistently put what is human before what is of God, at my children who, despite everything that surrounds them and despite all the signs that are sent to them, think that they can walk without My Son. They cannot! They are walking to eternal perdition" **(Mary to Mirjana Dragicevic, Medjugorje, March 2, 2011)** (45:79).

Jesus feels crucified all over again by the overwhelming sins of the world today (photo by author of wooden statue in Florence, Italy).

As a good mother, the Blessed Virgin loves us and wants the best for us. She is weary of our sinful misbehavior. She tells us how she has intervened many times to delay a great punishment from the Father. *But she cannot delay such a chastisement for much longer.* As excerpts and messages are presented from historical encounters, note the incredible similarity in language and content.

"If my people will not obey, **I shall be compelled to loose My Son's arm. It is so heavy, so pressing, that I can no longer restrain it**. How long have I suffered for you! God is being dishonored with swearing. The price for such abuse would be costly. If the harvest is spoiled, it is your fault. A great famine is coming. Many young children will die from a serious disease" **(Mary to Maximin Giraud [11], Melanie Mathieu [14], La Salette, France, September 19, 1846)** (10:85).

"Pray—for a severe punishment will come, a heavy cross. **I cannot hold back My Son's anger** if the nation does not convert. Kneel every day from 12:00 until 3:00 p.m., from August 6 and ask for forgiveness for all the sins of the world" **(Mary to Wladyslawa Papis [12], Sierkierki, Poland, August, 1943)** (150).

"My little one, I am happy to see you. Don't be afraid. Pray much for the peace of the world, because it is now that it needs it more than ever. My little child, **I am holding back the arm of My Son.** Change and convert. I love you very much. Adios, my little daughter" **(Mary to Patricia Talbot [16], Cuenca, Ecuador, October 7, 1988)** (23:8).

"If you don't help me, the wrath of God shall fall upon mankind. **I can hardly hold the hand of My Son back.** If you don't repent, it will happen very soon" **(Mary to Judiel Nieva [15], Agoo, Philippines, May 23, 1992)** (97:2).

"God wants to inflict a terrible punishment on us, but He cannot because the **Mother of God is shielding us**" **(St. Faustina Kowalska [31], Warsaw, Poland, 1936)** (86:82).

"Know that He who speaks to you is your brother, Jesus Christ. Why do you sometimes doubt my presence? I have spoken to you many times, but my little souls, you are innocent in Divine Wisdom. Love My Mother because **She holds back the fury of heaven**. Love her in all the good that happens to you and be discreet. I am the Merciful Jesus; my heart is filled with mercy. Ask, children. I would like the day of my Mercy to be celebrated. Have in your homes an image of my Merciful Heart. Do not forget that the Father is good and that I came to the world for you, my beloved ones. I am Jesus, and know that all is in your hands. The time is short, and I am already very wounded with all that my stray children have done" **(Jesus to Patricia Talbot [16], Cuenca, Ecuador, December 28, 1988)** (23:27–28).

"**I have held back the angel's arm and the sword he carries**. But when God the Father decides to act, not even I will be able to stop him" **(Mary to Gianna Talone Sullivan [49], Emmitsburg, Maryland, July 2, 2006)** (86:83).

"At the left of Our Lady and a little above, we saw an **angel with a flaming sword** in his left hand. Flashing, it gave out flames that looked as though they would set the world on fire—but they **died in contact with the splendor that Our Lady radiated toward him** from her right hand. Pointing to the earth with his right hand, the angel cried out in a loud voice, 'Penance! Penance! Penance!'" **(Lucia Santos [9], Fatima, Portugal, July 13, 1917)** (29:121–122)

"My sweet beloved Mary, a humble servant and spouse to the Holy Spirit, **continues to hold back the sword of the angel**, preventing it from striking and revealing the bowls of purification. However, even my sweet Mary could not do this unless I allowed her, for I have been a patient and loving God. But now, without revealing a time or a date or a place, I will forewarn humanity to take a cautious look at your very selves..." **(God to Gianna Talone Sullivan [49], Emmitsburg, Maryland, July 8, 2006)** (86:82)

"My dear child, tell My Priest sons I am calling them together to prepare to do battle. The church and the world are about to be thrown into great turmoil. Pray very much for the

Holy Father (John Paul II), as He suffers greatly for the sins of humanity and is very distressed. He needs your constant support in prayer. Tell My sons I have chosen you to give these messages, which is the holy will of My Son. Prepare humanity now for the greatest battle since time began, which is about to begin. If you do not heed My warnings, you will not survive the terrible and evil time ahead: torrents of rain, hail, thunder, earthquakes, catastrophes, natural disasters, murders, corruption, incest, immorality, abortions, priests and religious losing faith and committing sacrileges against the Holy Name of My Son—these are taking place. How much more can He take? He is daily crucified. Help Me, please. **I cannot hold back the justice of My Son any more**. Please, My sons, prepare now as never before. I am gathering you now from the four corners of the earth to do battle. Put on the armor of God daily, and take up your cross and carry it with joy. Go in peace" **(Mary to Geraldine, Australia, October 7, 1993)** (14:106–107).

"Now, daughter, now I will reveal to you my great secret, which corresponds to the one revealed to the other visionaries. This secret you cannot write nor tell to anyone until I permit you. (Our Lady reveals the great secret to Patricia and then continues…) I put into your hands the great mission of the conversion and turnabout of the world. **I am holding back the hand of My Son** with the message that I have given you, and if My children convert, the Heart of My Son will soften and the intensity can be diminished or be lost forever. If not, the great trial will come" **(Mary to Patricia Talbot [16], Cuenca, Ecuador, October 11, 1988)** (23:10–11).

"Our Lord can no longer watch the many grievous sins against purity. He wants to send a flood of punishments. **I have interceded** that He may be merciful once more! Therefore, I ask for prayer and penance to atone for these sins" **(Mary to Pierina Gilli [40s], Montichiari, Italy, November 16, 1947)** (134:3).

"My Father is angry. If My children will not listen to My Heart, which is the Voice of Mercy and Instruction, punishment will come swiftly, and none shall be able to stay it. **The pleadings of My Heart have held back the divine justice** about to descend on an ungrateful and sinful generation. Woe to the parents who set a bad example to their children! Terrible will be their judgment. I will demand a strict accounting of every soul entrusted to their care. Woe to the children who disobey and show disrespect toward their parents! 'Honor thy father and thy mother.' On this shall they be judged most severely" **(Jesus to Sister Mildred Neuzil [38], midwest USA, July 11, 1954)** (144: Part II).

"Many men in this world grieve the Lord. I seek souls to console Him. In order to appease the anger of the Heavenly Father, I wish, with My Son to search for souls who will make reparations for sinners and for the ungrateful by offering up their sufferings and poverty to God on their behalf. In order that the world might know the wrath of the Heavenly Father toward today's world, He is preparing to inflict a great chastisement on all mankind. With My Son, many times I have tried to **appease the wrath** of the Heavenly Father. **I have prevented the coming of the chastisement** by offering the sufferings of His Son on the cross, His precious Blood, and the compassionate souls who console the Heavenly Father, a cohort of victim souls overflowing with love. Prayer, penance, honest poverty, and courageous acts of sacrifices can soften His anger. Obedience is the foundation of all things…" **(Mary to Sister Agnes Katsuko Sasagawa, Akita, Japan, August 3, 1973)** (11:198)

"Whoever prays on these tiles and weeps tears of penance will find a secure, heavenly ladder and receive protection and grace through my motherly heart.…The Lord is still protecting the good and is **holding back a great punishment because of my intercession**" (Mary to Pierina Gilli [40s], Montichiari, Italy, December 8, 1947) (134:5).

Similar visual imagery is seen in an unexpected spiritual visit during a near-death experience that occurred in a hospital during a dangerous childbirth in Australia:

An angry Jesus is ready to send a punishing chastisement to the world (photo by author of dome painting in the Basilica of the National Shrine of the Immaculate Conception in Washington DC).

"Then all of a sudden, one moment I am lying there (in the hospital) in agony, and the next—I am in a completely different place, standing up free from all pain. I did not know where I was; I looked all around me, and everything was brilliant light. In front of me to my left I saw a figure of a man, and it was as though the sun was shining from his face, but yet it did not hurt my eyes to look at him. He was brighter than the sun. At that moment, I felt his great compassion for me, as if he felt sorry for me, and then he said, 'Do not worry, this person (the insensitive hospital nurse) belongs to the Wicked One.' I knew he meant the nurse who had caused me to suffer much. Up until this moment in my life, I sometimes wondered if God or heaven really existed. Now, in Jesus' presence, I was in awe and remembered thinking, 'Oh, God, there really is a Supreme Being who watches over the whole earth and sees everything.' Now I know for sure that there is a God! Then he said, 'They are persecuting My people,' and **He raised His right hand as He wanted to punish the wicked people here on earth**. I then felt tremendous anger coming from him and also felt His Almighty Power. Just as He was about to strike, **something from my right stopped Him**. I looked across to see what it was, and **I saw a Lady sitting down**. Coming from this woman were oceans and oceans of love. So much love—a love I have never known. All the love I have for my family, children, husband, mother, grandparents, relatives, everyone—all this put together is only a tear-drop compared to the love coming from this Lady—and a serenity, peacefulness, and gentleness on the same scale. **Her love was stopping this Man from punishing the world**, and I knew I must go through this Lady to get to this Man. She had a tremendous hold over Him, which was Love. In this love that I felt coming from Her I experienced the greatest ecstasy and happiness I had ever known. **Then I realized He could refuse Her nothing**. At this moment She said to me, "You are going to have a baby girl. Go back, they need you." And I was back in the hospital **(visionary Geraldine, Australia, a near-death encounter, 1986)** (14:27).

"The sign will come; you must not worry about it. The only thing that I would want to tell you is to be converted. Make that known to all my children as quickly as possible. No pain, no suffering is too great for me in order to save you. **I will pray to My Son not to punish the world;** but I plead with you, be converted. *You cannot imagine what is going to happen*, or what the Eternal Father will send to earth. That is why you must be converted! Renounce everything. Do penance. Express my thanks to all my children who have prayed and fasted. **I carry all this to My Divine Son in order to obtain an alleviation of His justice** against the sins of mankind. I thank the people who have prayed and fasted. Persevere and help me to convert the world" **(Mary to teenagers in Medjugorje, Bosnia-Herzegovina, June 24, 1983)** (45:172–173).

"Mankind is currently abusing the graces received and is moving toward perdition, and if there is no change, he will succumb under fire, war, and death. But **I am being sent into the world by God to avert or mitigate** such a cataclysm" **(Mary to Maria Esperanza [55], Betania, Venezuela, 1984)** (11:279).

"Children, there is much sorrow in my heart, for many natural catastrophes and others created by man are coming. Hard times are already taking place, a short decade filled with suffering. Children, the **Third World War** is near. Do not frighten your hearts because the peace of God is with you…Forgive all men.

Understand the mercy of God. Understand my petitions. All that I have told you is because God the Father has asked me to. Children, the time is short, very short. Conversion must be faithful. Remove all evil sentiments because Satan penetrates in them. Remove them with the Presence of God in your souls. Children, give thanks to God for what you have…you must fill your hearts with the Light of My Son, so that a desolation of faith will not exist…Children, My Son Jesus imposes his hands on your heads to take away hatred, pride, bitterness" **(Mary to Patricia Talbot [18], Cuenca, Ecuador, January 6, 1990)** (23:92–93).

"I am your Mother. Love each other. Forgive each other. Pray, pray, pray. I love you very much.…It is not enough to ask for peace, but make peace. Do not turn peace to violence. Ask for faith that you may be patient. If you do not change your ways, you will provoke the **Third World War**" **(Mary to Judiel Nieva [15], Agoo, Philippines, November 14, 1992)** (97:3).

"Do not fear because the kingdom is near. Do not allow Satan to penetrate the heart which loves God. Little children, know that all that you do benefits the world. Your prayers, penances, and fasts are impeding the **Third World War**. You, my little souls, *do you forget that with prayer and fasting you can deter wars and natural catastrophes*? It is in your hands. It depends on you whether the chastisement be as strong as the pain that My Son feels, or that it be appeased with prayers" **(Mary to Patricia Talbot [16], Cuenca, Ecuador, December 26, 1988)** (23:93).

"The times are coming which have been foretold as being those in the end times. See the desolation which surrounds the world…the sin, the sloth, the genocide. Pray for Russia. Oppression and wars continue to occupy the minds and hearts of many people. Russia, despite everything, continues to deny My Son. Russia rejects real life and continues to live in darkness. If there is not a return to Christianity in Russia, there will be a **Third World War**; the whole world will face ruin" **(Mary to Marina Kizyn [12], Hrushiv, Ukraine, 1987)** (2:275).

BE NOT AFRAID TO FOLLOW THE FOOTPRINTS FROM HEAVEN

"The earth will be struck with calamities of all kinds. There will be a series of wars until the **last war**, which will then be fought by the ten kings of the anti-Christ, all of whom will have one and the same plan. Before this comes to pass, there will be a time of false peace in the world. People will think of nothing but amusement. The wicked will give themselves to all kinds of sins. And so, my children, make this known to all my people" **(Mary to Maximin Giraud [11], Melanie Mathieu [14], La Salette, France, September 19, 1846)** (10:90).

"There will come a Great Chastisement for all mankind—a chastisement the likes of which have never been seen. If you do not hear me, there will be thousands of deaths, and the church will suffer a great decay. There will be no work, and **a new Great War** will come. The pope will be martyrized. You are very near the Last Times. The judgment over nations is very near. The Creator's Day is coming" **(Mary to Luz Amparo Cuevas, El Escorial, Spain, 1980–1992)** (107).

"Dear daughter, My Beloved Mother and I are present—be not afraid, I hold you in the palm of My hand. We are so very much offended, My child, by the sins of the world. Many souls are doomed to perdition. How it grieves Me to see this. Why are they so blind? Why do they not listen to Me and My Blessed Mother, who loves them with a love beyond their imagination? The greatest joy awaits them in paradise if only they would repent and turn away from sin. My children, why do you deceive yourselves? Don't you know the Kingdom of God is upon you? Repent now while there is still time. Weep, My children, for your families, as the earth and heavens above will shake to their very foundations with a terror the world has never known. Woe to the wicked as their fate is terrible. Pray, pray, pray continuously to lessen the punishment as you cannot imagine what God will send. But fear not—be not afraid, I will be with you in all things....**Arm yourselves urgently with My Holy Mother's Rosary**—as the Prince of Darkness is unchained from the abyss. In the Rosary you will find protection and consolation. The time is at hand—comfort one another, pray with and for each other. Suffer for souls, and the greatest joy in heaven will be yours for all eternity" **(Jesus to Geraldine, Australia, April 4, 1992)** (14:49).

"My dear children, God sends me on earth to come to save all because the whole world is in danger. I come among you to bring peace to your hearts. God wants that peace to reign in the hearts of all mankind, and He wants the conversion of all peoples. Therefore, my children, pray, pray, pray! If you do not pray, you will receive nothing. The time that you have left is short; there will be earthquakes, disasters, and famines for the inhabitants of the earth" **(Mary to Mrs. Mafalda Caputo, Oliveto Citra, Italy, 1986)** (86:41).

"A loss of mankind is that sign of punishment from heaven in the near future, my people. My children, whoever loves Me, carries his cross in suffering and does not complain, who is exhausted in dirty word from human word, who gives his glory to the Glorification of Great God, who suffers humiliations, who does not find relief—I am with you. I send you sufferings, but I also send you strength, grace, and the quiet in your soul" **(Jesus to Yulia [9], Ternopil, Ukraine, March 19, 2005)** (152).

"I urge my people to fulfill my wishes quickly, because today more than ever such fulfillment of my will is necessary for God's greater honor and glory. The Father pronounces a dreadful woe upon all who refuse to obey His Will" **(Mary to Barbara Ruess [12], Marienfried, Germany, June 25, 1946)** (130).

"Woe to the inhabitants of the earth! God will exhaust His wrath upon them. The leaders of the people of God have neglected prayer and penance, and the devil has bedimmed their intelligence. They have become wandering stars which the serpent will drag along with his tail to make them perish.... There will be bloody wars and famines, plagues and infectious diseases. There will be thunderstorms which will shake cities, earthquakes which will swallow countries. Voices will be heard in the air. **The fire of heaven will fall** and consume three cities" **(Mary to Maximin Giraud [11], Melanie Mathieu [14], La Salette, France, September 19, 1846)** (10:88, 91).

"In those times, the atmosphere will be saturated with the spirit of impurity which, like a filthy sea, will engulf the streets and public places with incredible license....Innocence will scarcely be found in children, or modesty in women. There shall be scarcely any virgin souls in the world. The delicate flower of virginity will seek refuge in the cloisters...Without virginity, **fire from heaven** will be needed to purify these lands" **(Mary to Mother Mariana de Jesus Torres y Berriochaoa, Quito, Ecuador, 1610)** (141).

"I am weeping because humanity is not accepting my motherly invitation to conversion. The (public) signs of my immense sorrow...are not believed in. Man is becoming ever more corrupt, godless, wicked, and cruel. A chastisement worse than the flood is about to come upon this poor and perverted humanity. *Fire will descend from heaven*. This will be the sign that God in His justice has—as of now—fixed the hour of His great manifestation....I am weeping because the church is continuing along the road of division, of loss of the true faith...I am weeping because, in great numbers, the souls of my children are being lost and going to hell.... Prepare yourselves to receive Christ in the splendor of His glory, because the great day of the Lord has even now arrived" **(Mary to Sister Agnes Katsuko Sasagawa, Akita, Japan, September 29, 1973)** (11:200–201).

"There are punishments drawing near like a cloud that will grow and extend itself to such a point as to cover everything. Everywhere **sparks will submerge people in fire** and blood. What an awful vision! My motherly heart would despair if I did not know how the justice of God needs to show itself for the salvation of souls and the purification of peoples!" **(Mary to Berthe Petit [30], Belgium, around 1900)** (86:59)

"...We must make many sacrifices, perform penance, and visit the Blessed Sacrament frequently. But first, we must lead good lives. If we do not, a chastisement will befall us. **The cup is**

already filling up, and if the people do not change, a very great chastisement will come upon us" **(Mary to Conchita Gonzalez [12], Mari Cruz Gonzalez [11], Mari Loli Mazon [12], Jacinta Gonzalez [12], Garabandal, Spain, July 4, 1961)** (34:27).

"**The cup of divine justice is full—is more than full, is flowing over**. Iniquity covers the whole earth. The Church is darkened by the spread of apostasy and sin. The Lord, for the triumph of his mercy, must as of now purify you with his strong action of justice and love" **(Mary to Father Don Stefano Gobbi, Milan, Italy, 1987)** (86:4) (94:357).

"As my message of October 18 has not been complied with and has not been made known to the world, I am advising you that this is the last one. **Before, the cup was filling up. Now, it is flowing over.** Many cardinals, many bishops, and many priests are on the road to perdition—and are taking many souls with them. Less and less importance is being given to the Eucharist. You should turn the wrath of God away from yourselves by your efforts. If you ask His forgiveness with sincere hearts, He will pardon you. I, your mother, through the intercession of St. Michael the Archangel, ask you to amend your lives. You are now receiving the last warnings. I love you very much and do not want your condemnation. Pray to us with sincerity and we will grant your requests. You should make more sacrifices. Think about the passion of Jesus" **(Mary to Conchita Gonzalez [16], Garabandal, Spain, June 18, 1965)** (34:27–28).

"This world, which has become as corrupt as it can ever be and violates even the stern dignity of God the Father, cannot escape the **disaster of the sulfuric fire that flames up violently**, but because the sounds of prayers have been soaring to the sky, which have been offered up by the souls who pray in imitation of a little soul like you—who prays with the most earnest devotion, God the Father is delaying to **release the cup of just wrath**" **(Jesus to Julia Kim [64], Naju, Korea, April 22, 2011)** (135).

"I gave the Savior to the world; as for you, you have to speak to the world about His great Mercy and prepare the world for the Second Coming of Him who will come, not as a merciful Savior, but as a just Judge. Oh, how terrible is that day! Determined is the day of justice, the day of divine wrath. The angels tremble before it. Speak to souls about this great mercy while it is still the time for mercy" **(Mary to St. Faustina Kowalska [31], Warsaw, Poland, 1936)** (86:60).

"The devil will be possessed of such power that those who are not firmly established in me will be deceived…You should establish everything in confidence to my Immaculate Heart. The devil has power over all people who do not trust in my heart" **(Mary to Barbara Ruess [12], Marienfried, Germany, May 25, 1946)** (3:201).

"My daughter, as previously in Fatima, today my visits are renewed on earth. *They are more frequent and more prolonged because humanity is passing through very dramatic times.* Has mankind not understood that they must be uniquely at the service of God? If they resist, their souls are going to perish. Many hearts do not accept my invitation to prayer and conversion. That is why the work of the devil is growing and expanding. My dear children, it is only through prayer and conversion that you will return to God. May He not find your hearts dry" **(Mary to Gladys Quiroga de Motta [52], San Nicolas, Argentina, May 13, 1989)** (149:3).

"God is trying desperately to get the attention of man. He has used miracles and graces beyond belief. At no other time in history has God tried so desperately to get the attention of His children" **(Mary to Ruth Ann Wade [54], Bloomington, Indiana, USA, January 14, 1994)** (86:33).

"My maternal action in these last times is being exercised in a manner which is open and always more powerful. My light is becoming bright in every part of the earth. For this reason, I am manifesting myself today everywhere by means of my numerous apparitions and of my extraordinary manifestations" **(Mary to Father Don Stefano Gobbi, Milan, Italy, December 8, 1990)** (86:41) (94:438).

"In the beginning, you had fear and distrust of the children I have chosen. Later, the majority accepted me in their hearts and started to carry out my motherly requests, but unfortunately, that didn't last long...It is because I am your mother that I love you and that I warn you. There are secrets, my children. This is what is not known—and when it will be known, it will be too late" **(Mary to Mirjana Dragicevic [23] "for the world," Sarajevo, Bosnia, January 28, 1987)** (52:231).

"God weeps over mankind, but mankind remains deaf. They pay no attention to My heavenly messages...God weeps over His Church..." **(Mary to Luz Amparo Cuevas, El Escorial, Spain, 1988)** (107)

"Child, the messages for the most part are no longer listened to. That is why, eventually, they too, will cease. These messages are much like the messages given to you for the world. How many of those who have read them have taken them to heart? How many of My children have begun saying the Rosary daily as a result? How many have returned to church and the sacraments? How many receive the Body of My Jesus as frequently as possible?...Not many have taken the messages, given to them from heaven, very seriously. A blueprint for salvation has been put before each of My children for their salvation, and they choose to ignore.... *God is going to remove the messages and try something more drastic to get the attention of His children.* God has a plan. His plan is perfect. There is to be great suffering come to your country as a result of the complacency of God's children to the evil going on around them...My children need to be awakened from their sleep. To do so will take drastic measures" **(Mary to Ruth Ann Wade [54], Bloomington, Indiana, USA, September 14, 1994)** (86:48–49).

"I am the sign of the Living God. I place my Sign on the foreheads of my children (those who consecrate themselves to my Immaculate Heart). Lucifer will persecute the sign, but my sign will conquer…Substitute my Immaculate Heart in place of your sinful hearts…Fulfill my request so that Christ may reign as the King of Peace" **(Mary to Barbara Ruess [12], Marienfried, Germany, May 25, 1946)** (3:200).

"Blessed are the homes that honor My Name and the Name of My Father. Blessed are the homes where I am loved, for there the Holy Trinity dwells. Blessed are the parents and children who have made a home for God in their hearts…Return My people, for My Heart hungers and thirsts for your love. **If you will not return, the just anger of My Father will descend upon you**. What would you choose—My love or My Father's anger? Choose, and as you choose, so shall it be done. I will not force your free will, for that is yours to use as you desire" **(Jesus to Sister Mildred Neuzil [38], midwest USA, July 12–14, 1954)** (144: Part II).

"At these moments, all humanity is hanging by a thread. If the thread breaks, many will be those who do not reach salvation…Hurry, because time is running out" **(Mary to Gladys Quiroga de Motta, San Nicolas, Argentina, January 8, 1984)** (149:2).

A weary, saddened Blessed Mary dreads the loss of any of her children's souls to hell.

Are you headed back to church now? Do we dare NOT to consider these messages? Are we bold enough to ignore them and safely remain in denial? **That would be much easier**. Just close this book and try to convince yourself that there is really *nothing to any of this*—and nothing to be concerned with…despite all the supernatural evidence and accurate predictions.

Perhaps, you are not impressed or convinced yet. Perhaps, when *your* dad came home, the dreaded punishment *never happened* after all. Perhaps, your mother used "scare tactics" as a clever tool to gain your compliance and obedience. Maybe that is all that heaven is really attempting to accomplish: Compliance through fear. Perhaps, you now believe that ***nothing is ever going to really happen*** on such a worldwide level.

But…*what if…you are wrong* this time?

Could this *really* be the end of the world? Or is it just more fear and hysteria from insecure human beings? For decades people have marched on the streets with homemade signs with the boldly printed message: Repent, the End of The World Is Coming! *And nothing ever happened*. Therefore, why should it **now**?

Do we have any further messages or "footprints" to make this proposed chastisement more specific, detailed, and credible? What if the predicted "purification" is actually the beginning of something new and better?

The final clues are straight ahead…**be not afraid** to *see* them… and *learn* from them.

CHAPTER 19

DARKNESS...THEN LIGHT

It has been an overwhelming joy to awaken and *feel* the reality of Jesus, Blessed Mary, God, the angels, and saints! Unfortunately, I have also had to admit to the existence of another entity—Satan. *I was not wanting to find out that he was real, too*—nor was I prepared to accept that. **Why did *he* have to be real?** I could have done without that chilling awareness.

However, understanding the genuine existence of the devil becomes a very important reality. I began to truly learn how he constantly works to undo the devotion to God with seemingly harmless distractions, pleasant temptations, and obsessions with wealth, material possessions, and other enjoyable self-indulgences. Being blind, deaf, oblivious, or avoidant of this reality is *not really* such a good idea! Satan lures us into a complacency, a comfortable apathy, and a growing doubt *that God is truly there* for us. Satan wants us to be content and enjoy all of our self-absorbing activities that give us no reason or any obvious need for God.

This leads to generations of technology-based, self-focused individuals who place much less importance on the quality of family life, the helping of others, living a moral life, or seeking spiritual growth. Hard-core science now seeks to define our reality—not intangible faith or any mystical belief in a Divine Creator. That blind faith or hopeful belief in an invisible, all-powerful God in such a troubled world racked with evil activity and violent behavior is shattered by the younger generations crying out for physical proof, tangible evidence, and a stronger need for trust and security rather than faith in what seem to be uncertain, intangible, and elusive concepts.

Furthermore, an acceptance of the reality of Satan and his dark angels adds credibility to reported cases of malevolent hauntings, satanic rituals, and "demonic possession"—with the actual need for exorcisms, an accepted Catholic service. The Catholic church would not take such matters seriously if they did not take Satan and his demonic influences seriously.

On **October 13**, 1884—*exactly thirty-three years to the day* prior to the great Miracle of the Sun in Fatima—Pope Leo XIII had a remarkable vision. The aged pontiff had just finished celebrating Mass in his private Vatican chapel, attended by a few cardinals and members of the Vatican staff. He suddenly stopped at the foot of the altar. He stood there for about ten minutes, appearing as if in a trance. His face was an ashen white color. Startled, the others asked him what had just happened. He explained that as he was about to leave the foot of the altar, he suddenly heard voices—two voices, one kind and gentle, the other guttural and harsh. The voices seemed to have come from the direction of the tabernacle. He described the following conversation (139):

> The guttural voice of Satan to Our Lord: **"I can destroy your Church."**
>
> The gentle voice of Our Lord: **"You can? Then go ahead and do so."**
>
> Satan: **"To do so, I need more time and more power."**
>
> Our Lord: **"How much time? How much power?"**
>
> Satan: **"Seventy-five to one hundred years, and a greater power over those who will give themselves over to my service."**
>
> Our Lord: **"You have the time. You will have the power. Do with them what you will."**

As soon as this disturbing conversation ended, Pope Leo XIII went immediately from the chapel to his office. He felt compelled to do something within his power to help—and composed the prayer to St. Michael with the instructions that it be said after all low Masses everywhere.

The debate continues today as to whether there *really was* a "one hundred-year deal" made—and, if so, **when** did the one hundred-year reign of Satan begin? Some note that exactly seventy-five years after 1884, Pope John XXIII publicly summoned the Second Vatican Council on January 25, 1959. Others state that the incredible scientific inventions and amazing technological advances of the twentieth century really have distracted and consumed mankind to turn further away from a less tangible God. Every day, children and their parents are consumed by iPads, MP3 players, computer screens, big-screen televisions, video games, Internet websites, digital tablets, Facebook, Apple watches, electronic books, as well as endless texting or "tweets" on cell phones—instead of really interacting with each other face-to-face. This is evidence of the devil's pleasurable means of replacing God with self-focused and distracting devices that seem to meet all of our needs now. Have you taken a "**selfie**" photo recently?

And if those "feel good" distractions are not enough, then alcohol, drugs, gambling, shopping sprees, food addictions, pornography, online dating, and sexual affairs seem to nurture and soothe human souls rather than our seeking comfort and trust in God. Family relations are distant, divorce rates high, child abuse rampant, prayer banned from schools, gay marriages legalized, empty churches forgotten, and dreadful abortions are abundant whenever convenient. Recent statistics indicate that only a small, 15 percent of Catholics actually attend church regularly (80:24). As many as 80 percent of young people do not even believe in God. Did the devil succeed in his efforts? Was there anything quite like this in any previous century?

We actually have a confirmation of this alleged deal with the devil from Blessed Mary in one of her messages to the teenagers in Medjugorje on February 14, 1982:

> "You must know that Satan exists. One day, he presented himself before the throne of God and asked permission to try the Church for a period of time. God permitted him to try

it during one century. **This century is under the power of the devil**, but when the secrets which have been confided to you have been fulfilled, his power will be destroyed. Already now, he is beginning to lose his power, and he has become aggressive. He destroys marriages, stirs up division between priests, and brings about obsessions and murders. You must protect yourself by fasting and prayer, especially community prayer. Carry blessed objects with you. Place them in your houses. Return to the use of holy water" **(Mary to Mirjana Dragicevic, Medjugorje, Februray 14, 1982)** (52:188–189).

Paul Regan, a Eucharistic apostle of Divine Mercy blessed by Pope John Paul II, spoke to the 2012 Marian Conference in Springfield, Missouri, and discussed Pope Leo XIII's encounter. According to Mr. Regan, certain events in Russia in 1917 fit the criteria for the beginning of the one hundred years. He states that as many as fourteen other prominent theologians are in agreement. They cautiously predict that the year 2017 will be the end of that evil one hundred-year era and shall usher in a new period of peace after some drastic changes occur (87). What exactly happened in 1917 that would create such agreement among those theologians?

The mysterious and sinister Rasputin who led to Russia's downfall into Communism.

Grigori Rasputin was a mysterious figure who created much controversy and influence over the Russian government, especially after 1915 when Tsar Nicolas II left to take command of the army at the front. Historians agree that Rasputin's presence played a significant part in the increasing unpopularity of the Tsar and Alexandra Feodorovna, his wife. He eventually was murdered when everyone began to see that he was the cause of the downfall of the Russian Monarchy and the root cause of Russia's despair during World War I.

Rasputin was not all that he seemed to be. Not a true monk but more of a mystic, his behavior and beliefs were despised by the Russians. However, he had gained favor with the royal family because he had actually healed their young prince, Tsesarevich, from Hemophilia through mystical prayers. But his "sinful attention" to young girls and many women created a negative stir in the press. He believed that those deliberately committing fornication but then repenting bitterly would be closer to God. Prime Minister Kokovtsov tried to get the Tsar to exile him, but the Tsar was still in favor of him. Kokovtsov offered Rasputin the Russian equivalent of $100,000 to leave the capital as Rasputin had become one of the most hated people in Russia. He was accused of spreading false doctrines—while kissing and bathing at the brothel with many women.

An effort to ordain him as a priest was attacked by the Holy Synod, who accused him of evil and immoral practices. Anyone bold enough to criticize Rasputin found condemnation from the Tsarina, mother of the mystically healed prince. By May 1914, Rasputin had become an influential factor in Russian politics. After a woman stabbed him on the street in 1914, and he recovered, he became even more evil and distrusting. And now, most of Rasputin's enemies had disappeared, fallen from power, or been banished. It appears that Rasputin's influence over the Tsarina became so great that it was he who ordered the destinies of Imperial Russia while she compelled her weak husband, the Tsar, to fulfill them. By 1915, Tsarina Alexandra and her trusted Rasputin were advising the military strategies and dominating the Holy Synod. Opposing officials would be quickly replaced. The public now saw Rasputin as the actual ruler and "evil genius" of Russia! Plans began to form for the elimination of his evil presence.

Rasputin was invited to the Yusupov palace in December 1916 for a party. He was offered snack cakes *laced with a large amount of cyanide*. After an hour of waiting, Rasputin had not yet collapsed.

He was then invited to play pool in a downstairs sound-proof room as Felix Yusupov became nervous that Rasputin might somehow survive the cyanide poisoning. Taking a gun and shooting Rasputin at close quarters, one bullet entered his left chest, penetrating his stomach and liver. A second bullet entered the left back and penetrated the kidneys. But Rasputin jumped back up and lunged at Yusupov, apparently not bleeding anywhere. They jumped Rasputin and clubbed him with a bladed weapon, beating him severely. Yet, he escaped up the stairs to the ground floor, opening a door to the courtyard. Rasputin was shot twice more by Vladimir Purishkevich and fell into the snow. To contain him further, he was then wrapped and tied inside curtains from the palace and thrown into the icy Malaya Nevka River. When his frozen corpse was retrieved the next day, it was clear that he had not died quickly because he had been clawing his way out if the bundled drapes (142).

Two months later in 1917, the February Revolution caused the ruling party to step down. A man named Vladimir Lenin started working against the provisional government that had overthrown the tsarist regime. ***The Virgin Mary began appearing in Fatima, Portugal, three months later on May 13, 1917.*** By October 1917, the Bolshevik Revolution began, evolving into the Communist Party and socialist form of a godless government. In fact, it was **October 13**, 1917, when the Bolsheviks tore down the Catholic Basilica in Red Square in Moscow (2:325). **October 13**, 1917 was also *the exact same day that the Virgin Mary made her final appearance in Fatima to the three shepherd children with over seventy thousand observers present and witnessing the Miracle of the Sun.* **Knowing what was happening in Russia that very day**, Blessed Mary said,

> "If humanity does not turn back to God, Russia will spread errors and terrors worldwide....I shall come to ask for the Consecration of Russia to my Immaculate Heart...If my requests are heeded, Russia will be converted, and there will be peace. If not, she will spread her errors throughout the world, causing wars and persecutions of the Church..." (11:146)

BE NOT AFRAID TO FOLLOW THE FOOTPRINTS FROM HEAVEN

In a 1957 interview with Fatima visionary, Lucia Santos, she explained that the Holy Virgin is engaged in a decisive battle with Satan—who knows his time is growing short and is determined to steal as many souls as possible. By the time this struggle is finished, Lucia said that people would be "either of God or of the Evil One." She added that if Russia were not converted, the country would be an instrument of God's chastisement for the entire world, and that many nations would be annihilated (8:177).

Did the devil select Russia as the "godless" country to oppose Christianity and heavily influence other nations toward Communism and away from God? Did he work through Rasputin, **who seemed possessed by evil**, impossible to eliminate, and the cause for the downfall of Russia's ruling party? With heaven knowing these disturbing matters, what better time to have the Virgin Mary make a historically memorable effort through multiple appearances in Fatima toward renewing faith, inspiring thousands, and warning us of such evil? Does this not seem like the obvious start of the devil's hundred years?

Of course, nobody can be certain of any exact dates or precise timing because heaven can change the rules or add more time any time it wishes. The blink of an eye in the eternity of heaven might be another hundred years on earth. But there are clues that something critically important is approaching us at this point in time. Listen to some of these heavenly validations:

> "Satan has been the uncontested dominator of the events **of this century of yours**…The struggle between the Woman Clothed with the Sun and the Red Dragon has, during these years, reached its highest peak. Satan has set up his kingdom in the world. He is now ruling over you as a sure victory" **(Mary to Father Don Stefano Gobbi, Fatima, Portugal, May 13, 1972)** (86:31– 32) (94:425, 495).

> "I greatly desire to help poor sinners. A catastrophe is imminent—just as in the time of Noah. Many will die—not from flood **but by fire**, because certain of God's children have so seriously disobeyed Him. Their offense has consequences that will harm many innocent people. Never in its history

has humanity fallen so low. **This is the age of the kingdom of Satan**" **(Mary to Anna, a young girl, Seredne, Ukraine, 1954)** (2:269).

"Daughter, the Prince of Evil pours out his venom today with all his might because he sees that **his sorry reign is ending;** little is left to him. His end is near" **(Mary to Gladys Quiroga de Motta (49), San Nicolas, Argentina, March 7, 1986)** (149:3).

"Satan will rule until the first secret is unfolded…**The hour has come when the demon is authorized to act with all his force and power.** The present hour is the hour of Satan" **(Mary to Mirjana Dragicevic [17], Medjugorje, Bosnia-Herzegovina, 1982)** (86:31).

"**You are living in the time of the last efforts of evil** against Christ. Satan has been released from his prison. He occupies the entire face of the Earth" **(Mary to Madeleine, Dozule, France, November 2, 1973)** (86:31).

"My daughter, the evil one is triumphant now, it is true, but it is a **victory that will last briefly. The Lord is only giving him time**, the same time that He gives man for him to return to God. That is why vices and worldly madness increase every day. The weaknesses will have to become strengths and in this way will be able to get rid of evil. As yet, man's heart is not totally invaded. Glory be to God" **(Mary to Gladys Quiroga de Motta [49], San Nicolas, Argentina, October 11, 1986)** (149:3).

"**This century of yours, which is about to end, has been placed under the sign of a strong power conceded to my Adversary.** Thus, humanity has been led astray by the error of theoretical and practical atheism. In the place of God, idols have been built which everyone adores: pleasure, money, amusement, power, pride, and impurity. Truly, **Satan**, with the cup of lust, **has succeeded** in seducing all the nations of the earth" **(Mary to Father Don Stefano Gobbi, Milan, Italy, December 31, 1997)** (86:32) (94:604).

"The world will have to drain the cup of wrath to the dregs because of the countless sins through which His heart is offended. The devil of the infernal regions will rage more violently than ever and will cause frightful destruction because **he knows that his time is short**, and because he sees that already many have gathered around my sign. Over these he has no spiritual power, although he will kill the bodies of many; but through these sacrifices my power to **lead the remnant** Host to victory will increase…" **(Mary to Barbara Ruess [12], Marienfried, Germany, 1946)** (3:200–201)

"Satan has succeeded in entering into the church, the new Israel of God. He has entered there with the smoke of error and sin, of the loss of faith and apostasy, of compromise with the world and the search for pleasure. **During these years, he has succeeded in leading astray bishops and priests, religious and faithful**" **(Mary to Father Don Stefano Gobbi, Milan, Italy, May 13, 1993)** (86:13) (94:495).

"My children, listen to me—the Lord your God speaks. Let not your sins be numerous because there will soon be a great chastisement. Turn back to Me, My children, quickly as Satan is very strong. This is his kingdom. **He now rules over much of the world, but My Kingdom is coming**. There really is another life. You are just passing through here. Do not let the world deceive you—it does not have anything to offer that is lasting. Store up in heaven your treasures, and soon, you will be with Me in paradise. Believe, My children, justice will come. Take refuge in Me. Do no harm and you will receive a peace this world cannot give you. Come to Me, My children, and I will give you rest. The people of this world will hate you as they hated Me before you, but do not fear, My child, I have overcome the world. Satan is very powerful, My children. **Pray the Rosary often. This is a very powerful weapon.** Do not concern yourselves with material things. Live simply and go to church as this is the only time when you are in My real presence. Go to confession at least once a month with the intention of changing afterwards" **(Jesus to Geraldine, Australia, February 15, 1991)** (14:34–35).

"All humanity is contaminated. It does not know what it wants, and **it is the evil one's chance**, but he will not be the winner. Christ Jesus will win the great battle, my daughter. You must not let yourselves be surprised; you must be alert. For this reason, daughter, I ask for so much prayer, so much obedience to God. I say this for the whole world" (**Mary to Gladys Quiroga de Motta [46], San Nicolas, Argentina, December 27, 1983**) (149:2).

"All children of this world, you must be wise. Use this time for your salvation, because it is very short. Do not be amused by the kindness of those who are going to decline—who are sent to you **by the devil in order to distract you from your salvation**. You have so short a time. All of your savings, accumulated buildings and possessions, reserved for the future for your children—that you planned all for yourselves will be **scattered by winds of fire** on this sinful earth, which will be devastated by the people" (**Jesus to Yulia [9], Ternopil, Ukraine, June 8, 2004**) (152).

"But mark this: There will be terrible times in **the last days***. People will be lovers of themselves, lovers of money, boastful, proud, abusive, disobedient to their parents, ungrateful, unholy, without love, unforgiving, slanderous, without self-control, brutal, not lovers of the good, treacherous, rash, conceited, lovers of pleasure rather than lovers of God, having a form of godliness but* denying *its power. Have nothing to do with such people"* (**2 Timothy 3:1–5**).

"The enemy will not advance; **the hand of God Our Father will stop him**. When the time comes, He will uproot all evil, purify you, and you will become good Christians. Glory be to heaven" (**Mary to Gladys Quiroga de Motta [47], San Nicolas, Argentina, February 25, 1984**) (149:2).

"But when [evil] seems triumphant and when authority abuses its power, committing all manner of injustice and oppressing the weak, their ruin shall be near. They will fall and crash to the ground. Then will the Church, joyful and triumphant like a young girl, reawaken and be comfortably cradled in the arms of my most dear and elect son of those times" **(Mary to Mother Mariana de Jesus Torres, Quito, Ecuador, 1610)** (141).

As details of a predicted series of chastisements from heaven are gathered, they all seem to indicate that the first wave of punishment is an increase in natural disasters. But are we *really* having any more natural disasters than the usual amount? And are they *really* more severe than at other times in the past? The following messages and acquired statistics might answer these questions.

> "Launch forth into the world a message to make known to all that the scourge is near at hand. The justice of God is weighing upon the world. Mankind, defiled in the mire, soon will be washed in its own blood by disease, famine, earthquakes, cloudbursts, tornadoes, floods, terrible storms, and by war. But men ignore all these warnings and are unwilling to be convinced that My tears are plain signs to serve notice that tragic events are hanging all over the world, and that the hours of great trials are at hand. If men do not amend their ways, a **terrifying scourge of fire will come down from heaven** upon all the nations of the world, and men will be punished according to the debts contracted with Divine Justice. There will be frightful moments for all, because heaven will be joined with the earth, and all ungodly people will be destroyed. Some nations will be purified while other nations will disappear entirely" **(Mary to Sister Elena Aiello, Italy, April 8, 1955)** (86:106–107).

"You will be saved if you do not ignore my tears and tears of blood, accept my words well, and live a life based on the Gospels. But if you fail to do so, major calamities from the sky, on the ground, and in the seas will continue to happen. The world will experience all kinds of disasters. Therefore, *do not think that these are accidental happenings*. Be awake and pray" **(Mary to Julia Kim [56], Naju, Korea, August 31, 2003)** (135).

"…In the United States, a major, horrific earthquake with a number of offshoots will lead to widespread devastation.

All the weather abnormalities will go on increasing and will culminate in **fire coming from the sky**....I do not know this with the same certainty as when I was shown the tsunami (2004) in the Indian Ocean beginning in 1992, and which I published that prediction the same year. I know this with the same certainty as when I publicly stated the collapse of the twin towers (World Trade Center) on September 11, 1999—two years to the exact date before they were destroyed" **(Christina Gallagher, Ireland, February 21, 2005)** (86:110).

"God's punishment will strike out **two-thirds of all humanity**. The sun will cease to warm; there will be cold summers with poor harvests. There will be terrible floods and other misfortunes through the elements. There will be earthquakes and mountains will move. Churches will collapse; houses will move and will be carried away by the floods. The nonbelievers will blaspheme in their despair. **The air will be filled with demonlike forms**, the incorporations of sins and vices. These phantoms will terrify humanity" **(Mary to Matous Lasuta, Turzovka, Slovakia, 1958)** (86:109).

"Every year you can count on forest fires in the Western USA, but recently there has been an enormous change in Western fires. In truth, we've never seen anything like them in recorded history. It appears we're living in a new age of mega-fires— forest infernos **ten times bigger** than the fires we're used to seeing" **(CBS News: 60 Minutes, October 18, 2007)** (86:158).

"One third of all the natural disasters in this century (1900–1999) have come in the 1990s. The world has an average of seven hundred natural disasters every ten years; there have been 2,400 natural disasters just between 1990 and 1999— **more than three times that average**. 130 million people have been affected by floods in the 1990s—a **700 percent increase** compared to those affected in the 1970s. Similarly, there has been a **600 percent increase** in those affected by hurricanes or tornadoes, a **400 percent increase** in those affected by volcanoes, and a **200 percent increase** in mudslides. In the twenty-nine years, 1960—1989, there was only one year when the United States had more than one thousand tornadoes reported. But in the 1990s, there have been one thousand or more tornadoes *every year*" **(Fox TV Special: "Signs from God," July 28, 1999)** (86:158–159).

In 2004, Hurricane Charley blasted Florida, causing 15.4 billion dollars in damage. Then, on December 26, 2004, a 9.1 earthquake struck Indonesia, lasting a **record ten minutes** and causing the massive tsunami that killed 230,000 people. In November 2007, Bangladesh experienced its **worst cyclone in one hundred years** that killed ten thousand people and left over a million others without homes or jobs. In 2008, the cyclone Nargis ravaged Myanmar, leaving 134,000 dead or missing and another million people homeless. In April 2010, Pakistan had the **worst flood in its history** leaving seven million homeless, twenty million injured, and 1,800 dead. In October 2010, flooding in central Africa affected nearly two million people, including 64,500 children under the age of five. The 7.6 earthquake near Izmit, Turkey killed seventeen thousand people in 1999. The Kashmir earthquake in 2005 killed over 74,500 people. The Sichuan earthquake in 2008 killed over 74,500 Chinese people with another 1,800 reported missing and over five million left homeless. On January 12, 2010, Haiti was rocked by a terrible earthquake that killed an estimated 376,000 people and displaced another 410,000 from their homes. An earthquake in Western China on April 14, 2010, killed at least 2,187 people and injured more than twelve thousand others. On March 11, 2011, an off-shore earthquake launched a tsunami that devastated the coast of Japan, killing 12,800 residents with another fifteen thousand still missing and three hundred thousand more having to evacuate their homes (86:159–162).

It is significant that the following three-phase predictions of (1) the Warning, (2) the Miracle, and (3) the Chastisement involving three days of darkness have been consistently reported with similar details by vastly different, numerous sources: a mother of seven in Spain, six teenagers in Bosnia-Herzegovina, four grade-school girls in Garabandal, a respected priest in Milan, Italy, a middle-aged woman in Argentina, a seventeen-year-old model in Ecuador, a religious sister in Japan, a young woman in Indiana,

and even a nine-year-old girl in the Ukraine. And there are many more as well. Here is a collection of their comments from their supernatural encounters and divine inspiration. The collective details go well beyond any fantasy, delusion, or hoaxing in their amazing similarity, detail, and correlation with each other:

THE WARNING

The Warning: a moment of interior reflection with God: "your latest spiritual grade card" (Photo-Art created by author).

In the early months of the Medjugorje apparitions in 1981, Blessed Mary presented a strange parchment to Mirjana that contained all ten secrets **written in an unknown language**. The parchment was neither cloth nor paper, but of a material "unknown" on earth. It could be balled and wrinkled but not torn. As of this date, only Mirjana, Ivanka, and Jakov have been given all ten secrets, including the day and date of each. Mirjana was to select a priest, Father Petar Ljubicic, who is to be given the parchment ten days before the first secret is to be revealed. He will only be able to read the first one. After seven days of fasting and prayer and three days before the event, he *must* announce it to the world in whatever method he chooses to do so (45:207).

Secret #2: There will be an interior "illumination" of the soul, experienced by every living human being at a specific designated time. Through the Holy Spirit, it will suddenly permit every person to see his or her soul *exactly as God sees it*. Every sin and every good deed will be visible to each of us—as the world will literally stand still for a matter of time. Those who believe in God will experience great benefits. Those without belief will suffer the pain of the undeniable truth that *God is real*. Some will die from the shock of seeing themselves as God sees them (45:208–209). In fact, Mother Mary later commented on this,

> "Tongues of fire (Holy Spirit) will come down upon you all, my poor children, so ensnared and seduced by all the evil spirits who, during these years, have attained their greatest triumph, and thus, you will be illuminated by this divine light, and **you will see your own selves** in the mirror of the truth and the holiness of God. It will be like a **judgment in miniature**, which will open the door of your heart to receive the great gift of Divine Mercy" **(Mary to Father Gobbi, Milan, Italy, Pentecost Sunday, June 4, 1995)** (86:99) (94:546).

> "There will come a sign, which everyone in the world—in an interior way—will experience, and it is not far away. Everyone will experience an inner awareness, and they will know that this is from God, and **they will see themselves as they really are in the sight of God**" **(Mary to Christina Gallagher, Ireland, Fall, 2003)** (86:99).

> "The Warning is something supernatural and will not be explained by science. It will be seen and felt. It will be a **correction of the conscience** of the world. For those who do not know Christ, they will believe it is a warning from God" **(Conchita Gonzales, Garabandal, Spain, October, 1968)** (86:98).

GARABANDAL, SPAIN (1965)

The Blessed Virgin revealed that a three-stage process would occur in the future. First, there will be a Warning that will "draw the good closer to God and warn the wicked that the end of time is coming." The Warning will be seen and experienced by everyone everywhere. **Each person will find himself alone with his conscience before**

God, able to know all his sins and what his sins have caused. One would not only become aware of his sins but would *feel* them deeply and their impact upon others. Hopefully, this could influence a worldwide "purification" before The Miracle happens. The year that this will happen was only revealed to Mari Loli. The Miracle would follow the Warning within the same year (34:31–34). Other visionaries report similar messages and visions:

> "Before the punishment, there will be a warning from heaven. Everybody will see it. **It will seem as if the whole world is in flames.** It will last twenty minutes, and many will die because of the shock. Those who believe in God and the Virgin will fall into a sort of ecstasy. After the warning and before the punishment, there will be a miracle" **(Mary to Luz Amparo Cuevas, El Escorial, Spain, 1981)** (107).

> "The Warning is something that is **first seen in the air** everywhere in the world and immediately is transmitted into the interior of our souls. It will last for a very little while, but it will seem a very long time because of its effect within us. It will be for the good of our souls, in order to see in ourselves our conscience…the good and the bad that we have done… **It will come upon us like a fire from heaven, which we will** *feel profoundly in our interior*. **By its light, each one will see the state of his soul with complete clarity**; he will experience what it is to lose God; he will feel the purifying action of the cleansing flame. Briefly, it will be like having the particular Judgment in one's very soul while still alive" **(Jacinta Gonzales, Garabandal, Spain, March, 2007)** (86:99).

> "If the world does not change, I will send the warning. The earth will shake. The sun will spin with a **big explosion**, and the moon will appear in the morning and the sun at night. The **miraculous phenomenon will be visible all over earth**, and all of this will happen within half an hour. Big storms, floods, volcanic eruptions, earthquakes, and changing weather conditions are already on their way" **(Mary to Judiel Nieva [15], Agoo, Philippines, June 11, 1992)** (97:2).

"Soon the illumination of your conscience and the **state of your soul** will occur!" **(Mary to Sadie Jaramillo, Santa Maria, California, August 25, 1998)** (86:176)

"The Warning will be like **two heavenly bodies** or stars colliding, that make **a lot of noise** and a lot of light, but they don't fall. We are going to see it. It will horrify us because at that very moment we will see our souls and the harm that we have done. In that moment we are going to **see our conscience**, everything wrong that we are doing, and the good that we are not doing. **It will be like fire**. *It will not burn our flesh, but we will feel it bodily and interiorly*" **(Conchita Gonzales, Garabandal, Spain, Fall, 2003)** (86:98).

"My children, you draw close to the illumination of soul" **(Mary to Christina Gallagher, Ireland, July 25, 2005)** (86:176).

"The Blessed Mother says that God is giving so much time for these apparitions so that all may come to conversion. She can't help anybody who doesn't want to change, who doesn't come back to God, who doesn't put God first. If you don't do this now, it will be too late" **(Vicka Ivankovic, Medjugorje, Bosnia-Herzegovina, 1995)** (51:75–76).

THE MIRACLE

The Miracle: a sign for all to see and believe, before it's too late (Photo-Art created by author using Perryville, Missouri grotto).

Secret #3: A permanent sign will be visible at the site of the first apparition in Medjugorje (and perhaps at the sites of all apparitions worldwide). It can be seen and photographed but not touched. It is mostly a sign for atheists and others to convert, and that God is indeed real. Mirjana says, "When the permanent sign appears, unbelievers will run to the hill and pray for forgiveness…" **(Mirjana Dragicevic, Medjugorje, Bosnia-Herzegovina, 1982)** (45:212–213)

Other visionaries report similar impressions and visions from heavenly messages:

> "Today is the day of my physical departure, but my spiritual retreat will never be. I will be with you always, little children. Help those in most need. Love one another, and love God above all things. Young people, be examples of light. Carry the Cross in your hearts. Put on humility. Children, white doves of peace, be the light. Come always to visit me here. Never abandon me, little ones, because I love you so much, so much. **At the end of all the apparitions in the world, I will leave a great sign in this place and in all those where I have been**. Goodbye, my little ones, my children" **(Mary to Patricia Talbot [18], Cuenca, Ecuador, March 3, 1990)** (23:62–63).

> "It will be visible to all those who are in the village or on the surrounding mountains…the sick who are present will be cured and the incredulous will believe. It will be the greatest miracle that Jesus has performed for the world. There won't be the slightest doubt that it comes from God, and that it is for the good of mankind. A sign of the miracle, which will be possible to film or televise, will remain forever at the pines…It will be like smoke. You can touch it but not feel it" **(Conchita Gonzales, Garabandal, Spain, 1965)** (34:34–35) (86:102).

> "All these signs are designed to strengthen your faith until I leave you the visible and permanent sign" **(Mary to teenagers in Medjugorje, October 22, 1981)** (45:165).

> "My children, there will be many signs here at my house to prove to the world that it is I, your Immaculate Mother, who is calling you. The signs will be great. The great sign will last for

three days and three nights for all to see" **(Mary to Christina Gallagher, Achill Island, Ireland, Summer, 2002)** (86:104).

"The great sign will be seen by all. A **great cross** will illuminate the sky and all eyes will see it. This will be a great chance for everybody to repent and return to the God of salvation and peace" **(Mary to Pedro Regis, Anguera, Brazil, October 24, 2007)** (86:105).

"Write this last warning! **People will see a big cross**. It will be seen by the whole world for seven days" **(Jesus to Yulia [9], Ternopil, Ukraine, 2005)** (152).

"Before the great tribulation, there is going to be a sign. We will see in the sky the **great red cross** on a day of blue sky without clouds…This cross will be seen by everyone—Christians, pagans, atheists, etc.…" **(Brother David Lopez, San Benito, Texas, 1989)** (86:105)

"Soon the sign that will be given will be My Face. My Face will radiate in the skies and throughout the world more brilliantly than a thousand suns" **(Jesus to Christina Gallagher, Ireland, Fall, 2003)** (86:104).

GARABANDAL, SPAIN (1965)

The Miracle will be a supernatural public display in the area of the pines "that will prove and manifest God's love to us in a most outstanding way." It will be visible to all in the village and surrounding areas. The sick that will be present shall be cured; the sinners present will all be converted. A sign of the Miracle will remain forever at the pines—but cannot be touched—just photographed. Conchita Gonzales is the only visionary to know the year, month, and day of the Miracle—and can announce when it will happen, eight days in advance. It is supposed to happen within twelve months of the Warning and occur on a Thursday evening at 8:30 p.m., probably between April 8 and 16. It will be in Conchita's lifetime, and she is approximately sixty-five years old, now, in 2015 (34:34–35).

The purification of the earth with a rain of fire that will eliminate all the sinners (Photo-Art created by author).

THE CHASTISEMENT / THREE DAYS OF DARKNESS

GARABANDAL, SPAIN (1962)

The Chastisement is conditional and can be lessened if the world heeds the messages of the Blessed Virgin. Conchita has seen a preview and warns that when it comes it will be "**worse than being enveloped in fire.**" Mari Loli and Jacinta were also given a preview during a vision on June 21, 1962. Their screams of terror and gestures to fend off some frightening danger greatly affected all the observers, who then began praying (34:35).

> "The earth will go out of its orbit for three days, which would be **three terrible days of darkness" (Mary to Patricia Talbot, Cuenca, Ecuador, 1989)** (86:122).

> "If men do not amend their ways, a terrifying scourge of **fire will come down from heaven** upon all the nations of the world, and men will be punished according to the debts contracted with Divine Justice. There will be frightful moments for all, because heaven will be joined with the earth,

and **all the ungodly people will be destroyed**. Some nations will be purified while other nations will disappear entirely" **(Mary to Sister Elena Aiello, Italy, April 8, 1955)** (86:107).

"People do not realize that **there is an era of peace coming**. However, many shall be lost. **At this time, 80 percent of this world shall be lost and killed** if they do not accept what is coming before this peaceful tomorrow" **(Mary to Julia Kim [56], Naju, Korea, August 31, 2003)** (86:61).

"God is going to send a **double purification** to the earth. On the one hand, there would be earthquakes, plagues, revolutions, riots, massacres, battles, black airships traversing the skies and **covering the earth with fire**. On the other hand, **impenetrable black darkness** covering the earth for **three days**, during which time only **blessed candles** would give light" **(Blessed Anna Maria Taigi, Italy around 1800)** (86:121).

"Because this humanity has not accepted my repeated call to conversion, to repentance, and to a return to God, there is about to fall upon it the greatest chastisement which the history of mankind has ever known. It is a chastisement much greater than that of the flood. **Fire will fall from heaven**, and a great part of humanity will be destroyed" **(Mary to Father Don Stefano Gobbi, Milan, Italy)** (86:119) (94:332).

"There will come a time when all motors and machines will stop. A **terrible wave of heat will strike the earth** and men will begin to feel a great thirst. In desperation, they will seek water, but this will evaporate from the heat. Then, almost everyone will despair, and they will seek to kill one another. But they will lose their strength and fall to the ground. Then it will be understood that it is God alone who has permitted this. Then we saw a crowd in the midst of the flames. The people ran to hurl themselves into the lakes and seas. But the water seemed to boil and in place of putting out the flames, it seemed to enkindle them even more" **(Mari Loli, Garabandal, Spain, June, 1962)** (86:118–119).

"Make haste to wake up and pray so that you may be saved from the chastisement and disaster of the **blazing fire of sulfur** which is to fall upon the world" **(Mary to Julia Kim, Naju, Korea, November 9, 2001)** (86:120).

"There would be a **time of darkness** when the day would begin by being very dark and overcast, but that people would not associate it with anything unusual, even though it would be abnormal. Between 4:00 p.m. and 8:00 p.m., everything would go 'black-dark'—and remain in that darkness for a time. There would be an **explosion of fire or light in the sky**, and people would tremble. Many would die as they would look at the sky. The earth would begin to shake, and a **great sound would be heard** like an enormous groan that would reach the ends of the earth" **(Mary to Christina Gallagher, Ireland, January, 2006)** (86:122– 123).

"I will purify the earth with **fire**" **(Jesus to Luisa Piccarreta, Corato, Italy, November 2, 1917)** (86:118).

"Then the day of the Lord shall arrive like a thief. On that day, the heavens shall pass away with great violence, and truly the elements shall be dissolved with heat; then the earth, and the works that are within it, shall be completely burned up. Therefore, since all these things will be dissolved, what kind of people ought you to be? In behavior and in piety, be holy, waiting for, and hurrying toward, the advent of the day of the Lord, by which the burning heavens shall be dissolved, and the elements shall melt from the heat of the fire. Yet truly, in accord with his promises, we are looking forward to the new heavens and the new earth, in which justice lives. Therefore, most beloved, while awaiting these things, be diligent, so that you may be found to be immaculate and unassailable before him, in peace" **(2 Peter 3:10–14)**.

With demons released from hell during the Three Days of Darkness, the final battle between good and evil will be fought (Photo-Art created by author).

"Before I come as the Just Judge, I am coming first as the King of Mercy. Before the day of justice arrives, there will be given to people a sign in the heavens of this sort: All light in the heavens will be extinguished, and there will be **great darkness** over the whole earth. Then the sign of the **cross will be seen in the sky**, and from the openings where the hands and the feet of the Savior were nailed will come forth great lights which will light up the earth for a period of time. This will take place shortly before the last day" **(Jesus to St. Faustina)** (96:42:#83).

SAN NICOLAS, ARGENTINA (1988)

On March 21, 1988, Gladys reported having a vision in which she saw the earth divided into two parts. **One part represented two-thirds** (67 percent) and the other part equaled one-third. She saw the Blessed Virgin in the smaller part. Our Lady then responded to Gladys,

> "**You are seeing the world half-destroyed**. These rays of light are sent from my heart, which wants to save as many hearts as it can. My heart is all-powerful, but it can do nothing if hearts are unwilling. The means to save souls are prayer and conversion. Every soul must prepare so as not to be imprisoned

eternally by darkness" **(Mary to Gladys Quiroga de Motta [51], San Nicolas, Argentina, 1988)** (149:3).

"What is to come, sooner than you know, could result in the **death of 70 percent of this world's population**. When you see **two suns in the sky**—wherever you are, come home to your Center of My Immaculate Heart. There you are protected" **(Mary to Gianna Talone Sullivan, Emmitsburg, Maryland, May 26, 2008)** (86:117).

"The end of the era will last thirteen years. **Two comets will fall down to the Earth**, one of them to the southern part, and the other to the eastern hemisphere into the ocean. Thirty-seven earthquakes will take place. **Sinners will explode in the atmosphere** and righteous people will be **saved in the Holy Places (where Our Lady appeared)** in Lourdes, Fatima, Garabandal, Zakarpattya, and here in Prykarpattya—and also in their own houses. You must cover doors and windows with white material. During this time, electric power and clocks will not work. Simple candles will not give light. Only **candles blessed** on the Candlemas Day will give some light. After the end of the era, people will return and believe in God; they will also go to the Church" **(Jesus to Yulia [9], Lishnya, Ukraine, 2005)** (152).

"People will see their guardian angels and also devils. **Those who listen to devils will explode in the atmosphere**. But those who listen to their guardians will be saved" **(Angel Gabriel to Yulia [9], Lishnya, Ukraine, 2005)** (152).

"Events are happening due to the world's wickedness, selfishness, lack of love, rejection of God's Word, hypocrisy, and godlessness. The earth is in danger and will **suffer with fire**. God's wrath cannot be sustained any longer, and it will fall on them because man refuses to break with sin. That God's Mercy all of these years was to draw as many as possible to Him, extending His arm to save them—but only a few understood and listened. That His time of mercy will not hold much longer and the time is coming where everybody will be tested, and the earth will spew out from within it rivers of fire, and the people of the world will understand their worthlessness and their helplessness without having had God in their hearts...The time has come where the household of God will be tested, and **those who refused His mercy will taste God's fire**" **(Mary to Vassula Ryden, Switzerland, 3:10 a.m., January 2008)** (86:174–175).

"**Three days of darkness** are to come upon the world because of the increase of sin" **(God to Therese, Vietnam, 1979)** (86:121–122).

"Forgive one another and remove resentment from your heart. **Days of darkness are near**, but greater than the darkness of the earth is the darkness of the soul. Why? Because you do not keep lit the lamp of the heart with the light of My Son Jesus. You must learn how to make amends for your faults. When you fall, you must not remain sitting, but you must get up. The greatest fault is when you realize that you have fallen and you don't get up" **(Mary to Patricia Talbot [17], Cuenca, Ecuador, December, 1989)** (23:54).

"In secret I shall work marvels in souls until the required number of victim souls will be filled. Upon you it depends to shorten the **days of darkness**. Bishops and priests should consecrate themselves to me...Pray always. Pray the Rosary. Keep the Saturdays which have been dedicated to me" **(Mary to Barbara Reuss, Marienfried, Germany, May 25, 1949)** (3:201).

"God the Father will send two very big punishments. One will include wars, revolutions. The other one comes from heaven. There will be great earthquakes in several nations. All Earth will be in **darkness for three days**. Nothing will be visible. The air will be unbreathable, and during those dark days, the *only light will be provided by holy candles*. The believers must stay at their homes, saying the Holy Rosary and asking God for Mercy. **The punishment will end two-thirds of Mankind**. Nothing will happen to those who are with God and the Virgin" **(Mary to Luz Amparo Cuevas, El Escorial, Spain, 1981)** (107).

"A night of **great darkness** will come with such obscurity that everyone will tremble" **(Mary to "Mama Rosa" Quattrini, San Damiano, Italy, 1969)** (86:121).

Then the Lord said to Moses, "Extend your hand into the sky. And let there be darkness over the land of Egypt, so dense that they may be able to feel it." And Moses extended his hand into the sky. And there came **horrible darkness** in the entire land of Egypt for **three days**. No one could see each other, nor moved himself out of the place where he was. But wherever the sons of Israel were living, there was light (**Exodus 10: 21–23**).

"**The Cup of Justice is full**. It's more than full—it's flowing over! It is time for My Son to come with His mercy and to cleanse the world. Even my Church is darkened by apostasy in sin…Yes, My children, the hour is nearer than you think… The time of chastisement and the bloody hour is closer than you think. It is being prepared for you! But remember, I am your mother. I am the Mother of Consolation, and I will be there for you….This will all come about through the Holy Spirit. He will be given to you by the Father and the Son. **He will come as fire and will purify the earth**—like a farmer burns his field to get rid of the weeds, and, in the spring, lush green comes up….After the time of suffering, there will be a new rebirth, and My Son, himself, will come upon the earth and take over **His reign again**. My Son with His own hands will form a new creation. There will be a new rebirth, and all humanity will recognize Him and will pay Him homage" **(Mary to Sally Steadman [84], Oregon, Ohio, July 3, 2004)** (86:56–58).

The Chastisement: God's warrior-angels are sent to punish the evil in mankind (Photo-Art created by author).

"An intense darkness will come upon the earth, lasting three days and three nights. Nothing will be visible; the air will become harmful and pestilential…No artificial light will work… During this darkness covering the universe, all the enemies of the Church, visible or unknown, will perish everywhere in the world, except for a few who will be converted…" **(Mary to Amparo Cuevas, El Escorial, Spain, 1981)** (86:122)

"The nonbelievers will blaspheme in their despair. **The air will be filled with demonlike forms**, the incorporations of sins and vices. **These phantoms will terrify humanity**" **(Mary to Matous Lasuta [42], Turzovka, Slovakia, 1958)** (86:109).

"During these **three days of darkness**, there is **not going to be one demon left in hell**. All are going to be on earth. The three days are going to be so dark that we will not be able to see our own hands before our faces. In those days, the ones who are not in the state of grace are going to **die of fright because of the horrible demons that they will see**. The Virgin told me to close all the doors and windows and not to respond to anyone who calls from the outside. The biggest temptation we will have is that the devil is going to **imitate the voices of our**

loved ones. She told me, 'Please do not pay attention because those are not your loved ones; those are demons, trying to lure you out of the house.... The hours of darkness will be exactly seventy-two, and the only way to count them is with mechanical clocks, because there won't be any electricity" **(Mary to Brother David Lopez, San Benito, Texas, August, 1992)** (86:120–121).

"Take care to guard your blessed objects, My children. They will serve you when the **day of darkness** comes. During those **three days and these three nights**, those objects will shine, My child. They will shine no matter where they go" **(Jesus to Amparo Cuevas, El Escorial, Spain, 1984)** (86:122).

Saint Padre Pio, a Capuchin priest in Italy who bore the stigmata and lies with an incorrupt body in death, wrote a personal letter to the Commission of Heroldsbach which was appointed by the Vatican. In this letter, he details the two revelations given to him by Jesus concerning these Three Days of Darkness:

"Keep your windows well covered. Do not look out. Light a blessed candle, which will suffice for many days. Pray the Rosary. Read spiritual books. Make acts of Spiritual Communion, also acts of love, which are so pleasing to Us. Pray with outstretched arms or prostrate on the ground in order that many souls be saved. Do not go outside the house. Provide yourself with sufficient food. The powers of nature shall be moved, and a rain of fire shall make people tremble with fear. Have courage! I am in the midst of you" **(Jesus to St. Padre Pio, Italy, January 28, 1950)** (89).

"Take care of the animals during these days. I am the Creator and Preserver of all animals as well as man. I shall give you a few signs beforehand, at which time you should place more food before them. I will preserve the property of the elect, including the animals, for they shall be in need of sustenance afterwards as well. Let no one go across the yard, even to feed the animals; he who steps outside will perish! Cover your windows carefully. My elect shall not see My wrath. Have confidence in Me, and I will be your protection. Your confidence obliges Me to come to your aid. The hour of My coming is near! But I will show mercy. A most dreadful punishment will bear witness to the times. My angels, who are to be the executioners of this work, are ready with their pointed swords! They will take special care to annihilate all those who mocked Me and would not believe in My revelations.

Hurricanes of fire will pour forth from the clouds and spread over the entire earth! Storms, bad weather, thunderbolts, and earthquakes will cover the earth for two days. An uninterrupted rain of fire will take place. It will begin during a very cold night. All this is to prove that God is Master of Creation. Those who hope in Me and believe in My words have nothing to fear because I will not forsake them, nor those who spread My message. No harm will come to those who are in a state of grace and who seek My Mother's protection.

That you may be prepared for these visitations, I will give you the following signs and instructions: The night will be very cold. The wind will roar. After a time, thunderbolts will be heard. Lock all the doors and windows. Talk to no one outside the house. Kneel down before a crucifix, be sorry for your sins, and beg My Mother's protection. Do not look during the earthquake, because the anger of God is holy. I do not want you to behold the anger of God because God's anger must be contemplated with fear and trembling.

Those who disregard this advice will be killed instantly. The wind will carry with it poisonous gases which will be diffused over the entire earth. Those who suffer and die innocently will be martyrs, and they will be with Me in My Kingdom. After three nights, the earthquake and fire will cease. On the following day, the sun will shine again. Angels will descend from heaven and will spread the spirit of peace over the earth. A feeling of immeasurable gratitude will take possession of those who survive this terrible ordeal.

This catastrophe shall come upon the earth like a flash of lightning—at which moment the light of the morning shall be replaced by black darkness. No one shall leave the house or look out of a window from that moment on. I shall come amidst thunder and lightning. The wicked shall behold My Divine Heart. There shall be great confusion because of this utter darkness in which the entire earth shall be enveloped, and many, many shall die from fear and despair.

Those who shall fight for My cause shall receive grace from My Divine Heart, and the cry, 'Who is like unto God' shall serve as a means of protection to many. However, many shall burn in the open field like withered grass. The godless shall be annihilated—so that afterwards, the just shall be able to stand afresh. On the day, as soon as complete darkness has set in, no one shall leave the house or look from out of the window. The darkness shall last a day and a night, followed by another day and a night, and another day—but on the night following, the stars will shine again, and on the next morning the sun shall rise again, and it will be springtime! In the days of darkness, My elect shall not sleep as did the disciples in the garden of olives. They shall pray incessantly, and they shall not be disappointed in Me. I shall gather My elect. Hell will believe itself to be in possession of the entire earth, but I shall reclaim it" **(Jesus to St. Padre Pio, Italy, February 7, 1950)** (89).

Secret #10: This will be an unavoidable "purification" of the world through "**three days of darkness.**" Wayne Weible, apparitions researcher for thirty years, summarizes the impressions of these three days from the words of the six visionaries in Medjugorje, Bosnia-Herzegovina:

"It will begin on a bitterly cold winter night in the Northern hemisphere. The wind will howl and roar with lightning and **thunderbolts of an unprecedented magnitude will strike the earth**. The whole earth will shake. The moon and the stars will be disturbed and not be seen in a normal way. Then, **every demon**, every spirit **will be released from hell and allowed to roam the earth**. Terrifying apparitions will take place. Many will die from sheer fright. **Fire will rain forth from the sky**; all large cities will be destroyed and poisonous gases will fill the air. Cries and lamentations will be heard everywhere. The

unbelievers will burn in the open like withered grass. The entire earth will be afflicted; it will look like a huge graveyard.

We are to go indoors, lock all doors and windows, pull down the blinds, and stick adhesive paper on vents and around windows and doors. **We are not to answer calls and pleas from outside**—which sound like our relatives, our children, and our friends—even though the temptation will be overwhelming to respond. In order to protect ourselves, we are to light **blessed wax candles**, which can be obtained by asking a priest to bless any wax candle. Nothing else will burn, but the candles will not be extinguished once lit. Nothing will put them out in the houses of the faithful, but they will not burn in the houses of the godless. Second, we should sprinkle holy water about the house and especially near doors and windows. The devils fear holy water. We are to bless ourselves with it and anoint our five senses with it—eyes, ears, nose, mouth, hands, feet, and forehead.

We should kneel and pray incessantly with outstretched arms—or prostrate on the floor. Pray the Rosary and meditate on the Sorrowful mysteries. Mercifully, some people, especially children, will be taken up to heaven beforehand to spare them the horror of these days. **People caught outdoors will die instantly. Three-quarters of the human race will be exterminated**, more men than women. When all seems lost and hopeless, in the blink of an eye, the ordeal will be over. The sun will rise and shine as in springtime over a purified earth" (45:214–217).

Jesus said to his disciples: "There will be signs in the sun, the moon, and the stars, and on earth nations will be in dismay, perplexed by the roaring of the sea and the waves. People will die of fright in anticipation of what is coming upon the world, for the powers of the heavens will be shaken. And then they will see the Son of Man coming in a cloud with power and great glory. But when these signs begin to happen, stand erect and raise your heads because your redemption is at hand. Beware that your hearts do not become drowsy from carousing and drunkenness and the anxieties of daily life, and that day catch you by surprise like a trap. For that day will assault everyone who lives on the face of the earth. Be vigilant at all times and pray that you have the strength to escape the tribulations that are imminent and to stand before the Son of Man." **(Luke 21:25–28, 34–36)**

But in those days, after that tribulation, the sun will be darkened, and the moon will not give her splendor. And the stars of heaven will be falling down, and the powers that are in heaven will be moved. And then they shall see the Son of Man arriving on the clouds, with great power and glory. And then he will send his angels, and gather together his elect, from the four winds, from the limits of the earth, to the limits of heaven. Now from the fig tree discern a parable. When its branch becomes tender and the foliage has been formed, you know that summer is very near. So also, when you will have seen these things happen, know that it is very near, even at the doors. Amen I say to you, that this lineage shall not pass away, until all these things have happened. Heaven and earth shall pass away, but my word shall not pass away. But concerning that day or hour, no one knows, neither the angels in heaven, nor the Son, but only the Father. Take heed, be vigilant, and pray. For you do not know when the time may be. **(Mark 13:24–33)**

PEACE ON A PURIFIED EARTH

> "Yet, I tell you, my daughter, even should such a destruction happen because there were not enough souls who took my warning seriously, **there will remain a remnant**—untouched by the chaos who, having been faithful in following me and spreading my warnings, will gradually **inhabit the earth again** with their dedicated and holy lives. These will renew the earth in the power and light of the Holy Spirit. These faithful ones of my children will be under my protection and that of the Holy Angels, and they will partake of the life of the Divine Trinity in a most remarkable way" **(Mary to Sister Mildred Neuzil [68], midwest USA, 1984)** (86:80).

"After this purification, there will be spring. Everything will be green, and **everything will be clean. The water will be crystal** clear—even the water from the faucets in houses. There will be no contamination in the water, nor the air, nor the river…" **(Mary to Brother David Lopez, San Benito, Texas, August, 1992)** (86:121)

"The Church must be opened to His divine fire in such a way that, completely purified, it will be ready to receive the splendor of His **new Pentecost**, in preparation for the **second, glorious coming** of My Son, Jesus" **(Mary to Father Don Stefano Gobbi, Milan, Italy)** (86:129).

"To be delivered from the slavery of these heresies, those whom the merciful love of My Son has destined for this restoration will need great will-power, perseverance, courage, and confidence in God. To try the faith and trust of these just ones, there will be times when all will seem lost and paralyzed. It will then be the **happy beginning of the complete restoration…**" **(Mary to Mother Mariana de Jesus Torres, Quito, Ecuador, 1610)** (141).

"My Son will destroy any bad herb, and He will prepare a **glorious rebirth** in His mercy's time. Then will come **peace** and reconciliation between men, mankind, and God. He will be served, adored, and glorified. Charity will shine everywhere. The new kings will be the right hand of the church. Gospel will be preached everywhere, and **men will live in awe of God**. The Holy Church will be mild, pious, strong, poor, and meticulous in imitating Jesus Christ's virtues" **(Mary to Luz Amparo Cuevas, El Escorial, Spain, 1981)** (107:4).

"Focus on the result of this cleansing, the return of My Son to a land purified by the blood of martyrs for the greater honor and glory of God. Focus on a purified earth, and the gift of My Son's **Second Coming and peace that will reign for a thousand years.** These are the things that My children must focus on. The evil one would have you so afraid for what is to come that you will despair and not be able to pray and do all that is asked of you. Children, pray for peace that can come only from God. Once you have peace in your heart, nothing else matters" **(Mary to Ruth Ann Wade [54], Bloomington, Indiana, USA, January 14, 1994)** (86:138).

"I have come to comfort you and to tell you that your suffering will end soon. I shall protect you for the glory and the **future of God's kingdom on earth, which will last for a thousand years**. The Kingdom of Heaven and Earth is close at hand. It will come only through penance and the repentance of sins" **(Mary to Marina Kizyn [12], Hrushiv, Ukraine, 1987)** (2:275).

"The time is coming, little ones, when Jesus will create **a new heaven on earth**. Pain and suffering will cease. His people will live not only a mere few years but rejoice in the fullness of life. Your merciful Lord is coming and **shall renew the face of the earth**. You, beloved children, will leap with joy. Your hardships will be forgotten; you will no longer grieve or go hungry. The Lord will be your delight. The time is approaching when the world will be renewed. First, however, this world will be purged of its crimes against God" **(Mary to Gianna Talone Sullivan, Emmitsburg, Maryland, April 16, 1998)** (86:127).

"Today this world is full of hatred, and you will know that the time of My return is near—that I am on My way when you hear of and *see the wars of religion*. Know then, that I come, for nothing will be able to stop these wars. Know, too, that it will not be easy to recognize Me, but here are the signs that will help you to know that it is I. I will come like a traveler, but if I walk past a deaf man, he will hear. If I walk past a blind man, he will open his eyes and see...If I walk past a mother, she will be full of joy. The one who loves Me—even if he is under a bridge—I will find him. Go and tell men to be ready...assure them, that I am on My way back. All you people who search—not for heavenly treasures—but who think only of your earthly goods and riches—know that you will have to account for all My words. For, as I have already said once before to this world, all things will pass, but My words will never pass away. All that I have planned *will be realized*" **(Jesus to teenagers in Kibeho, Rwanda, 1981–1989)** (39-CD).

"**I will send you My Holy Spirit in full force on all mankind**, and as a foresign I will display portents in heaven as never before. There will be a **second Pentecost** so that **My kingdom on earth will be restored**…" **(Jesus to Vassula Ryden, Egypt, around 1985)** (86:129)

"After the time of great suffering, there will be the time of the **great rebirth**. Humanity—a new garden of life and of beauty. The Church—a family, O yes! Enlightened by truth, nourished by grace, and consoled by the presence of the Spirit. **Jesus will restore His glorious reign**. He will dwell with you. You will know the new times, the new era. You will see a new earth and new heavens. His kingship will be welcomed and exalted. This will be a universal reign of grace, of beauty, of harmony, of communion, of holiness, of justice, and of peace…These are times of the great mercy. They are therefore the times of the triumph of My Immaculate Heart" **(Mary to Father Don Stefano Gobbi, Milan, Italy)** (86:126–127).

"BE NOT AFRAID"

"If we are afraid of these kinds of things, we don't have confidence in God. Fear of this kind does not come from God. It can only come from Satan who wants to disturb us so that we close ourselves to God and are not able to pray. With God, you can only have confidence and strength to go through any troubles" **(Vicka Ivankovic, Medjugorje)** (51:74–75).

"Tell the pilgrims not to be afraid of the messages. They have nothing to fear because they believe in My Son" **(Mary to Tarcisio de Biasi, Oliveto Citra, Italy)** (86:58).

"Pray, fast, and do penance, but do not be consumed with the doom and gloom…Do not focus on the pains and suffering of the cleansing of your earth. Concentrate on the rebirth of your earth" **(Jesus to Ruth Ann Wade [54], Bloomington, Indiana, USA, January 14, 1994)** (86:3).

"Warn the people about Satan's power. He wants to steal heaven from us. Tell them to pray and fast. Tell them of God's immense love for us. Tell them nothing of the earth has value unless it leads us to God. Tell them our true home is heaven. No suffering on earth is too much when the true reward is heaven. I've seen heaven! It is such a gift of God's love! We are God's children. Nothing of this earth is worth one moment of worry. If people only realized how much He loves us, and what He has prepared for us, they would be filled with such peace!" **(Mirjana Dragicevic, Medjugorje)** (51:34)

"All that I have told you is because God the Father has asked me to. Children, the time is short, very short. Conversion must be faithful. Remove all evil sentiments because Satan penetrates in them. Remove them with the Presence of God in your souls. Children, give thanks to God for what you have… you must fill your hearts with the Light of My Son, so that a desolation of faith will not exist…" **(Mary to Patricia Talbot [18], Cuenca, Ecuador, January 6, 1990)** (23:57–58)

Although the terrifying and gloomy nature of this chastisement sounds so scary and depressing, *think about what it is really saying*: All evil will be abolished. The end of the devil's influence on earth. Only sincere believers in God remaining. No crime, no deceit, no abuse—truly like a new Garden of Eden—an age of peace with love and harmony…truly a **"world without end."** The Virgin Mary said to not waste energy worrying about the secrets. Believe in God, consider her messages, and practice the teachings from Jesus. This is how we should live our lives. In conclusion, Our Blessed Mother tells us:

"Resist everything that wants to distance you from My Son…" (Nov.2, 2012) (45:218)

"Dear children! Give thanks with me to the Most High for my presence with you. My heart is joyful watching the love and joy in the living of my messages. Many of you have responded, but **I wait for, and seek, all the hearts that have fallen asleep to awaken from the sleep of unbelief**. Little children, draw even closer to my Immaculate Heart so that I can lead all of you toward eternity. Thank you for having responded to my call" **(Mary to Medjugorje, June 25, 2011—the thirtieth anniversary of first appearance)** (45:11).

Are you still with me?
Are you overwhelmed from these messages?
Are you ready now to run out and obtain blessed candles?

During the Three Days of Darkness one should stay inside, light blessed candles, and pray continuously and sincerely (Photo-Art created by author which includes a miraculous face of Jesus which appeared in a Eucharistic miracle in Argentina between 1983 and 1990).

"**DO NOT BE AFRAID**." Those words have appeared 365 times in the Bible. Heaven *knows* that there is much that we cannot understand yet—and seeing supernatural beings, signs, or miraculous events can be scary, confusing, mystifying, or mysterious. *But none of this is meant to frighten us.* God just wants our love—just as *any* father wants his children to not forget him and stay in touch. But we have basically ignored him, denied him, forgotten him, or even cursed him. What kind of children have we become? Would we want our own children to treat us in the same manner? As disobedient, disrespectful and sinful children…we truly have earned a punishment.

Heaven wants us to wake up, come back to the Father, and live better lives. Is it too late?

The "footprints" that we have been tracking have led us to many of the puzzle pieces. Much of that puzzle has now been assembled… We have followed the directions to where the repeating patterns of data have led us. There were many unexpected surprises…There are teachings and lessons to be learned…and there are specific ways to save our souls…if we are listening…and if we even care—and if we put any credence in any of this information.

What is it that we have seen and learned?

The kind of future you have in eternity…may depend upon this…

Read on—but without fear.

CHAPTER 20

THE MEANING OF LIFE

"Love is patient and kind; love is not jealous or boastful; it is not arrogant or rude. Love does not insist on its own way; it is not irritable or resentful; it does not rejoice at wrong, but rejoices in the right. Love bears all things, believes all things, hopes all things, and endures all things. Love never ends; as for prophecies, they will pass away; as for tongues, they will cease; as for knowledge, it will pass away. For our knowledge is imperfect and our prophecy is imperfect; but when the perfect comes, the imperfect will pass away...So faith, hope, love abide, these three; **but the greatest of these is love**." (1 Corinthians 13: 4-10, 13)

I feel that I have sorted through thousands of puzzle pieces in an effort to fit them together and make sense out of the mystery of our existence on this earth. Like a gigantic jigsaw puzzle, all of these pieces are coming together to reveal an accurate portrayal of our reality. The repeating patterns of data are significant down to the smallest of details. They create a vivid picture of truth supported by comprehensive historical validation. So what does this portrait of Truth tell us? And are you *ready* to see this?

Loving partners enjoy a beautiful sunset over the peaceful waters (photo by author in Charlevoix, Michigan).

Like the busy, self-absorbed ants in an "ant farm" enclosed in its case between two clear plastic panels, we have stopped looking for the Creator who placed us here. We just continue our daily routine and schedule of tasks—*as if it really means anything*. We earn our money so that we can pay our bills and obtain more things—so then we can enjoy our pleasurable yet meaningless distractions. Open and permissive sexual contact becomes a superficial playground for selfish and creative pleasuring of the flesh. And if you are too shy to do this in person, you can now see whatever sexual acts you desire with endless Internet pornography. Electronic devices absorb our attention in every way. Texting on phones replaces face-to-face communication. Listening to our favorite music with headphones helps us to stay within ourselves and avoid the outside world. Hundreds of cable TV channels give us endless entertainment for hundreds of hours. We could "surf the Internet" endlessly as there is truly an infinite number of possible paths to pursue. We can even bully someone better on the new playgrounds of Facebook and Twitter where gossip, drama, slander and verbal abuse from cyberbullies is so much easier. *Is **any** of this meaningful?*

What *is* the meaning of life?

Is it all the precious and sentimental stuff that we accumulated over the course of our lives?

Is it the power, status, achievements, or level of fame we acquired?

Is it how much money or valuables we earned during our lives to guarantee our security?

You may say no rather quickly—yet, where is your current focus *still placed* every day?

Have you ever seen a U-Haul hooked up behind a funeral hearse? You can't take ANY of this with you when you die! Perhaps, you don't worry about that because you assume that there is nothing beyond death to have to face or deal with. *Besides, you really want to live to the fullest while you are still here*—right? But what if you are wrong about *not having to account later* for your present lifestyle? And what if that *does* determine where you spend eternity?

How healthy is your soul? Or do you even worry about that?

How do we improve the health of our souls? What are we to do?

From all that we have learned in this book, here is your "to-do" list:

1. **LOVE GOD**. Love God and thank him for ALL that you have: every breath of life; a beautiful planet filled with amazing natural wonders; loving friends, partners, and family; the food that nourishes us; the water that cleanses and sustains life; the shelter and materials provided for our lives. Appreciate ***all*** that Our Father has provided. Know that He loves you much more than you could ever comprehend. He knows that the bad events and misfortunes of life challenge you but enhance your growth; protecting you or sheltering you from those trials would not develop your soul as well.

2. **LOVE YOUR FAMILY**. Parents may not have been perfect or even successful at parenting, but they brought you into this life and did the best that they knew how to do.

Honor their efforts—even if they fell short. Your brothers and sisters have their problems—but always need your love and understanding. Listen to their hurts and needs and focus much less on yourself.

3. **LOVE YOUR SPOUSE.** It was no accident that you found each other. Some might argue that it was Satan who sent this partner to you—not God. But if it was meant to be the right union under God, both of you will put God first and learn how to love each other to the fullest. Work hard to listen to each other and understand your spouse's experiences. You will always have differences, but you can grow together into new directions where you can feel as one. Do not abuse, neglect, control, dominate, demean, manipulate, deceive, or ignore your God-given partner—a beautiful gift for you to learn from, nurture, and treasure.

4. **LOVE YOUR CHILDREN.** They are miracles from God given to you *when God decided to do so*—not exactly whenever you had planned it. Do not alter God's plan by killing that gift. Treasure these innocent souls as they look to you for love, nurturing, protection, guidance, and knowledge. Teach them how to love by *showing* them your love every day. Raise them to know God, love God, and worship God—so that their souls may be guided toward heaven and not lost to hell. Spoiling them with cash or material wants only promotes more materialistic desires and a hunger for wealth—*and no obvious need for God in their lives*. Teach them with rules and discipline—not candy and toys to silence their manipulative emotional fits. Let the light of your Christian soul shine for them to see how to live and love.

5. **LOVE YOUR FELLOW MAN.** Do not discriminate against or judge your neighbor. *He did not choose* to be poor, disabled, mentally challenged, or of a different race. He cannot be blamed for how God chose for him to exist. Nor can any of those conditions be easily changed. Perhaps he is unfriendly, unkind, abusive, or selfish. He will be

judged later by the Father and appropriately punished, so do not waste *your* energy or time on that. Help the less fortunate to find resources and how to improve their lives. Share what you have—and *find a greater joy* in doing so. If *you* should suffer such problems one day, you know how wonderful it would feel to experience an unsolicited kindness and unexpected generosity from strangers who shine with God's love.

6. **LOVE THE ANIMALS**. They are precious gifts to love and enjoy. Recall how a dog will happily greet you every day with the same unconditional love and sincere appreciation. Do not kick or beat these innocent creatures just because you have had a bad day. Do not imprison them on chains or in cages for your convenience; they can become sad from feeling neglected or unwanted. They seem like children and hurt like children, too.

7. **LOVE YOURSELF**. *This does **not** mean to spoil yourself selfishly or self-indulge in numerous, materialistic ways.* Respect yourself—do not demean or verbally abuse yourself with negative thoughts, self-recrimination, or discrediting your positive efforts. Do not judge or condemn yourself unfairly. Do not swallow and accept the judgments from others. Be kind to your body. **It is your personal temple for the Holy Spirit**. Do not soil it with drugs, alcohol, needles, sexual diseases, or self-mutilation—including excessive consumption of unhealthy foods. Keep your "temple" clean. Can you imagine throwing bags of garbage, used condoms, and beer cans through the front doors of your church? Be humble and appreciative of the life and body that God has given you.

8. **LOVE JESUS**. *How do you really do that?* Well, you have to get to know Him before you can truly love Him. To know Him, you have to spend time with Him. You can spend time with Him in prayer, at Adoration, in Confession, and in the Mass. Science has validated (but yet to explain) the existence of *the real blood and real body of Jesus* appearing

in the consecrated wine and bread of the Holy Eucharist (Communion). Take Him into you with the promise of eternal life. Let His Light shine through you to attract others to the truth. They will see the Christ in you with your sincere compassion, caring, and genuine love for others. Come to His table in the Mass for His spiritual meal.

9. **LOVE BLESSED MARY.** She is the Queen of Heaven and the Mother for all of us—whether you believe in her presence or not. Ask for her help, her protection, and especially her intercession with Jesus, Her Son, for your needs and prayers. We do not worship her; we honor her as the Mother of Jesus. Just like you would ask a friend to pray for you, you can ask Her to put in a good word with Jesus as you pass along your prayer requests. "Never was it known that anyone who fled to thy protection, implored thy help, or sought thine intercession was left unaided." She loves you as one of her children—no matter what race or culture you come from on this planet.

10. **LOVE THE ROSARY.** Identified as the queen of all prayers and the chief weapon against Satan and all of his evil, the praying of the Holy Rosary has proven throughout history to bring about miraculous results, incredible healing, dramatic changes in history, and the destruction of evil wherever it flourishes. Reflecting on the Rosary's twenty mysteries from the New Testament keeps us focused daily on the most important Biblical events—which drives the devil crazy every time he hears us praying to Jesus through Mary.

11. **LOVE CONFESSION.** *Do not be afraid.* This is a wonderful gift and blessing from God. You will not be judged, embarrassed, or condemned. Instead, after you humbly share your imperfections, wrongful actions, or guilty thoughts, you will be forgiven and your sins forgotten. Imagine that your loving Jesus is standing with open arms to embrace you right behind the priest that you see before you. Welcome this precious gift of forgiveness. Hiding and

holding your faults within you just burdens you and festers within you like an infection. Lift the heaviness from your shoulders and give it to God. *He already knows* that you are not perfect! Going to Communion during the Mass without Confession is like going to dinner without bathing or washing your hands. Come clean and free your heart.

12. **LOVE PRAYER.** This is where you become closely acquainted with God and His Son, Jesus. The more time you spend in prayer, the deeper your relationship will develop. No time for prayer? If you have time to worry about things, then you have time that you could be praying instead. *Worry never accomplished or changed anything.* Prayer has been proven numerous times to have a positive impact and often miraculous results. So, **PRAY**. Just talk with God or recite basic prayers (Our Father, Hail Mary, Glory Be, Apostles Creed, Divine Mercy). The Blessed Virgin has reminded us that heaven cannot always send graces if you don't ask for them. She said, "If you only knew the power of prayer, you would never cease praying!"

What about the Ten Commandments? If you practice the kinds of love as outlined above, then following these commandments from God should be much easier. You would honor God and not curse him. You would keep Sunday holy and visit Him in church while treasuring the gift of His Son's spiritual supper. You would appreciate your parents and family. You would not harm, kill, steal, or commit meaningless sex which is lacking true Christian love. You would not lie, slander, or cheat your fellow man, nor strongly desire his wife or his possessions. That summarizes the Ten Commandments and how you could follow them by practicing all the dimensions of love that I just described.

The trails of "footprints" and the piles of historical evidence that I presented in this book are the reasons that I *caught fire* with the Holy Spirit and grew with enthusiasm and passion for my faith in the Catholic church. I am **not** saying that you have to be Catholic to be right with God! **Anyone on this planet who believes in God,**

worships and appreciates God, and truly practices His love for mankind in his life—will succeed in avoiding the eternal fires of hell. Sound too dramatic? Are you really wanting to take that chance—and possibly be wrong?

Remember, the Catholic Church was started by Jesus Christ with Peter as His first "rock" or pope. The word Catholic means "universal." All other religions that have evolved since then have edited, removed parts, streamlined, altered or shifted the focus away from this original version that Jesus began. Catholics have just tried to carefully preserve and stay true to the original church.

Many Catholics are not very active Catholics; almost 80 percent do not attend regularly these days. As in many other religions today, people have lost their spark, drive, or enthusiasm. ***They don't SEE or FEEL a NEED*** for their religion anymore. But if mankind derails off the tracks like an out of control, speeding train, where are we going to be in God's eyes when that terrible crash happens—and Judgment Day is suddenly here? Will preparing your soul for eternity be as delayed as the list of household projects that you have procrastinated in starting? And now, unexpectedly and unfortunately, ***it will really be too late.*** How ready would you be if your moment of judgment in front of the Divine Creator comes at 3:00 p.m. tomorrow afternoon?

Maybe you still find it hard to believe that Jesus is *really alive* in the tabernacles of all the churches of the world. Perhaps you need to consider this historic account:

> "On the evening of the last day of his October 1995 visit to the United States, Pope John Paul II was scheduled to greet the seminarians at Saint Mary's Seminary in Baltimore. It had been a very full day. The schedule was tight so the plan was simply to greet the seminarians while they stood outside on the steps. But the pope made his way through their ranks and into the building. His plan was to first make a visit to the Blessed Sacrament. When his wishes were made known, security flew into action. They swept the building, paying close attention to the chapel where the pope would be praying. For this purpose, highly trained dogs were used to detect any person who might be present. The dogs are trained to locate survivors in collapsed buildings after earthquakes and other

disasters. These highly intelligent and eager dogs quickly went through the halls, offices and classrooms and were then sent to the chapel. They went up and down the aisles, past the pews and finally into the side chapel where the Blessed Sacrament is reserved. Upon reaching the tabernacle, the dogs sniffed, whined, pointed, and refused to leave, **their attention riveted on the tabernacle**, until called off by their handlers. *The security dogs were convinced that they had discovered someone in the tabernacle.* (We know the dogs were right—they had found a real, living presence in the tabernacle!)" (90) (95)

This last puzzle piece just fits right in with all the others that have been presented in this book.

1. As a psychiatric therapist, I have explained how the visionaries do not fit any possible category of psychological disorder. Furthermore, those psychological professionals who *have* evaluated them found all of them to be free of disorders and declared as psychologically "normal."
2. I have shown how appearances of the Virgin Mary have actually been frequent occurrences around the world and often well-documented with credible witnesses and occasional evidence from 40 AD until today.
3. I have presented a method of studying supernatural phenomena in which repetitive details and patterns of data help create a valid picture of reality that surpasses hoaxes, fantasy, religious obsession, mass hysteria, imagination, delusions, or hallucinations. None of those explanations would have such a coherent, specific, and matching pattern of details that are well beyond chance—and thus promote validity and reality.
4. I have presented how the experiences of the visionaries are unique and indeed supernatural. Scientists and medical experts cannot explain what is happening to them.
5. I have described how many innocent bystanders have suddenly become witnesses to extraordinary events, miracu-

lous sights, and supernatural signs that validate the claims of the visionaries.
6. I have also shown how the famous Miracle of the Sun at Fatima in 1917 was not a one-of-a-kind event—but actually was repeated worldwide numerous times since 1917.
7. I have outlined how the Blessed Virgin had a distinct purpose and clear set of consistent goals in getting churches built, promoting prayer, penance, humility, attending church, conversion, and worshipping Her Son. She would even approach hard-core opponents, atheists, and people from all cultures around the world.
8. I have described how predictions given by Our Lady have remarkably come true, thus validating the reality and credibility of her visits with Her children on earth.
9. I have even shown where the power of a prayer like the Rosary has had a great impact on changing the course of human events in wars, natural disasters, threats of evil, politics, and deadly illnesses.
10. Countless, miraculous healings have been documented and listed as "unexplained" or "impossible" by experts—*unless it was performed by the hand of God.* This adds much more proof for the belief in the supernatural existence of God.
11. Generations in today's world demand proof for these supernatural claims, so I detailed several kinds of evidence that exist today that serve as proof for those encounters.
12. I have also included scientific and medical investigations that were able to validate the existence of these supernatural events—but unable to explain them in any fashion whatsoever or even suggest how such miracles could happen.
13. I have provided strong testimony for the existence of *heaven, hell,* and *purgatory* which is powerful in the very similar descriptions and details coming from a variety of sources.

14. Because angels have been reported numerous times by witnesses, I set out to detail their actions, duties, and apparent roles in dealing with mankind.
15. Some types of angels are described as having protective roles in keeping humans safe. I have included some intriguing accounts that seem to confirm that type of role.
16. Assuming that the visionaries are truly receiving messages from heaven's representatives, I presented a comprehensive collection of heavenly wisdom and advice.
17. Many of these heavenly messages developed into a pattern comprised of stern warnings toward mankind—and what might happen as punishment if we do not listen and change our ways of living.
18. Numerous messages from vastly different sources are warning us in similar and specific details of an impending purification of the earth which would eliminate all sinners and disbelievers. This should be of great concern for every human being on this planet.

These points summarize my process of presenting credible evidence for your consideration and inspiration. Historical accounts, credible testimonies, supernatural events, miraculous proof, and scientific evidence have given you much to contemplate, absorb, and potentially ignite your spiritual growth. For some, your eyes will be opened wide, your heart will be set on fire, and you will be awakened to a new reality. Welcome that Holy Spirit to live within you! Even Blessed Mary made similar comments in her three recent messages from 2015:

> **"Dear children, I am calling you to spread the faith in My Son—your faith. You, my children illuminated by the Holy Spirit, my apostles, transmit it to others, to those who do not believe, who do not know, who do not want to know, but for that you must pray a lot for the gift of love, because love is the mark of true faith—and you will be apostles of my love. Love always, anew, revives the pain and the joy of the Eucharist, it revives the pain of the Passion of my Son, by which he showed you what it means to love**

immeasurably; it revives the joy for having left you his body and blood to feed you with himself—and in this way, to be one with you. Looking at you with tenderness, I feel immeasurable love which strengthens me in my desire to bring you to a firm faith. Firm faith will give you joy and happiness on earth and in the end the encounter with my Son. This is his desire. Therefore, live him, live love, live the light that always illuminates you in the Eucharist. I implore you to pray a lot for your shepherds (priests), to pray so as to have all the more love for them because my Son gave them to you to feed you with his body and to teach you love. Therefore, you are also to love them. But, my children, remember, love means to endure and to give, and never, ever to judge. Thank you" (**Mary to Medjugorje, July 2, 2015) (131b).**

"Dear children, I desire to work through you—my children, my apostles—so that in the end, I may gather all of my children there where everything is prepared for your happiness. I am praying for you, that **through works you can convert others, because the time has come for acts of truth, for my Son.** My love will work in you—I will make use of you. Have trust in me because everything that I desire, I desire for your good, the eternal good created by the Heavenly Father. You, my children, my apostles, are living an earthly life in union with my children who have not come to know the love of my Son, who do not call me 'mother'—**but do not be afraid to witness the truth. If you are not afraid and witness courageously, the truth will miraculously win, but remember, strength is in love.** My children, love is repentance, forgiveness, prayer, sacrifice and mercy. **If you will know how to love, by your works you will convert others, you will enable the light of my Son to penetrate into souls.** Thank you. Pray for your shepherds (priests). They belong to my Son. He called them. Pray that they may always have the strength and the courage to shine with the light of my Son" (**Mary to Medjugorje, June 2, 2015) (131b).**

"Dear children, I, as a mother who loves her children, see how difficult the time in which you live is. I see your suffering, but you need to know that you are not alone. My Son is with you. He is everywhere. He is invisible, but you can see Him if you live Him. He is the light which illuminates your soul and gives you peace. He is the church which you need to love and to always pray and fight for—but not only with words, instead with acts of love. My children, bring it about for everyone to come to know my Son, bring it about that He may be loved because the truth is in my Son born of God—the Son of God. Do not waste time deliberating too much; you will distance yourselves from the truth. With a simple heart accept His word and live it. If you live His word, you will pray. If you live His word, you will love with a merciful love; you will love each other. The more that you will love, the farther away you will be from death. For those who will live the word of my Son and who will love, death will be life. Thank you" (Mary to Medjugorje, August 2, 2015) (131b).

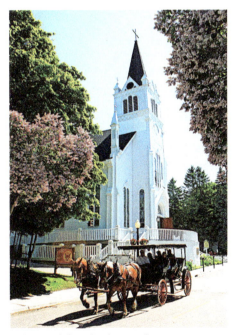

A less hectic lifestyle: horse-drawn carriage trots by the small-town Catholic church on Mackinac Island, Michigan (photo by author).

I could not imagine a more fitting close to this chapter than words from God the Father, written to you in the form of a letter—as precisely quoted only from biblical scriptures. Thank you for "not being afraid" to read this book and to open your eyes to new information which has the exciting potential of changing your life forever. **God bless you.** Enjoy your letter from God, *written just for you...*

My Child,

You may not know me, but I know everything about you.	(Psalm 139:1)
I know when you sit down and when you rise up.	(Psalm 139:2)
I am familiar with all your ways.	(Psalm 139:3)
Even the very hairs on your head are numbered.	(Matthew 10:29–31)
For you were made in my image.	(Genesis 1:27)
In me you live and move and have your being.	(Acts 17:28)
For you are my offspring.	(Acts 17:28)
I knew you even before you were conceived.	(Jeremiah 1:4–5)
I chose you when I planned creation.	(Ephesians 1:11–12)
You were not a mistake, for all your days are written in my book.	(Psalm 139:15–16)
I determined the exact time of your birth and where you would live.	(Acts 17:26)
You are fearfully and wonderfully made.	(Psalm 139:14)
I knit you together in your mother's womb.	(Psalm 139:13)

BE NOT AFRAID TO FOLLOW THE FOOTPRINTS FROM HEAVEN

And brought you forth on the day you were born. (Psalm 71:6)

I have been misrepresented by those who don't know me. (John 8:41–44)

I am not distant and angry, but am the complete expression of love. (1 John 4:16)

And it is my desire to lavish my love on you. (1 John 3:1)

Simply because you are my child and I am your Father. (1 John 3:1)

I offer you more than your earthly father ever could. (Matthew 7:11)

For I am the perfect father. (Matthew 5:48)

Every good gift that you receive comes from my hand. (James 1:17)

For I am your provider and I meet all your needs. (Matthew 6:31–33)

My plan for your future has always been filled with hope. (Jeremiah 29:11)

Because I love you with an everlasting love. (Jeremiah 31:3)

My thoughts toward you are countless as the sand on the seashore. (Psalms 139:17–18)

And I rejoice over you with singing. (Zephaniah 3:17)

I will never stop doing good to you. (Jeremiah 32:40)

For you are my treasured possession. (Exodus 19:5)

I desire to establish you with all my heart and all my soul. (Jeremiah 32:41)

And I want to show you great and marvelous things. (Jeremiah 33:3)

If you seek me with all your heart,
you will find me. (Deuteronomy 4:29)

Delight in me and I will give you
the desires of your heart. (Psalm 37:4)

For it is I who gave you those desires. (Philippians 2:13)

I am able to do more for you than
you could possibly imagine. (Ephesians 3:20)

For I am your greatest
encourager. (2 Thessalonians 2:16–17)

I am also the Father who comforts you
in all your troubles. (2 Corinthians 1:3–4)

When you are brokenhearted,
I am close to you. (Psalm 34:18)

As a shepherd carries a lamb,
I have carried you close to my heart. (Isaiah 40:11)

One day I will wipe away every tear
from your eyes. (Revelation 21:3–4)

And I'll take away all the pain you
have suffered on this earth. (Revelation 21:3–4)

I am your Father,
and I love you even as I love my son, Jesus. (John 17:23)

For in Jesus, my love for you is revealed. (John 17:26)

He is the exact representation of my being. (Hebrews 1:3)

He came to demonstrate that I am for you,
not against you. (Romans 8:31)

And to tell you that I am not
counting your sins. (2 Corinthians 5:18–19)

Jesus died so that you
and I could be reconciled. (2 Corinthians 5:18–19)

BE NOT AFRAID TO FOLLOW THE FOOTPRINTS FROM HEAVEN

**His death was the ultimate expression
of my love for you.** (1 John 4:10)

**I gave up everything I loved that
I might gain your love.** (Romans 8:31-32)

**If you receive the gift of my son Jesus,
you receive me.** (1 John 2:23)

**And nothing will ever separate
you from my love again.** (Romans 8:38–39)

**Come home and I'll throw the biggest party
heaven has ever seen.** (Luke 15:7)

**I have always been Father,
and will always be Father.** (Ephesians 3:14–15)

My question is…Will you be my child? (John 1:12–13)

I am waiting for you. (Luke 15:11–32)

**Love,
Your Dad
Almighty God** (85)

APPENDIX 1

EIGHTY-NINE MARIAN APPARITIONS CHART

89 APPEARANCES OF THE VIRGIN MARY
(3.5% of 2,554 reported visits)

DATE	PLACE	CONTACTS	APPROVAL DATE / STATUS
40, Jan. 02	Zaragoza, Spain	St. James	Traditional approval
352, Aug. 05	Rome, Italy	adult couple, Pope Liberius	Traditional approval
1061	Walsingham, England	Richeldis de Faverches	Papal approval - 1150
1206-1214	Spain / Southern France	St. Dominic Guzman (36)	Traditional approval
1251, 1322	Aylesford, England	St. Simon Stock (86)	Implicit approval – 3 popes
1291, May 12	Loreto, Italy	priest, hermit, shepherds	Traditional approval
1426, 1428	Vicenza, Italy	Vincenza Passini (70)	Bishop approved - 1428
1467, Apr. 25	Albania / Genazzano, Italy	two men, crowd of people	Implicit approval - 1467
1490, Aug. 29	Genoa, Italy	Benedict Pareto	Bishop approval - 1582

Date	Location	Visionary	Approval
1491, May 03	Orbey, France	Thierry Schoere	Bishop approval - 1495
1531, Dec. 9-12	Mexico City, Mexico	Juan Diego (57), his uncle	Vatican approval - 1555
1536, Mar. 18	Savona, Italy	Antonio Botta – old farmer	Bishop / Cardinal approval - 1536
1541	Tlaxcala, Mexico	Juan Diego Bernardino	Papal approval - 1746
1557, July 02	Rapallo, Italy	Giovanni Chichizola	Archbishop approval - 1558
1579, July 08	Kazan, Russia	young girl (9)	Traditional approval
1580-1620	Vailankanni, India	2 boys, 2 men, sailors	Papal approval – 1960's
1605, summer	Siluva, Lithuania	children, adults	Papal approval - 1775
1610	Madrid, Spain / Quito, Ecuador	Mother Mariana de Jesus Torres	Bishop approval - 1611
1610	Manaoag, Philippines	one man	Papal approval - 1926
1641-1642	Kevelaer, Germany	Hendrick Busman, his wife	Bishop approval - 1642
1649, Mar. 25	Vinay, France	Pierre Port-Combet	Papal approval - 1856
1652, Aug. 15	Querrien, France	Jeanne Courtel (12)	Archbishop approval - 1652
1664-1718	Laus, France	Benoite Rencurel (17)	Bishop / Vatican approval - 2008
1754	Guaitara Canyon, Colombia	Maria Mueses, Rosa (3)	Traditional approval - 1951
1798	La Vang, Viet Nam	crowd of refugees	Implicit approval with papal visits
1813, 1850	Lichen, Poland	soldier, farmer	Papal approval - 1967
1830, July 18	Paris, France	Sr. Catherine Laboure	Vatican approval - 1836
1834, Aug. 02	Valmala, Italy	4 girls (ages 10-12)	Bishop approval - 1946

BE NOT AFRAID TO FOLLOW THE FOOTPRINTS FROM HEAVEN

Date	Location	Visionaries	Approval
1842, Jan. 20	Rome, Italy	Alphonse Ratisbonne (28)	Vatican approval - 1842
1846, Sept. 19	La Salette, France	2 children (ages 11 & 14)	Vatican approval - 1851
1858, Feb - July	Lourdes, France	Bernadette Soubirous (14)	Vatican approval - 1862
1859, Oct. 8-9	Champion, Wisconsin, USA	Adele Brice (28)	Bishop approval - 2010
1871, Jan. 17	Pontmain, France	at least 8 children (12 & under)	Vatican approval - 1871
1872-1884	Pompeii, Italy	Bartolo Longo, Fortuna Agrelli	Papal approval - 1891
1873, June-July	Herault, France	Auguste Arnaud (30)	Bishop approval - 1876
1874, May-Oct.	Pra, Italy	4 girls (12-13), 2 adults	Implicit approval
1876, Feb-Dec.	Pellevoisin, France	Estelle Faguette (33)	Papal approval - 1878
1877, June-Sept.	Gietrzwald, Poland	2 girls (12, 13)	Vatican approval - 1977
1879, Aug. 21	Knock, Ireland	18 people	Vatican approval - 1936
1888, Mar-Nov.	Castelpetroso, Italy	many people, skeptics, heretic	Bishop approval - 1889
1900, April	Dong Lu, China	thousands of rebels	Papal approval - 1932
1917, May-Oct.	Fatima, Portugal	3 children (ages 6-9)	Vatican approval - 1930
1919, 1938	Wigratzbad, Germany	2 girls (20 and under)	Archbishop unofficial approval
1932-1933	Beauraing, Belgium	5 children (ages 9-15)	Vatican approval - 1949
1933, Jan-Mar.	Banneux, Belgium	Mariette Beco (11)	Vatican approval - 1949
1937-1940	Heede, Germany	4 girls (ages 11-13)	Vicar approval - 1959; implicit

Date	Location	Visionary	Status
1943-1944	Vicksburg, Mississippi, USA	Claude Newman (20), inmate	positive: awaiting approval
1943-1949	Siekierki, Poland	Wladyslawa Papis (12)	awaiting approval
1944, May 13-31	Ghiaie di Bonate, Italy	Adelaide Roncalli (7)	Bishop approval - 2002
1945, May-July	La Codosera, Spain	2 girls (10, 17)	Bishop approval - no date
1945-1959	Amsterdam, Holland	Ida Peerdeman (39)	Bishop approval - 2002
1946, Apr-June	Marienfried, Germany	Barbara Reuss (12)	Bishop approval - 2000
1947, April 12	Tre Fontane, Rome, Italy	skeptic & 3 kids (10, 7, 4)	Vicar approval - 1947; implicit
1947, Dec. 8-14	L'Ile Bouchard, France	4 girls (ages 7, 8, 10, 12)	Bishop approval - 2001
1947-1966	Montichiari-Fontanelle, Italy	a nurse - Pierina Gilli	uncertain decision
1948, Sept-Nov.	Lipa, Philippines	Teresita Castillo (21)	Archbishop approval – 2015
1954-1955	Seredne, Ukraine	young girl – Anna	awaiting approval
1955-1971	Ngome, South Africa	Sr. Reinolda May (54)	Bishop approval - 1992
1956-1958	Rome City, Indiana, USA	Sr. Mildred Neuzil (40)	Implicit Papal approval - 1959
1961-1965	Garabandal, Spain	4 girls (11-12), a priest	awaiting approval; no negatives
1962, July 13-25	Janonis, Lithuania	Ramute Macvyte (18)	awaiting approval
1964-1981	San Damiano, Italy	Mama Rosa (55)	unclear decision initially
1968-1971	Zeitoun, Egypt	approx. 40 million people	Coptic Pope approval - 1968
1973-1981	Akita, Japan	Sr. Agnes Sasagawa (42)	Vatican approval - 1988

1976-2001	New South Wales, Australia	"Geraldine"	Bishop approval - 1996
1980, Apr-Oct.	Cuapa, Nicaragua	Bernardo Martinez (50)	Bishop approval - 1982
1980-1992	El Escorial, Spain	Luz Amparo Cuevas	awaiting approval
1981-- present	Medjugorje, Bosnia	6 youth (ages 10-17)	Vatican investigated*
1981-1989	Kibeho, Rwanda	8 youth (ages 14-24)	Vatican approval - 2001
1982	Luson, Philippines	500 children, 1 teacher	awaiting approval
1982-1990	Damascus, Syria	Myrna Al Akharas (18)	Syrian church approval - 1982
1983-1990	San Nicolas, Argentina	Gladys Quiroga de Motta (46)	Bishop approval - 1990
1984, Mar. 25	Betania, Venezuela	Maria Esperanza (55), 108 others	Bishop approval - 1987
1985-1997	Naju, Korea	Julia Kim (40's)	awaiting approval
1986, Feb. 25	Manila, Philippines	crowd of people, soldiers	Archbishop approval - 1986
1986-1991	Shoubra, Egypt	hundreds of people	Coptic Pope approval - 1986
1987, Apr-Aug.	Hrushiv, Ukraine	Marina Kizyn, (12), 500,000 others	awaiting approval
1988-1990	Cuenca, Ecuador	Patricia Talbot (16)	awaiting approval; no negatives
1989-1993	Agoo, Philippines	Judiel Nieva (12)	unfairly rejected / personal **
1990, May	Santa Maria, California	Sadie Jaramillo	awaiting approval
1990, Jul-Aug.	Litmanova, Slovakia	two girls (both 13)	awaiting approval
1992-1995	Steubenville, Ohio, USA	Tony Fernwalt	awaiting approval

1994-1998	Itapiranga, Brazil	Edson Glauber (22), his mom	Archbishop approval - 2009
1995, May 23	Dong Lu, China	30,000 people	Implicit papal approval
2000-2001	Assiut, Egypt	thousands	Coptic Pope approval - 2000
2002, August	Zakarpattya, Ukraine	two girls (9 & 10)	awaiting approval
2003-2005	Ternopil / Lishnya, Ukraine	Yulia (age 9)	awaiting approval
2003--present	Perryville, Missouri, USA	Neal (40's) – a farmer	awaiting approval
2009, Dec. 11-22	Warraq el-Hadar, Egypt	over 200,000 people	Coptic Pope approval - 2010

*(Medjugorje) The final report from the three-year Vatican investigation rests with Pope Francis at this moment. Bishop Zanic (1981-1993) was initially thrilled and supportive of the appearances of Mary, but totally changed his position when threatened with imprisonment by the Communist government. Bishop Peric (1993-present) does not believe in ANY apparitions of the Virgin Mary anywhere in the world. In an unprecedented move in 2009, the Vatican took the matter out of the hands of the bishop to do their own study (2010-2013). They would not be likely to even take the time to do this study if they did not suspect that it had some merit and was worth their time.

**(Agoo, Philippines) The Bishop gave no explanation for his abrupt rejection of this apparition. It was known that he distrusted the character of the visionary's family and did not approve of the visionary's own gender identity issues. However, nearly one million people witnessed amazing supernatural events and signs; the religious witnessed a Eucharistic miracle; all details closely match all other approved apparitions.

APPENDIX 2

"DESSERT FOR CATHOLICS"

This additional chapter is presented for the consideration of researchers, theologians, avid Catholic readers, and dedicated Marianologists. When research uncovers interesting data that supports, challenges, or promotes theological concepts, I feel the responsibility to share this information so that it can be potentially useful to the reader of this work.

ACTUAL BIRTHDATE OF THE VIRGIN MARY?

Although the Catholic Church celebrates the birth of the Blessed Mother every year on September 8, the Virgin, herself, has indicated that her birthdate is actually August 5. When I first heard of this from the visionaries in Medjugorje, I had great concern because no other visionary had ever stated this—and this would stir the church to doubt the authenticity of those apparitions. However, no person has ever confirmed September 8, either! As I have indicated throughout this book, credibility is established with repetition in the occurrence of such data. I finally got the breakthrough that I was hoping to find in order to help validate the report from Medjugorje. The information unexpectedly came from the obscure encounters in Cuenca, Ecuador. With 365 days in the year, what are the odds that another visionary on a different continent would also claim August 5 as the birthdate of Mary—unless Mary had told them herself?

MEDJUGORJE, BOSNIA-HERZEGOVINA (1984)

At the end of May 1984, Our Lady told Ivan that August 5 would be the two thousandth anniversary of her birthday (the church actually celebrates it on September 8). That would make Our Lady about fifteen to sixteen years old when she gave birth to Jesus. Our Lady told Ivan that Jesus would present her with a special gift of many conversions throughout the world. In preparation for this day, Our Lady asked for three days of prayer and fasting just prior to August 5, 1984. She also requested that her birthday be a special day of prayer,

> "I have dedicated all my life to you through the centuries. Let it not be too much to give that day to me. There will be conversions, changes in the lives of people, in those who are psychologically ill, in sinners. Young people especially will accept me" (52:104).

The area responded with great enthusiasm; close to forty thousand followers came for Mary's birthday. The children stated that Our Lady appeared "more brilliant than ever," glowing, very happy, and very pleased with the widespread response to her request for prayer and fasting. *"Pray, pray—never stop praying!"* Around 7:00 a.m. that morning, a number of people reported seeing Blessed Mary on Mount Krizevac for fifteen minutes. Her hands were uplifted, and she turned slowly, dressed in brilliant white. Somewhere around this time, the huge concrete cross was seen *spinning* for about one minute. Two American women reported that many pilgrims saw the "sun spinning furiously" and not hurting their eyes at all. Mary's birthday was truly a spiritual celebration in many ways! (52:108–109)

CUENCA, ECUADOR (1989)

On August 5, 1989, Patricia and a large number of pilgrims gathered at El Cajas because that was the day Our Lady said was her birthday. The Virgin appeared for her birthday, dressed completely in white. Patricia presented her with a birthday cake and the birthday song, hoping she wouldn't laugh at them. Blessed Mary smiled and replied,

"One day I was also human, my little one. The singing of my little ones is from their hearts. Their songs arrive to my soul. I am happy when you sing, my little ones."

Jesus also appeared again to Patricia and commented on his mother's birthday, stating that she is the most beautiful lady both on earth and in heaven.

"She is My Mother. Love My Father more than anything else. Love My Mother because She will take you to My Heart. Tell all of them that I love them. Tell them all to convert faithfully, humbly, and with simple hearts…I want you to pray the Way of the Cross and the Rosary by foot…" (23:46)

ROME, ITALY (352 AD)

It should be noted that Blessed Mary's request for a church to be built—and the location selected with her predicted miraculous snowfall on Mt. Esquiline, **occurred on August 5** as well. Today, it is called the Church of Santa Maria Maggiore (St. Mary Major near the Vatican) and is one of the largest basilicas in the world. They celebrate the Miracle of the Snow every year on August 5 (4:118).

THE ASSUMPTION OF THE VIRGIN MARY INTO HEAVEN

There has been a longstanding theological debate as to whether Blessed Mary died or was simply taken, body and soul, into heaven. Here are some clues from my research.

TRE FONTANE, ROME, ITALY (1947)

After this momentary blindness, Bruno saw in the most illuminated part of the cave a woman of indescribable celestial beauty. She was dressed in a long, brilliantly white dress with a rose-colored sash. Over her black hair was a green mantle which extended to her bare feet. Her head was adorned by a halo of brilliant golden light. Her face had an expression of motherly kindness, although cloaked by sadness at times. She was holding a dark gray Bible close to her heart. At her bare feet lay a black cloth which had a smashed crucifix on it. Her hands were crossed at her breast, but she unfolded them once to point to the broken pieces of the crucifix.

> "I am the one who is of the Divine Trinity. I am Daughter of the Father, Mother of the Son, and Spouse and Temple of the Holy Spirit. I am the Virgin of Revelation.
>
> (Then she turned on Bruno.) You persecute me. Enough of it now! Enter into the true fold, God's Kingdom on Earth. The Nine First Fridays of the Sacred Heart have saved you. You must be like the flowers which Isola picked. They make no protest—they are silent and do not rebel."

Mary then spoke at length about many things with Bruno that afternoon, including her Assumption into Heaven. **"My body could not decay and did not decay. My Son came for me with His Angels"** (153:2–3).

QUITO, ECUADOR (1629)

Visionary Mother Mariana received these prophetic words from the Child Jesus:

> "They ought to obey and recognize the pope as My representative on earth and render him blind obedience. He will be the blessed pope of My Heavenly Father and will reign with Me in heaven."

> "The dogma of faith of My Mother's Immaculate Conception will be proclaimed when the church is fought against more, and My vicar (Pope Pius IX) is a captive."

> "The de fide dogma of My Blessed Mother's Passage and **Assumption in body and soul** to heaven (will be defined) in the same way. But you, My spouses and chosen souls, ought to believe it always, as if it were already a dogma." (Done by Pope Pius XII, November 1, 1950)

> "This gives me much happiness because it is an act of recognition of My power and love as the Son for His **Immaculate Virgin Mother, whose immaculate and blessed body, for My own honor and dignity, I would never have permitted to be reduced to the dust of the earth**, as happens with the generality of mankind…"
>
> "I know…that the preservation of the incorrupt bodies of some of My servants is beyond comprehension to human beings; with greater reason would I not preserve the body of My Mother, the Immaculate Virgin?" (56:73)

"I AM THE IMMACULATE CONCEPTION"

Many Catholics may recall that young Bernadette Soubirous of Lourdes was told this phrase by the Blessed Virgin as a form of "proof" for the religious to believe that the apparitions were genuine. My research has uncovered many other occasions in which she used this same title.

LOURDES, FRANCE (1858)

Bernadette decided to meet the priest's request, so she dared to ask Mary four times,

> "Mademoiselle, would you be good enough to tell me who you are?"

The Blessed Mother slipped the rosary over her right arm, unfolded her arms, extended her hands toward the ground, and then folded them at her breast. She then raised her eyes toward heaven and finally answered,

> "I am the Immaculate Conception."

Bernadette had *absolutely no idea what that meant*, but she kept repeating the strange words to herself all the way to Father Peyramale's residence so that she would not forget this precious response that they had all been waiting for. After she reported to him what Mary had told her, he was simply astonished. How could this uneducated girl, whose catechist had described her as "a blank slate," know that the Virgin Mary had been born without sin? Pope Pius IX had proclaimed the dogma of the Immaculate Conception *only four years earlier*. When she left, Father Peyramale was now a believer and broke down and wept (42:11–12).

PRA, ITALY (1874)

On October 25, a thirteen year old and her friend Maria Valley Pegollo visited the site of the apparitions and saw the Virgin Mary dressed in black. They lowered their eyes and prayed. After a while, they saw angels surrounding the Blessed Mother, who now wore a blue cape, fastened on her chest with a shining star. Her hands were folded on a cross upon her breast. Two people were at her sides, benign and friendly. The girls began asking questions. The Virgin stated that she was "**the Immaculate Conception**." The two people with her were Saint Clare and Saint Elizabeth. The angels were reported as having come to assess the innocence of the girls. Mary explained that the star on her chest which served as a clasp for her cape was given by Her Son, Jesus, to recognize his mother as the "Queen of Heaven and Earth" (140).

GIETRZWALD, POLAND (1877)

The fourth apparition happened on the day of Justyna's first Holy Communion, July 1. When Justyna asked who she was, Mary replied, "I am the Most Holy Virgin Mary **Immaculately Conceived**." (112:2)

L'ILE-BOUCHARD, FRANCE (1947)

On the next day, December 9, the four girls assembled at the appointed time and began praying the Rosary. The Blessed Virgin appeared in a shining golden sphere, about three feet across that came out of the wall and unfolded itself as a rectangular curtain of silvery light on which the rocky grotto stood out in relief. Her long hair was now hidden by her veil. Written across her breast in gold letters was the word "Magnificat." The words on the block of stone underneath her feet had changed. Now the words on the rock read, **"I am the Immaculate Conception"** (3:205).

MONTICHIARI, ITALY (1947)

Seventh Apparition (December 8, 1947) - Countless priests were present for this anticipated event—so many that Pierina Gilli had trouble getting into the church! Pierina knelt in the center of the church, praying the Rosary, when Our Lady appeared on a large white staircase decorated with a white, red, and yellow rose. She said, with a smile,

> "I am the Immaculate Conception...(took a few more steps)...I am Mary, full of grace, Mother of My Divine Son Jesus Christ..." (134:4)

KIBEHO, RWANDA (1982)

On August 4, 1982, Agnes Kamagaju (twenty-one) had her first visions. Lying on her bed in her room, she began feeling an intense happiness that caused her to start giggling and laughing so loudly that it woke her parents. Then the Virgin Mary emerged from a spectacular glowing light. She was young and very beautiful, dressed in a white dress with a blue veil. The light surrounding her glowed like a crown about her head. She soon identified herself as "**the Immaculate Conception.**" She told her to start praying the rosary, and when she did, they were both transported to a beautiful field of flowers (39:116) (4:145).

BETANIA, VENEZUELA (1989)

Thirtieth Apparition: December 8, 1989 - 6:30 p.m.

> "My children, today we have lived a great day of light...with the hope that all My children who have come to celebrate by My side, My Feast of Angels, **as the Immaculate Conception**, may have received the supreme purity of the divine spirit... and as a result you may have felt in your hearts, not only My presence, but the presence of My Divine Son...discovering the reason why in these times of great calamity for mankind, we are calling all Our scattered children from different places of the world to receive Our message" (9).

THE PROPOSED FIFTH MARIAN DOGMA

The idea for a fifth Marian dogma actually originated with the Virgin Mary herself. Here is when, what, why, and where that she proposed this:

> "I am standing on the globe, and both of my feet are set upon it firmly. You also see my hands clearly as well as my face, hair, and veil. The rest is as in a haze...Now, I will explain to you why I come in this form. I stand as the Lady before the Cross—with head, hands, and feet of a human being—but with the body, however, of the Spirit, because the Son came through the will of the Father. The Father and the Son want to bring me into this world as **Co-Redemptrix, Mediatrix, and Advocate. This will be the new and final Marian dogma**. This image will precede. This dogma will be much disputed, yet it will be carried through" (Mary to Ida Peerdman [39], Amsterdam, Holland, 1945) (99:2).

> "I was **Co-Redemptrix** from the moment of the Annunciation. The Mother has been constituted **Co-Redemptrix** by the will of the Father. Tell this to your theologians. Tell them likewise that **this dogma will be the last in Marian history**" (Mary to Ida Peerdman [45], Amsterdam, Holland, November 15, 1951) (99:3).

> "Ask the Holy Father to pray the prayer…and to lead all the nations in praying it…(to the pope) Apostle of the Lord Jesus Christ, teach your peoples this simple yet profound prayer. It is Mary, the Lady of All Nations, who asks this of you. You are the shepherd of the Church of the Lord Jesus Christ. Tend your sheep. Know well, great threats are hanging over the Church, are hanging over the world. Now the time has come for you to speak of Mary as **Co-Redemptrix, Mediatrix, and Advocate,** under the title, Lady of All Nations. Why is Mary asking this of you? Because she has been sent by her Lord and Creator **so that under this title and through this prayer, she may deliver the world from a great world catastrophe. She is now asking that the people may hear this title from *you*, the Holy Father"** (Mary to Ida Peerdman [47], Amsterdam, Holland, May 10, 1953) (99:3).

Co-Redemptrix means that the Blessed Virgin is a partner or participant with Jesus in the plan of redemption for mankind. **Advocate** means that she is an intercessor for our prayers, a mediator between man and heaven, or the one who carries our needs to Jesus—much as she did at the Wedding at Cana when she let Jesus know the needs of the wedding for more wine. **Mediatrix** means the one who passes on numerous graces to mankind after receiving them from God—along with her directions from Him for dispensing them. Here are further examples of Mary being referred to by these titles in her appearances to people on earth.

> "I entrust you from My Holy Heart, to which you consecrate your sweet heart in every coming day of God's, to spread all over the world the Majesty of Holy Glory of Our Queen of Heaven and the Earth as Our Protectress and **Co-Redemptrix** of the whole world" (Jesus to Yulia [9], Ternopil, Ukraine, May 21, 2005) (152:6).

> "The Lady of All Nations is now permitted to come in order to banish Satan. She comes to announce the Holy Spirit. The Holy Spirit will only now descend over this earth. But you should say my prayer: Lord Jesus Christ, Son of the Father, send now your Spirit over the Earth. Let the Holy Spirit

live in the hearts of all nations. That they be preserved from degeneration, disaster, and war. May the Lady of All Nations, known as Mary, be our **Advocate**" (Mary to Ida Peerdman, Amsterdam, Holland) (1:154–155).

"In these times of so much confusion and so little light in souls, my most pure light will be the one to guide you in the midst of so much darkness. Many are the children who do not admit that the Mother is the **Mediator** before the Son; many resist going to the Son through the Mother. I tell all mankind: I will help you to overcome every uncertainty; this Mother will make your encounter with the Son possible. For this it is necessary to become little and abandon yourself in My heart. I assure you, do not doubt" (Mary to Gladys Quiroga de Motta [51], San Nicolas, Argentina, December 8, 1988) (149:3).

"**I am the powerful Mediatrix of Graces**. As the world can find Mercy only through the sacrifice of the Son with the Father, so can **you find favor with the Son through my intercession**. Christ is unknown because I am not known. It is true that the world was consecrated to my Immaculate Heart, but this consecration has become a fearful responsibility for many men. I demand that the world live the consecration" (Mary to Barbara Reuss [12], Marienfried, Germany, May 25, 1946) (3:200).

"I have placed myself as the **Mediatrix** between my Divine Son and mankind, especially for the soul consecrated to God. Tired of the continuous offenses, He already wants to dispense His justice....Live out of Love!" (Mary to Pierina Gilli, Montichiari, Italy, October 22, 1947) (134:3).

"I am Mary, **Mediatrix** of All Grace..." (Mary to Teresita Castillo, Lipa, Philippines, September 26, 1948) (126:6)

"The ball which you see (in my hands) represents the whole world, especially France and each person in particular. These rays symbolize **the graces I shed upon those who ask for them**. The gems from which rays do not fall are the graces for which souls forget to ask" (Mary to Catherine Laboure, Paris, France, November 27, 1830) (54:13).

SEREDNE, UKRAINE (1954)

On the vigil of the Feast of the Immaculate Conception, December 21, 1954, a young girl, Anna, saw the Virgin Mary in a small church as she prayed after Mass. Mary was so beautiful that Anna cried with joy. Mary wore a glorious dress "all of white like shining lights" and a blue sash. On her head was a golden crown with twelve stars that twinkled with dazzling light. Mary said to her,

> "My daughter, you see that **I hold so many graces for my children** which I am unable to give them because they do not ask for them. Our Father in heaven respects the freedom of His beloved sons and daughters. Only if you turn to me and ask, am I permitted to bless you with **the graces my Son has given to me** for each of you" (2:268–269).

Other appearances by the Blessed Virgin also mention Her role as dispenser of graces.

> "I will work **miracles of grace** only in those who ask for them and empty their souls of the love and attachment to sin and all that is displeasing to my Son. Souls who cling to sin cannot have their hands free to receive the **treasures of grace** that I hold out to them" (Mary to Sister Mildred Neuzil, Midwest USA, August 1957) (146:3).

> "After my ascension into heaven, I have always acted as **Mediatrix** between my Son Jesus and the whole of mankind. How many graces I have been able to obtain in all these centuries! How many graces were shown. How much punishment was prevented. How many dialogues did I hold with souls" (Mary to Pierina Gilli, Fontanelle, Italy, August 6, 1966) (134:8).

> "Pray, make sacrifices for sinners. Pray the Rosary—not for external things; weightier things are at stake in these times. Expect no signs and wonders. I shall be active as the **powerful Mediatrix** in secret…**It is the will of the Father that the world acknowledge this position of His Handmaid**" (Mary

to Barbara Reuss [12], Marienfried, Germany, May 25, 1946) (130) (3:201).

MONTICHIARI, ITALY (1947)

Countless priests were present for the anticipated seventh apparition on December 8, 1947—so many that visionary Pierina Gilli had trouble getting into the church! Pierina knelt in the center of the church, praying the Rosary, when Our Lady appeared on a large white staircase decorated with a white, red, and yellow rose. She said, with a smile,

> "I am Mary, full of grace, Mother of My Divine Son Jesus Christ…It is my wish that every year, on the 8th of December, at noon, the Hour of Grace for the World be celebrated. Many divine and bodily graces will be received through this devotion. Jesus will send His overflowing mercy if good people will pray continuously for their sinful brother. One should very soon notify the Holy Father of the Church, Pope Pius XII, that it is my wish that the HOUR OF GRACE FOR THE WORLD be made known and spread throughout the world. If anyone is unable to visit his church, yet will pray at noon at home, he will also **receive graces through me**. Whoever prays on these tiles and weeps tears of penance will find a secure, heavenly ladder and receive protection and grace through my motherly heart.…Soon, one will recognize the greatness of this Hour of Grace."

> "I have already prepared a **flood of graces for all the children** who listen to my words and keep them in their hearts" (134:4–5).

The first supernatural event took place in Marienfried, near Paffenhofen, Germany on April 25, 1946. Barbara Reuss, age twelve, was amazed when an angel appeared to her. The angel announced that he was the Angel of the **Great Mediatrix of Graces**. He instructed Barbara to kneel while he introduced a prayer to be addressed to the Blessed Virgin Mary. This was his prayer:

"Act as the Mother of Grace; act as the thrice miraculous Mother; the thrice admirable Mother of Grace, Thou **Great Mediatrix of Graces!**" (3:199)

"**I do not dispose all graces. I receive from God what I obtain through prayer**. God has placed His complete trust in me. I particularly protect those who have been consecrated to me" **(Mary to teenagers in Medjugorje, Bosnia-Herzegovina, August 31, 1982)** (45:171).

From researching such historical accounts, these messages and events are presented in the hope that other researchers or proponents of certain movements in the Catholic Church may find them useful. Petitions are being presented to the pope for consideration for approving this fifth Marian dogma.

BIBLIOGRAPHY

MULTIPLE APPARITIONS / SHRINES

1. Roy Abraham Varghese, *God-Sent: A History of the Accredited Apparitions of Mary* (The Crossroad Publishing Company, New York, NY, 2000).
2. Janice T. Connell, *Meetings with Mary / Visions of the Blessed Mother* (Ballantine Books, Random House Publishing Group, New York, NY, 1995).
3. Joan Carroll Cruz, *See How She Loves Us: 50 Approved Apparitions of Our Lady* (TAN Books, St. Benedict Press, LLC, Charlotte, NC, 2012).
4. Peter Mullen, *Shrines of Our Lady* (St. Martin's Press, New York, NY, 1998).
5. Bob and Penny Lord, *The Many Faces of Mary: A Love Story* (Journeys of Faith, 1-800-633-2484, 1987).
6. *The Marian Library / International Marian Research Institute, University of Dayton, Dayton, OH, accessed online at "The Mary Page."* (http://campus.udayton.edu/mary/aboutmary2.html)
7. *The Mary Pages: Apparitions and Pictures, accessed online at www.marypages.com*
8. Randall Sullivan, *The Miracle Detective* (Grove Press, New York, NY, 2004).

9. *The Miracle Hunter (lists apparitions from 40 AD to 1900 along with approvals)*, accessed online at www.miraclehunter.com
10. David Michael Lindsey, *The Woman and the Dragon / Apparitions of Mary* (Pelican Publishing Company, Gretna, LA, 2000).
11. Catherine Odell, *Those Who Saw Her* (Our Sunday Visitor Publishing Division, Our Sunday Visitor, Inc., Huntington, IN, revised 2010).
12. Julie Dortch Cragon, *Visiting Mary / Her U.S. Shrines and Their Graces* (Servant Books, Franciscan Media, Cincinnati, OH, 2014).

SPECIFIC APPARITIONS

AMSTERDAM, HOLLAND

13. Dr. Richard Russell, "Messages on War and Peace from the Lady of All Nations." *Signs and Wonders for Our Times*, Vol. 22, No. 3–4 (Signs of the Times Apostolate, Inc., Herndon, VA, Fall 2012), pp. 24–41.

AUSTRALIA

14. Geraldine, *Divine Inspirations from Jesus and Mary: For Love of Many, Volume I* (First American Edition, Queenship Publishing Company, Goleta, CA, 1999).
15. Geraldine, *Divine Inspirations from Jesus and Mary: For Love of Many, Volume II* (First American Edition, Queenship Publishing Company, Goleta, CA, 2002).
16. Geraldine, *Divine Inspirations from Jesus and Mary: For Love of Many, Volume III* (First American Edition, Queenship Publishing Company, Goleta, CA, 2006).
17. Geraldine, *Divine Inspirations from Jesus and Mary: For Love of Many* (Divine Inspirations, Guidford, NSW, Australia).

BETANIA, VENEZUELA

18. MarCom Enterprises, *Betania, Land of Grace*, Green Bay, WI.

CASTELPETROSO, ITALY

19. William James Walsh, *The Apparitions and Shrines of Heaven's Bright Queen in Legend, Poetry, and History: From the Earliest Ages to the Present Time* (Carey-Stafford, New York, 1906), pp. 173–174.

CHAMPION, WISCONSIN

20. Judith M. Albright, *Queen of Heaven / Our Lady of Good Help* (Queenship Publishing Company, Goleta, CA, 2012).
21. Shrine of Our Lady of Good Help, *The Shrine of Our Lady of Good Help*, 2011.

CUENCA, ECUADOR

22. *"Apparitions in Ecuador,"* edited by Michael Cain, appearing in *The Daily Catholic* (vol. 10, 58 and 63, Daily Catholic, 2001).
23. Sister Isabel Bettwy, *I am the Guardian of the Faith* (Franciscan University Press, Steubenville, OH, 1991).

FATIMA, PORTUGAL

24. *Fatima*, EWTN Classic Documentary (EWTN Home Video, Irondale, AL, 2006.
25. Father Jason Brooks, LC, *Fatima: Living the Message* (Lighthouse Catholic Media, www.lighthousecatholicmedia.org, 2011).

26. Ian & Dominic Higgins, *Finding Fatima* (Major Oak Entertainment / Ignatius Press, 2010).
27. John M. Haffert, *Meet the Witnesses of the Miracle of the Sun* (The American Society for the Defense of Tradition, Family, and Property, Spring Grove, PA, 1961).
28. French of Chanoine Barthas and Pere Da Fonseca, SJ, *Our Lady of Light / World-Wide Message of Fatima* (The Bruce Publishing Company, Milwaukee, WI, 1947).
29. Leo Madigan, *The Children of Fatima* (Our Sunday Visitor Publishing Division, Our Sunday Visitor, Inc., Huntington, IN, 2003).
30. Father Frederick L. Miller, *The Messages of Our Lady of Fatima* (Catholic Information Service, Knights of Columbus Supreme Council, New Haven, CT, 2001).
31. Ian & Dominic Higgins, *The 13th Day* (13th Day Films / Ignatius Press, 2009).
32. John de Marchi, I.M.C., *The True Story of Fatima* (The Fatima Center, Constable, NY, 2009).

GARABANDAL, SPAIN

33. *Garabandal: The Eyewitnesses*, MFJ Productions, Auckland, New Zealand, 2003, and St. Michael's Garabandal Centre, Pasadena, CA.
34. Judith M. Albright, *Our Lady at Garabandal* (Queenship Publishing Company, Goleta, CA, 2009).

GUADALUPE, MEXICO

35. Father Christopher Rengers, OFM Cap, *Mary of the Americas, Our Lady of Guadalupe* (Society of St. Paul / Alba House, Staten Island, NY, Revised & Updated Edition 2007).

KIBEHO, RWANDA

36. Immaculee Ilibagiza, *A Visit from Heaven / The Last Apparition of Alphonsine* (Immaculee Ilibagiza, New York, NY, 2010).
37. Immaculee Ilibagiza & Sean Bloomfield, *If Only We Had Listened*, 2011.
38. *Immaculee: Discovering Kibeho*, a collection of ten short documentaries, Immaculee Ilibagiza.
39. Immaculee Ilibagiza with Steve Erwin, *Our Lady of Kibeho* (Hay House Inc., New York, NY, 2008). (39-CD) Immaculee Illibagiza with Greg Amaya, *Immaculee Shares the Messages of Our Lady of Kibeho* (Mary Our Mother Foundation, New York City, NY, 2009).

KNOCK, IRELAND

40. Tom Neary, *I Saw Our Lady* (Custodians of Knock Shrine, Cashin Printing Services Ltd., Castlebar, Mayo County, Ireland, 1977).

LOURDES, FRANCE

41. Jean Delannoy, *Bernadette* (Ignatius Press / CEA Films, 1990).
42. Kerry Crawford, *Lourdes Today / A Pilgrimage to Mary's Grotto* (Servant Books, St. Anthony Messenger Press, Cincinnati, OH, 2008).

MEDJUGORJE, BOSNIA-HERZEGOVINA

43. Dr. Mark Miravalle and Wayne Weible, *Are the Medjugorje Apparitions Authentic?* (New Hope Press, Hiawassee, GA, 2008).
44. *Medjugorje: A Message of Peace for You, Center for Peace*, Boston, MA.

45. Wayne Weible, *Medjugorje: The Last Apparition / How It Will Change the World* (New Hope Press, Hiawassee, GA, 2013).
46. Wayne Weible, *Medjugorje: The Message* (Paraclete Press, Brewster, MA, 1989).
47. Wayne Weible, *Medjugorje: The Mission* (Paraclete Press, Brewster, MA, 1994).
48. James Mulligan, *Medjugorje: What's Happening?* (Paraclete Press, Brewster, MA, 2011).
49. Sean Patrick Bloomfield, *Miracles of Medjugorje*, Queen of Peace Productions, 2006.
50. Bambiina, LLC, *Queen of Peace*; www.medjfilms.com, 2012.
51. Jan Connell, *Queen of the Cosmos / Interviews with the Visionaries of Medjugorje* (Paraclete Press, Brewster, MA, Revised Edition 2004).
52. Joseph A. Pelletier, *The Queen of Peace Visits Medjugorje* (Assumption Publications, Worcester, MA, 1985).

NAJU, KOREA

53. *Messages of Love*, the Blessed Mother's Messages to Julia Kim, translated by Sang M. Lee (Mary's Touch By Mail, Gresham, OR, 1996).

PARIS, FRANCE

54. *A Light Shining on the Earth / The Message of the Miraculous Medal*, edited by Rev. Edward Udovic, CM and Keith Piche (Editions du Signe, Albagraf, Rome, Italy, 1997).

QUITO, ECUADOR

55. *Our Lady of Good Success: History, Miracles & Prophecies*, Pro Multis Media, CA, 2008.

56. Rev. Father Manuel Sousa Pereira, *The Story of Our Lady of Good Success and Novena*, an abridged version translated by Rev. Paul M. Kimball (Dolorosa Press, Camillus, NY, 2013).

ROME, ITALY (TRE FONTANE)

57. *"The Virgin of the Revelation,"* in *Marian Shrines of Italy* (Franciscan Friars of the Immaculate, EWTN).

SAN DAMIANO, ITALY

58. Harry Faulhaber, *Miraculous Lady of the Roses at San Damiano, Italy* (Miraculous Lady of the Roses / MLOR Corporation, Hickory Corners, MI, 1970, 1992, 2002).

ZEITOUN, EGYPT

59. Pearl Zaki, *Before Our Eyes / The Virgin Mary, Zeitun, Egypt, 1968 & 1969* (Queenship Publishing Company, Goleta, CA, 2002).

HEAVEN / ANGELS

60. Father Joshua Waltz, *All Things Are Possible for God* (Lighthouse Catholic Media, www.lighthousecatholicmedia.org, 2014).
61. *"Angel in the Hospital,"* reported by Mike Celizic (NBC's *Today Show*, December 23, 2008).
62. Dr. Mark Miravalle, *Angels Explained / What You Should Know about the Nine Choirs* (Lighthouse Catholic Media, www.lighthousecatholicmedia.org, 2013).
63. *Heaven Is for Real*, by Todd Burpo as told by Colton Burpo (Thomas Nelson Inc., Nashville, TN, 2011).

64. *Heaven Is for Real for Kids*, as told by Colton Burpo to his parents, Todd & Sonja Burpo (Tommy Nelson, Thomas Nelson Publishers, Nashville, TN, 2011).
65. Don Piper with Cecil Murphey, *90 Minutes in Heaven* (Revell, Grand Rapids, MI, 2015).
66. Eben Alexander, MD, *Proof of Heaven / A Neurosurgeon's Journey into the Afterlife* (Simon & Schuster Paperbacks, New York, NY, 2012).
67. Mary Kathleen Glavich, SND, *The Catholic Companion to the Angels* (ACTA Publications, Chicago, IL, 2014).

SCIENTIFIC INVESTIGATIONS

68. Professor Courtenay Bartholomew, MD, *A Scientist Researches Mary, the Ark of the Covenant* (The 101 Foundation, Asbury, NJ, 1996).
69. Elizabeth Ficocelli, *Bleeding Hands, Weeping Stone / True Stories of Divine Wonders, Miracles, and Messages* (St. Benedict Press, Charlotte, NC, 2009).
70. Joan Carroll Cruz, *Eucharistic Miracles* (TAN Books, Charlotte, NC, 1987 / 2010).
71. *Guadalupe: A Living Image*, Studio3 TV & Janson Media, 2010.
72. Brother Thomas Sennott, *Not Made by Hands* (Franciscan Friars of the Immaculate, Our Lady's Chapel, New Bedford, MA, 1998).
73. Ron Tesoriero and Michael Willesee, *Science Tests Faith / Following the Trail of the Blood of Christ* (Love and Mercy Publications, Hampstead, NC, 2010).
74. *The Eucharistic Miracles of the World (Catalogue of the Vatican International Exhibition)*, Institute of St. Clement I, Pontifical Academy Cultorum Martyrum, and Real Presence Eucharistic Education and Adoration Association (Eternal Life, Bardstown, KY, 2009).
75. Joan Carroll Cruz, *The Incorruptibles* (TAN Books: St. Benedict Press, LLC, Charlotte, NC, 1977).

76. Father Francis Peffley, *The Passion of Christ in the Light of the Holy Shroud of Turin* (Lighthouse Catholic Media, www.lighthousecatholicmedia.org, 2011).
77. Larry Schauf, *The Shroud of Turin Exhibition Book* (a Larry Schauf publication, based on the Trial of the Shroud Presentation, larry@theschaufs.com, or www.shroud.com, 2011).
78. Ron Tesoriero and Lee Han, *Unseen: New Evidence* (Ron Tesoriero, Kincumber, New South Wales, Australia, 2013).

OTHER RESOURCES

79. *"A Medal, a Vision, a Conversion," Crusade Magazine* (bi-monthly publication of The American Society for the Defense of Tradition, Family and Property, www.tfp.org, March/April 2013), pp. 22–23.
80. Sherry A. Weddell, *Forming Intentional Disciples* (Our Sunday Visitor, Inc., Huntington, IN, 2012).
81. Rice Broocks, *God's Not Dead / Evidence for God in an Age of Uncertainty* (W Publishing, Nashville, TN, 2013).
82. *God's Not Dead*, Check the Gate Productions and Red Entertainment Group (Pure Flix Entertainment, LLC., Scottsdale, AZ, 2013).
83. *Interview with Donald Hartley*, during *"Journey with Mary,"* an Internet radio program (Deeper Truth website, blog talk radio, 2014).
84. *Interview with Neal* (John Carpenter/Marian Association, Perryville, MO, May 12, 2013).
85. *"Letter from God"* arranged from Biblical scriptures by unknown source, appearing in Immaculee Ilibagiza's daily *"Uplifting Messages"* from her website, http://immaculee.biz, 2015.
86. Father Edward O'Connor, *Listen to My Prophets, Divine Mercy and Divine Justice* (Queenship Publishing Company, Goleta, CA, 2011).

87. *Marian Conference* (Marian Association of Springfield / Cape Girardeau, Missouri Diocese, Saturday, October 13, 2012).
88. Mark Miravalle, *Meet Your Mother* (Lighthouse Catholic Media, Sycamore, IL, & Marian Press, Stockbridge, MA, 2014).
89. *"Padre Pio and the Three Days of Darkness,"* by Saint Padre Pio from a translation of his personal letter addressed to the Commission of Heroldsbach, appointed by the Vatican (*These Last Days News*, December 18, 2012 at www.tldm.org/news/darkness-11-13-98.htm).
90. Father Arthur Byrne, *"Police Dogs Recognize Christ in the Eucharist?" Garabandal Journal*, January-February 2007.
91. Father Charles Arminjon, *The End of the Present World and the Mysteries of the Future Life*, translated by Susan Conroy and Peter McEnerny (Sophia Institute Press, Manchester, NH, 2008).
92. Edward Sri, *The New Rosary in Scripture* (Servant Books, St. Anthony Messenger Press, Cincinnati, OH, 2003).
93. Father Michael Gaitley, MIC, *The Second Greatest Story Ever Told* (Marian Press, Stockbridge, MA, 2015).
94. *To the Priests, Our Lady's Beloved Sons*, messages received by Father Don Stefano Gobbi (The Marian Movement of Priests, St. Francis, ME, 1995).
95. Linda Brenegan, *"Who Can Doubt the Real Presence?"* as told by Martha Chai in *Gospel Mission News Letter*, Baltimore, MD, 2007.
96. St. Faustina, *Divine Mercy in My Soul: Diary of Saint Maria Faustina Kowalska* (Marian Press, Stockbridge, MA, 2008).

OTHER INTERNET REFERENCES

AGOO, PHILIPPINES

     97. www.miraclehunter.com/marian_apparitions/messages/agoo_messages.htm

     98. www.catholicrevelations.org/PR/judiel%20nieva.htm

AMSTERDAM

     99. www.marypages.com/AmsterdamEng.htm

ASSIUT, EGYPT

     100. www.zeitun-eg.org/assiut.htm

BEAURAING, BELGIUM

     101. www.theotokos.org.uk/pages/approved/appariti/beaurain.html

CUAPA, NICARAGUA

     102. http://allformary.org/our-lady-of-cuapa-nicaragua/

CUENCA, ECUADOR

     103. www.piercedhearts.org/hearts_jesus_mary/apparitions/guardian_faith.html#historia

DAMASCUS, SYRIA

     104. http://www.unitypublishing.com/damascus.html

     105. http://www.catholicdigitalstudio.com/miracleofdamascus.htm

DONG LU, CHINA

106. www.miraclehunter.com/marian_apparitions/approved_apparitions/donglu/index.html

EL ESCORIAL, SPAIN

107. www.marypages.com/ElEscorialEng.htm

GENAZZANO, ITALY

108. http://www.traditioninaction.org/religious/a004rp.htm

GHIAIE di BONATE, ITALY

109. www.marypages.com/Bonate.htm
110. www.madonnadelleghiaie.it/inglese/insegnamenti.asp
111. http://ghiaie.net/index.html

GIETRZWALD, POLAND

112. www.marypages.com/GietrzwaldEng.htm

HEEDE, GERMANY

113. www.myetherworld.com/heede.html
114. www.users.qwest.net/~slrorer/HeedeVisions.htm
115. www.miraclehunter.com/marian_apparitions/approved_apparitions/heede/index.html

HIROSHIMA MIRACLE

116. http://holysouls.com/sar/rosarymiracle.htm

HRUSHIV, UKRAINE

117. www.motherofallpeoples.com/Articles/Marian_Private_Revelation/our-lady-of-hrushiv
118. http://mrosa.szm.com/341998/angl/ukrajina.htm
119. www.dzhublyk.org.ua/index-en.htm

HUMAN BODY DECAY

120. http://www.exploreforensics.co.uk/the-rate-of-decay-in-a-corpse.html

ITAPIRANGA, BRAZIL

121. www.miraclehunter.com/marian_apparitions/approved_apparitions

KEVELAER, GERMANY

122. www.marypages.com/KevelaerEng.htm

LAUS, FRANCE

123. www.catholictradition.org/Mary/laus.htm

LA VANG, VIETNAM

124. www.marypages.com/LaVang.htm

LICHEN, POLAND

125. www.marypages.com/LichenEnglish.htm

LIPA, PHILIPPINES

126. www.catholicrevelations.org/PR/novice%20teresita%20lipa.htm

LORETO

127. http://catholictradition.org/Mary/loreto1.htm
128. http://www.newadvent.org/cathen/13454b.htm

LUZON, PHILIPPINES

129. http://miracles.mcn.org/motherx.htm

MARIENFRIED, GERMANY

130. www.salvemariaregina.info/SalveMariaRegina/SMR-091.html

MEDJUGORJE

131. 131a. www.ourmedjugorje.com
131b. http://www.medjugorje.com/medjugorje-messages/
132. www.ourmedjugorje.com/The%20changing%20medjugorje.htm

"Michael in the Morning"

133. http://www.tfpstudentaction.org/resources/prayers-for-students/incredible-miracle-us-marine-saved-by-saint-michael.html

MONTICHIARI, ITALY

134. www.mgr.org/rosamystica.html

NAJU, KOREA

135. www.marys-touch.com/introduction/miracles.htm

NGOME, S.AFRICA

136. www.icon.co.za/~host/ngome/messages.htm

PELLEVOISIN, FRANCE

137. www.marypages.com/PellevoisinEng.htm

POMPEII, ITALY

138. www.marypages.com/OurLadyofPompeii.htm

POPE LEO XIII

139. www.stjosephschurch.net/leoxiii.htm

PRA, ITALY

140. www.mariadinazareth.it

QUITO, ECUADOR

141. http://www.onepeterfive.com/400-years-ago-our-lady-sent-us-a-message-from-ecuador/

RASPUTIN

142. https://en.wikipedia.org/wiki/Grigori_Rasputin

RATISBONNE (Rome)

143. www.traditioninaction.org/SOD/j112sdOLMiracles_1-20.htm

ROME CITY, INDIANA

144. www.ourladyofamerica.com
145. http://allformary.org/our-lady-of-america/
146. www.marypages.com/OurLadyofAmerica.htm

ROME, ITALY (Snows)

147. www.snows.org/DevotionalAreas.aspx?path=root/english/AboutUs

SAN NICOLAS, ARGENTINA

148. www.miraclehunter.com/marian_apparitions/approved_apparitions/sannicolas/index.htm
149. www.motherofallpeoples.com/2006/05/apparition-of-our-lady-of-the-rosary-san-nicolas-argentina/

SIEKIERKI, POLAND

150. www.marypages.com/Siekierki.htm

SILUVA, LITHUANIA

151. www.marypages.com/LadyofSiluva.htm

TERNOPIL / LISHNYA

152. www.marypages.com/ApparitionsUkraine.htm

TRE FONTANE, ROME

153. www.marypages.com/TreFontaneEnglish.htm

VAILANKANNI, INDIA

154. http://en.wikipedia.org/wiki/Our_Lady_of_Good_Health

WALSINGHAM, ENGLAND

155. 155a. www.marypages.com/Walsingham.htm
155b. http://timetravel-britain.com/articles/churches/walsingham.shtml

WARRAQ el HADAR, EGYPT

156. www.wataninet.com/ArticleDetails.aspx?A=25232
157. http://weekly.ahram.org.eg/2009/977/fr2.htm
158. www.zeitun-eg.org

ZAKARPATTYA, UKRAINE

159. www.wumag.kiev.ua/index2.php?param=pgs20054/124

ZARAGOZA, SPAIN

160. http://en.wikipedia.org/wiki/Basilica_of_Our_Lady_of_the_Pillar

GUAITARA CANYON

161. http://www.traditioninaction.org/SOD/j145sdLasLajas_8-16.htm

SAVONA, ITALY

162. http://en.mariedenazareth.com/qui-est-marie/savona-shrine-our-lady-mercy

ST. DOMINIC

163. http://www.theholyrosary.org/rosaryhistory

MANILA, PHILIPPINES

164. http://en.wikipilipinas.org/index.php?title=1986_Apparition_-_Manila%2C_Philippines

HRUSHIV, UKRAINE

165. http://saints2beindallastx.blogspot.com/2014/03/apparitions-of-mother-of-god-in-ukraine.html

TIXTLA, MEXICO

166. deepertruthblog.com, posted by Donald Hartley, January 26, 2016

ABOUT THE AUTHOR
John S. Carpenter, MSW, LCSW

Raised in Evansville, Indiana, as the son of a Methodist minister, John loved the nurturing home his parents provided. He has fond memories of vacation trips to the family's rustic log cabin on a wilderness lake in Northern Michigan every summer. He loved the meditative beauty of calm waters, glowing sunsets, adventuresome trails, and mystical northern lights. These beautiful moments enhanced his interest in photography, music, poetry, and writing.

Carpenter received a degree in psychology from DePauw University in Indiana, followed by a Master in Psychiatric Social Work from Washington University in St. Louis. For the past thirty-seven years, he has served Southwest Missouri in the field of psychiatry providing psychological assessments, individual, group, and family therapy, marriage counseling, and clinical hypnotherapy. While performing those services, he also lectured and trained other healthcare professionals from Hawaii to Maine and Alaska to Key West on various disorders and forms of psychological treatment. His first book was entitled *Effective Strategies for Helping Couples and Families* (2002).

Having listened to details of thousands of people's life experiences, he has always been intrigued by some of their paranormal encounters and supernatural occurrences. Like a good detective, he has always approached those questionable events with a nonjudgmental, logical, and open-minded attitude along with investigative curiosity.

After his father retired, he drifted away from the church for years until his beloved Ruthie gently introduced him to Catholicism in 2006. He became Catholic in 2010 and then found fascination with documented, alleged appearances of the Virgin Mary. He delved deeply into this research, going well beyond what most Catholics had been taught. By 2012, he was sending out a free e-mail newsletter every weekend on Marian Apparitions. In 2013, he became the codirector of the Marian Association for the diocese of Springfield, Cape Girardeau, Missouri. By 2014, he was serving as the president of the Bishop's Diocesan Pastoral Council as well as on the parish council of Our Lady of the Lake in Branson. That same year, he was invited to broadcast an on-going, weekly, international radio show, Journey with Mary, through the Internet. Today, he continues to provide enthusiastic presentations on the evidence-based reality of God.

He can be contacted at: jcdivinemystery73@gmail.com or visit his website: "Divine Mysteries and Miracles" for more information, photos, artwork, and products (www.divinemysteries.info).

CPSIA information can be obtained
at www.ICGtesting.com
Printed in the USA
LVOW05s1736020517
533004LV00029B/516/P